ANTIQUE GLASS BOTTLES

Their History and Evolution (1500-1850)
A Comprehensive, Illustrated Guide
With a World-wide Bibliography of Glass Bottles

A group of five utility bottles from different countries dating from 1670 to1840. (See Plate 257, page 312.)

ANTIQUE GLASS BOTTLES

Their History and Evolution (1500-1850)
A Comprehensive, Illustrated Guide
With a World-wide Bibliography of Glass Bottles

Willy Van den Bossche

Photographed by Fred Weegenaar

ANTIQUE COLLECTORS' CLUB

ISBN 1 85149 337 9

British Library Cataloguing-in-Publication Data
A catalogue record for this book is available from the British Library

This book has been sponsored by:
SAINT-GOBAIN
Emhart Glass SA, Cham, Switzerland
Gerresheimer Glas, Düsseldorf, Germany
Maltha Holding B.V., Fijnaart/Heijningen, The Netherlands
Mr. J.R. Ritman, Amsterdam, The Netherlands
Mr. Karl-Heinz Poser, Neumünster, Germany
'Santos Barosa-Vidros S.A.', Marinha Grande, Portugal
'Glass Works Auctions', East Greenville, Box 187, PA 18041, U.S.A.
'BBR Auctions (British Bottle Review)', Elsecar Heritage Centre, Elsecar, South Yorkshire, England
The **Hugo van Win Glasfonds,** administered by the **Prins Bernard Cultuurfonds,** Amsterdam, The Netherlands
Mr. Willy Van den Bossche, The Netherlands

Printed and bound in Italy

ANTIQUE COLLECTORS' CLUB

The Antique Collectors' Club was formed in 1966 and quickly grew to a five figure membership spread throughout the world. It publishes the only independently run monthly antiques magazine, *Antique Collecting*, which caters for those collectors who are interested in widening their knowledge of antiques, both by greater awareness of quality and by discussion of the factors which influence the price that is likely to be asked. The Antique Collectors' Club pioneered the provision of information on prices for collectors and the magazine still leads in the provision of detailed articles on a variety of subjects.

It was in response to the enormous demand for information on 'what to pay' that the price guide series was introduced in 1968 with the first edition of *The Price Guide to Antique Furniture* (completely revised 1978 and 1989), a book which broke new ground by illustrating the more common types of antique furniture, the sort that collectors could buy in shops and at auctions rather than the rare museum pieces which had previously been used (and still to a large extent are used) to make up the limited amount of illustrations in books published by commercial publishers. Many other price guides have followed, all copiously illustrated, and greatly appreciated by collectors for the valuable information they contain, quite apart from prices. The Price Guide Series heralded the publication of many standard works of reference on art and antiques. *The Dictionary of British Art* (now in six volumes), *The Pictorial Dictionary of British 19th Century Furniture Design, Oak Furniture* and *Early English Clocks* were followed by many deeply researched reference works such as *The Directory of Gold and Silversmiths,* providing new information. Many of these books are now accepted as the standard work of reference on their subject.

The Antique Collectors' Club has widened its list to include books on gardens and architecture. All the Club's publications are available through bookshops world wide and a full catalogue of all these titles is available free of charge from the addresses below.

Club membership, open to all collectors, costs little. Members receive free of charge *Antique Collecting*, the Club's magazine (published ten times a year), which contains well-illustrated articles dealing with the practical aspects of collecting not normally dealt with by magazines. Prices, features of value, investment potential, fakes and forgeries are all given prominence in the magazine.

Among other facilities available to members are private buying and selling facilities, the longest list of 'For Sales' of any antiques magazine, an annual ceramics conference and the opportunity to meet other collectors at their local antique collectors' clubs. There are over eighty in Britain and more than a dozen overseas. Members may also buy the Club's publications at special pre-publication prices.

As its motto implies, the Club is an organisation designed to help collectors get the most out of their hobby: it is informal and friendly and gives enormous enjoyment to all concerned.

For Collectors — By Collectors — About Collecting

ANTIQUE COLLECTORS' CLUB
5 Church Street, Woodbridge Suffolk IP12 1DS, UK
Tel: 01394 385501 Fax: 01394 384434
or
Market Street Industrial Park Wappingers' Falls, NY 12590, USA
Tel: 845 297 0003 Fax: 845 297 0068

CONTENTS

ACKNOWLEDGEMENTS

In essence, this book is a collation of information supplied by many museums, archaeological services, libraries, historical societies, historians, researchers, writers, bottle manufacturers, institutions, collectors, dealers in antique bottles and glass, auctioneers and many other private persons.

For many years numerous collectors all over the world have opened their houses and collections to me and shared their knowledge about the bottles and jars in their collections. I am gratefully indebted to all those persons and institutions who have contributed in one way or another to our knowledge of the history and evolution of utilitarian glass bottles and jars (1500-1850) to provide the basis of this book.

Their names are as follows★:

Museums, libraries, archaeological services, historical societies, public services, institutions, bottle clubs, bottle manufacturers, auctioneers… etc.

David Whitehouse, Corning Museum of Glass (bottles)★★, Corning, NY (USA); Formsammlung der Stadt Braunschweig (bottles), Brunswick (D); Ingeborg Krueger, Rheinisches Landesmuseum Bonn, Bonn (D); Museum für Kunst und Gewerbe Hamburg, Hamburg (D); Römisch-Germanisches Museum, Cologne (D); Kunstgewerbemuseum der Stadt Köln, Cologne (D); Helena Horn, Museum für Glaskunst, Lauscha (D); Österreichisches Museum für angewandte Kunst, Vienna (A); Stefan Vandenberghe, Gruuthusemuseum (bottles), Bruges (B); Janette Lefrancq, Musées Royaux d'Art et d'Histoire/Koninklijke Musea voor Kunst en Geschiedenis, Brussels (B); Michèle Thiry and Isabelle Laurent, Museé du Verre (bottles), Charleroi (B); Aalborg Historiske Museum, Aalborg (DK); Det danske Kunstindustrimuseum (Museum of Decorative Arts), Copenhagen (DK); The National Museum of Finland, Helsinki (SF); Karhulan Lasimuseo (Karhula Glass Museum), Karhula (SF); Riihimäen valtakunnallinen Lasimuseo (The Finnish Glass Museum, bottles), Riihimaki (SF); Musée des Arts et Traditions populaires, Paris (FR); Musée du Louvre, Paris (FR); Musée archéologique, Strasbourg (FR); National Museum of Ireland, Dublin (IRL); Museo Vetrario di Murano, Murano (I); Kunstindustrimuseet i Oslo (N); Hugh Tait, British Museum, London (GB); London Museum (bottles) (GB); Science Museum, London (GB); Reino Liefkes, Victoria and Albert Museum (bottles), London (GB); Ashmolean Museum (bottles), Oxford (GB); Nordiska museet, Stockholm (S); Kunstgewerbemuseum der Stadt Zürich, Zürich (CH); Musée du Petit Palais, Avignon (FR); Clasina Isings, Provinciaal Oudheidkundig Museum, Utrecht (NL); Harold E. Henkes, Museum Boymans-van Beuningen (bottles), Rotterdam (NL); Museum Het Vleeshuis, Antwerp (B); Pharmacie Historique XVIIe Siècle (bottles), Baugé (FR); Art Gallery of Ontario, Toronto (CDN); Musée Paul-Dupuis (bottles), Toulouse (FR); Johan Veeckman, Archeologische Dienst, Kunsthistorische Musea der Stad Antwerpen, Antwerp (B); National Portrait Gallery, London (GB); Staatliche Kunsthalle, Karlsruhe (D); Germanisches Nationalmuseum, Nürnberg (D); Hans-Joachim Kruse, Museum des Kreises Plön (bottles and seals), Plön (D); Musée des Beaux Arts de Rennes, Rennes (FR); Scheepvaartmuseum, Amsterdam (NL); Jaap Cottman, Rijksdienst voor Oudheidkundig Bodemonderzoek, Amersfoort (NL); Jan Baart, Afdeling Archeologie -

Dienst Stadsbeheer, Amsterdam (NL); Pieter C. Ritsema van Eck, Rijksmuseum, Amsterdam (NL); Musée de la Ville d'Eaux, Spa (B); Gemäldegalerie der Akademie der bildenden Künste in Wien, Vienna (A); Ivor Noël Hume, Colonial Williamsburg Foundation (bottles and seals), Williamsburg, VA (USA); Mark Davis, Somerset County Museum (sealed bottles), Taunton (GB); Topkapi Palast Museum, Istanbul (TR); Toledo Museum of Art, Toledo (USA); Musée de la Chartreuse, Douai (FR); Stiftelsen Smalands Museum (Glassmuseum), Växjö (S); Museo Nacional del Prado, Madrid (E); Deutsches Apothekenmuseum (bottles and jars), Heidelberg (D); Hermitage Museum, St. Petersburg (RUS); Musée Ingres (bottles), Montauban (FR); Heimatmuseum, Sternberg (D); Staatsgalerie, Stuttgart (D); The Arts and Crafts Museum of Norway, London (GB); Schweizerisches Pharmazie-Historisches Museum (bottles and jars), Basel (CH); Budapesti Történeti Muzum, Budapest (H); Instituut voor het Archeologisch Patrimonium, Ministerie van de Vlaamse Gemeenschap, Zellik (B); Heimatmuseum (bottles), Goldberg (D); Deutsches Medizinhistorisches Museum, Ingolstadt (D); Musée du Verre (bottles), Liège (B); Hunterian Art Gallery, Glasgow (GB); Museum and Art Gallery, Bristol (GB); Kulturhistoriska Museet, Lund (S); Karin Friese, Stadt- und Kreismuseum (bottles and seals), Eberswalde (D); Musée Borely, Marseille (FR); Musée historique lorrain (bottles), Nancy (FR); The J. Paul Getty Museum, Malibu, CA (USA); Die Österreichische Gallerie, Vienna (A); Schlossmuseum, Arnstadt (D); M.C. Laleman, Stadsarcheologie der stad Gent, Ghent (B); Norbert Bastin, Musée de Groesbeeck de Croix, Namur (B); Thüringer Museum, Eisenach (D); Staatliche Kunstsammlungen Dresden, Grünes Gewölbe, Dresden (D); Museum der Schottenabtei, Vienna (A); Worcester Art Museum, Worcester (USA); Hessisches Landesmuseum, Darmstadt (D); Bürgerspital, Würzburg (D); Badisches Landesmuseum, Karlsruhe (D); Groot Constantia Wine Museum, Capetown (SA); Nationaal Glasmuseum (bottles), Leerdam (NL); Ralf Wendt, Mecklenburgisches Volkskundemuseum (bottles), Schwerin-Muess (D); Musée départemental des Antiquités, Rouan (FR); Cecil Higgins Art Gallery and Museum, Bedford (GB); Frans Hals Museum, Haarlem (NL); Chantal Fontaine, Institut Royal du Patrimoine Artistique/Koninklijk Instituut voor het Kunstpatrimonium, Brussels (B); Glasmuseum Wertheim, Wertheim (D); Olga Drahotová, Umeleckprumyslové Muzeum (Museum of Applied Arts, bottles), Prague (CZ); Royal Institution of Cornwall, The County Museum (bottles), Truro (GB); Provinciaal Museum Sterckshof (bottles), Deurne, Antwerp (B); Schlossmuseum Göbelsburg, Österreichisches Museum für Volkenkunde, Vienna (A); Museu da Farmacia (bottles), Lisbon (P); Museu Nacional de Arte Antiga, Lisbon (P); Württembergisches Landesmuseum, Stuttgart (D); Nederlands Gedistilleerd Museum (bottles), Schiedam (NL); Eric Van Schoonenberghe, Nationaal Jenevermuseum (bottles), Hasselt (B); Museo del Carmen (bottles), Perelada, Gerona (E); House of Sandeman (bottles), Vila Nova de Gaia, Oporto (P); Alan Blakeman, Coddswallop (Bottle Museum), Elsecar, Nr. Barnsley (GB); Pilkington Glass Museum (bottles), St. Helens (GB); Michael Funk, Westfälisches Industriemuseum (bottles), Glashütte Gernheim, Gernheim (D); José Barosa, Santos Barosa Vidros (bottle-making), Lisbon and Marinhe Grande (P); Emhart Glass S.A. (bottle-making), Cham (CH); Gerresheimer Glas A.G. (bottle-making), Düsseldorf (D); Norma Jenkins and Virginia Wright, The Rakow Library (thousands of books on glass), c/o Corning Museum of Glass, Corning, NY (USA); British Library Documentation Supply Center, Wetherby (GB); Württembergische Landesbibliothek (2,000 books on glass), Stuttgart (D); Olive

Jones, Material Culture Research (bottles), Archeological Research Division, National Historic Parks and Sites Branch, Parks, Ottawa (CDN); Maria Mucha, Instytut Prahistorii Uniwersytetu im.A.Mickiewicza (bottles), Poznán (PL); Danièle Foy, Centre National de la Recherche Scientifique, Laboratoire d'Archéologie Médiévale Méditerranéenne (glass), Aix-en-Provence (FR); Archiv zur Geschichte des Markenartikels, Institut für Absatzwirtschaft, Universität München, Munich (D); Staatliche Akademie der Bildenden Künste, Lehrstuhl für Produktgestalltung, Stuttgart (D); Jean-Luc Olivier, Centre du Verre du Musée des Arts Décoratifs, Paris (FR); Genaeologisch Instituut, The Hague (NL); Het Koninklijk Penningkabinet, Leiden (NL); Het Koninklijk Huis Archief, The Hague (NL); Library of the Society of Antiquaries of London, London (GB); Instituto per lo studio del vetro e dell' arte vetraria di Altare, Altare (I); Stadsarchief, Vlissingen (NL); Stadsarchief, Maastricht (NL); Koninklijke Bibliotheek, The Hague (NL); Stadsarchief, Bruges (B); Thüringisches Hauptstaatsarchiv, Weimar (D); Service photographique de la Réunion des musées nationaux, Paris (FR); Bibliothèque nationale, Paris (FR); Riksarkivet (National archives of Norway), Oslo (N); Sächsische Landesbibliothek, Dresden (D); Accademia Carrara di Belle Arti, Bergamo (I); Claus Grimm, Haus der Bayerische Geschichte, Munich (D); André Deflorenne, Cercle d'Histoire et d'Archéologie de la Thiérarche, Momignies/Beauwelz (B); Bibliotheek Universiteit Leiden, Leiden (NL); Bibliotheek Universiteit Amsterdam, Amsterdam (NL); Rijksbureau voor Kunsthistorische Dokumentatie, The Hague (NL); Niedersächsisches Hauptstaatsarchiv, Hanover (D); Brandenburgisches Landeshauptarchiv, Potsdam (D); Archivo Storico di Montecassino, Montecassino (I); Archives de l'Etat, Liège (B); La Biblioteca Apostolica Vaticana, Vatican City; Koninklijke Bibliotheek Albert I/Bibliothèque Royale Albert I, Brussels (B); The Frick Art Reference Library, New York (USA); Société d'Histoire Régionale de Rance, Rance (B); Association Internationale pour l'Histoire du Verre, c/o Rijksmuseum, Amsterdam (NL); Bibliothèque universitaire de Nancy II, Nancy (FR); Archives de Meurthes-et-Moselle et des anciens Duchés de Lorraine et de Bar, Nancy (FR); La Biblioteca Ambrosiana, Milano (I); Österreichische Akademie der Wissenschaften, Institut für Realienkunde des Mittelalters und der frühen Neuzeit, Krems a/d Donau (A); Biblioteca da Ordem dos Farmacêuticos, Lisbon (P); Library of the European Patent Office/Office Européen des Brevets/Europäisches Patentamt, The Hague (NL) and Munich (D); British Patent Office, Swansea (GB); United States Patent Office, Washington DC (USA); Sheldon Baugh, 'Federation of Historical Bottle Collectors' (FHBC), Russellville, KY (USA); Federation of Historical Bottle Collectors (Carl Sturm), publisher of *Bottles & Extras,* Longwood, FL (USA); Peter Vermeulen, Verzamelaarsclub 'De Oude Flesch', Ravenstein (NL); Jim and Janice Hagenbuch, publishers of *Antique Bottle and Glass Collector,* East Greenville, PA (USA); Alan Blakeman, publisher of *British Bottle Review,* Elsecar, Nr. Barnsley (GB); Russell and June Dunn, publishers of *Australian Bottle & Collectables Review,* Whittlesea, Vic, (Aus); Jörg Sachse, editor of *Der Glasfreund,* Neustrelitz (D); Sotheby's London (GB); Christie's London (GB); Phillips London (GB); British Bottle Review Auctions (Alan Blakeman), Elsecar Nr. Barnsley (GB); Norman C. Heckler & Company Auctioneers, Woodstock Valley, CT (USA); Glass Works Auctions (Jim Hagenbuch), East Greenville, PA (USA); Heilbronner Kunst- und Auktionshaus Dr. Jürgen Fischer, Heilbronn (D); Wiener Kunst Auktionen, Vienna (A).

Collectors, historians, researchers, writers, antique glass dealers and other persons.

Fred and Elly Weegenaar, The Hague (NL) for their excellent photography; my son Karl Van den Bossche for patiently measuring the dimensions, capacities and weights of hundreds of bottles over a period of two months and without breaking one bottle(!). Jeremy Stroud, Amsterdam (NL), who proofread my English manuscript; Neil Willcox, Twickenham (GB) and Karl-Heinz Poser, Neumünster (D) for our more than twenty years' exchange of know-how and experience on antique bottles; Claude Laydu, Paris (FR); Robert McNulty, Washington DC (USA); Roger Dumbrell (†), East Sussex (GB); Paul Hanrahan, Nepean (CDN); Gordon Litherland, Burton-upon-Trent, (GB); Roy Morgan (GB); Ethleen Lastovica, Cape Town (SA); Fay Banks, Oxford (GB); Geoffrey Wills (†), Truro (GB); Eugen Leitherer, Munich (D); Thomas Dexel, Brunswick (D); José Barosa, Lisbon (P); Germaine Rose-Villeqeue, Laxou (FR); Gabriel Ladaique, Villers-lez-Nancy (FR); Johan Soetens, Rotterdam (NL); Theo and Frans Laurentius (experts in engravings), Voorschoten (NL); Erwin Baumgartner, Basel (CH); Albert Schwiezer, Hessisch Oldendorf (D); Peter Vermeulen, Ravenstein (NL); Alfred Holl (†), Wendelstein (D); Gregory Koslow, Moscow (RUS); Hans (†) and Joachim Wiegand, Steinbach am Wald (D); Glasantiquariat dr. Michael Bauer, Kronberg im Taunus (D); James Barrelet (†), Paris (FR); N.R.A. Vroom (†), Baarn (NL); Axel von Saldern, Starnberg (D); J.R. Ritman, Amsterdam (NL); Mrs. Raymond Chambon, Marcinelle (B); Hans-Dieter Kreft, Salzhemmendorf (D); Arlene Palmer, Yarmouth, ME (USA); David Walker Barker, Elsecar, Nr. Barnsley (GB); Kenneth M. Wilson (USA), Frans Smit, Peterborough (GB); Rudolf Hoffmann, Lauscha (D); Matthew Shade, The Hague (NL); Peter Savage (Codd bottles), Warwick (GB); A.J. van der Horst, Zaandam (NL); Count J.L. Goethals de Mude de Nieuwland, Ghent (B); Jorge Barrera, Paris (FR); Joseph Philippe, Ellemelle (B); Jacqueline Bellanger, Paris (FR); Ada Polak, London (GB); Mogens Schlüter, Naestved (DK); Roger Monmélien(†), Saussey (FR); Walter Rigling, Brookville, FL (USA); Karl Amendt, Krefeld (D); Oskar Kiesling, Nürnberg (D); Torbjorn Fogelberg, Åkarp (S); Sibyll Kummer-Rottenhausen (†), Zürich (CH); Jacob Seela, Turku (SF); Glasgalerie Michael Kovacek, Vienna (A); Bernard Dragesco, Paris (FR); Pierre Poulus, Brussels (B); Henk van Vliet, Frides Laméris, Peter Korf de Gidts and Constant Vecht, all from Amsterdam (NL); Jonathan Horne, Jeanette Hayhurst and Christopher Sheppard, all from London (GB); Karl Stimm, Antwerp (B), and last but not least Twigger Book Finding Service, Reading (GB).

Willy Van den Bossche

★ Identification codes of the cited countries:
(A) Austria. (AUS) Australia. (B) Belgium. (CDN) Canada. (CH) Switzerland. (CZ) Czech Republic. (D) Germany. (DK) Denmark. (E) Spain. (F) France. (GB) Great Britain. (H) Hungary. (I) Italy. (IRL) Ireland. (N) Norway. (NL) The Netherlands. (P) Portugal. (PL) Poland. (S) Sweden. (SA) South Africa. (SF) Finland. (RUS) Russia. (TR) Turkey. (USA) United States of America.

★★(bottles) indicates that this museum or institution has a significant collection of bottles.

† deceased

FOREWORD

To the reader already familiar with antique glass utility bottles and their history, it will be self-evident that this in an important book – a major contribution to the literature, destined to become one of those few key, indispensable, reference works.

This is the first major reference book on early blown bottles since the 1983 publication of Roger Dumbrell's *Understanding Antique Wine Bottles* – still the standard reference work. That this was predominantly devoted to British bottles was inevitable: from the short chapter on 'European Wine Bottles' it is clear just how fundamental was the lack of knowledge available at the time (a situation which the author readily admits, stating 'In conclusion, the further investigation of European wine bottles is much needed…').

While the general level of knowledge has increased somewhat since then, it remains the case that there are still no reference guides to assist collectors world wide in the dating and attribution of early Continental bottles. While research has continued into increasingly specialised aspects of early British bottles, it has become all the more apparent that there is a major gap in knowledge regarding the history and evolution of bottles throughout the rest of Europe.

Just how major was this gap in knowledge can now be seen: Willy Van den Bossche has undertaken to redress this in a consistently thorough and structured way. Considering that it would be a daunting task to produce the first comprehensive illustrated study of the utility bottles in just one of the countries or regions puts into clear perspective the magnitude of the author's achievement in undertaking no less than such a study into each and all of the main bottle producing regions across Europe, noting the influences and inter-relationships, in order to present a comprehensive, illustrated, comparative guide covering, in effect, the entire bottle producing world at that time.

Happily, Willy Van den Bossche is supremely qualified to undertake this ambitious project. His early interest in bottles has given him the benefit of long experience; his training and daily work in glass technology has allowed a greater insight into the relevance of chemical and technical processes involved; his command of Dutch, English, French and German is an obvious advantage; even his geographical location in Belgium (the area which presented at the time the main competition to Britain in the export of bottles). All these combine with personal qualities of dedication and thoroughness to ensure the best chance of success in achieving an understanding of 'the big picture' as concerns the history of the glass utility bottle and its use, for wine, beer, oil and all manner of other liquid and dry wares.

The bibliography in itself illustrates well the author's thorough and systematic approach: in order to assimilate all the relevant information (in any language and from every period) he has sought assiduously to make this as comprehensive a listing as possible, and this alone will prove to be an indispensable reference for future generations of researchers.

The consolidation of all the knowledge and information makes this a singularly useful reference work; there is also, however, every evidence of a great deal of original research and new insight. The text and glossary allow the reader a firm understanding of every aspect of the background and history as well as the processes and factors involved in making bottles in the different European areas.

Although British bottles are the one 'known' element in this story, they have, quite rightly, been granted a fully comprehensive analysis. Britain played such a central role in the early development and evolution of the commonplace glass bottle that it is essential first to gain a working knowledge of her products, providing as they do a yardstick against which to compare subsequent developments across Europe.

The plates display a full evolution of the English 'wine' bottle, with an exceptional range of sealed or dated sealed examples for each decade from the 1660s to the 1880s. These are the bottles at the heart of the story of the development of the modern glass bottle. The glass industry went on to create the hugely influential position it holds in modern life, providing a vast variety of commercial packaging for everyday products, but it was this, the invention in England of the standard, thick-walled, blackglass 'wine' bottle, that started the whole process by proving the suitability of this fragile medium, glass, for such use.

These 'wine' bottle provide much of the story in terms of their evolution of form and their variety of shapes, as well as being the basis of comparison, throughout the period covered, with their equivalent counterpart produced at the same time in the various bottle glasshouses of Europe. The illustrations are carefully selected to show to best advantage the salient features and differences.

All of the other types of glass bottles and jars that were produced are included. Across Europe a great variety of generic forms and colours appeared for different products or purposes – this book best tells: their story, but the distinctive shapes do enhance considerably the vocabulary of form available to the collector.

Apart from their historical significance and romantic status as artefacts providing clues to our past, early glass bottles can have great aesthetic appeal. The fluidity of glass as a medium, its frozen molten quality, combines well with the earthy shades of green and degrees of translucency intrinsic to 'blackglass', 'forest glass' (the most natural of glass, the closest to its origin of basic natural ingredients processed in the simplest way). That the desired product was in fact no more than a container for some product, subject to every constraint of economy and usefulness in its competition with stoneware and other ceramics (and to the limitations of technology at a time when everything was made by hand) helps to explain the 'naturalness of form' that is often exhibited in early blown glass bottles, and which is their particular charm. Despite their mass-production as essentially disposable commonplace objects, all display a handmade individuality and many have a striking sculptural presence, man-made yet seemingly less designed than natural, organically evolved, forms.

In each category, examples of the rarest and most important bottles are illustrated and described, as well as those most likely to be encountered – in each case the best of its type available, the most fit for its purpose: to illustrate a point, represent a type, show the colour or form. The items chosen for illustration have been subject to the same meticulous selection process shown throughout the book, with the same attention to detail in ensuring that the colour plates reflect accurately the original colours of the bottles and that the photographs themselves are taken with a special technical camera to show the true shapes of the bottles with no distortion of image.

Taken as a whole, the items illustrated combine to form a uniquely complete collection encapsulating the history of the utilitarian glass bottle in Europe. In text and image, the reader is presented with a serious study that is well conceived in its presentation and in terms of its usefulness and accessibility as a reference guide.

Few new books on a specific, established field of antiques break new ground to this extent – Willy Van den Bossche has made a great contribution to our understanding of antique bottles, one that will hopefully inspire others with interests in the bottles from a specific region, to publish fully comprehensive, in-depth reference. guides for each region.

This is a 'landmark' book, the fruit of diligent study and intensive work in bringing together all of the bottles here shown. With its publication, there is a strong sense that the study of, and interest in, early blown bottles has now 'come of age'.

Neil Willcox
Twickenham, England

PREFACE

This book contains **368** colour plates and **26** black and white figures describing in total **773** antique bottles and glass seals including **572** plain bottles, **165** sealed bottles and **36** seals from broken bottles. The origins of the bottle and the seals are as follows:

Great Britain: **156** bottles (including **71** sealed bottles) and **7** glass seals

Holland and Belgium: **139** bottles (including **17** sealed bottles) and **12** glass seals

Belgium (Supplement): 70 bottles (including **14** sealed bottles) and one glass seal

France: 162 bottles (including **21** sealed bottles) and one glass seal

Italy, Spain and Portugal: 11 bottles (including **4** sealed bottles)

Germany and the Alpine countries: 149 bottles (including **19** sealed bottles) and **13** glass seals

Scandinavia: 19 bottles (including **13** sealed bottles) and **2** glass seals

U.S.A.: 25 bottles (including **2** sealed bottles)

Other countries: 7 bottles (including **2** sealed bottles)

INTRODUCTION

Collecting antique drinking glasses has been far more popular in Europe than collecting utility bottles (1500-1850), which have been very much neglected on the Continent in spite of their wide variety of artistic shapes and colours. The reason for this may be explained by the facts that early, blown bottles made before the Industrial Revolution (starting in the 1850s) are very difficult to find and are more complicated to understand than drinking glasses. The utility bottle has been missing the 'prestige' and 'status' that it merits. Many Roman bottles were found in tombs and are thus much more common than their successors which were 'reinvented' after the Dark Ages.

Collecting antique bottles and jars became popular from the 1950s onwards in English-speaking countries, especially England, America and Australia, and the Continent has followed this trend progressively since the 1970s, although on a much smaller scale.

In collectors' jargon, early utility bottles are frequently wrongly described as 'wine' bottles, a term too restrictive for bottles used for wine, beer, oil, vinegar and all other liquid and powder wares. Extensive iconographic research and a study of many archaeological excavations from all over the world have helped to date and locate the origins and use of the bottles described.

This book has been written for collectors, archaeologists, museums, libraries, historians, writers, researchers, institutions, bottle-makers, dealers, wine and beer lovers, pharmacists and all other persons interested in collecting antiques. In order to render it as comprehensive as possible, the selection of bottles illustrated has been carefully chosen from different private collections. Only three bottles from museums are illustrated, which underlines the lack of interest in bottles shown by museums in the past. The complete history and evolution of utility bottles in Europe is explained. Twenty-five American bottles are illustrated to show the differences in style, colour and blowing techniques from European bottles. One colour photograph can say more than a thousand words.

Each bottle has been briefly described including its colour, blow technique used, dimensions, capacity and weight. The references cited support the description or refer to other similar bottles known. The chapters are cross-referenced to aid the reader in locating related bottles that have been included in other chapters.

Bottle related items such as seal dies and corkscrews are also illustrated at the end of the book for completeness.

The glossary of bottle-making terms and the extensive bibliography (1,151 titles) on bottle books and selected bottle articles from literature world-wide and in many different languages will give the reader a good overview of the state of the art in bottle literature.

This comprehensive, illustrated guide will provide the reader with a better insight into a neglected part of European cultural, commercial and pre-industrial history and will enable him or her to conclude that the collecting of antique bottles is one of the most exciting of all hobbies.

Willy Van den Bossche

NOTES ON THE FIGURES AND PLATES

Description and terminology

The descriptions of the antique bottles and bottle related items in the captions comprise as far as possible the following: name, approximate age, origin of production, area of use, glass colour, shape, capacity, weight, contents, dimensions, technology (pontil scar, etc.), short history, seals, application, bottle protection means and references.

For the interest of the collector and for scientific research, the weight and capacity (bottle filled to the brim) of most bottles have been measured in order to help to identify their origin of production, the area of use and their original contents.

Many bottles described are of dark olive green, dark grass green or dark amber colour. In bottle jargon these colours are known as 'black glass', in Dutch (Holland and Belgium) as 'zwart glas', in French (France and Belgium) as 'verre noir' and in German as 'schwarzes Glas'.

In order to become familiar with certain bottle terms such as 'utility bottle' (for beer, wine, oil, vinegar and all other liquid or powder wares), 'black glass', 'coal firing', 'wood firing' etc., these terms are repeated several times mixed with other terms or definitions to understand better the application, colour, melting method etc. of the bottles.

The glossary of bottlemaking terms at the end of this book helps the reader better to understand 'bottles'. In addition there is a comprehensive bibliography, referred to for most illustrations, which gives a worldwide survey of the literature on bottles and their related artefacts.

Bottles illustrated are described in order from left to right, unless otherwise indicated.

Abbreviations

H (height):	cm (centimetre)
Dim (dimensions):	height x width x thick in cm
Wt (weight):	gr (grams)
Ø (diameter):	cm (centimetre)
L (length):	cm (centimetre)
Cap (capacity):	cl (centilitre) or litre
	(bottles were filled with water to the brim)
	1cl = 0.61023 cu.in. (cubic inch)
	1cu.in. = 1.6387 cl (centilitres)
mm:	millimetre (1mm = 0.03937 inch)
cm:	centimetre (cm = 0.3937 inch)
in.:	inch (1 inch = 25.4mm = 2.54cm)

HISTORY AND EVOLUTION OF UTILITY GLASS BOTTLES (1500-1850)

Chronology of bottle-making (1500BC-AD1929)

In order to understand the craft of bottle-making from 1500 until the beginning of the Industrial Revolution in 1850 in its historical context, a complete overview of bottle-making from 1500 BC until the Great Depression of 1929 has been made. Economic, political and social events of particular relevance are also mentioned to give a clearer picture of the circumstances in which bottles were made and used.

Numbers in italics between brackets refer to publications cited in the Bibliography. The figures and plates referred to are those in this book.

1500BC–50BC: Production of the earliest glass bottles (alabastrons, flasks, emphoriskos, etc.) by the core forming technique in Egypt, Syria, Greece and Cyprus. A gather of molten glass is wound around the already shaped core, such as sand mixed with clay and straw supported by a rod, and then rolled on a stone slab. After forming, the bottle is annealed and the core then removed by scraping.

50BC: Discovery of the blowpipe for glass-blowing, probably in Syria. It is now possible to blow bottles of many different shapes and at a much greater speed than before.

50BC–400AD: Roman period. Thanks to the invention of the glass-blowing pipe successful production of many thin-walled, free-blown and mould-blown bottles, jars and vials of all shapes, such as kuttrolfs, case bottles, balsam bottles and baby feeders. Bottles are plain or embossed, with glass seals or masks, handled, optically blown by the half-post method, engraved, decorated with rigarees or glass threads on the body; colours are bluish, azure, amethyst, amber, etc. The techniques used have remained unchanged to the present day.

End of the West Roman Empire in 476 and decline of glass-making in Europe.

400-1250: The Dark Ages. Great degeneration of bottle-making in Europe.

451: The Council of Chalcedon, the fourth ecumenical council of the Christian Church, is held in Chalcedon (now Kadiköy, Turkey). Gifts to the dead in tombs are forbidden from now onwards so that finding bottles made between 451 and the 17th century becomes very hard.

9th-13th century: At first glass is mainly made in monastic glasshouses, but later glass-making becomes independent of the church and glasshouses making 'Waldglas' (forest glass) appear in Northern France, Belgium and north of the Alps.

800-814: Charlemagne conquers nearly all the Christian lands of Western Europe and rules as emperor (Aachen 800-814).

11th century: The Catalonian Bible of the Abbey of San Pedro de Roda, Spain illustrates a meal where the guests drink from 'round bottles with long necks'.

11th-13th century: The thin-walled 'shaft and globe' is a common bottle in the Middle East. Its style is the forerunner of the thick-walled English and Continental 'shaft and globe' (Figure 18).

12th-17th century: Revival of the art of alchemy. Use of bottles, vials, flasks and other glassware in medicinal chemistry and pharmacy.

1110-1140: Oldest description in literature for making a 'shaft and globe' by the German monk Theophilus Presbyter *(1019, 1020)* in his treatise *Schedula diversum artium* (in Latin).

> 'If you wish to make bottles with a long neck, this do. When you have gathered some hot glass on the end of a blowing-tube and blown it in the form of a large bladder, swing the tube with the glass appended to it, beyond your head as if you intended to throw it, and the neck will be stretched by this action: then separate it with a wet stick and put it in an annealing furnace.' (Liber II, cap. XI 'De ampullis cum longo collo')

Two parts of sand are mixed together with one part of tree ash, then roasted (sintered) in a first furnace and finally molten in a second separate pot furnace. This method is used until the end of the eighteenth century. Broken glass is often added to the batch.

1199: 'Privilege of Bordeaux'. The Bordeaux wine-makers possess for more than six centuries the sole right to sell their wines to England before Christmas. This competition suppressing system makes Bordeaux an important and reputed wine-making area needing many 'wine'-bottles and containers.

13th century: Revival of the half-post method for making optically blown bottles and flasks, a technique already used in Roman times and in the Middle East. The technique is brought to Germany by crusaders returning from the crusades (1095-1270) (Figure 38).

1250: Revival of glass-making in Europe with Venice and Altare (Italy) being the main centres for making glass.

During the 16th and 17th centuries, many Italian glass-makers were to emigrate to Northern Europe to make luxury glassware 'à la façon de Venise'. Hall in the Tirol (Austria), Antwerp and Liège (both in Belgium) were to be the most important 'Venetian' glasshouses in Northern Europe in the 16th century.

1270: Oldest illustration of a 'kuttrolf' (Figure 7).

1300-1700: Bottles and decanters are stoppered with a spill of paper, a wooden plug, or covered with a cloth and a cord. 'Violles were stopped with waxe or bombase [cotton wool or raw cotton] and parchment over it'. Wool dipped in wax is used as a bottle stopper into the late 17th century.

1348-1400: Catastrophic halving of the population in Europe mainly due to the Black Death which first struck Europe in 1348. The survivors were burying the dead. Very few bottles were made and survived.

1400-500: The Burgundy-style bottle, a cylindrical bottle with sloping shoulders, is used in the Burgundy area and made in Lorraine and La Vôge (North-east France). Called 'feulette', it is mostly made in 'verre noir'. A 'kuttrolf' survives from the late Middle Ages (Plate 190(2)).

1425: Miniature of a German medieval glass-making furnace illustrated in the encyclopaedia *De Universo* by Rabanus Maurus, dating from 1023. The miniature, added in 1425, shows a typical German conical upset bottle and a pear-shaped bottle (Figure 29).

1450-1850: Belgium is the most important bottle-making area on the Continent. It mainly exports flasks, bottles, vials and jars to Holland and France (Champagne and Burgundy areas). For 400 years the leading bottle-making dynasty is the Colinet family. Their most reputed glasshouses are situated in Momignies (Beauwelz) and Macquenoise, both in Hainault. The name Colinet is also written as Collinet, Colinet, Colenet, Colnet, etc.

1453: Fall of Constantinople, end of the Roman Byzantine Empire in the East.

1490-1500: Painting from an unknown Austrian Master depicting three dark brown transparent forest glass bottles or 'black glass' bottles (Figure 17).

16th century: Illustration of one of the earliest bottles made in Germany or Bohemia by the German half-post method. First quarter 16th century (Plate 191).

1500: Oldest 'shaft and globe' is produced in Belgium (Figure 3.2).

1506/1507: Englebert Colinet obtains from Margaret of Austria, Regent of the Dutch and Belgian Netherlands, permission to erect, at the already existing glasshouse at Surginet, Beauwelz, Hainault (Belgium), a glass furnace for making 'des verres à la vénitienne décorés d'émaux et autre biaux verres, objets et ornements transparents' (glasses à la façon de Venise decorated with enamel and other beautiful glasses, objects and transparent ornaments). Colinet is the first glass-maker outside Italy to make glass 'à la façon de Venise'; vials, flasks, jars, bottles and German style glasses in 'Waldglas' are already being produced.

1517: Martin Luther publishes his Ninety-five Theses, an attack on various ecclesiastical abuses in the Roman Catholic Church. The Protestant Reformation begins. Calvinism begins with John Calvin in 1536.

1519-1556: The Hapsburg Emperor Charles V (Ghent, Belgium 1500-Spain 1558) rules Austria, Hungary, Bohemia, Spain, the Netherlands (including Belgium), Italy and Spanish America.

1530-1615: Important bottle-making in Lorraine and La Vôge, North-east France. Export to Germany, Switzerland and Holland mainly via the Rhine.

1530-1630: Stoppering of bottles, mostly vials, with a cork. 'Stoppe the bottle with a corke'.

1534: King Henry VIII (England) breaks with papal rule from Rome and forms the independent Church of England, with himself at its head.

1540: The Italian Vannoccio Biringuccio *(168, 169)* describes bottle-making in *De la Pirotechnia*. The technique is identical to that described by Theophilus *(1019, 1020)* between 1110 and 1140.

1556: The German Georgius Agricola *(509)* illustrates in his *De re Metallica* a beehive-shaped glass-making furnace with bottle-makers using copper moulds and blowpipes made of brass, bronze or iron, three feet long. The technique for making bottles is identical to that described by Theophilus *(1019, 1020)* between 1110 and 1140.

1560-1648: Wars of religion widespread on the European Continent. Inquisition by the Roman Catholic Church. Decline of bottle-making on the European Continent.

1567: A very important date for bottle and glass-making in England and France. The Spanish King Philip sends his troops to Brussels to subject the Low Countries (Holland and Belgium). Jean Carré of Arras (Atrecht) and glass-maker in Antwerp emigrates to Fernfold, Wisborough Green, Sussex, England to make Norman, Burgundy and Lorraine glass, including bottles. Due to religious wars in France the first large scale emigration of Norman and Lorraine glass-makers to the Wealden in Sussex and Surrey, England takes place. The style of bottles and glasses made in England is mainly Continental.

1568-1648: Eighty Years War of the Netherlands (present Holland and Belgium) independence from Spain. Decline of glass-making.

1571-1887 ... Sealed bottles. Wax-sealed bottles made in '1571', '1604' and '1608' are first mentioned and illustrated in the *Journal d'Amandt Colinet (261* and Figure 22). An archive document in Liège, Belgium from '1606' states that Spa mineral water bottles have to be provided with a green wax seal to prove the true origin of the mineral water from Spa, a town in

Belgium. From c.1630–1640 onwards bottles are sometimes sealed with glass seals. Seals on bottles may indicate the private owner, a merchant, the bottle-maker or the bottle house, the bottle capacity or its contents, the commemoration of somebody or something, and any other information. Sometimes the seals are blank to be inscribed later with a diamond tool.

1572: St. Bartholomew's Day Massacre in France when several thousands of Huguenots (French Protestants) are murdered. More Norman, Lorraine and Belgian glass-makers emigrate to England. Production of the earliest known square-moulded bottle or case bottle with enamel decoration, pewter screw stopper and dated '1572'. See Von Saldern *(930,* Figure 51 and Plates 192, 253(4)).

1574: Earliest dated flattened ovoid-shaped bottle known. Made in Venice. Collection of the 'Staatliche Kunstsammlungen Dresden, Germany – Albertinum, Grünes Gewölbe'. Forerunner of the Belgian Spa mineral water bottles as illustrated in Plate 135.

1575: *The English-Housewife* refers to 'round bottles with narrow necks for bottle ale, the corks being tied down with stout string'.

1579–1585: The priest Johannes Rhenanus *(601)* experiments with the use of brown coal (lignite) as a fuel for melting glass in Kassel and Habichtswald, Hesse, Germany. Although successful, difficulties in selling the unusual coloured 'black' glassware combined with fears of competition from bottle-makers of Hainault County, Belgium, stop the making of 'black glass' in Germany. The Hainault bottle-makers are the main suppliers of bottles to Hesse during this period; they also have access to a lot of coal. See also date '1701'.

1600: The European discoveries of America (1492: Columbus), Africa, Asia, etc. between 1450 and 1600 lead to a commercial revolution in some parts of Europe from c.1600 onwards. Export of bottles to the colonies.

1602: The Flemish painter Jan Bruegel the Elder (1568-1625) depicts on the 'Allegory on the Fire' many early bottles, flasks, vials and jars common in Belgium at that time. Many bottles and other glassware are used in alchemy (Figure 9).

1602–1799: The Dutch East India Company, a trading company, export bottles and other wares overseas, hence the name 'Dutch bottles' which does not mean 'made in Holland'.

1608: Engraving from 'The funeral of Charles III of Lorraine' by Matheus Merian, depicting one of the many glasshouses producing bottles in the forest of Darney, La Vôge, North-east France (Figure 30).

1612: The Italian monk Antonio Neri *(778)* writes *L'Arte Vetraria* (in Italian), the first book in the world devoted to the art of making glass. The book is first translated into French (Jean Bonhomme, Liège, Belgium, in 1652), then into English (Merrett in 1662), Latin (in 1668),

German (in 1678 by Geissler and in 1679 by Kunckel) and Spanish (in 1776), and is used as a guide for most glass-makers until the mid-19th century.

1615: An important date for bottle-making in England and on the Continent. King James I *(303)* prohibits the use of wood to make glass in England and Wales. Sea-coal or pit-coal has to be used. The forest glasshouses disappear and the glass-makers move en masse to the coal areas such as Stourbridge and Newcastle-upon-Tyne to make 'black' glass bottles. 2400 kilograms of wood is needed to make one kilogram of glass by wood-firing!

1616: First use of coal as a fuel for making bottles in Rouen, France. Experiments have already been going on for twenty years.

1618–1648: Thirty Years War, between Germany, Denmark, Sweden, Poland, France and Russia. Second large scale emigration of Lorraine glass-makers to England and Belgium. Definitive decline of glass-making in Lorraine.

1620–1630: Very thin-walled (1mm or less) side-flattened onion bottles in dark brown colour or 'verre noir' are first made. Made in La Vôge or Lorraine, North-east France (Plate 255(2)).

1621–1794: The Dutch West India Company export bottles and other wares to the West Indies and South America. Bottles there are named 'Dutch bottles', which again does not mean 'made in Holland'. Trading in slaves becomes very profitable.

1623: On 22 May 1623, Sir Robert Mansell, Vice-Admiral of England, is granted the exclusive patent in England for making glass such as bottles and vials with coal.

1627: First archive document relating to the use of coal as a fuel for making glass in Belgium by Henri Bonhomme and Guy Libon from Liège. Charleroi first uses coal in 1654.

1630: Bottles are now provided with a string rim to reinforce the lips and to facilitate corking the bottle. The corks are conical and therefore easy to withdraw. The lips of the bottles made before c.1630 are flared or finished with a narrow flange but no string rim is laid on the neck.

1632: Introduction in England of the 'Belgian'-style shaft and globe bottle, probably at the bottlehouse of Newnham-on-Severn, near Gloucester, where bottle-makers John Colnett, John Vinion and Edward Percival (notice the French-Belgian names) assist Sir Kenelm Digby to make coal-fired 'English bottles'. In contrast to the 'Belgian' shaft and globe, the 'English bottle' is black, thick-walled (3-7 mm) and thus strong in order to compete with the mass imported 'stone bottles and jugs' (bellarmines) from Cologne. Many seals, described as 'rough buttons' and black glass slag have been found on the bottlehouse site (near the Old Quay) in Newnham. See also date '1661', Figure 19.1 and 19.2 and Plate 1.

1632–1887: The start of the modern bottle industry in Europe. Gradual evolution in England and on the Continent of the new utility bottle from 'shaft and globe' to the 'onion', the 'mallet' and the 'cylinder'. The bottles are mostly thick-walled, strong and black. Their design evolves from the decanter 'all-round' bottle to a cylindrical bottle for specific uses, such as for wine, beer, mineral water, milk, soft drinks, etc. Plates 1-28 show for each decade from 1632 to 1887 a (dated) (sealed) bottle in England. The trend of this evolution on the Continent is roughly similar to that of the English bottles.

1640: Earliest known glass seal on the European Continent. Made in Schleswig-Holstein, North Germany (Figure 23).

1640-1730: Bottle-making in Schleswig-Holstein, North Germany. Many sealed bottles exported to Holland.

1643-1715: Louis XIV, King of France. Triumph of Absolutism.

1648: The Peace of Westphalia brings an end to the Eighty Years War (1568-1648) and to the Thirty Years War (1618-1648). The Northern Netherlands, now The Netherlands, were definitively separated from the Southern Netherlands, now Belgium. Disintegration of Germany. The map of Europe is irrevocably changed. End of the Hapsburg supremacy in Europe. The date '1648' may be considered as the revival of bottle-making on the whole Continent.

1648: Earliest antedated sealed bottle known. Seal reads: 'OLD HOCK – 1648'. Bottle made c.1848 (Plate 265(1)).

1650: Earliest known authentic dated bottle seal in the world. The English seal reads: 'WE – 1650' (Figure 24.1).

1650: Unusual Belgian onion bottle provided with two seals. Made c.1750. Antedated 1650 (Plates 131 and 132).

1650-1750: The use of cheap cork extractors in the form of a prong becomes popular in Europe until the middle of the 18th century (Plates 322(2) and 322(4)).

1650-1850: England is the most important bottle-making country in Europe and Belgium on the Continent. Many small bottlehouses are spread all over Europe supplying bottles for local needs. They are mainly situated at locations where most conditions are fulfilled for making and transporting bottles, such as the presence of wood (forests) or coal (coal areas), glass-making ingredients, rivers, etc.

1659: Original German manuscript from glass-maker Mathias Wenzel *(1095)* with a poem and a line drawing of a handled 'Bocksbeutel', probably added afterwards in the 20th century.

1660: Restoration of the monarchy in England. Charles II, King of England (1660-1685). Extension of bottle-making in England.

1661: British 'Letters Patent' *(262)* of 6 September 1661 granted to John Colnett (Jean or Jan Colnet) – a member of the famous Belgian bottle-making dynasty Colnet, Colinet, etc. – for the 'Manufacturing of glass bottles and for preventing of frauds and abuses in the making and public vending thereof'. The patent claims

'the perfection of making glass bottles which shall contain the full measure of gallons, pottles, quarts and other measures according to the standard, and that the bottles shall be marketed with the particular stamp or mark of John Colnett'.

'The 'Bill of parliament for Glass Bottles' *(701)* of 10 April 1662 declares the withdrawal of the Patent. It is alleged that bottle-maker John Colnett assisted Sir Kenelm Digby – a scientist, writer and diplomat – in making these 'English bottles' (read 'shaft and globes') thirty years earlier, in 1632, probably at the glasshouse of Newnham-on-Severn, near Gloucester. The 'Letters Patent' is the earliest document relating to a 'shaft and globe', to the bottle capacity and to sealing bottles with the name of their maker, a typical Continental custom which had not been practised in England in the 17th and 18th centuries. Jean or Jan Colnet was a bottle-maker who probably owned the glasshouse at Savenel, Nethen, Belgium, from 1600-1640 (Figure 31).

1662: Christopher Merret *(747)*, London, 1662, states in *The Art of Glass* that the same bottles were used for all possible purposes. 'Bottles and other vessels to keep Wine, Beer, Spirits, Oyls, Powders…' (Figure 5). 'Wine' bottles are also used for containing beer, liquor, vinegar, cider and chemicals, and for all other applications.

1663: Earliest known dated Continental bottle seal. The German (Schleswig-Holstein) seal reads 'PIKE•FEDES•VON•SCHLOTT ★1663★' (Figure 24(2)).

1669: Earliest known Continental bottle seal with the name of its German glass-maker 'HINRICH BRVWER' (Figure 25).

1670: Bernard Perrot *(342)* of the Verreries Royales du Duché d'Orléans, France makes perfume bottles and flasks in honey colour. He makes embossed bottles by means of two-part and three-part moulds.

1670-1699: Christian V, King of Denmark and Norway. The bottle-making area Schleswig-Holstein, now Germany, is a part of Denmark at this time.

1674: George Ravenscroft from the Henley-on-Thames Glass Works, England obtains a patent from the King of England to make bottles and glassware in flint glass (lead glass or crystalline glass). Closed glass-melting pots are used. A conical building to exhaust the smoke from the coal-fired furnaces is used for the first time in the history of glass-making (Figure 34). This 'English' cone-furnace becomes widespread in England and Germany, such as Gernheim (in 1826) and Obernkirchen (in 1827).

1677: The London 'Company of Glass Sellers' *(854)* publishes on 1 January 1677 its *SCHEDULE of Wholesale Rates and Sizes of Green-Glass Vessels*. Plain bottles, marked bottles, square bottles and handled bottles of different sizes between double gallons and half-pints are priced between 32 shillings and 1s.10d (one shilling and ten pence). A 'marked quart bottle' (sealed shaft and globe) costs 4 shillings, a plain quart bottle 3 shillings.

1679: The German Johann Kunckel *(634)* publishes *Ars Vitraria Experimentalis oder Vollkommene Glasmacher-Kunst,* a German translation with personal comments on A. Neri's *L'Arte Vetraria* (published in Italian in 1612). Kunckel invents, in 1679, the famous gold ruby glass (Figure 6 and Plate 233).

1679: Earliest engraving of an overground dip mould in copper for fast blowing square and rectangular case bottles of all sizes. Illustrated in Johann Kunckel's *(634) Ars Vitraria Experimentalis oder Vollkommene Glasmacher-Kunst* (Figure 39).

1680-1690: The first 'shaft and bladder' made in France and Europe. A very rare and attractive bottle (Plate 141).

1681-today: A 'Steel Worme' or 'cork-drawer' or 'bottle-screw' is used for extracting corks from bottles. The use of cheap cork extractors in the form of a prong was more popular those days (Plate 322).

1682-1725: 'Westernizing' of Russia by Tsar Peter The Great.

1683: First production of crystal glass in Bohemia. The glass is made by adding chalk to the glass instead of lead.

1689-1702: William III of Orange (1650-1702) becomes King of England (1689-1702) and Stadtholder of Holland and Zeeland (Plate 64.1).

1690: Dom Pérignon, a French monk at the Hautvillers Abbey near Epernay, Champagne, invents champagne and corks the bottles with a cork and a metal wire.

1690-1720: Earliest known glass seal indicating the contents of the bottle. The German seal reads: 'PIERMONT WATER' (Plate 197).

1691-1760: The glasshouse 'SKÅNSKA GLASBRUKET' in Henrikstorp *(790)* is the first and most important bottle-maker in Sweden, using mostly German glass-makers.

1692: First glass stoppers used for bottles and decanters in Paris.

1695: The *Tracts relating to Trade* quotes that: 'in 1695 it was computed that 240,000 dozens (2.88 million) of bottles were made in England every year'.

1696: Thirty-seven so-called 'bottlehouses' in England and Wales are making bottles, nine in the London area, five in Bristol, five in Stourbridge, four in Newcastle, and many others scattered about the country.

1697: Earliest known dated sealed Belgian onion bottle (Plate 120).

1701: Reintroduction of the use of coal as a fuel for making glass in Germany at the Glasshouse of Osterwald (1701-1827), Hanover area. See also dates '1579-1585'.

1701-1713: Frederick I, King of Prussia.

1702: Earliest known English bottle (onion) bearing a date '1702' only.

1702: First dated silver corkscrew (England, 1702).

1704: Latest known dated sealed 'shaft and globe' in the world. French (Figure 21).

1705: The Thuringian glass-maker Hans Schmidt in Stützerbach produces 298,000 pieces of 'holländisches Glas' ('Dutch glass') for Holland.

1711: Decree of the city of Bruges, Belgium *(308)* on gauging bottles for wine, beer, brandy and all other liquid wares with a pewter gauge-ring to certify the correct capacity of the bottle sold within the city of Bruges (Figure 27 and Plate 124).

1713: English onion indicating its full provenance and date (Ann Tomlinson, the Three Tuns Tavern, Oxford, 1713) (Plate 16).

1714-1837: Hanoverians, Kings of England and Hanover. English made bottles were exported to Hanover and Hanoverian made bottles exported to England.

1715-1774: Louis XV (the 'Sun King'), King of France.

1716: Jonathan Swift (Dublin 1667-1745), author of *Gulliver's Travels,* owns an English bladder onion sealed with his private mark, his initials 'I.S.' and the date '1716' (Plate 30).

1718: Decree ('Anordnung') in Hanover *(304),* Germany, on sealing bottles to prove their correct capacity.

1720-1750: The first vertical straight-sided case-gin bottles appear on the market in Holland and Belgium. From c.1750 onwards the case-gin bottles become tapered (Plate 83).

1720-1750: First 'Dutch onion' (made in Belgium or Germany) with a blank glass seal on its neck (Plate 258(3)).

1720-1780: Bottle-production in Thuringia, Hesse and Mecklenburg, Germany. Export to Holland.

1722: Decree *(310)* proclaiming that bottles filled with wine for public sale have to be gauged with a pewter gauge ring to certify their correct capacity in the city of Maastricht, Holland (Figure 27).

1730: First English bottle seal indicating the contents of the bottle. Seal reads: 'H.EYRE – PURVEYOR FOR MINERAL WATERS TO HER MAIESTY – HOLT MINERAL WATERS' (Plate 61).

1730: Dutch merchants negotiate a contract for the delivery from a Mecklenburg (North Germany) bottlehouse of 600,000 'Netherlands-Hamburg style' bottles per annum for a period of four years. The bottles are side-flattened onions as illustrated in Plates 274 and 275.

1730-1746: Earliest bottle seal known on the Continent impressed twice. The Holstein (Germany) made seal shows the monogram 'C6' under a king's crown relating to King Christian VI (1730-1746) of Denmark. See Kruse *(630)* and Plate 207.A for another later seal.

1730-1750: Earliest known bottle used for Maraschino, a cherry liqueur in Zara, Croatia (Plate 183).

1730-1835: The glasshouse of Amersfoort is the first and most important bottle-maker in Holland.

1732: Earliest antedated bottle made in a Ricketts mould c.1830 and bearing the name of its contents on the seal, 'SHERRY – 1732' (Plate 48).

1734: England's most perfect and complete mallet bottle. The seal carries the full provenance and date of the bottle, 'The Revd Doc † Rumney – St. Albans – 1734' (Plate 21).

1734: The first round and flat octagonal black glass bottles made in England appear on the market. Octagonal bottles with a flat bottom are blown in a dip mould in an attempt to make bottles with the correct capacity.

1735: First price-list named 'GLAS-TAXA' *(858)* published by a cartel of Thuringian (Germany) glasshouses indicating the original names of bottles and other glassware with prices for export to the Dutch and German markets.

1736-1787: Swedish bottle with four glass seals bearing its capacity '1 QVART' and the name of the glasshouse 'BIÖRKNAS'. Plate 243 illustrates a similar '1850' dated example. See also H. Seitz *(962),* (Figure 8).'

1739-1777: The first American glasshouse is set up in Jamestown, USA in 1608 and produces for a couple of years. The German immigrant Caspar Wistar founds in 1739 the 'Wistarburg Glass Works' in Alloway in Salem County, New Jersey. Most sorts of bottles, gallon, half gallon, quart and pint, case bottles, snuff and mustard bottles, pocket bottles and window glass are their primary products. The wood-firing glasshouse operates until the American Revolution.

1740: The earliest known sealed and dated rectangular utility bottle in the world. Sealed 'IHH – 1740'. Made in the Baltic Sea area (Plate 201).

1740: A French 'gourde' (drinking flask) provided with 18 raspberry prunts and 16 medallions each showing a mask (Plate 162).

1740-1763: The Great British-French Colonial War: America and India. The British overseas empire triumphs over the French. English bottles made at that period are very hard to find today.

1741: Decree by the King of Prussia *(312)* that 'Quart' bottles must be sealed with the name of the bottlehouse and their year of production. Marking the sealed bottles was already 'exercised' in 1739 (Plate 201).

1741-1777: The glasshouse of Nøstetangen is the first glasshouse in Norway to produce bottles and other glassware. The Norwegian glasshouses are suppliers of glass for Denmark and Norway. Before 1753 the glass-blowers at Nøstetangen were mostly Germans.

1748: Date of the earliest known embossed and dated medicine vial. The embossing reads: 'ROBERT TURLINGTON – BY THE KINGS PATENT – MAY 2ᵈ 1748'. The vial contained Turlington's 'Balsam of Life', a multi-ingredient cure-all first patented in England in 1744.

1750: The bottle-makers of Charleroi, Belgium possess a special patent for making all types of black glass bottles for the Dutch market ('Bouteilles de Hollande').

1750: The Belgian glasshouse of Arnould de Colnet in Bruges, the most important bottle-maker at that time, produce yearly 400,000-500,000 bottles for Amsterdam and Middelburg in Holland.

1750: The first wide-mouth jars become popular in Europe in the second half of the eighteenth century.

1750: Belgian 'onion' bottle bearing two seals, one antedated '1650' (Plates 131 and 132).

1750-1770: The earliest pinched waisted 'case'-bottle ('kuttrolf') with a plain seal (Plate 205).

1751-1772: The Frenchmen Diderot and D'Alembert *(328, 330)* publish their *Encyclopédie, ou Dictionnaire raisonné des Sciences, des Arts et des Métiers.* Bottle-making at the 'Verrerie Royale de Sèvres', one of the three most important bottlehouses in France, is extensively illustrated.

1757: Earliest dated sealed 'London gin' bottle. Seal reads: 'LONDON – 1757' surmounted with a king's crown. See Figure 14(1) for a similar bottle.

1760: A flat octagonal handled sealed bottle is produced in 1760, the only one of its kind known in the world. The seal reads: 'AF' surmounted with a king's crown and dated '1760'. The bottle is made by the glasshouse at Henrikstorp, Sweden. The initials are those of Adolph Frederick, King of Sweden (1751-1771) (Plate 239.2).

1760: First English sealed bottle indicating its 'wine'-contents ('PORT') (Figure 12).

1760: First Continental sealed bottle indicating its 'wine' contents ('CONSTANTIA WYN') (Plate 80(2)).

1760-1830: First Industrial Revolution, mainly in England.

1761-1764: Production of 1.5 million bottles a year – vials not included – in Belgium.

1763: Illustration of many bottles, jars and other glassware in the Ip Olufsen Weyse price-list, known as the *Nøstetangen Catalogue (1100),* published in Copenhagen, 1763 (Figure 13).

1769: Decree of 5 September *(309)* by the United Netherlands to protect the Dutch glasshouses against the mass import of glass bottles made in the Austrian Netherlands (Belgium). An import tax of 50% is imposed. Two years later, in 1771, the decree is extended to bottles imported from England and Germany. The decree is cancelled some years later due to limitations in capacity for making bottles in Holland.

1773: Decree *(305)* of George III, Hanover, proclaiming the sealing of bottles with the initials 'GR' (George Rex), the name of the glasshouse and their capacity.

1776-1783: The original thirteen British colonies become the United States of America in 1776 (American Revolution). War of American Independence (1776-1783).

1785: The name 'Bocksbeutel' (capacity 22cl) appears for the first time in a price-list of a bottlehouse (Gehlberger Glashütte in Thuringia, Germany) (Plate 218).

1789: French Revolution.

1789: Five glasshouses in Bordeaux produce together 3.2 million bottles a year (coal-firing).

1789: George Washington, first President of the United States of America.

1791: The smallest known (H: 15.7cm) black glass sealed bottle bearing a date only (England, 1791) (Plate 46(1)).

1792: First French Republic established.

1793: Introduction of the 'litre' (100 cl) in France, 7 April 1793, in use from 1809 onwards.

1794: Jacob Schweppe, in Bristol, first uses earthenware bottles for containing mineral water, but they were not watertight and he soon found that glass bottles were indispensable.

1795: The earliest known French bottle seal indicating its full provenance, contents and date: 'M. CASTILLON Jᵒ – BORDEAUX – COGNAC CHAMPAGNE – 1795' (Figure 26(4)).

1795–1820s: Cylindrical stoneware bottles for beer become popular in England. Oldest dated stoneware beer bottle known: '1795' (England).

1797: A cylindrical bottle sealed 'Col: Wood – Maderia – 1797' is one of the rare English 18th century bottles indicating its 'wine' contents (Madeira wine) (Plate 25(3)).

1800–1900: Due to bad sanitation and impure drinking water many people in Europe die of cholera. Development of special bottles, jars and closures to hygienically preserve beer, mineral and soda water, soft drinks, milk, fruits, food, etc. Syphons, Hamiltons, Codds, medicine and poison bottles become popular.

1802: Charles Chubsee of Stourbridge, England visits some Bohemian glasshouses and introduces to England a Bohemian 'open-and-shut' mould for pressing glass stems of complicated motifs for drinking glasses. The mould should not be confused with the famous three-part Ricketts mould (Figure 41), invented in 1821, for producing bottles.

1814: The Englishman William Hamilton patents an egg-shaped bottle (Hamilton bottle). It had to be stored on its side and thus the cork was always kept moist.

1815: Napoleon Bonaparte rules France from 1804 until 1815. His far-flung military ventures end in Waterloo, Belgium, in 1815.

1816: Introduction of the 'litre' (100cl) in Holland and Belgium on 21 August 1816, in use from 1820 onwards.

1818: 'Ribbon' sealed bottles used for the first time in the world by the Danish distiller Peter Herring (Plate 240(3)).

1820: The Frenchman Nicolas Leblanc succeeded in making unrefined soda ash, an essential ingredient for making cheaper bottles of better quality.

1820: Smallest sealed pontilled bottle (H: 7.2cm) in the world (Holland). Sealed: 'RYKSEIGENDOM' (Property of the State) (Plate 300(1)).

1821, 5 December: Henry Ricketts of Bristol, England *(880)* invents a revolutionary three-part mould for the 'Manufacturing of Glass Bottles, such as used for Wine, Porter, Beer, Cyder or other Liquids' (English Patent No. 4623). The mould determines the shape of the whole bottle including the neck. The lip of the bottle is finished with a tool afterwards. Bottles are still pontilled. This invention was a revolution in hand-blowing glass bottles (Figure 41).

1821–1930s: Use of two-part and three-part movable metal moulds all over Europe for hand-blowing bottles.

1825: George Stephenson invents the railroad locomotive in England. Glasshouses are no longer dependent on transport by water. Decline of the 'forest glasshouses' on the Continent and their removal to more practical areas such as coal areas.

1825, 1 May: Introduction of the 'Imperial Quart' (113.6cl) in England.

1825–today: Holmegaards Glasværk is the first bottle-maker in Denmark.

1830–1860: Use of the bare iron pontil all over the world (Figure 47(2)).

1832–1855: The cholera epidemic in Paris in 1832 forces the people to drink pure water. The syphon bottle for containing Selzer water or English soda water is developed in France between 1832 and 1855. Production: 500,000 bottles a year.

1842: The American Charles Goodyear invents a vulcanisation process that made possible the commercial use of rubber. Bottles provided with rubber parts date from 1842 onwards.

1848: Social revolutions on the European Continent. Marx and Engels' Communist Manifesto. Governments collapse all over the Continent from Paris to Budapest and from Copenhagen to Palermo.

1850–1920: Industrial Revolution in England and Europe. Mechanisation of bottle-making.

1855: The American Amasa Stone obtains the first patent No. 13402, 7 August 1855, for forming screw threads inside the necks of glass bottles. The internal screw stoppers are still used extensively today.

1858: The American John Mason obtains the first patent No. 22129, 30 November 1858 for his mould for blowing an external screw thread on jars for closing them with a one-piece metal screw cap.

1858: French wine bottles with two different seals, one as a 'ribbon'. One seal reads 'MARGAUX BEL-AIR – MARQUIS D'ALIGRE', the ribbon reads: 'DEFENDU D'EN LAISSER'. (Plates 266(2) and 266(3)).

1860–1870: French bottle provided with five glass seals. Another bottle in the Lincolnshire City and County Museum, England has seven(!) seals (Plate 155).

1860–1920: Use of the 'sabot' or 'case' instead of the pontil iron to hold the bottle during and after making.

1861–1865: American Civil War.

1864: An early dated French 'CHATEAU CHALON' sealed bottle as an example for the use of a 'snap case' or a 'sabot'. No pontil scar (Plate 151(1)).

1865: The Belgian Ernest Solvay invents and produces sodium carbonate on a large scale for the manufacture of glass and soap. His method is adopted in Europe and the United States and supplants the Leblanc process. Bottles are now made of higher optical quality and are cheaper than those made by Leblanc's method.

1867: Friedrich Siemens in Dresden, Germany develops the first continuous tank furnace for continuous melting of bottle glass. It is now possible to use machines all over Europe for making 100,000s of bottles a day.

1870: The Frenchman Louis Pasteur invents in 1863 a method for preserving food with heat. In 1870 a Copenhagen brewery produces the first pasteurised bottled beer.

1870–1871: German victory over France in the Franco-German War. William I, King of Prussia, becomes in 1871 the first emperor of Germany.

1872: British Patent No. 2612 describes the important invention made by Hiram Codd for his most successful closure for 'Bottles to Contain Aerated Liquids', such as mineral waters, soda water, lemonade, etc. The glass bottle is sealed with a captive glass marble inside the neck (Figure 43 and Plate 312).

1874: Earliest semi-automatically made dated sealed wine bottle known, 'CHATEAU LAFITE – 1874 – GRAND VIN' (Plates 149(4) and 149(5)).

1886: Coca-Cola is invented in the USA by John Pemberton. In 1894, the Hutchinson-stoppered bottle is the first bottle to contain Coca-Cola. The classical contoured bottle embossed 'BOTTLE PAT'D NOV. 16 – 1915' becomes the world's most famous bottle.

1887: First use of a semi-automatic bottle-making machine in England by Howard Ashley. British Patent No. 8677 published 27 May 1887.

1890: Oscar Ehrbeck is granted German Patent No. 55012 for the first invention of a porcelain cork swing stopper for bottles.

1892: The American William Painter of Baltimore is granted German Patent No. 68350, 2 February 1892, for a 'crown cork', the most widely used closure in the brewing and soft drink trades. His cork was protected in the USA in 1890.

1892: The German Friedrich Siemens patents the first porcelain-rubber swing stopper.

1894: Bottling of milk in swing-stoppered bottles.

1894: M. Boucher, bottle-maker of Cognac, France invents a bottle-making machine (13 French patents) which becomes very popular in France.

1896: The first American automatic bottle-blowing machine, known as the Beatty or the Blue machine, is installed in Washington, Pennsylvania, USA. By this year, bottle-making has assumed a definite commercial pattern in the USA. Some fruit jars were made by this machine as early as 1896 at the Atlas Glass Co., Washington, PA.

1900–1920: Largest machinery-made sealed octagonal bottle in the world (Germany). H: 57cm. Cap: 11 litres (Plate 213(3)).

1903: The American Michael Owens invents a six arm rotary bottle machine (US Patent No. 774.690). This machine has been acclaimed as one of the most brilliant inventions in the history of inventions. By 1911 in the United States, 103 Owens-machines are installed with a production capacity of 102,000 bottles per machine every twenty-four hours. The machine revolutionises bottle-making, and is the most popular bottle machine in Europe in the first half of the 20th century.

1910: The introduction of automatic bottle-making machines means that the old small bottlehouses are replaced by large industrial factories with expensive machinery.

1914–1918: First World War or Great War.

1917: Russian Revolution.

1924 and 1928: Henry Ingle obtains American Patents No. 1.843.159 and No. 1.911.119 for an Individual Section machine to make bottles and jars. This machine has been improved much since then and today has become the most important bottle-making machine in the world (3,000 machines; the most modern I.S. machine produces 720,000 bottles every twenty-four hours).

1929: In his book *A History of English and Irish Glass,* W.A. Thorpe *(1028)* mentions for the first time the name 'shaft and globe' for the 'English bottle' from about 1650 with a long neck and a round body. In the 1650s their name was simply 'bottles' or 'English bottles'.

1929: The Crash of 1929 or The Great Depression. Collapse of the world economy.

Capacity of antique bottles in the eighteenth and nineteenth century in Europe

The capacity of antique bottles may be an extra indicator of their original contents, the period or date of use and the market or area for which the bottles have been made. Except in England and some Scandinavian countries, such as Sweden and Finland in the 18th and early 19th century, the official capacity of bottles may vary from one area or city to another on the Continent and can be related to their contents, such as wine, beer or other liquids. Note that a bottle may have been made in one area to export to another area where other capacity standards are used. Because bottles are free-blown or hand-blown their capacity may sometimes vary up to 20% from the official standard. Examples from different areas, cities and countries are now given to illustrate the system.

Great Britain (until 1 May 1825)

English Queen Anne 'wine' Quart = 94.63cl (one Gallon = 2 Pottles = 4 Quarts = 8 Pints).
English 'ale and beer' Quart = 115.53cl.
Scotch Pint (officially) = 172.06cl.
Scotch 'ale' Pint (in trade) = 182.88cl.
Irish Quart (from 1695) = 111.53cl.
Irish Quart (from 1736) = 89.15cl.
English 'reputed' Quart (popular for all liquids from c.1680 until the mid-19th century) = 75.77cl.
English Imperial Quart (from 1 May 1825) = 113.57cl.

Holland and Belgium (until 21 August 1816, in use from 1820)

Amsterdam Bottle or Fles = 88cl.
Amsterdam Pint = 57.5cl.
Amsterdam Stoop = 243cl.
Rotterdam Pint = 64cl.
Rotterdam Stoop = 255cl.
Utrecht Fles = 85cl.
Maastricht Fles = 3 Pinten = 100cl.
Bruges Pot or Kan = 2 Pints = ½ Stoop = 112.96cl.
One Litre = 100cl (from 21 August 1816, in use from 1820).

Germany

Berlin Quart (1722-1816) = 117cl for Brandenburg and Prussia.
Berlin Quart (after 1816) = 114.5cl for Prussia (¾ Berliner Quart = 85.87cl).

Hamburg Quartier = 90cl.
Hanoverian Quart = 97.2cl (1 Quart = 2 Nösel = 4 Ort).
Bavarian Kanne or Maß = 107cl.
Rostock Kanne = 2 Pott = 4 Oeßel = 8 Ort = 181.1cl (for Mecklenburg-Schwerin).
Brunswick Quartier = 93.5 cl.
Hesse Maß = 200cl.
One Litre = 100cl (in Lower Saxony from 19 August 1836, in Bavaria from 17 August 1868 and in Mecklenburg from 1 January 1872).

France (until 7 April 1793, in use from 1809)

Lorraine Pinte = 122cl (1 Pot = 2 Pintes = 4 Chopines = 4 Demi-pintes = 244 cl).
Paris Pinte = 93cl.
Toul Pinte = 107cl.
One Litre = 100cl from 7 April 1793, in use from 1809).

Miscellaneous

Stockholm Stop = 2 Halvstops = 4 Kvarters (quarts) = 130.8cl (common in Sweden and Finland).
Austrian Maß = 2 Halben = 4 Seidel = 141cl.
Swiss Maß = 4 Seidel = 150cl.
Danish, Norwegian and Schleswig-Holstein Pott = 96.6cl.
Portuguese Melo = 68.6cl.
Russian Kruschka = 12 cl.

Main characteristics for identifying the origin, date and use of antique bottles

The following characteristics – alone or in combination – may help to identify an antique bottle. The bottle 'style' or shape, the technique used to make the bottle, the glass colour of the bottle and its condition, such as corrosion and wear. Further, the bottle dimensions, such as its capacity and wall thickness. Glass seals, pewter gauge-rings, embossings, closures, engravings, decorations and remains of the contents may help a lot, as well as comparing a bottle with other similar bottles with known characteristics. Last but not least, we may not underestimate experience in collecting bottles.

ILLUSTRATED HISTORY OF BOTTLES

(Figures 1–48)
Their origin, evolution, use, capacity, seals and gauge-rings.
The raw materials, furnaces, technology, tools and empontilling used in
bottle-making

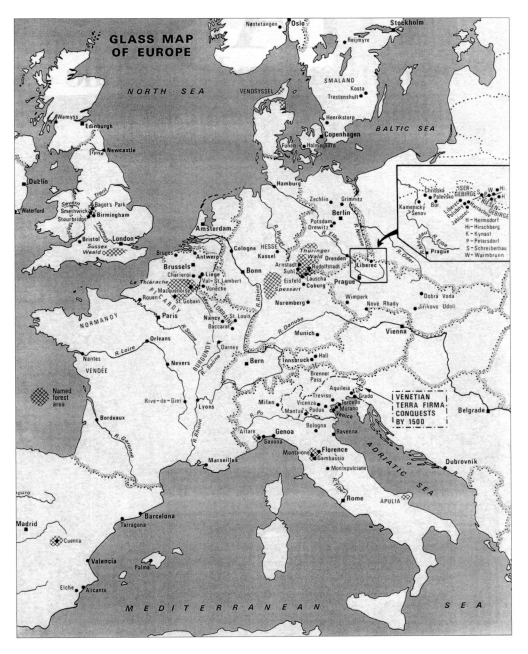

Figure 1. Glass map of Europe showing the most relevant glassmaking areas. Note that the most important bottle and vial making area from the 16th century to the mid-20th century was Belgium which exported millions of bottles/vials to Holland and France, especially the Champagne and Burgundy regions.

Bohemia, which specialised in Bohemian crystalware, was of minor importance for making 'black glass' utility bottles.

As it is not possible to show all regional bottle-makers on a single map, as many areas of production as possible are indicated with the figures and plates in the book.

Courtesy of Ada Polak

29

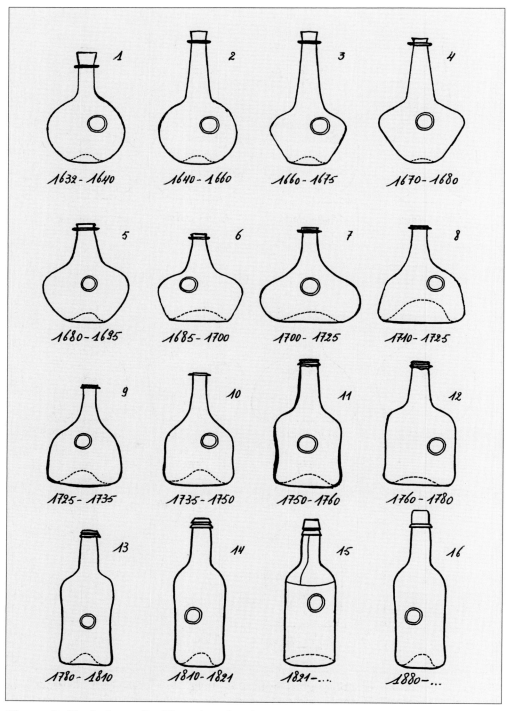

Figure 2. Evolution of utility glass bottles in England (1632–1880) for wine, beer, spirits, oil, vinegar and all other purposes. The bottles are mostly thick-walled (3-6mm) and made of black glass.

    The dates are approximate. Each sealed bottle also existed unsealed.

    Note that this illustration shows the pre-industrial evolution of the 'shaft and globe' of 1632 to the 'cylinder' of c.1880. Parallel to this evolution in the 18th century other bottle types were made such as round and flat octagonal, square, side-flattened onions, bladders, etc.

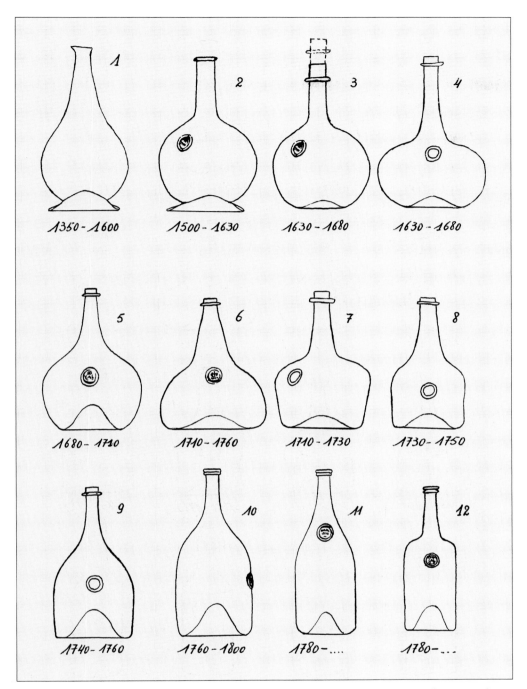

Figure 3. Evolution of utility glass bottles in Belgium (1350-1780) for wine, beer, spirits, oil, vinegar and all other purposes except the mineral waters of Spa.

The illustration shows the evolution of the 'pear'-shaped bottle of c.1350 to the 'cylinder', based on surviving bottle types. The authenticity of the shapes was checked, based on iconographic, archivic and archaeological research. Several of the bottle types shown were the predominant bottle types made in England, France, North Germany and Belgium at the time.

Bottles (1) and (2) are very thin-walled (less than 1mm) and made of clear, yellowish or olive green forest glass. Bottles (3)-(12) are mostly made of olive green, grass green or black glass ('verre noir') and are of lighter weight (wall thickness 2-4mm) than their English counterparts.

The seal of bottle (2) is probably made of wax; the other seals are glass.

'Shaft and globe' (3) also exists with a long neck.

STUART PERIOD		HANOVERIAN PERIOD	
1625-1649	Charles I	1714-1727	George I
1649-1660	Commonwealth	1727-1760	George II
1660-1685	Charles II	1760-1820	George III
1685-1688	James II	1820-1830	George IV
1689-1702	William III and Mary II	1830-1837	William IV
1702-1714	Anne	1837-1901	Victoria

Figure 4. Kings and Queens of England from 1625 to 1901. During the Hanoverian period (until 1837) the Kings of England were also Kings or Electors (Kurfürsten) of the Electorate Hanover, Germany and greatly influenced bottle making in Hanover, such as the introduction of the art of coal firing.

Of the use of Glass.

IN Domestick affairs it makes drinking vessels, infinite in fashion, colour, largness, the Romer for Rhenish wine, for Sack, Claret, Beer, plain, moulded, coloured in whole, or in part, Bottles and other vessels to keep Wine, Beer, Spirits, Oyls, Powders, wherein you may see their Fermentations, separations, and whatsoever other changes nature in time worketh in any liquours, the clearness and goodness of them.

Figure 5. Excerpt from *The Art of Glass* by Christopher Merret (747), London, 1662, stating 'Bottles and other vessels to keep Wine, Beer, Spirits, Oyls, Powders…'

The same bottles were used for all possible purposes.

This also declares that until c.1750 – all over Europe – bottle seals rarely mention the contents of the bottles.

Due to widespread cheating regarding the quality of mineral waters (at that time named 'medicinal' waters), the bottles were sealed with wax seals (from c.1600 onwards) or with glass seals (from c.1690 onwards) to distinguish them from the fraudulent mineral waters. (See Plates 61(1), 136 and 197-199.)

Ref: Willy Van den Bossche (188)

Vom Gebrauch des Glaſes.

Es werden zu dem Hauswesen aus dem Glaß mancherley Geschirr/ von unterschiedlicher Farb und Gröſ/ verfertiget : als da sind flache und zugespitzte Becher/ gantz oder nur zum Theil gefärbet ; dienende zum Reinischen und Spanischen Wein/ zum Claret oder Bier : Jngleichen Flaschen und andere Geschirr/ darinnen man Wein/ Bier/ Spiritus, Oehl oder Pulver auffbehalten/ und in welchen man die Durchsichtig= keit der Liqvorum, derselben Güte/ Jährung/ Scheidung und andere Verwunderungssachen sehen kan/ welche mit der Zeit von der Natur in denselben gewürcket werden.

Figure 6. Excerpt from *Ars Vitraria Experimentalis oder Vollkommene Glasmacher-Kunst* by Johann Kunckel (634), Frankfurt/Leipzig, 1679 which is a translation from Christopher Merret's (747) remark on 'The use of Glass' in his book *The Art of Glass* (1662). (See Figure 5.)

The German translation reads: '…Ingleichen Flaschen und andere Geschirr darinnen mann Wein/Bier/Spiritus/Oehl oder Pulver auffbehalten hat…'

Until at least the middle of the 18th century bottles were common utility bottles used for all purposes.

Ref: Willy Van den Bossche (188)

Figure 7. Flemish miniature dated c.1270 showing a monk, called a 'Piskijker' (a urine examiner), analysing the urine of a female patient, contained in a kuttrolf, with a view to diagnosing any ailment. This illustration from the Psalmbook of the Gwijde van Dampierre, created Count of Flanders (Belgium) in 1270, shows the oldest kuttrolf ever pictured. It proves that this drinking bottle was also used as a urinal. For a 15th century kuttrolf see Plate 190(2). *Courtesy of the Koninklijde Bibliotheek Albert I, Brussels, Belgium. Manuscript HS. 10607, folio 16v-17*

Figure 8. Illustration of a side-flattened kidney-shaped Belgian/French utility bottle as depicted in *Black Jacks and Leather Bottells* by O. Baker (116), London, 1921.

The front of this leather covered glass bottle has a heart-shaped ornament in the centre, with the initials 'ST' to the left and 'L' to the right. Below is the date '1600'. This bottle was presented to Sir Thomas Leigh in 1600 by the City of London.

From Roman times onwards until the development of the English thick-walled (3-7mm) shaft and globe in c.1630, glass bottles were thin-walled (0.5-2mm) and very fragile. Even until the 20th century some types of thin-walled bottles such as demijohns and Chianti wine bottles were made and needed to be protected against damage. Covering bottles with leather, straw, wood, wickerwork etc. was a very common practice.

See also Plate 117 for a similar glass bottle, but without its protective covering.

Figure 9. Detail of a painting from Jan Bruegel the Elder or 'Velvet Bruegel' (Brussels 1568-Antwerp 1625), dated 1602, depicting the 'Allegory on the Fire' (one of his 'Four Elements'). It is amazing to see so many early bottles, flasks, vials, jars and alembics in one painting. *Courtesy of the Pinacoteca Ambrosiana, Milano, Italy*

Figure 10. Engraving from Jan van der Velde III (Rotterdam 1593-Enkhuizen 1641) depicting a quack selling his products to credulous people. The accompanying motto says: 't'volek wil bedrogen zyn' (people want to be cheated).

The giant kidney-shaped bottle, the three onion-shaped, long-neck vials, the three case bottles and the long-neck, tubular vial are pictured in Plates 118(1), 248(5), 249(1-3), 253 and 301(3). *Courtesy of the Boymans-van Beuningen Museum, Rotterdam, Holland*

Figure 11. Woodcut of 'The Alchemist in his Laboratory' by David Teniers the Younger (Antwerp 1610–Brussels 1690).

Note the different shapes, closures and uses of the bottles and jars pictured.

Courtesy of the Bibliothèque Nationale, Paris

Figure 12. An English common utility bottle for port wine, sealed: 'Port', c.1760. Sand pontil scar. H: 23cm. Cap: 90cl. Excavated and patinated.

This bottle shows the earliest known English wine seal indicating its contents. Plate 80(2) shows a Dutch/Belgian wine bottle sealed 'CONSTANTIA WYN' of the same period (1760). Plate 61(1) shows the oldest known (c.1730) English glass seal referring to mineral water.

This style of bottle, combined with its correct capacity, was in the 19th century mainly used for beer and porter.

Dumbrell (346, fig. 172) illustrates another cylindrical bottle for wine and sealed 'TV – 1771' encircled by vines, leaves and grapes. The bottle owner may have been Thomas Vyvyan of Trelowarren and later of Trewan (England).

Ref: Willy Van den Bossche (188), Abb.16

Photo: Bernd Hardy

Figure 13. Bottles and a jar as illustrated in the famous Ip Olufsen Weyse price list for all sorts of utility glasswares, known as the *Nøstetangen Catalogue* (published in Danish, Copenhagen, 1763, 348 pages, about 290 glass items illustrated, mostly of North German origin).

The Nøstetangen glasshouse (1741-1777) was situated in Nøstetangen, Norway, which was a part of the Danish kingdom until 1814, similar to the situation of Schleswig-Holstein, which became a part of Germany from 1864.

The illustrated bottles and jar are described as follows:

No. 145: 'cantin eller kluk flasker', case or kuttrolf bottles. Cap: 2 Pott (193.2cl). See Plate 88(3).

No. 109: 'ronde Boutellier, round bottles. Cap: ½ Pott (48.3cl). See Plate 260(2).

No. 143: 'cantin flasker", case flasks. Cap: 1½ Pott (145cl). See Figures 14, 26(1) and Plates 206-208.

This bottle type exists in the following colours: dark olive green, light olive green, aqua, clear, cobalt blue, light blue, amethyst and forest green.

No. 164: 'syllte glas', preserving or storage jars. Cap: 2 Potts (193.2cl). See Plate 289(1).

Refs: I.O. Weyse (1100); A. Polak (843)

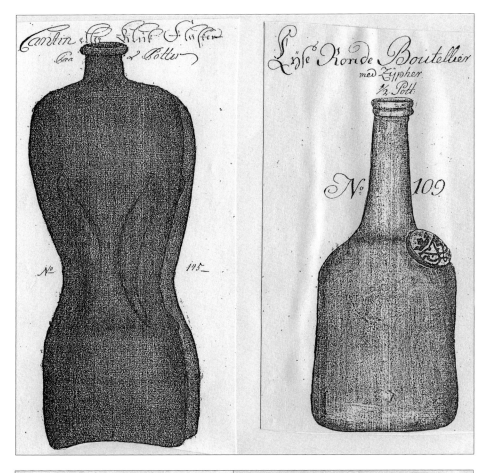

Figure 14. A modern and two very rare 'London gin' case bottles sealed: 'LONDON' surmounted by a king's crown (left) and a noble crown (right). No initials of the glasshouse or the glassmaker on the seal. The bottles were made in the areas around the Baltic Sea where they were filled with 'London gin' and then sold locally or exported to the neighbouring countries.

Note the colours and shapes at different periods. The capacities of the illustrated mouth-blown bottles approach 87cl (⅔ Swedish, Finnish or Russian Stop) and 96.6cl (1 Danish, Norwegian or Holstein Pott).

(1) c.1750-1760. The king's crown refers to Frederick V, King of Denmark and Norway (1746-1766) or to Adolf Frederick, King of Sweden (1751-1771) and indicates that the glasshouse had the royal privilege or patent to produce these bottles. Bottle blown in a strongly tapered dip mould. Forest green glass colour. Dim: 16.6 x 8.1 x 8.7cm (base). Cap: 81.8cl (⅔ Stop). Wt: 540gr.

(2) A modern 'LONDON DRY GIN' bottle. H: 28cm. Cap: 1 litre.

(3) c.1780. Light olive green colour. The noble crown refers to the nobleman who gave the privilege to the glasshouses to produce bottles on his territory. Dim: 20 x 9 x 8cm. Cap: 92cl (⅔ Stop or 1 Pott). Wt: 500gr.

See also Figures 13 (No. 143) and 26(1) and Plates 83-91 ('Dutch' gin bottles), 206, 208(4).

Refs: K-H. Poser (847), bottle (1) illustrated on Abb. 34, lot 324; K. Friese (418) illustrates a similar bottle as (1) sealed: 'No. 3-GRIMNITZ-1768'; I.O. Weyse (1100), illus. No. 143 ('cantin flasker'); A. Polak (843)

Figure 15. Two English 'black glass' bottles showing the comparison between a 'beer and porter' style bottle and a 'wine and cider' style bottle from the same date (1809) and the same owner. Both with disc pontil scar. Deep olive green colour.

> (1) Sealed: 'SIR WILL.ᴹ STRICKLAND BAR.ᵀ – 1809'. H: 24cm. Ø: 11cm. Cap: 105cl. Wt: 850gr. A large 'beer and porter' style quart bottle.
>
> (2) Sealed: 'SIR W.ᴹ STRICKLAND BAR.ᵀ – 1809'. H:26.5cm. Ø: 9cm. Cap: 75cl (1 reputed quart = 76cl). Wt: 750gr. A 'wine and beer' style quart bottle. The seal on the shoulder of cylindrical bottles is unusual in England between 1740 and 1850.

Sir William Strickland (1753-1834)was a baronet who came from Boynton Hall, near Bridlington, Yorkshire (U.K.). In England, until the mid-18th century, utility bottles were used for beer, wine, liqueur and all other liquid or powder wares. Since that time such bottles have evolved to a short, wide body for beer and porter and a tall slender body for wine and cider. Note that porter is a beer and should not be confused with port wine. See also Plates 26(3) and 28(1).

Ref: O. Jones (578)

Figure 16. Three 19th century European beer bottles. From c.1800 onwards the common utility bottle develops for containing specific drinks such as beer. The combination of the bottle style and a fixed beer capacity determines the beer or porter bottle.

    (1) England, c.1810. Blown in a dip mould. Clear olive green colour. Sand pontil scar. H: 18.5cm. Ø: 8cm. Cap: 44cl. Wt: 395gr.

    (2) England, c.1860–1870. Blown in a Ricketts three-part mould. No pontil scar; a sabot, case or snap-case was used to hold the bottle during finishing. Black glass. H: 23cm. Ø: 9.6cm. Cap. 73cl. Wt. 890gr.

    (3) English seal: 'P.G. & OLD BRISTOL PORTER C°.' c.1800. Die Ø: 38mm. The seal was near the base of the porter bottle. Porter was a strong, dark brown beer mainly drunk by the 'porters' at the ports in England.

    (4) Belgium, c.1860. Bare iron pontil scar. Deep olive green colour (black glass). Sealed. H: 21cm. Ø:7.8cm. Cap: 35cl. Wt. 480gr.

Refs: O. Jones (580) for (1) and (2); H. Tait (1009) for (3)

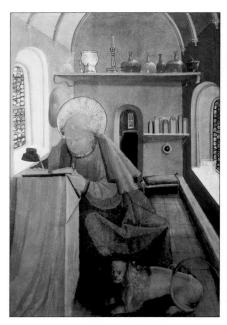

Figure 17. Painting from an unknown Austrian master depicting the Holy Markus and three dark brown transparent forest glass bottles. Between 1490 and 1500.

In the 15th and 16th centuries glass bottles in this colour were mainly made in Lorraine, North-east France, and are described in the archives as 'verre noir' (black glass).

Courtesy of the Institut für Mittelalterliche Realienkunde Österreichs, Krems a/d Donau, Austria

Figure 18. This bottle may be considered as the forerunner of the English and Continental 'shaft and globe'. Produced in the Middle East (Iran, Iraq or Syria) between the 11th and 13th century. Dark honey colour (wood firing). Glass-tipped pontil scar.

H: 21cm. Cap: 112cl. Wt: 162gr. Wall thickness: 1-1.5mm. The funnel-shaped lip facilitates filling and drinking from the bottle.

In comparison to this medieval bottle the English 'shaft and globe' is strong (wall thickness: 7mm!), heavy (1200gr!) and of 'black glass' as illustrated in Plate 2.

Ref: A similar bottle (Inv. Nr. P. 1966-96) is displayed at the Kunstmuseum, Düsseldorf, Germany

Figure 19.1. One of the earliest known 'reinvented' shaft and globes in Europe. Made in Belgium from c.1625–1630. Bottle made in almost clear glass with a greenish tone (wood firing).

Note the use of a 'string rim' around the lip of the bottle adopted in Europe since c.1625–1630. Bottle excavated at Utrecht, Holland and is the property of the Oudheidkundig Museum in Utrecht (Inventory No. 6825). See also Figures 2, 3, 19.2 and Plates 2–6.

Ref: Bottle illustrated in R. McNulty (735), fig.36, no.3.   *Courtesy of the Oudheidkundig Museum, Utrecht, Holland*

Figure 19.2. Illustration of the earliest known 'reinvented' shaft and globes. Produced in Belgium from c.1630 until c.1680 by one of the many bottle-houses of the Colinet glassmaking dynasty (1450-1850).

Bottles are thin-walled (max. 2mm), lightweight and in clear olive green or dark bluish green forest glass. Because at that time in Belgium there was no need or legal obligation to use coal as a fuel most bottles were made using wood firing only. About 2,400 kilograms of wood was needed to make one kilo of glass!

Jean Colinet (John Colnett) assisted Sir Kenelm Digby to make the bottle-type figured on the left, in England, by using coal instead of wood as a fuel; this darkens the original glass colour. Such an 'English bottle' is illustrated in Plate 1. Bottles are now provided with a string rim to facilitate corking the bottle.

The illustrated bottles were excavated at the Bishopric Palace in Antwerp and are the property of the 'Archeologische Dienst' of the city of Antwerp, Belgium.

(1)   H: 20.5cm. Ø: 13.5cm. Wt: 800gr (estimate). Wall: 2mm. Bottom: 4mm thick. Glass-tipped pontil scar. A similar bottle sealed with a Maltese cross has been excavated in The Hague, Holland. See also Plate 1.

(2)   H: 22cm. Ø: 14cm. Wt: 430gr (estimate). Blowpipe pontil scar.

(3)   H: 19cm. Ø: 13.5cm. Wt: 430gr (estimate). Blowpipe pontil scar. 'Verre bleu' or 'Verre fougère'.

See also the 'Chronology of bottle-making', dates 1450-1850, 1632 and 1661 and Figures 2, 3, 19.1 and 31.

Photo: Willy Van den Bossche.

Figure 20. A very rare, late, handled English 'shaft and globe' c.1700. The seal depicts the Chetwynd arms, a chevron between three mullet. This bottle belonged to Walter Chetwynd, Member of Parliament for the boroughs of Stafford and Lichfield (1703-1735). He was nominated Viscount of Chetwynd in 1717. Compare the string rim and the shape of this late shaft and globe with its earlier counterparts made between 1660 and 1675 as illustrated in Plates 3-6. H: 17.1cm.

Photo: Willy Van den Bossche.

Courtesy of the Trustees of the Cecil Higgins Art Gallery, Bedford, England

45

Figure 21. A French utility bottle sealed with three fleurs-de-lis (the arms of the French crown) surmounted with the date '1704'. The reverse pictures the enamel painted text: 'Essence Specifique'.

This bottle is the youngest known dated shaft and globe in the world. The text shows that it was not only used for wine, beer, oil, vinegar etc., but also for pharmaceutical purposes. It is 21cm high, of dark grass green colour and has a blowpipe pontil scar. See also Plates 139, 140 and 178 (seal).

Ref: Bottle displayed at the Pharmacie Historique XVII⁰ Siècle in Baugé, France   *Photos: Willy Van den Bossche*

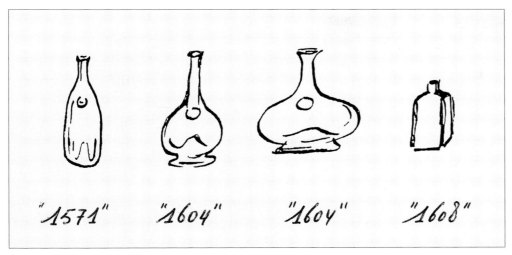

Figure 22. Four early Belgian bottles as illustrated in the Belgian *Journal d'Amandt Colinet* (261) written by glassmaker Amandt Colinet (Beauwelz 1530-1613) from 1567 onwards until 1613. He was director of the famous glasshouses 'Surginet' in Beauwelz and 'Formathot' in Macquenoise, both in Hainault, South Belgium. The 'Formathot' glasshouse specialised in making bottles.

Note that the bottles (1), (2) and (3) were made in 'verre noir' (black glass), a dark olive amber transparent glass as can be seen in the painting and from excavated bottles of that period.

The use of wax seals on bottles was not uncommon in Belgium from the last quarter of the 16th century onwards.

The bottles illustrated by A. Colinet in his diary (written in French) were ordered by his customers and are described as follows:

(1)   In '1571': '1350 bottles in ver noir [black glass] with a place for a wax seal'. (Note: for Reims.) This burgundy bottle type turns up in Burgundy, France, from c.1500.

(2) (3) In '1604': 'black bottles with a seal and a bottom [foot], 400 of each type.' Note that many bottles made before c.1630 do have a foot and flanged folded-in or tapered down lips to reinforce the lip. After c.1630 bottles are provided with a string rim better to reinforce the lip. These bottle types were excavated or seen in Flemish and Dutch paintings in clear and black glass, unfortunately without a seal in either wax or glass.

(4)   In '1608': '80 square bottles with chamfered corners and a screw stopper.' These case bottles were very common all over Europe.

Courtesy of the Corning Museum of Glass, Corning, New York, U.S.A.

Figure 23. Detail of the earliest known glass seal on the European Continent, c.1640.

This seal – from a broken drinking glass – depicts a shield in the centre surrounded by three leaves of the nettle plant, at that time the coat of arms of Holstein, North Germany.

In 1640 1416 'Spitzgläser mit dem Nesselblatt gezeignet' (goblets signed with the nettle leaf) were ordered for Duke Frederick III in Gottorf, Holstein.

Seal excavated on the site of the Rixtorf glasshouse, near Plön, Holstein. Seal Ø: 20mm, die Ø:14mm. Greenish Waldglas.

Refs: H-J. Kruse (630), pls.B1 and B2; K-H. Poser (697). Heft 10, p.196, 1992
Collection: Peter Besel   *Photo: K-H. Poser*

Figure 24.1. Detail of the earliest known dated glass seal in the world. 'WE – 1650.' From an English broken shaft and globe as pictured in Plate 2. The seal diameter is 42mm. The glass colour is pale green.

Several seals, antedated 1650 or before 1650, exist as pictured in Plates 131, 132 and 265(1). In these cases neither the bottle shapes nor the technology correspond to the date on the seals. *Courtesy of the Museum of London*

Figure 24.2. Detail of the earliest known dated Continental glass seal from a broken bottle. The seal reads 'PIKE•FEDES•VON•SCHLOTT ★1663★ around coat of arms depicting a triangular buoy and a bird.

Pike Fedes von Schlott or Pike Fedes van der Sloot was of Dutch origin and lived as a glassware merchant at Itzehoe, Holstein, North Germany, well situated for the glass trade from Holstein to Holland.

The seal comes from a large onion-shaped thin-walled (2-3mm) bottle in forest green glass ('Waldglas') and was excavated in Holland.

The bottles were made at the glasshouses of Bossee, Wittenberg and Testorf in Holstein, North Germany. *Courtesy of H-J. Kruse (630)*

Refs: H-J. Kruse (630), pp.12, 45 and illustrations C1 (p.3) and A1 (pp.5,9); Dumbrell (346), p.185, pl.106 illustrates an English seal (probably 1665-1670) that also shows a buoy

Figure 25. Glass seal from a broken bottle dated '1669' with the name of its glassmaker 'HINRICH BRVWER' and three bottles or jars as his trade mark. Hinrich Brvwer, named today Brauer, possessed the glasshouses in Ascheberg, Wittmold and Lammershagen, Holstein (North Germany). Seal excavated in Holland and has a light grass green colour with bluish tone (forest glass). Indicating the glassmakers' references on a bottle seal was non-existent in England but widespread on the European Continent. Die Ø: 42mm.

Refs: H-J. Kruse (630); Willy Van den Bossche (188)

Figure 26. A collection of 17th-18th century glass seals from broken bottles. Excavated and patinated. Note the differences of style, quality and colour compared with the other seals illustrated in Plates 61, 115, 116 and 214.

(1) Seal of a 'London gin' case bottle. Embossed: 'LONDON' surmounted with a noble crown. The five-pointed star or pentagram symbolises the protection of the drinker against demonic beings. The initials 'G-G' are those of Georg Grimm, owner of the 'Lehtse Fabrique' glassworks (in German: 'Glas- und Boutellen-Fabrique unter den Gute Lechts') operating from 1776 to 1808 at Rekka, Estonia, Baltic Sea area.

The name 'LONDON' refers to 'London gin' to differentiate this London-made dry gin from the Netherlandish gins known as 'Hollands', 'genever', 'geneva' or 'Schiedam'. The London dry gins have more added flavouring ingredients than Dutch types and are very popular for making cocktails such as 'gin and tonic' etc.

Thus, 'LONDON' seals are very unusual seals referring to the contents of the bottle ('gin') as well as to the quality and the taste of the gin.

The seals appear only on the widespread case bottles (in Danish: 'cantin flasker') popular in the 18th-19th century in the areas around the Baltic Sea (Norway, Sweden, Denmark, Finland, Estonia, Latvia, Lithuania, Russia, Poland and North Germany).

Many of the 'London gin' bottles were produced in these countries (except Denmark), for example in the glasshouses of Rekka and Gorondyonka (both in Estonia), Biri Glasværk in Norway and of Urzecze in Poland. Often, although not always, the 'LONDON' or 'LONDEN' seals are embossed with the initials of the glasshouses or the glassmaker.

The pictured seal is of dark green 'forest glass' colour with a bluish tone (black glass). Made c.1780. Die Ø: 24mm. See also Figures 13 and 14 and Plates 83-91 ('Dutch' gin bottles), 206, 207 and 208.

(2) Seal illustrating 'Fortuna' standing as a goddess on the terrestrial globe symbolising prosperity, good (or bad) luck. The Fortuna is surrounded by the name 'FRANTZ ★ GVNDELACH', glassmaker at the glasshouses of Grünhaus, Perdoel, Rumohrhütte and Glasau, all in Holstein, North Germany. c.1670-1700. Seal excavated in Holland. Forest green glass colour. Die Ø: 32mm.

(3) Seal 'I.C. HOFFMANN'. England c.1830. Black glass. Die Ø: 28mm. See also Plate 45(1).

(4) French seal: 'M. CASTILLON J° – BORDEAUX' and 'COGNAC CHAMPAGNE – 1795'. One of the first French seals to indicate the full provenance of the bottle, its contents and its date. Dark olive green colour. Die Ø: 32mm.

(5) Portrait of Prince William III of Orange (1650-1702) surrounded by the device: 'VIVAT DE PRINCE VON ORANGIE' (Long live the Prince of Orange). Produced for the Dutch market from 1672 until 1690 in the Holstein (North Germany) glasshouses of Wittmoldt, Perdoel and Lammershagen. Seal excavated in Holland. Forest green glass colour. Die Ø: 42mm. See Plate 64.1 for a complete bottle with its extended description.

(6) Seal bearing the coat of arms of Amsterdam surrounded with :'CAROLUS ORBEM SIC NOSTRAM CAESAR LUSTRAVIT' (In this way Emperor Charles favoured our city). The device refers to Charles V (born in Ghent 1500–died 1558), Emperor of Germany (1519-1556), King of Spain (1516-1556) and Governor of the Netherlands (Holland and Belgium).
     Bottle produced for the Dutch market in the glasshouses of Lammershagen, Rostdorf and Wittenberg, all in Holstein (North Germany). Seal excavated in Holland. Forest green glass colour. c.1670-1700. Die Ø: 38mm.

Refs: M. Roosma (903) for (1); A. Polak (841), p.271, ref.35 for (1); I.O. Weyse (1100), Flasker no. 143 for (1). H-J. Kruse (630) for (2), (5), (6); H. Henkes (490) for (2), (5), (6). K. Humbsch (536)

De vtro et origine eʒ. Capᵒ. x.

jtrum dñm eɟ uisibᷢ perspicui-
tate tᷤluceat iu aliis eui
metallis qᷣd iutiliseɟ con-
tuieɟ. abscondiᷢ iu uitro

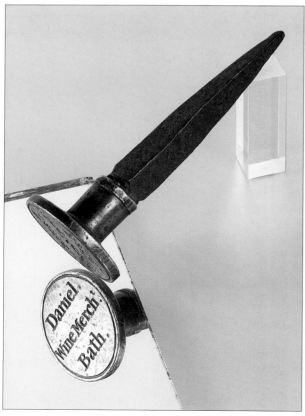

Figure 27. (top left) Neck of a broken utility bottle with a 'pewter gauge-ring' to mark off the correct capacity of the bottle. In Belgium and Holland in the first half of the 18th century many towns or cities such as Ghent, Bruges, Charleroi, Rotterdam and Maastricht had their own measures standards.

When sold within the town or city, to avoid fraud with the capacity of the bottles for 'beer, wine, brandy, vinegar, oil…and all other liquid wares…' they had to be measured and marked with a metal (pewter, iron…) gauge-ring by the local inspector of weights and measures.

The picture illustrates a pewter gauge-ring embossed with 'MASTRICHT' and the five pointed star of the city of Maastricht, Holland, as was decreed by the local act of 16 September 1722 known as the 'REGLEMENT Voor de Wyn-koopers ontrent de maete van haere Bouteilles'. In this city only bottles for selling wines to the public, or in pubs or restaurants, had to be gauged. 'Wine' bottles for private use were exempted from gauging.

The use of a gauge-ring is not related to a specific bottle style but only to the capacity of the utility bottle.

See also Plates 124, 135 and 173–175 and their references.

Figure 28. (left) A bronze seal die for impressing the references on the glass seal of a bottle for Mr. Daniel, Wine Merchant in Bath, England. c.1830–1850. Die Ø: 28mm, L: 7.5cm. Wooden handle missing. See also Plates 316(1), 317 and 318.

Figure 29. (top) Miniature of a medieval glassmaking furnace as illustrated in the encyclopaedia *De Universo* by Rabanus Maurus, dating from 1023 and preserved in Monte Cassino, Italy.

The copy from 1425 ordered by Ludwig III of Palatinate for the library in Heidelberg, Germany, depicts a typical Rhenish-Main double conical upset bottle and a pear-shaped bottle as pictured in Plates 188(2) and 190(3). The annealing oven is separated from the melt oven. A similar furnace was also used for smelting metals such as lead, silver, iron and bronze.

Courtesy of the Bibliotheca Apostolica Vaticana, Manuscript Palat. Lat. 291, fol. 211V.

Figure 30. Engraving from 'The funeral of Charles III of Lorraine' by Matheus Merian, dated 1608, depicting one of the many glasshouses of that period in Lorraine, North-east France.

The Latin text reads: 'Glass-houses, in which vessels and other glassware are made, in particular glass-sheets which are so large, transparent and in so many colours they they cannot be compared with others and for this reason are wanted and sold all over Europe'. The bottles produced were a dark brown colour, named 'verre noir' (black glass).

From 1500 onwards the Lorraine glassmakers made bottles in 'verre noir' using wood as a fuel for melting the glass ingredients which contained many impurities such as iron and carbon.

Because of the Thirty and Eighty Years wars in Europe from the end of the 16th century until the mid-17th century many reputed glassmakers such as de Thysac, de Hennezel and de Thietry emigrated from the forests of Darney, Lorraine to England (Stourbridge, Sussex, Newcastle-upon-Tyne) and Belgium to start a new life as glassmakers for bottles, window glass, etc.

Courtesy of the Musée historique lorrain, Nancy, France

Figure 31. Dark olive green glass and a broken part of a glass melting pot excavated on the site of an early 17th century (1600-1640) glasshouse at Savenel, Nethen, Belgium where Jean Colinet (John Colnett) and his sons were making glassware of all types.

At that time Colinet used beechwood fuel to melt a mixture of yellowish sand, limestone and unwashed ash from burned beeches which produced the natural dark olive green colour of his bottles termed 'black glass' (verre noir). Coal firing is not a must for producing 'black glass'. The reducing atmosphere of coal firing in the glass melting furnace darkens more molten glass than the oxidising atmosphere of wood-firing for glass of the same composition. Depending on the quantity of impurities such as iron present in the sand and/or in the other glassmaking ingredients, the final natural glass colour as a result of wood-firing may also be olive amber or brownish amber known as 'black glass'.

Courtesy of Mr. Alexis-Michel Terlinden, Nethen, Belgium
Photo: Willy Van den Bossche

Figure 32. Woodcut of a 'beehive' type glass furnace for making bottles or other glassware. Illustrated in *L'Art de la Verrerie* by A. Neri, C. Merret and J. Kunckel (779), 1752.

This furnace was in widespread use on the European Continent from the 15th to the 19th century. The wood fire was in the lower compartment, the glass pots were heated by flames rising through the bottom hole of the middle compartment and the finished articles were slowly cooled in the upper compartment or in a separate annealing furnace. Note that from 1556 (509) the moulds (E) were made of copper.

Figure. III.

Figure. IV.

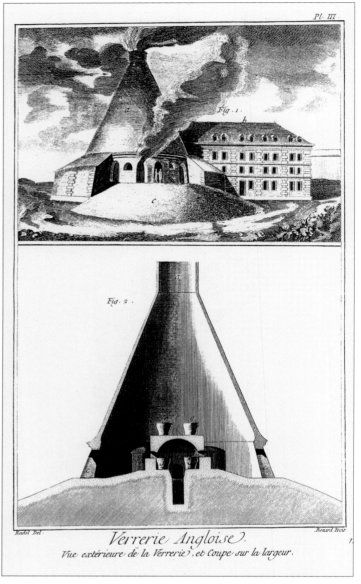

Figure 33. Woodcut of the frontispiece of *De Arte Vitraria* (778), Amsterdam, 1686. The book is a translation from Italian into Latin of Antonii Neri's *L'Arte Vetraria* first published in Florence, Italy, in 1612, and is one of the earliest and most famous books on glassmaking.

The woodcut illustrates the Italian style glass furnace of Amsterdam situated at the Rozengracht (1657-1676) which mainly produced glass 'à la façon de Venise'.

Figure 34. Woodcut of an English 18th century glasshouse for making 'black glass' bottles. From the *Encyclopédie* (1751-1772) of Diderot and d'Alembert (330).

The conical building, often over thirty metres high, functions as a huge chimney to exhaust the smoke from the coal-fired furnace.

These glasshouses were very popular in England for making bottles from c.1674 until c.1930. They also appeared on the Continent from the late 19th century until c.1930. See also Figure 35.

Pl. II

Verrerie Angloise

Plan du premier étage d'une Halle avec son Four et le Batiment de Service.

R.adel Del.

Benard Fecit.

Figure 35. Plan view of an 18th century English coal-fired cone glasshouse for making 'black glass' bottles as illustrated in the *Encyclopédie* (1751-1772) of Diderot and d'Alembert (330).

a) glass melting furnace; b) grating for coal; c) glass melting pots; d) ovens for firing the melting pots before placing them in the furnace; e) calciner or sintering oven for preheating the batch before melting it in the pots; f) small annealing furnaces for slowly cooling the bottles after they have been formed; g) doors; i) entrances of the glasshouse.

This furnace type for blowing bottles and window glass was already popular on the European Continent from the 16th century onwards. A similar glass furnace dating c.1600 was excavated at Savenel, Nethen, Belgium, where Jean Colinet (John Colnett) produced glassware such as bottles in dark olive green or brownish colour known as 'verre noir' (black glass).

The use of a grating in the furnace permits melting glass with coal at high capacity. See also Figure 34.

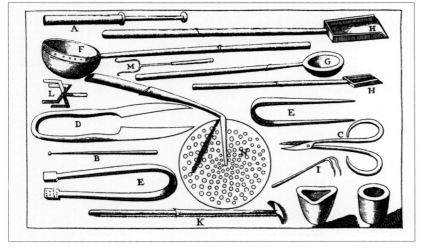

Figure 36. 17th-19th century glassmaking tools, as illustrated in Haudicquer de Blancourt's (475) *L'Art de la Verrerie,* 1697.

A: blowpipe or blowing-iron; B: pontil or puntee; C: scissors; D: shears or shaping tool; E-K and N: pincers, ladles, shovels, drainers and other implements; L: 'case' or 'sabot' for holding urinals or unpontilled bottles; M: fork for bringing the blown glass articles to the annealing furnace.

Figure 37. Woodcuts from the *Encyclopédie* (1751–1772) of Diderot and d'Alembert (330), *'Verrerie en Bouteilles',* illustrating the technique for making bottles.

Planche IV: blowing a parison (b) on a marver (c) followed by blowing the body of the bottle in a dip mould.

Planche V: rolling the body of the bottle on a marver after a push-up in its bottom has been made with a 'molette'.

Planche VI: applying a string rim around the lip of the bottle and tooling it with shaping pincers. The blowpipe is used as a pontil rod and produces a tubular pontil scar. Any type of empontilling may be used.

Figure 38. An American Pitkin-flask showing clearly the result of blowing an optical thin-walled flask by the 'German' half-post method. The resulting ridge is very apparent near the neck and shows that the flask is in fact a container with an 'overlay' of the same glass as the inside flask.

The term 'inserted neck' is a widespread misconception. From the 16th-17th century the half-post method was very popular in the Alpine regions of Europe such as Austria, South Germany and Switzerland. In the 18th-19th century German glassmakers emigrated to America and introduced their 'half-post' method, hence the 'German' half-post method. The Pitkin Glassworks in East Manchester, Connecticut, produced flasks mainly by the half-post method. Other American glasshouses also produced these 'Pitkin-style' flasks (and jars). The German half-post blowing technique is an important indicator of the area where the bottle, flask or jar was made.

The illustrated Pitkin-flask has a 36-rib pattern swirled to the right and was produced between 1780 and 1810. Light green colour. Blowpipe pontil scar. Dim: 13.5 x 8.6 x 5.2cm. Cap: 26cl. Wt: 140gr. See also Plate 309(1). For the terms 'German half-post', 'half-post' and 'Pitkin-flask' see the Glossary of Bottlemaking Terms.

Figure 39. Engraving of an overground dip-mould dated '1679' for fast blowing square and/or rectangular case bottles of all sizes.

The four 1cm thick movable copper plates (B, C, E, G) permit a quick change to the desired dimensions of the case bottle. Examples of case bottles of the type blown in this mould are depicted in Plates 192 and 253.

The illustration is from Johann Kunckel's (634) *Ars Vitraria Experimentalis oder Vollkommene Glasmacher-Kunst,* Frankfurt/Leipzig, 1679.

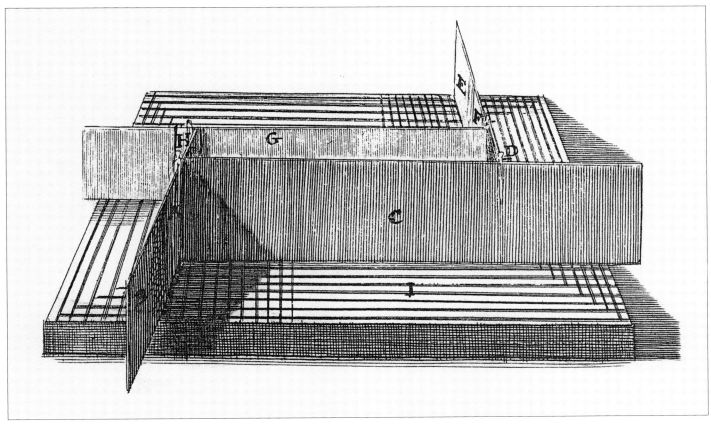

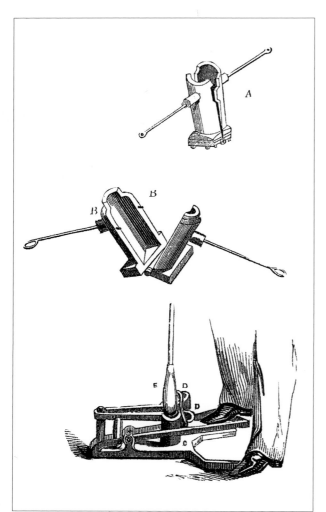

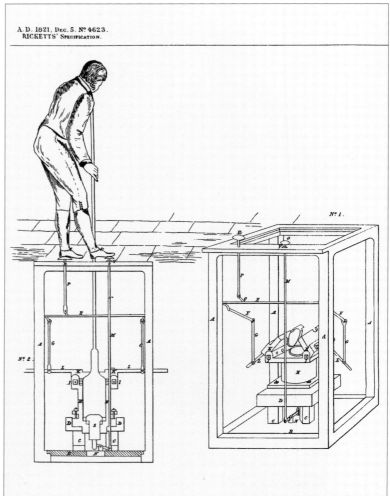

Figure 40. Illustrations of three bottle moulds used in the mid-19th century as shown in Apsley Pellatt's *Curiosities of Glassmaking* (822), London, 1849.

A: an 'open and shut mould' constructed in two exact halves connected by a bottom hinge in which round bottles are blown.

B: an 'open and shut mould' to make square bottles.

C: a foot-operated three-part mould with one piece (C) for the bottle body and two movable pieces (D, D) for the neck. Very popular mould for blowing cylindrical bottles (after 1821).

The illustrated moulds were very popular all over the world from c.1821-1830 onwards until the early 20th century. They were mostly made of cast iron.

Figure 41. Drawing from Ricketts' British Patent No. 4623 from 5 December 1821 showing 'An Improvement in the Art or Method of Making or Manufacturing Glass Bottles, such as are used for Wine, Porter, Beer, Cyder or other Liquids.

Henry Ricketts of Phoenix Glass Works, Bristol, England was the first glassmaker using a three-part mould for making bottles with a great degree of regularity or conformity to each other. This mould became extremely popular all over the world until the early 20th century.

Bottles made by Ricketts in his three-part moulds are often embossed on the shoulder with the word 'PATENT' or 'IMPERIAL PATENT' (until 1835). The bottoms of the bottles are embossed with: 'H. RICKETTS & CO. GLASSWORKS BRISTOL' or with one of six variants thereof.

Georges Bontemps (183) mentions that in 1828 he saw 'three-piece' moulds being used in England and that three workers could make ninety to one hundred bottles in an hour. Sealed Ricketts bottles dated '1821' are extremely rare.

For an example of a bottle made in a Ricketts mould see Figures 42(1) and 42(2).

Figure 42. Two English bottles of great historical value because they are blown before and after '1821' in a three-part Ricketts mould (British Patent No. 4623 from 1821). Note also the different style of the lips: handmade (1) and using a neck finishing tool.

(1) Blown before '1821' in an experimental Ricketts mould. Bottle made between 1804 and 1815. Sealed: **'H.C'** and a dexter hand appaumée. The bottle belonged to Sir **H**enry **C**arew, 7th Baronet of Haccombe (1779-1830), Newton Abbot, Devon (U.K.). No embossings. Black glass. Sand pontil scar. H: 26cm. Cap: 76cl (1 reputed quart). Wt. 804gr.

(2) Blown after '1821' in a Ricketts mould. Sealed: **'D.B.D.'** and dated '1826'. Shoulder embossed with 'PATENT' and the bottom with 'H. RICKETTS & Cᵒ GLASSWORKS – BRISTOL'. This bottle belonged to **D**aniel **B**ishop **D**avy, a shipbuilder in Topsham, Devon (U.K.). Unusual clear green glass colour. Disc pontil scar.

See also Figure 41 and Plate 27(3).

Refs: R. Dumbrell (346), bottle (1) illustrated in pls.34 and 77; Truro Exhibition Catalogue (70), p.190 for bottle (2)

A.D. 1872, 3rd September. N° 2621.

Bottles for Aërated Liquids.

LETTERS PATENT to Hiram Codd, of Grove Lane, Camberwell, in the County of Surrey, for the Invention of "IMPROVEMENTS IN BOTTLES TO CONTAIN ÆRATED LIQUIDS."

Sealed the 17th December 1872, and dated the 3rd September 1872.

PROVISIONAL SPECIFICATION left by the said Hiram Codd at the Office of the Commissioners of Patents, with his Petition, on the 3rd September 1872.

5 I, HIRAM CODD, of Grove Lane, Camberwell, in the County of Surrey, do hereby declare the nature of the said Invention for "IMPROVEMENTS IN BOTTLES TO CONTAIN ÆRATED LIQUIDS," to be as follows :—

This Invention has for its object improvements in bottles to contain aerated liquids. Bottles for aerated liquids are now sometimes constructed with an internal stopper of a globular or other form which by 10 the pressure of the gas is held up to a seat of vulcanized india-rubber in the mouth of the bottle. Now my Invention consists in so constructing such bottles that when they are opened by forcing back the stopper the

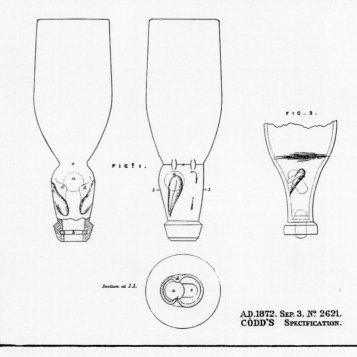

Figure 43. Hiram Codd's patent No. 2621 from 3 September 1872 describing his invention of 'Improvements in Bottles to Contain Aerated Liquids' such as mineral water, soda waters, lemonade, etc.

This most important Codd patent is known as 'Codd patent number four' from a series of Codd patents which were used under licence all over Europe between 1872 and 1950.

For 'Codd' bottles see Plates 312–315.

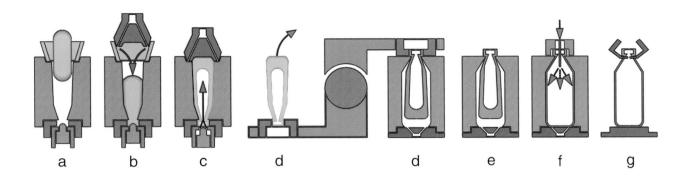

Blow-and blow process

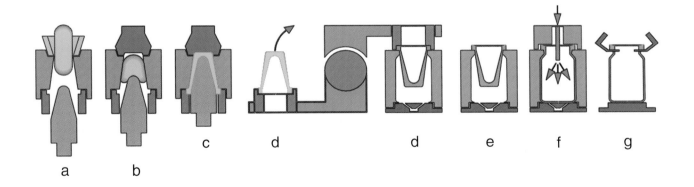

Press-and-blow process

Figure 44. Basic principles for making modern bottles and jars by means of the most popular Individual Section (I.S.) machine:

    (a) feeding a gob of molten glass into a preform or blank mould.
    (b) settle blowing/plunger pressing the gob to form the neck of the bottle/jar.
    (c) counter blowing/pressing a preformed bottle/jar.
    (d) transferring the blown/pressed preform from the blank mould to the blow mould.
    (e) reheating the preformed bottle/jar.
    (f) blowing the preformed bottle/jar to its final shape.
    (g) taking out the blown bottle/jar from the blow mould.

The I.S. machine was first protected on 2 February 1932 by the U.S. Patent No. 1.843.159 (Henry Ingle) and has been improved since then hundreds of times. It can produce 200,000–700,000 bottles a day or about 500 bottles a minute, depending on their weight.

Courtesy of Emhart Glass, Switzerland

Figure 45. Woodcut from the *Encyclopédie* (1751-1772) of Diderot and d'Alembert (329) illustrating the method for making a 'disc pontil' and a 'sand pontil'.

First, a young glassmaker takes an iron pontil rod (a) on the end of which he gathers a small mass of molten glass which he rolls on a marver (b) until a cylindrical 'post' is formed. Then, this preformed 'plain glass pontil' is upset to form a 'disc pontil' by pushing the pontil rod (a) axially on to the marver (b). Its final shape is circular or elliptical, mostly of irregular circumference.

The produced 'disc pontil' is then partially cooled by being plunged into a bath of water (e) just long enough to stiffen it so that it does not deform during sticking at the − previously made − conical push-up of the bottle bottom.

A 'sand pontil' is formed when cold glass or sand particles are sprinkled on to the marver (b) before the upsetting operation. Its temperature is a little bit higher than for the 'disc pontil' in order to deform during formation of the bottle push-up and sticking to the bottom of the bottle at the same time.

Figure 46. Illustration of five **empontilling techniques** and a 'case' for supporting a bottle during its manufacture.

    (1) blowpipe pontil (see Figure 47.3)
    (2) plain 'glass-tipped' pontil (see Figure 47.1)
    (3) disc pontil (see Figures 45 and 48.2)
    (4) sand pontil (see Figures 45 and 48.1)
    (5) bare iron pontil (see Figure 47.2)
    (6) a 'sabot' or a 'case'. Illustrated by Neri (778) as long ago as 1612. Became popular again all over the world from c.1860 until 1920. See Figure 36(L).

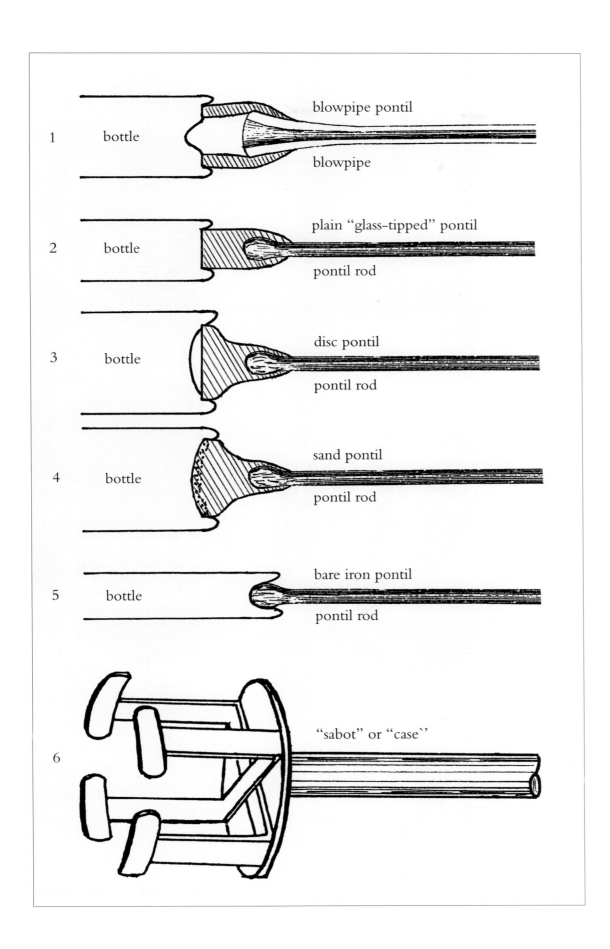

1   bottle   blowpipe pontil

blowpipe

2   bottle   plain "glass-tipped" pontil

pontil rod

3   bottle   disc pontil

pontil rod

4   bottle   sand pontil

pontil rod

5   bottle   bare iron pontil

pontil rod

6   "sabot" or "case"

Figure 47. Close-ups of three different pontil scars on the bottoms of Continental made bottles.

(1) **Plain 'glass-tipped' pontil scar** (Ø: 3cm). Common throughout the centuries, particularly in Belgium and France; also in England during the second half of the 17th century. Note the iron deposits remaining from the iron pontil rod. Bottle illustrated in Plate 264(1).

(2) **Bare iron pontil scar** (max. Ø: 3.5cm). Used all over the world between c.1830 and 1860. Note the white lead oxide deposits on the pontil scar. Sometimes the pontil rod was coated with lead, tin, zinc or other materials in order to avoid sticking too strongly to the bottom.

(3) **Blowpipe or ring pontil scar** (Ø: 3.6cm). The blowpipe being used as a pontil rod. Common since Roman times all over the world, although its use became extremely rare in England from c.1650 onwards. Bottle illustrated in Plate 146(3).

Figure 48. Close-ups of two different pontil scars on the bottoms of English made bottles. The large pontil diameters (between 5 and 7cm) are mainly used for supporting heavy or high capacity bottles to prevent bending of the bottom. These pontils could be used many times for different bottles.

(1) **Sand pontil scar** (Ø: 4.8-5.2cm). Note the remaining sand grains within the circular/elliptical outer line of the pontil scar preventing the pontil from sticking too strongly to the bottom. The dome-shaped push-up of the bottle is formed using the sand pontil itself. System mainly used in England in the 18th and early 19th century. Bottle illustrated in Plate 27(1).

(2) **Disc pontil scar** (Ø: 5.5-6cm). Note the remaining rough chips of glass of the pontil forming an irregular elliptical shape on the bottom. This pontil scar only appears on bottles where, before empontilling, a conical push-up of the bottom was formed using a metal tool called a 'molette'. The pontil may also be of square or rectangular shape. The practice of this method is known for English as well as Continental bottles of the 18th and early 19th century. Bottle illustrated in Plate 39(1).

I
GREAT BRITAIN

In order to make it easier for the reader to understand the history and evolution of utility bottles on the European Continent we first start with Great Britain.

This chapter shows the evolution of bottles for wine, beer, oil, liqueur and all other liquid and powder wares from the beginning as a 'shaft and globe' c.1632 to the end of the hand–blown 'cylindrical' bottle c.1860 (Plates 1-28). A dated sealed bottle 'style' is shown for each decade.

Plates 29–61 show other bottle styles such as 'bladders', 'octagonals', etc., made and used in Great Britain in the 18th and early 19th century. These shapes exist in parallel to the English 'onion' evolving to the 'cylinder'.

The evolution of bottles in different countries or areas of the European Continent such as North Germany, Denmark, Sweden, Holland and France is very similar to that of England and Belgium. In general, each English style bottle has its Continental counterpart. Some bottle styles were developed first in England, others first on the Continent.

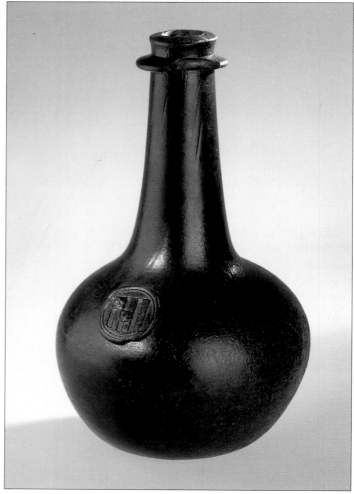

Plate 1. Earliest known example of an 'English bottle' known today as a 'shaft and globe'. Made in England from c.1632 until 1640/1660. Bottle type introduced in England by the Belgian bottle-maker Jean Colinet (John Colnett) as illustrated in Figure 19.2(1).

Notice the cylindrical neck in comparison to the later English shaft and globes which have a longer and strongly tapered neck. Dark grass green colour (coal firing). Glass-tipped pontil scar. H:19.3cm. Cap: 92cl. (about 1 English quart). Wt: 620gr.

See also Figures 2 and 3.

Ref: Ivor Noël Hume (538), p.176, pl.78 illustrates an identical half-size bottle sealed with a Tudor Rose and the owner's initials 'W.M.H.' from the Rose Tavern in Nottingham, England. Date c.1650-1660. H: 15.5cm.

Plate 2. An early English sealed 'shaft and globe' bottle, c.1660 (bottle type popular between 1640 and 1660). Excavated in Aylesbury (England), the surface condition showing the result of burial in the ground for a long time.

This bottle belonged to Baron John Trott (1614-1672) of Laverstoke Manor, Hampshire, Member of Parliament for Andover (1660-1672). John Trott was created a baronet by letters patent dated 12 October 1660, hence the baronet's mark – the left hand – upon the centre of the arms. He died on 14 July 1672 and was buried at Laverstoke where his monument survives in the chancel of St. Mary the Virgin.

Coat of arms: paly of six or and gules on a canton argent a cross flory sable charged with a bezant. Black glass (coal firing). Glass-tipped pontil scar. H: 24cm. Cap: 95cl (about 1 English quart). Wt: 1200gr!. Wall thickness 7mm! Compare with the medieval 'shaft and globe' in Figure 18.

A similar English sealed shaft and globe c.1655 with unknown initials 'EB' was sold on 9 July 2000 at BBR (British Bottle Review) - Auctions in Elsecar, UK for an absolute world record price of £18,000 (hammer price).

Ref: Dumbrell (346) fig.14

Plate 3. English 'shaft and globe' c.1660 (bottle type popular between 1660-1675).
Coat of arms: argent, a bend engrailed and gules under a baron's crown, of Lord John Colepeper, 1st baron of Thoresway, Lincoln (1600-1660) who was at that time an important politician. He lived in Wigsell and Hollingbourne, Kent, where he was buried. Olive green colour (wood firing). Glass-tipped pontil scar. H: 23.3cm. Cap: 107cl. (about 1 English quart). Wt: 1070 gr.
 As we can see on the photograph, this 'shaft and globe' has been blown in a funnel-shaped dip-mould in an attempt to produce bottles with the correct capacity and a greater degree of regularity. See also Plates 7 and 140.
Refs: R. Green (448), photographed on p.13; R. Dumbrell (346) figs.21 and 25

Plate 4. An English 'shaft and globe' c.1660 (bottle type popular between 1660-1675). Olive green colour (wood firing). Dug bottle. Coat of arms: a terrestrial globe and capitals 'W I S', the initials of the owner of a tavern or ale-house somewhere in England named 'The Globe'. Glass-tipped pontil scar. H: 23cm. Cap: 96cl. (about 1 quart). Wt: 945gr.
Ref: R. Dumbrell (346) figs.21 and 25

Plate 5. An English half-size 'shaft and globe' bottle, c.1660 (bottle type popular between 1660–1675). Coat of arms: a fleur-de-lis surmounted by a lion. The bottle belonged to William Brock of Upton, Cheshire (1622-1663), a nobleman. Dug bottle. Patinated. Restored. Glass-tipped pontil scar. H: 18.5cm. Cap: 46cl. (about ½ a quart or 1 pint). Wt: 535gr.
Ref: R. Dumbrell (346) figs.21 and 25

Plate 6. Three English 'shaft and globes', all in black glass.

(1) A miniature c.1650-1655. Glass-tipped pontil scar. H: 11.5cm. Cap: 13cl. Wt: 220gr.

(2) A magnum (2 full-sizes) c.1675. Disc pontil scar. H: 24cm. Cap: 188cl. (about 2 quarts = 1 pottle = ½ gallon) Wt: 1510gr.

(3) A common full-size c.1660-1675. Glass-tipped pontil scar. H: 23.5cm. Cap: 86cl. (about 1 quart). Wt: 905gr. These bottles are listed on the sales list (dated 1677) of the London Company of Glass Sellers (854) as 'plain bottles'.

Refs: R. Green (448) pl.6(1) pictured on p.15; R. Dumbrell (346) figs.4, 21, and 24

Plate 7. An English 'shaft and globe', c.1670. Crest: a unicorn. Dark olive green colour. Glass-tipped pontil scar. H: 18.5cm. Cap: 76cl. (1 reputed quart = 75.7cl). Notice that this bottle type was blown in a funnel-shaped dip mould in an attempt to produce bottles of a greater degree of regularity and conformity with each other.
Refs: R. Dumbrell (346), fig.23; A. Simon (979) pl.LXXXVIII (No. 215A), bottle c.1670-1675, antedated '1661'

Plate 8. A later English 'shaft and globe' of a shape between the 'shaft and globe' and the 'onion'. Dated 1681. Capitals 'W M' intertwined on the seal and the digits '81' for 1681. Probably the seal of William Morrell who held the Crown Tavern (1604-1766) in Oxford. Listed on the sales list (dated 1677) of the London Company of Glass Sellers (854) as a 'marked bottle'.
Refs: Dumbrell (346) pls.8, 60, and 110, fig.31; F. Banks (123) pp.55-70

Plate 9. An early English full-size 'onion' bottle. Sealed: 'W.S' (intertwined) surmounted by a crown and dated '1692'. Black glass. Sand pontil scar. H: 15cm. Cap: 90cl. Wt: 1030gr.
Ref: R. Dumbrell (346) fig.42

Plate 10. An early English half-size 'onion' bottle. Sealed: 'I.S.F.' and dated '1701'. Olive green colour. Sand pontil scar. H: 13.5cm. Cap: 51cl. Wt: 490gr.
Ref: R. Dumbrell (346) fig.52

Plate 11. A common shaped English 'onion'. Sealed: 'Robt. Smith' and dated '1710'. Black glass. Disc pontil scar. This original English bottle shape became very common on the European Continent where it is known as a 'Dutch onion'. H: 16.5cm. Cap: 93cl (1 English quart = 94.6cl). Wt: 1045gr. See also Plates 70(3), 72 and 200.
Ref: R. Dumbrell (346) fig. 67

Plate 12. An English decanter bottle (c.1705-1715). Black glass. Sand pontil scar. H: 15cm. Cap: 64cl. Wt: 810gr. See also Plates 38(3) and 296(1).
Ref: R. Dumbrell (346) fig.218 and pl.45

Plate 13. Three English 'onions' of different colours and capacities.
  (1) Black glass onion. Full-size. c.1705-1720. Sand pontil scar. H: 13.5cm. Cap: 80cl. Wt: 960gr.
  (2) Olive green straight-sided onion. Half-size. c.1710-1725. Sand pontil scar. H: 13.cm. Cap: 45cl. Wt: 370gr.
  (3) Blue-greenish small onion. Lead glass. c.1710-1725. Engraved 'Mary Mellor – Died 10th May 1820 – Aged 66'. Blowpipe pontil scar. Unusual bottle colour. H: 12cm. Cap: 30cl. Wt: 410gr. See also Plate 38(3).
Refs: R. Dumbrell (346) pl.12 and figs.55, 81 for bottle (1); fig.68 for bottle (2); U. Zischka (1150), pp.216 and 217 bottle (3) on a painting 'The Love Dinner' from Jean Baptiste Coclers (Liège 1741-Liège 1817) dated c.1780. Bottle used as a decanter bottle filled with white wine.

Plate 14. Three English 'onions' of different capacities. Black glass. All with sand pontil scars.
(1) Sealed: 'Inº. Bray – 1719' (Jonathan Bray) surmounted by a star. H: 14.2cm. Cap: 66cl. Wt: 710gr.
(2) A double magnum (four times a full-size) onion, sealed with a coat of arms. H: 27.7cm. Cap: 358 cl. Wt: 2920gr.
(3) A later type full-size onion. Sealed: 'Ioⁿ Sanford – 1725' (John Sanford) H: 18.2cm. Cap: 108cl. Wt: 965gr. See also Plate 42 for a similar bottle type dated '1745' (very late).
Refs: R. Dumbrell (346) fig.80 for bottle (1) and fig.90 for bottle (3); R. Morgan (762) bottle (2) p.50

Plate 15. An English straight-sided onion. Dark olive green glass. Sealed: 'James Anderson – 1714'. Disc pontil scar. H: 15.8cm. Cap: 100cl. Wt: 955gr. See also Plates 17, 70(1), 71(1), 71(4) and 75.
Ref: R. Dumbrell (346) fig.68

Plate 16. An English half-size 'onion'. Sealed: **'A.T. – OXON – 1713'** and a chevron between three tuns (the arms of the Vintners' Company in London). **A**nn **T**omlinson ran the Three Tuns tavern, High Street, Oxford, from 1712-1719. Bottles indicating their full provenance and date are very rare. Sand pontil scar. H: 13cm. Ø: 12cm. Cap: 42cl. Wt: 525gr. A similar bottle sealed with a crown, **'OXON'** and the initials **REW,** of **R**ichard **W**alker and his wife **E**lisabeth of the King's Head Tavern, Oxford, 1687-1704, dated **1689,** was sold at Sotheby's London on 30 November 1999 for a price of £12,350 (a hammer price of £10,500) or about Euro 20.000. See also Plate 61(2).
Refs: D.C. Davis (290) p.24 (top); F. Banks (122); F. Banks (123) pp.42-51 and fig.5.12 (bottom) for a '1715' dated bottle

Plate 17. Two English straight-sided onions. Dark olive green glass.

(1)　With an unknown coat of arms. c.1710-1715. Sand pontil scar. H: 15.6cm. Cap: 86cl. Wt: 855gr. This original English bottle type was copied on the European Continent. Copies in Holland were named 'buikje' or 'kattekop', in North Germany 'Englische Bouteillen' (English bottles) and in England 'Dutch onions' because at that time Holland exported them – filled with wine, beer, etc. – all over the world. See Plates 15, 70(1), 71(1), 71(4) and 75.

(2)　Sealed: 'E. Herbert – 1721' Disc pontil scar. H: 18cm. Ø: 14cm. Cap: 84.5cl. Wt: 865 gr.

Refs: R. Dumbrell (346), fig.68 for (1); G. Wills (1115) for (2)

Plate 18.

    (1) An English bottle made for the American market. Sealed: 'David Provost – 1723'. David Provost was Mayor of New York/Bronx in 1699. Black glass. Disc pontil scar. H: 18.5cm. Cap: 95cl. (1 U.S. quart). Wt: 995gr.

    (2) An English over-sized bottle sealed: 'WB – 1723'. Black glass. Sand pontil scar. H: 18.5cm. Cap: 138cl. Wt: 1100gr.

Refs: D.L. Murschel (772) p.90 for (1); R. Dumbrell (346), fig.85 for (1)

Plate 19. Three English 'mallets' of different sizes and capacities. Black glass.
  (1) A half-size bottle. Sealed: 'B. Greive – 1727'. Sand pontil scar. H: 15cm. Cap: 50cl. Wt: 585gr.
  (2) A triple-size bottle (a 'Marie-Jeanne'). Sealed: 'Ben. Iennings – 1728' (Benjamin Jennings). Sand pontil scar. H: 26.5cm. Cap: 276cl. Wt: 1750gr.
  (3) A full-size bottle. Sealed: 'Ths. Smith – Kingston – 1735' (Thomas Smith). Disc pontil scar. H: 18.8cm. Cap: 84cl. Wt: 975gr.
Ref: R. Dumbrell (346) pp.83-86

Plate 20. An English straight-sided nearly cylindrical bottle. Sealed: 'I. RUMBOLD – CALNE – 1731'. Calne is a village in Wiltshire. Black glass. Sand pontil scar. Half-size. H:15.5cm. Cap: 47cl. Wt: 800gr.

Ref: R. Dumbrell (346) p.79, fig.b

Plate 21. A perfect English 'mallet' bottle. The sharply defined seal carries the full provenance and date of the bottle. 'The Revᵈ Doc † Rumney – St. Albans – 1734'. (The Reverend Doctor † Rumney – Saint Albans – 1734.) Robert Rumney was the son of Job Rumney of Kirkoswald, Cumbria. He went to the Queen's College, Oxford in 1704 at the age of seventeen. He obtained his Bachelor of Arts degree in 1707 and his Master of Arts degree from St. John's College, Cambridge in 1714. He became a Doctor of Divinity in 1728. He became Vicar of St. Peter's, St. Albans in 1715.

The † refers to the Roman St. Alban carrying a cross (the 'Alban Cross') during his execution to remember the way Jesus died. Notice that in England seals never mention the capacity or the contents of the bottle, at least not before c.1750. Black glass. Sand pontil scar. H: 19cm. Cap: 68cl. Wt: 600gr.

Ref: R. Dumbrell (346), front p.2; personal communication Fay Banks

Plate 22. An English mallet bottle. c.1730-1735. Sealed with a coat of arms (three lions rampant). Dark olive green colour. Blowpipe pontil scar (very unusual). The same bottle exists with a sand pontil scar. H: 20cm. Cap: 96cl. Wt: 870gr.
Ref: R. Dumbrell (346), figs.106 and 112

Plate 23. An English mallet bottle with a silver closure. Used as a decanter bottle. Sealed: 'Thos. Holdsworth – Dartmouth – 1735'. Thomas Holdsworth was a member of a prominent merchant-mariner family in Dartmouth (Devonshire) at the time. From 1713 (Arthur Holdsworth) until 1820 (Robert Holdsworth) we find bottles all belonging to the same family which is unique. H: 17.5cm. Cap: 67cl. Wt: 730gr.
Refs: R. Dumbrell (346) figs.103, 143 and pp.272, 273; S. Ruggles-Brise (920) pp.112, 113, 159 and pl.3, centre lower row

Plate 24. Four English squat cylindrical bottles. Black glass.
    (1) Sealed: 'J: ILOYD – CAERWAYES – 1739'. Sand pontil scar. H: 23cm. Cap: 103cl. Wt: 965gr.
    (2) Sealed: 'I. CHINNOCK – 1744'. Sand pontil scar. H: 22.5cm. Cap: 96.5cl. Wt: 1115gr.
    (3) Sealed: 'B.W. – 1756'. Sand pontil scar. H: 24cm. Cap: 137cl. Wt: 1365gr.
    (4) Sealed: 'John Feast – 1761'. Disc pontil scar. H: 23cm. Cap: 104cl. Wt: 1175gr.
Ref: R. Dumbrell (346), pp. 91-99 and pl.69 (bottom left)

Plate 25. Three English cylindrical bottles. Black glass.
  (1) Sealed: 'Inº. Pomeroy – Farway – 1773' (Jonathan Pomeroy). Squat cylinder. Sand
      pontil scar. H: 23.4cm. Cap: 109cl. Wt: 1070gr.
  (2) Sealed: 'JAˢ. OAKES – BURY – 1788'. James Oakes (1741-1829) was a wine
      merchant and banker at Bury St. Edmunds. Bottles belonging to him are recorded
      with several dates: 1770, 1771, 1777, 1783, 1785, 1787, 1788, 1793 and 1795. Disc
      pontil scar. H: 25.5cm. Cap: 78cl. Wt: 880gr.
  (3) Sealed: 'Col: Wood – Maderia – 1797'. One of the earliest English sealed bottles
      indicating its contents (Madeira wine). Disc pontil scar. H: 27.5cm. Cap: 80cl. Wt:
      890gr. The word 'Maderia' is a spelling error. See also Plate 131B.
Ref: R. Dumbrell (346) pl.29 for bottle (1); fig.171, pl.33 and p.293 for bottle (2); fig.199 for bottle (3)

Plate 26. Three English cylindrical bottles. Black glass.

    (1) Sealed: 'J.F. 1800'. Presumably the initials of John Fothergill from Yorkshire. Disc pontil scar. H: 26cm. Cap: 73cl. Wt: 840gr.

    (2) Sealed: 'I. Square – 1804'. Sand pontil scar. H: 28cm. Cap: 91cl. Wt: 890gr.

    (3) Sealed: 'SIR WM. STRICKLAND BT. – 1809' Sir William Strickland (1753-1834) was a baronet who came from Boynton Hall, near Bridlington, Yorkshire. Disc pontil scar. H: 26.5cm. Cap: 75cl. Wt: 750gr. Seal on shoulder is unusual on cylindrical bottles in England between 1740-1850. See also Plate 27(4) and Figure 15.

Refs: S. Ruggles-Brise (920) p.160 for bottle seal (1); R. Dumbrell (346) pp.219 and 261 for bottle (1); R. Morgan (762) pp.74, 76 and 77 for bottle (3)

Plate 27. Four English cylindrical bottles. Black glass. (1) (2) (3) with sand pontil scar. (1) (2) full-size. (3) double-size (magnum). (4) half-size.

(1) Sealed: 'R.H.C. – 1815'. Richard Hall Clarke (1750-1821) was a Justice of the Peace whose commissions were at Bridwell, Uffculme, Devon. H: 26.5cm. Cap: 81cl. Wt: 740gr. One of the last free-blown bottles before the use of the Ricketts mould in 1821.

(2) Sealed: 'John Colby – Fynone – 1822' and the word 'PATENT' embossed on the shoulder. On the base embossed with 'H. Ricketts & Cᵒ Glassworks – Bristol'. This is one of the first bottles blown in a Ricketts Patent mould (British Patent No. 4623, publ. Dec. 1821). John Colby was the owner of Flynnonau estate in North Pembrokeshire, Wales. H: 28cm. Cap: 81cl. Wt: 860gr.

(3) Sealed: 'D.B.D. – 1836'. Daniel Bishop Davy was a shipbuilder in Topsham, Devon. Other dated D.B.D. Bottles are 1820, 1826, 1828, 1830 and 1837. Shoulder embossed: 'PATENT'. On the bottom embossing: 'H. Ricketts & Cᵒ Glassworks – Bristol'. Bottle blown in a Ricketts mould by Ricketts Glassworks at Bristol. H: 31cm. Cap: 175cl. Wt: 1400gr.

(4) Sealed: 'BOYNTON – 1848' Boynton refers to Boynton Hall, near Bridlington, Yorkshire where Sir George Strickland, Baronet, son of Sir William Strickland, lived. Seal near the bottom (unusual). No embossing. Disc pontil scar. H: 24cm. Cap: 40cl. (half-size bottle). Wt: 410gr. Blown in a three-part mould. See also Plate 26(3).

Refs: R. Dumbrell (346), pls.36 and 67 for bottle (1), p.247 for bottle (2); British Patents; Truro Exhibition Cat. (70), p.190 for bottle (3); R. Morgan (762) p.77 for bottle (4); see p.74 for a '1809' dated bottle (4)

Plate 28. Four English cylindrical bottles of different sizes and capacities. Black glass. All blown in a three-part mould. Sealed bottles are rare in the second half of the 19th century in England. All bottles without a pontil scar – a snap case was used.

  (1) Sealed: '1858'. Bottles bearing dates only are very rare. H: 29.5cm. Cap: 149cl. (a double-size or magnum bottle). Wt: 1170gr. Ø: 11.4cm. See also Plate 46(1).

  (2) Sealed: 'MARCH 1867'. No embossing. H: 25.5cm. Cap: 36cl. (half-size bottle). Wt: 500gr.

  (3) Sealed: 'BORDER MAID – 1877' and embossing on the base: 'W. SHIELDS & C° – LEITH'. Border Maid is the brand name of a whisky, 1877 is the date of the bottle manufacture and W. Shields was a whisky dealer in Leith, near Edinburgh in Scotland. H: 29.5cm. Cap: 76cl. (a full-size bottle). Wt: 730gr.

  (4) Sealed: 'Rousdon Jubilee – 1887'. Made to commemorate Queen Victoria's (1837-1901) Golden Jubilee in 1887. One of the last three-part mould blown bottles. Probably used for port wine. H: 29.5cm. Cap: 79cl. (full-size) Wt: 680gr.

Ref: R. Dumbrell (346), p.119 for bottles (2) (3); pls.44, 75 and fig.214 for bottle (4)

Plate 29. An English small-sized side-flattened onion. Dark olive green colour. Disc pontil scar. Sealed: 'L.S – 1723'. Similar bottle shapes were produced in North France and Belgium in the 17th century. In the 18th century they were very popular in Germany and were named 'Blatte' (flat bottle). Dim: 16.5 x 12.5 x 9cm. Cap: 58cl. Wt: 630gr.
Ref: R. Dumbrell (346) pl.19

Plate 30. An English bladder onion. Sealed: 'I.S. – 1716' with bust of a man holding an arrow (quill pen) in his right hand. This bottle belonged to the noted writer Jonathan Swift (Dublin 1667-1745), author of *Gulliver's Travels*. He was made Dean of St. Patrick's, Dublin in 1713. Another bladder sealed: 'I Swift – Dean – 1727' is in the National Museum of Ireland in Dublin. Dark olive green glass. Sand pontil scar. Dim: 20.5 x 14.5 x 12cm. Cap: 105cl. Wt: 930gr.
Ref: C. Munsey (771) p.61; N.C. Heckler (480) pl.XX lot 2589 (ex Charles Gardner Collection); R. Dumbrell (346) figs.95, 98, pl.20 and pp.308, 309; R. Morgan (762), p.49 for the seal description and p.52 for a similar bottle 'I. Swift-Dean 1727'; S. Ruggles-Brise (920) p.2 for 'I. Swift-Dean-1727'

85

Plate 31.
  (1) An English bladder onion. Sealed: 'C. Hollister – 1736'. Black glass. Disc pontil scar. Dim: 19 x 12.5 x 10cm. Cap: 54cl. Wt: 635gr.
  (2) A very early dated English over-sized bladder onion. Sealed: 'I. Pitt – 1724'. Black glass. Disc pontil scar. Dim: 21 x 16 x 12.5cm. Cap: 130cl. Wt: 1080gr.
Ref: R. Dumbrell (346) fig.101 for (1) and pp.77, 297 for (2)

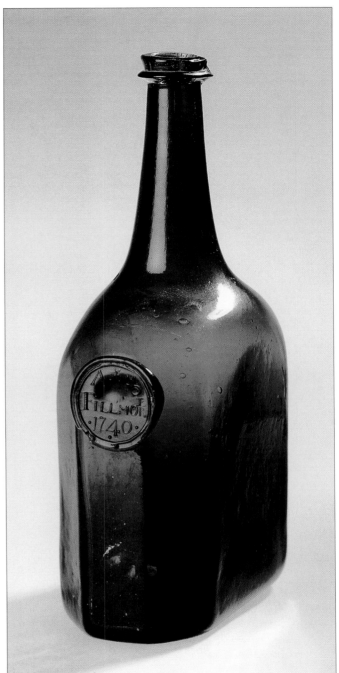

Plate 32. An English round octagonal bottle. Sealed: 'R.S. – 1739'. Black glass. Disc pontil scar. H: 25.5cm. Ø: 10.5/11.3cm. Cap: 90cl. Wt: 970gr.
Ref: R. Dumbrell (346) fig.128

Plate 33. An English flat octagonal bottle. Sealed: 'ABRM FILLMORE – 1740' (Abraham Fillmore). Rectangular sand pontil scar. Black glass. Dim: 25 x 12 x 7.5cm. Cap: 85cl. Wt: 935gr. See Plate 201 for a Continental dated '1740' rectangular sealed bottle.
Ref: N.C. Heckler (480) pl.XX lot 2926 ('Jno. Jackson – 1751') and lot 2957 ('Jno Collings – 1736') for similar bottle types

Plate 34. An English flat octagonal bottle in an unusual green–aquamarine colour. Half-size. Sealed: 'L.F. – 1740' Sand pontil scar. Dim: 21 x 8.8 x 6.5cm. Cap: 44cl. Wt: 540gr.
Ref: R. Dumbrell (346) fig.127

Plate 35. Three English octagonal bottles of different dimensions and capacities. All in black glass and with sand pontil scar.
   (1) Round octagonal c.1740. H: 16.5cm. Ø: 7cm. Cap: 19.5cl. (quarter-size). Wt: 375gr.
   (2) Flat octagonal c.1740. Dim: 25.5 x 12 x 7.5cm. Cap: 78cl (full-size). Wt: 830gr.
   (3) Flat octagonal c.1740. Dim: 21 x 8.5 x 6.3cm. Cap: 41cl (half-size). Wt. 470gr.
Ref: R. Dumbrell (346) figs.127, 128

Plate 36. An English round octagonal bottle in opaline turquoise blue glass originating from glassgall (see Glossary) in the molten glass. c.1760. Sand pontil scar. H: 23cm.Ø: 10.6/11.2cm. Cap: 90cl. Wt: 870gr.
Refs: R. Dumbrell (346) p.87, fig. right; A. Simon (979) pl.XCIV (No 224)

Plate 37. An English flat octagonal bottle embossed: 'IMPERIAL QUART' (1 Imp. quart = 113.6cl). Black glass. Blown in a two-part mould. c.1830. Disc pontil scar. Dim: 26 x 12 x 9cm. Cap: 130cl. Wt: 700gr. This bottle also exists as a half-size.

Plate 38. Three English decanter bottles.
 (1) Shaft and globe, c.1680. H: 17cm. Cap: 68cl. Wt: 1010gr. Sand pontil scar. Black
     glass. Listed in the sales list (dated 1677) of the London Company of Glass Sellers as a
     'Handle Bottle'.
 (2) Mallet c.1730-1735. H: 22.6cm. Cap: 92cl. Wt: 1020gr. Disc pontil scar. Black glass.
 (3) Onion c.1710-1725. H: 16.6cm. Cap: 56cl. Wt: 700gr. Blowpipe pontil scar. Blue-
     greenish aquamarine colour. See also Plates 12, 13(3) and 296(1).
Ref: Dumbrell (346) figs.215-218; A. Simon (979) pl.XCIIIA, lot No 222, pictures a sealed handled shaft and
globe, c.1700 with coat of arms of Chetwynd. See also Dumbrell (346) p.214. The bottle is in the Cecil Higgins
Museum, Bedford

Plate 39. Four English common utility bottles in black glass.
  (1) c.1690. Disc pontil scar. H: 17cm. Cap: 93cl. Wt: 1060gr.
  (2) c.1685. Disc pontil scar. H: 16cm. Cap: 77cl. Wt: 905gr.
  (3) A side-flattened onion, c.1720-1725. Sand pontil scar. Dim: 17 x 14 x 11cm. Cap: 71cl. (1 reputed quart = 75.7cl). Wt: 865gr.
  (4) A flowerpot-shaped onion, c.1750-1760. Sand pontil scar. H: 19cm. Cap: 109cl. Wt: 1030gr.

Plate 40. Three English wide mouth preserving/storage bottles. Black glass.
  (1) Wide mouth onion. c.1710-1725. Disc pontil scar. Half-size. H:13cm. Cap: 47cl. Wt: 630gr.
  (2) Wide mouth squat cylinder. Sealed: 'I. WATSON – ESQr – BILTONPARK' c.1780. Sand pontil scar. H: 22cm. Cap: 120cl. Wt: 1125gr.
  (3) Wide mouth flat octagonal. c.1740. Sand pontil scar. Half-size. Dim: 18 x 8.8 x 6.7cm. Cap: 38cl. Wt: 610gr.
Ref: R Dumbrell (346) pls.31 and 74 for bottle (2)

Plate 41.
(1) An English wide-mouth mallet, c.1735-1740. Olive green colour. Disc pontil scar. H: 18cm. Cap: 120cl. Wt: 910gr.
(2) An English side-flattened squat bottle, c.1780. Black glass. Rectangular sand pontil scar. Free blown. Dim: 18 x 14.5 x 7.5cm. Cap: 65cl. Wt: 580gr. For its German counterpart see Plate 217.
(3) A Scottish ship decanter bottle, c.1830. Black glass. Disc pontil scar. H: 23.5cm. Ø: 17.5cm. Cap: 160cl. Wt: 890gr. This bottle shape improves the stability of the bottle on ships.

Plate 42. A very late English onion. Sealed: 'W. Stinton – 1745'. Black glass. Disc pontil scar. H: 19.5cm. Cap: 116cl. Wt: 1210gr. See also Plate 14(3) for a '1725' dated example.

Plate 43. A very early English cylindrical bottle. Sealed: 'All Souls College – 1764'. The only known dated bottle from All Souls College, Oxford. All Souls was founded in 1438 by Archbishop Chichele as a memorial to those killed in the Hundred Years War. Olive green glass. Many carbon dioxide (CO_2) bubbles. Sand pontil scar. H: 27cm. Cap: 84cl. Wt: 855gr.
Refs: R Dumbrell (346) fig.167; F. Banks (123) fig.6.5; R. Morgan (762) p.84

Plate 44. A very early English cylindrical bottle. Sealed: 'MagCo – CR – 1769' (Magdalen College, Common Room, Oxford). The College was founded in 1448 by William of Wayneflete, Bishop of Winchester, and is perhaps Oxford's most beautiful college. Black glass. Disc pontil scar. H: 26.5cm. Cap: 88cl. Wt: 824gr.
Refs: R. Dumbrell (346) p.101, fig.d and p.286; F. Banks (123), fig.6.34 for a detached seal

Plate 45.

   (1) A small English bottle. Sealed: 'I.C. HOFFMANN' c.1830. Black glass. Disc pontil scar. Blown in a three-part mould. H: 21cm. Ø: 6.8cm. Cap: 38cl. Wt: 375gr. From 1748-1889 there was a glasshouse in Rotterdam making bottles ('De Rotterdamse Hut') founded by the German Johann Friedrich Hoffmann. This bottle is an English counterpart probably from the same family. A seal 'Hoffman – London' also exists. See also Figure 26(3).

   (2) A double-magnum squat cylindrical English bottle. Sealed: 'T – 1770'. Black glass. Sand pontil scar. H: 29cm. Ø:17.5cm. Cap: 3.2 litres. Wt: 2070gr.

Refs: F. Hudig (519) p.111 for bottle (1); R. Morgan (762) p.69 for bottle (2)

Plate 46.

    (1) An English small bottle. Sealed: '1791'. Black glass. Sand pontil scar. Bottles bearing date only are very rare. H: 15.7cm. Ø: 6cm. Cap: 23cl. Wt: 235gr. See also Plate 28(1).

    (2) A large English globular bottle ('carboy'). Sealed:'A.B.S – 1771'. Black glass. Disc pontil scar. H: 30cm. Ø: 24cm. Cap: 5.3 litres. Wt: 1780gr.

Refs: R. Morgan (762), p.69 for bottle (1); R. Dumbrell (346) fig.192 for bottle (1) and pl.54 for bottle (2); S. Ruggles–Brise (920) p.152 for bottle (1)

Plate 47. Three excavated English bottles with beautiful iridescent patination. Black glass.
All c.1780–1800. H: 22, 26 and 20cm.

Plate 48. Two antedated English bottles. Blown in a three-part Ricketts mould (British Patent No 4623 dated 1821). Both with sand pontil scar. Embossed on the shoulder: 'PATENT' and on the bottom 'H. RICKETTS & CO. GLASSWORKS – BRISTOL'.

    (1) Sealed: 'SHERRY – 1732'. This seal mentions the contents of the bottle which is very unusual. H: 23cm. Cap: 46cl. Wt: 412gr. This is the earliest antedated Ricketts bottle known. Blown c.1830.

    (2) Sealed: 'W. Leman – Chard – 1771'. H: 22cm. Cap: 40cl. Wt: 512gr. The date '1771' probably refers to the date that W. Leman, a brewer, founded the business in the Somerset town of Chard.

Ricketts claimed that the capacities of his bottles blown in these moulds could be made 'with a great degree of regularity or conformity to each other'. The difference of capacities of both bottles (46cl and 40cl) shows that it was impossible rigidly to control the capacities of bottles.

Refs: R. Dumbrell (346), Bottle (2) pl.64, p.281; O. Jones (581)

Plate 49. Two English decanter bottles. Green colour. Both glass–tipped pontil scars.
  (1) H: 16cm. Cap: 50cl. Wt: 425gr. A similar bottle is known with a seal: 'W. Trease –
      1821' (Cornwall).
  (2) H: 32cm. Cap: 3.8 litres. Wt: 2100gr.
Refs: R Dumbrell (346) fig.220 for bottle (1); Truro Exhibition Catalogue (70) fig.238 for bottle (1)

Plate 50. Two 'Nailsea' decanter bottles (jugs). White enamel flecks on black glass. Produced at the Nailsea Glass Works, near Bristol. Both with blowpipe pontil scar, c.1800–1815.

   (1) H: 11.5cm. Cap: 16cl. Wt: 170gr.

   (2) H: 32cm. Cap: 4.45 litres. (1 English Imperial gallon = 4.54 litres). Wt: 1570gr.

Bottles in 'Nailsea style' were produced at six different glasshouses in England.

Ref: R. Dumbrell (346) pl.47 for jugs (1) (2)

Plate 51. A 'Nailsea style' bottle attributed to Alloa Glass Works in Alloa, near Edinburgh, Scotland. Sealed 'MH – 1826'. Black glass globular bottle with white and blue enamelled flecks and four vertical rigarees. Disc pontil scar. H: 26cm. Cap: 2.6 litres. Wt: 1035gr.

Pre-'1800' dated Nailsea sealed bottles are extremely rare. A similar Nailsea bottle with the seal 'S.W. – 1792' was sold on 3 July 1999 at British Bottle Review Auction (694) for £3,575 or about 5,500 Euro!

Refs: R. Dumbrell (346) figs.221-223; K. Vincent (1072) pl.57

Plate 52. A 'Nailsea style' decanter bottle attributed to Alloa Glass Works in Alloa, near Edinburgh, Scotland. Sealed: 'E.F. – 1826' Black glass bottle with white and blue enamelled flecks. Sometimes made with vertical rigarees. Blowpipe pontil scar. H: 27cm. Cap: 1.6 litres. Wt: 728gr.

Refs: R. Morgan (762) pl, p.31; R. Dumbrell (346) fig.224

Plate 53. A decanter bottle attributed to Alloa Glass Works, Alloa, Scotland. Sealed: 'A.S. – 1828'. Black glass. Three vertical rigarees. Disc pontil scar. H: 31cm. Cap: 2.1 litres. Wt: 1340gr.

Plate 54.
Three bottles attributed to Alloa Glass Works, Alloa, Scotland. Black glass decorated with rigarees. Blowpipe pontil scars. All c.1820-1830. Clockwise from top:
   (1) A flask. Dim: 22 x 15 x 10cm. Cap: 140cl. Wt: 810gr.
   (2) A small decanter bottle. H: 20cm. Cap: 45cl. Wt: 370gr.
   (3) A snuff tobacco bottle. L. 11cm. Cap: 4cl. Wt: 125gr.

Plate 55. A masonic bottle. Triangular shape. Sealed with three standard masonic symbols: a pair of dividing compasses, a trowel and a set-square. Black glass. Blowpipe pontil scar. Probably made at Alloa Glass Works, Alloa, Scotland. H: 22cm. Cap: 30cl. (½ pint = 28.4cl from 1 May 1825 onwards). Wt: 555gr. Dim: base 8 x 8 x 8cm. c.1830.

The number three plays an important role in freemasonry. The bottle has three sides, the seal three emblems and symbolises mainly 'Belief, Hope and Love' or 'Wisdom, Force and Beauty' or 'Master, Mate and Apprentice'. See also Plate 56.

Ref: S. Ruggles-Brise (920) pl.1 (bottom row right) and pp.74, 75 picture the Dutch counterpart of this bottle

Plate 56. A Scottish masonic bottle sealed with masonic symbols: a pair of dividing compasses, a plumb line and a set-square, embossed underneath with 'LODGE ST. EBBE', all placed within a triangle. St. Ebbe is in Scotland. Notice the importance of the number three. Black glass. Sand pontil scar. c.1860. H: 21cm. Cap: 27cl. Wt: 530gr. Seal Ø: 35/45mm. See also Plate 55.

Ref: S. Ruggles-Brise (920) pl.1 (bottom row right) for a triangular Dutch item

Plate 57. An English pear-shaped 'carboy' used as a storage bottle in pharmacies. Green colour. Glass-tipped pontil scar. Metal cap closure. Label: 'TR:CAMPHORA' (tincture of camphor). c.1770. H: 37cm. Cap: 8.3 litres. Wt: 2800gr.
Ref: J.K. Crellin (277) fig.40

Plate 58. An English pharmaceutical storage bottle ('carboy'). Renewed capitals 'TR: SENEGAE' (tincture of Senega). c.1770. H: 35cm. Cap: 7 litres. Wt: 2700gr.

Plate 59. An English pharmaceutical storage bottle ('carboy'). Labelled: 'Spiritus Vini'. Black glass. Sand pontil scar. c.1770. H: 27.5cm. Cap: 5.5 litres. Wt: 1920gr. Ø: 23cm.
Ref: J.K. Crellin (277) fig.35

Plate 60. An English cylindrical pharmaceutical bottle. Label 'AQ. ROSE' (Aqua Rose, rose water). c.1800. Sand pontil scar. H: 27cm. Ø: 12.5cm. Cap: 2.6 litres. Wt: 1400gr. See also Plate 270(2).
Ref: J.F. Crellin (277) fig.25

Plate 61. Some examples of excavated and patinated glass seals from broken English bottles. Die Ø: between 38mm.(1) and 22mm (4). See also Plates 115, 116, 209 and 214. Row left from top to bottom etc.:

(1) 'H: EYRE – PURVEYOR FOR MINERAL WATERS TO HER MAIESTY – HOLT MINERAL WATERS'. In the centre of the seal is the coat of arms of Edward Lisle of Hoyles Court, Hampshire. The family was at one time Lord of the Manor at Holt. This is the private seal from Henry Eyre, merchant for mineral waters at Holt. He imported Pyrmont Water from Germany (see Plates 199A and 199B) and Spa Mineral Waters from Spa, a town near Liège, Belgium (see Plates 136A and 136B). This seal is the oldest known English glass seal referring to the contents (mineral water) of the bottle. c.1730. See also Figure 12 for the oldest sealed (c.1760) English 'Port' wine bottle.

(2) Seal from Ann Tomlinson who ran the 'Three Tuns' Tavern in Oxford from 1712 till 1719. See also Plate 16.

(3) Seal with the crest of 'The Most Noble Order of the Garter' with their device 'Honi Soit qui mal y pense' surmounted by an earl's coronet. The arms are those of John, first Earl Poulett (1663-1743), created an earl by Queen Anne in 1706. He became a Knight of the Garter in 1712.

(4) (5) (6) Three seals with a merchant's mark based on the 'rune four' symbol which refers, according to Christian and occult magic tradition, to the four Gospels, the four evangelists, the four quarters, the four seasons, the four elements (air, water, earth and fire), etc. The use of runes on bottle seals and as merchant marks was widespread in Europe in the 15th-18th century.

Seal (4) is a North German seal illustrated for comparison with the English seals. Plate 128 shows a Belgian made bottle with a merchant's mark.

Refs: H. Eyre (366) for (1); F. Banks (123) fig.5.12 (bottom) for (2); F.A. Girling (431) p.113 for (4) (5) and (6); S. Ruggles-Brise (920) p.167 for (4) (5) and (6); H. Henkes (489, 490), figs.2.40 and 2.41

II
HOLLAND and BELGIUM

In this part the words 'Holland' and 'Dutch' are used to make a clear distinction between 'The Netherlands' and 'Belgium', as they exist geographically today. Until the Peace treaty of Münster (or Westphalia), Germany in 1648, The Netherlands comprised the northern and southern Netherlands, also known as The Low Countries.

The seven northern provinces gained legal independence from Spain in 1648 and comprise The Netherlands of today. These provinces were Zeeland, Holland, Gelderland, Utrecht, Groningen, Friesland and Overijssel.

The southern provinces, which for the most part comprise Belgium today, were Flanders, Brabant, Luxemburg, Artois, Namur, Limburg and Hainault.

The Prince Bishopric Liège, now a part of Belgium, was not a part of The Netherlands at that time, but a very important source of glassmaking because of its geographical location, bordering on Holland, Germany and France.

When compared with Germany, Belgium or France in the 16th-18th centuries, Holland was not an important bottle-making country. Indeed, only a few small bottle houses (about fourteen) existed from the middle of the 18th century onwards.

Most glasshouses producing bottles on a large scale were situated in Belgium (more than 200!), especially the areas of Hainault (Beauwelz, Macquenoise, Charleroi), Liège, Bruges and Ghent.

The presence in Belgium (c.1450-1850) of the famous glassmakers' dynasty Colinet (or Colnet, de Colnet, Colenet etc.), many of whom specialised in making bottles and vials, together with the presence of forests, coal, sand, limestone, clay and transport routes (rivers) in the provinces of Hainault and Liège, provided ideal conditions for the production of very cheap high quality bottles for the Dutch market.

Arnould-Joseph 'de Colnet', the most important bottle glassmaker in those days, declared in 1745 that from the time of the Austrian War of Succession (1740-1748) onwards his glasshouse in Bruges exported 400,000 - 500,000 bottles (probably 'Dutch' onions) a year to Amsterdam, Holland and Middelburg, Zeeland. He also exported bottles to America and the French West Indies. See H: Schuermans (953), F. Hudig (519) and R. Chambon (242).

In 1750 Charleroi possessed a special patent for making 'bouteilles de Hollande' ('Dutch bottles') which means all types of bottles popular in Holland at that time such as 'onions', 'horse-hoofs', 'case-gin' bottles, etc.

Other glasshouses producing bottles for the Dutch market in the 16th-19th century were situated in Lorraine, North-east France (16th-early 17th century), England (second half 17th-18th century), Schleswig-Holstein (second half 17th-early 18th century), Thuringia, Mecklenburg and Hesse, Germany (all in the 18th-early 19th century).

Around 1730 Mecklenburg, North Germany, had a contract for delivering 600,000 'Netherlands-Hamburg' style bottles a year for four years to Holland (R. McNulty, 735, p.97). It is thought that the 'style' of these bottles was a 'side-flattened onion (in German 'Hamburger blatte Bouteille') as illustrated in Plates 278(2) and 280A(2).

Plate 62. A Dutch/Belgian oversize 'shaft and globe' with a silver mounted cork stopper. A common utility bottle used in this case as a decanter bottle. Emerald green colour. Blowpipe pontil scar. c.1670-1680. This bottle type exists also in blue and clear glass. Some are with a handle and/or sealed. They were often engraved by famous Dutch diamond-point engravers such as Willem Jacobsz. van Heemskerk (Leiden 1613-1693), Willem Mooleyser (1640-1700), François Crama and others. H: 25cm. Cap: 1.52 litres. Wt: 740gr. See also Plates 63 and 170.

Refs: K. Middlemas, *Antique Coloured Glass*, Ferndale Editions, London, 1979, p.55 for a handled example; P.C. Ritsema van Eck, *Glass in the Rijksmuseum*, Waanders, Zwolle, 1995, vol.II, pls.76-78 and 83-93; T. Dexel (326) pl.261

In order to avoid any misunderstandings about where the bottles were produced and the market where they were sold and used, the distinction between Holland and Belgium has been made. Many bottles produced in Belgium were used in Holland as well as in Belgium, some only in Holland, some only in Belgium. See also the notes on Belgium (Plates 117-138), Germany (Plates 188-243) and Miscellaneous (Plates 244-329).

Plate 63. A Dutch/Belgian full size 'shaft and globe' used as a common utility bottle. Emerald green colour. Blowpipe pontil scar. c.1670-1680. H: 22cm. Cap: 106cl. Wt: 484gr. See also Plates 62 and 170.

Refs: K. Middlemas *Antique Coloured Glass,* Ferndale Editions, London, 1979, p.55 for a handled example; P.C. Ritsema van Eck, *Glass in the Rijksmuseum,* Waanders, Zwolle, 1995, vol .II, pls.76-78 and 83-93

Plate 64.1. A very rare forest green (Waldglas) 'shaft and globe' produced in Holstein (Germany) for the Dutch market. Sealed with the portrait of Prince William III of Orange (1650-1702) and surrounded by the device 'VIVAT DE PRINCE VON ORANGIE' 'Long live the Prince of

'Orange', referring to his appointment as Stadtholder of Holland and Zeeland in 1672, known in Holland as the disastrous year. William III or 'Dutch William' married Mary II and was King of England from 1689 until 1702. This bottle type was blown at the glasshouses in Wittmoldt, Perdoel and Lammershagen in Holstein (North Germany). Other than Belgium, Holstein was one of the main suppliers of bottles to Holland in the 17th century. This bottle was produced from 1672 until c.1690. Blowpipe pontil scar. H: 23cm. Ø: 17cm. Cap: 1.9 litres (magnum or 2 full-size bottles). Wt: 840gr. Seal Ø: 50mm. Die Ø: 42mm. See also Plates 64.2, 98, 115, 116 and Figure 26(5).

Refs: H-J. Kruse (630) Typus B21; R. McNulty (735) fig.66; H. Henkes (489, 490) fig.3.04; Het Koninklijk Penningkabinet, Leiden, The Netherlands; Het Koninklijk Huis Archief, Den Haag, The Netherlands

Plate 64.2. A very rare and early North-German (Holstein) onion-shaped utility bottle made for the Dutch market, c.1690.

The seal shows a rider galloping across a field surmounted by the words: '•PRINS•★★★•IVRG•'. The rider, who wears a wig, a harness, a sword and spurs, commemorates the victory of the Protestant English King (1689-1702) and Dutch Prince William III of Orange (1650-1702) after the Battle of the (River) Boyne (July 1690), Northern Ireland at which William himself led the charge of the cavalry against the Roman Catholic James II (1633-1701), King of England (1685-1688) and Ireland (1688-1690) in his attempt to regain the English Crown.

The Battle of the Boyne is still remembered today as a victory for the Protestant cause

Plate 65. A half-size Dutch/Belgian (Liège) turquoise blue flask of ovoid horizontal section. Diamond-point engraved in the manner of Willem Mooleyser (1640-1700) c.1670. Blowpipe pontil scar. H: 18.5cm. Cap: 40cl. Wt: 120gr.

Ref: P.C. Ritsema van Eck: *Glass in the Rijksmuseum,* Waanders, Zwolle, 1995, vol.II, pl.90 for a similar shape and colour

through the Orange Marches in Northern Ireland. The meaning of 'IVRG' on the seal remains unsolved. The illustrated bottle was produced from 1690 until 1699 at the glasshouses of Schönhorst (until 1690) and Grünhaus (1690-1699) both in Holstein, North Germany.

The bottle, in forest green glass ('Waldglas'), has a pouring lip and a blowpipe pontil scar. H: 32.5cm. Ø: 27cm. Cap: 7 litres. Wt: 1.74kg. Seal Ø: 54mm. Die Ø: 46mm. See also Plates 64.1, 98, 115, 116, 196 and Figure 26(5).

Refs: H-J. Kruse (630), p.15, 16, 86 (text) and pp.8 and 12 (illust.) typus B24 for a similar seal and p.2 (illust.) col.pl. KMP 219 for a similar bottle-style; Het Koninklijk Penningkabinet, Leiden, The Netherlands; Het Koninklijk Huis Archief, Den Haag, The Netherlands

Plate 66. A Dutch/Belgian (Liège) small size turquoise blue coloured decanter bottle with silver-mounted stopper. The cork stopper with the cast finial figure of St. Peter. Blown by the German half-post method. Glass tipped pontil scar. c.1670. H: 18.5cm (with stopper). Cap: 35cl. Wt: 176gr.
Ref: A.E. Theuerkauff-Liederwald (1021) pl.544; Sotheby's cat. 'The Joseph Ritman Collection of 16th and 17th century Dutch Glass', London, 14 Nov. 1995, lot 29

Plate 67. A Dutch/Belgian (Liège) small cobalt blue decanter bottle. The body is decorated with 'nipt-diamond-waies'. Blown by the German half-post method. Glass tipped pontil scar. H: 13.5cm. Cap: 20cl. Wt: 110gr.
Ref: A.E. Theuerkauff-Liederwald (1021), pl.553; Sotheby's cat. 'The Joseph Ritman Collection of 16th and 17th century Dutch Glass', London, 14 Nov. 1995, lot 32

Plate 68. A Dutch/Belgian (Liège) decanter bottle. Amethyst colour. Decorated with eight pincered ribs c.1720–1750. Glass tipped pontil scar. H: 22.5cm. Cap: 107cl. Wt: 455gr.
Ref: P.C. Ritsema van Eck: *Glass in the Ryksmuseum,* Waanders, Zwolle, 1995, vol.II, pl.424

Plate 69. A Dutch/Belgian (Liège) decanter bottle. Clear glass. Body decorated with 'nipt-diamond-waies'. c.1670. German half-post method. Glass-tipped pontil scar. H: 24cm. Cap: 125cl. Wt: 530gr.

Ref: P.C. Ritsema van Eck: *Glass in the Rijksmuseum,* Waanders, Zwolle, 1993, vol.I, pl.299

Plate 70. Three typical common utility bottles mostly used in Holland throughout the 18th century. Blowpipe pontil scar.

(1) A straight-sided 'Dutch' onion ('buikje' or 'kattetop'). Clear green colour with bluish tone, produced in Schleswig-Holstein ('Englische Bouteille') for the Dutch market. This bottle type was reproduced from its English counterpart (see Plate 17). c.1720-1730. H: 18.5cm. Cap: 75cl. Wt: 745gr. Ø: 13.5cm.

(2) A 'horse hoof' bottle. Yellowish olive green colour, mainly produced in Belgium or in North Germany (Mecklenburg) for the Dutch market. c.1720-1750. A typical Belgian bottle shape. H: 21.5cm. Cap: 85cl. Wt: 855gr. Ø: 15cm.

(3) A 'Dutch' onion ('buikje'), dark grass green colour, mainly produced in Germany (Hesse, Thuringia) for the Dutch market. This bottle type was reproduced from its English counterpart (see Plate 11). c.1720-1750. H: 19cm. Cap: 85cl. Wt: 755gr. Ø: 14cm. A similar 'onion' is sealed 'Jakob van Veen'. Another sealed with the monogram 'L.R' of the Brunswick Duke Ludwig Rudolf (1731-1735) is in the City Museum of Brunswick, North Germany.

Bottles (1) (2) (3) were used for wine, beer, oil etc. and were shipped throughout the 18th century all over the world (including Surinam, Guyana...) hence the name 'Dutch' onion. They were used in pharmacies as decanters (especially the 'horse hoof' type) and for all manner of other applications.

Type (1) is relatively rare. Type (3) was produced for at least 100 years. A sealed onion dated '1804' is recorded. These bottles were of course also produced in Holland but on a much lesser scale because of the competition from Belgium and Germany which was very strong. Holland did not have a glassmakers' tradition, cheap raw materials and fuel. Notice the capacities of these 'onion' bottles. An 'Amsterdamse fles' had in the 18th century a capacity of 88cl. See also Plates 71-75.

Refs: T. Dexel (326) pl.281 for bottle (3); J. Koch (621) Abb. 25 for bottle (3); W. Klein (612, 613); A.J. van der Horst (512, 513)

Plate 71. Four 'Dutch' onions (buikfles, kattekop) used as common utility bottles for beer, wine, brandy, oil, vinegar, etc. Blowpipe pontil scar. Their capacities vary from 78cl-92cl. (1 Amsterdamse fles = 88cl). Bottles mainly blown in Belgium ('des bouteilles de Hollande') and Germany for the Dutch market. c.1720-1750. See also Plates 15, 17, 70 and 72-75.
Ref: W. Klein (612, 613); A.J. van der Horst (512, 513)

Plate 72. A collection of 'Dutch' onions (buikfles, kattekop). Capacities fluctuate from 78cl–92cl. (1 Amsterdamse fles = 88cl.). c.1720–1750. Blowpipe pontil scar. About 70% of these 'Dutch' onions were produced in Belgian glasshouses such as those of the Charleroi area and Bruges. Charleroi possessed a special patent for producing 'des bouteilles de Hollande' (bottles for Holland) and the Bruges glasshouse of Arnould de Colnet – a member of the famous Belgian glassmakers' dynasty – between 1745 and 1750 exported 400,000 – 500,000 bottles a year to Amsterdam and Middelburg, probably for further export by the V.O.C. (Vereenigde Oost-Indische Compagnie). Other important bottlemakers for the Dutch market were situated in Germany (Schleswig-Holstein, Mecklenburg, Thuringia, Hesse). Very few bottles came from England. See Plates 15, 17, 70, 71 and 73-75.

Refs: R. Chambon (242) p.138; F. Hudig (519), p.115; H. Henkes (489) pl.59.11; W. Klein (612, 613); R. McNulty (735, 736); W. Dorsman (338)

Plate 73. Four 'Dutch' bottles of different capacities, colour and shapes.
  (1) 'Dutch' onion. H: 15cm. Ø: 13cm. Cap: 61cl. Wt: 625gr. c.1720. Blowpipe pontil scar. Made in England.
  (2) A small 'horse hoof' (calcoentje). H: 15.5cm. Ø: 9.5cm. Cap: 26cl. Wt: 300gr. c.1750. A Belgian bottle for the Dutch market ('bouteille de Hollande'). Blowpipe pontil scar.
  (3) An English straight-sided onion (magnum). Disc pontil scar. H: 21cm. Ø: 17cm. Cap: 190cl. (1 English Queen Anne wine pottle = 189cl. or half a gallon or two quarts). c.1690-1700.
  (4) A straight-sided Dutch onion. H: 16cm. Ø: 12.5cm. Cap: 55cl. Wt: 660gr. c.1720-1750. Blowpipe pontil scar.
See also Plates 15, 17, 70-72, 74, 75 and 92.

Plate 74. Three patinated 'Dutch' onions with beautiful iridescence.
  (1) English origin. Sand pontil scar. c.1720. H: 14.5cm. Ø: 14cm. Cap: 78cl. Wt: 844gr.
  (2) North German origin (green forest glass). c.1720-1750. Sealed: 'H:P.' Blowpipe
      pontil scar. H: 17.5cm. Ø: 14cm. Cap: 71cl. Wt: 534gr. See ref. below.
  (3) Belgian or German origin (Hesse, Thuringia). c.1720-1750. Dark grass green colour.
      Blowpipe pontil scar. H: 17.7cm. Ø: 14cm. Cap: 87cl. Wt: 786gr.
See Plates 11, 70-73, 75, 200 and 258.

Ref: T. Dexel (326) pl.281 pictures a German 'Dutch' onion sealed with the monogram 'L.R.' of the Brunswick
Duke Ludwig Rudolf (1731-1735) H: 18.5cm. A similar 'Dutch' onion to (2) and sealed '1804 – I.B. -¾ St.' of
Scandinavian origin is known

Plate 75. An early straight-sided English style 'Dutch' onion with original contents (red wine). Excavated. Patinated. c.1720. Closed with a cork and wax (the copper wire string is gone). H: 16.5cm. Blowpipe pontil scar. This bottle style was also produced in Mecklenburg (North Germany) and denominated an 'Englische Buddel' or an 'Englische Bouteille'.

Refs: W. Klein (612, 613); A.J. van der Horst (512, 513)

Plate 76. A small early straight–sided wide mouth bottle. Flared lip for mounting a pewter screw closure or for tying a closing cloth with a cord. A preserving bottle for general purposes. c.1650–1700. Excavated in Holland. A North German (green forest glass) bottle for the Dutch market. Blowpipe pontil scar. H: 5.5cm. Ø: 8.5cm. Cap: 14cl. Wt: 156gr.

Plate 77. An English made black glass 'mallet' bottle produced for the Dutch market. Sealed:. 'Direk Vanveghten – 1728'. Disc pontil scar. H: 20.5cm. Cap: 88cl. (1 Amsterdamse fles = 88cl). Wt: 1065gr. Henkes (489, 490) mentions other English bottles made for the Dutch market, for example 'Jacobus Van Driel – Utreght – 1706' (fig. 2.02) and 'Rijkevorsel – 1716' (fig. 2.03), a merchant's family in Rotterdam.

Refs: R. Dumbrell (346) fig.112; H. Henkes (489, 490) figs. 2.02 and 2.03; R. McNulty (735) fig.51 and (736) fig.98

Plate 78. Three long neck utility bottles ('langhals') for the Dutch market. All blowpipe pontil scar.

    (1) Half-size. Belgian origin ('Bouteille de Hollande'). c.1770. H: 25cm. Cap: 38cl. Sometimes sealed. See Plate 79(2) for a full-size bottle.

    (2) Dutch or Belgian. c.1800. H: 28cm. Ø: 10.5cm. Cap: 79cl. Wt: 678gr.

    (3) German origin. c.1750. H: 25cm. Ø: 11cm. Cap: 75cl. Wt: 672gr.

See also Plates 79–82 and 130.

Ref: W. Klein (612, 613)

Plate 79. Three Dutch/Belgian 'long neck' utility bottles ('langhals') mostly used for containing all types of wine. c.1770-1840. Dark olive green colour ('verre noir', 'zwart glas').
  (1) A half-size bottle. Lady's leg neck. H: 24cm. Cap: 44cl. (1 Amsterdamse fles = 88cl.) Wt: 485gr.
  (2) A full size 'long neck' flowerpot bottle. H: 30cm. Cap: 88cl. (1 Amsterdamse fles!) Wt: 775gr. See Plate 78(1) for a similar half-size bottle.
  (3) A full-size 'long neck' cylinder. H: 28.5cm. Cap: 72cl. Wt: 660gr.
Notice that these bottles were common utility bottles. They were not made for any one particular wine type. The following types of wine have been registered on 'sealed' items: Constantia, Burgundy, Claret, Madeira, Hermitage, and Hobrion. See also Plates 80-82, 130 and 263.

Refs: W. Van den Bossche (187); W. Klein (612, 613); H. Henkes (489) §60 and (490); R. McNulty (735) fig.64; E. Leitherer (668) pl.p.33

Plate 80. Two Dutch/Belgian common utility bottles, in this case used for 'CONSTANTIA WYN'. This wine was so called after Constance, wife of the Dutch Governor Simon Van der Stel (died 1712) in South Africa, who possessed vineyards at the Cape from c.1680 onwards. The following eight seals relating to Constantia wine are registered on eleven different shaped utility bottles (1760-1840) 'CONSTANTIA WYN', 'CONSTANTIA WEIN', 'KONSTANTIA WYN', 'CONSTANCE' (name inverted on the seal), a sun above a vineyard and the name 'CONSTANTIA', 'GROOT CONSTANTIA' (sometimes inverted on the seal), 'J.P. CLOETE – CONSTANTIA WINE' and finally 'HAUT CONSTANCE – S. VAN REENEN – CAP DE BONNE ESPERANCE' (Sebastiaan van Reenen, from 1821).

   (1) Bottle with a 'lady's leg' neck in dark olive green glass colour (coal firing). c.1800. Blowpipe pontil scar. H: 22cm. Cap: 36cl. Wt: 385gr. Notice the remains of a wax seal on the lip. Wax was used to make the corked bottle airtight. Sometimes the wax was sealed with a merchant's mark or indicated the contents of the bottle (see Plate 319)

   (2) The oldest known sealed 'CONSTANTIA WYN' bottle. c.1760. This bottle type is also known sealed with 'BOERGONIE WYN' and 'BOURGOGNE WYN'. Blowpipe pontil scar. Bottle in olive green colour (wood firing) produced in Belgium. H: 25cm. Ø: 10.5cm. Cap: 84cl. Wt: 830gr. Before 1760 Constantia wine was bottled in full-size or half-size 'Dutch' onions.

See also Plates 78–82 and 130.

Refs: W Van den Bossche (187); G. Abrahams (2); Dumbrell (346), p.143, fig.q and p.247; H. Henkes (489, 490); R. McNulty (736), figs.109–111

Plate 81. Three Dutch/Belgian long neck utility bottles ('langhals'), ('zwart glas', 'verre noir'). c.1770. Blowpipe pontil scars for (1) and (3). (2) has a glass-tipped pontil scar.

1) Sealed: 'CONSTANTIA WYN'. H: 20.5cm. Cap: 35cl. Wt: 440gr.
2) Sealed: 'M.S.' (turns up only in Belgium). H: 28cm. Cap: 93cl. Wt: 760gr.
3) Sealed: 'CLARET'. H: 27cm. Cap: 80cl. Wt: 650gr.

See also Plates 78-80, 82, 130, and 263.

Refs: W. Van den Bossche (187); G. Abrahams (2); H. Henkes (489, 490); E. Leitherer (668) pl. p.33

Plate 82. Two long neck cylindrical utility bottles ('langhals'). Belgium/Holland. c.1770 (1) and 1820 (2). Blowpipe pontil scars. Black glass.

      (1) Sealed: 'ICC'. H: 26cm. Cap: 72cl. Wt: 660gr. The meaning of 'ICC' is still unsolved. A similar bottle sealed 'H I' exists.

      (2) A half–size bottle. H: 22.5cm. Cap: 40cl. Wt: 432gr. A French 'bottle ticket' shows the contents of the bottle when used as a decanter.

See also Plates 79, 81 and 263.

Refs: R. McNulty (735) fig.26 and (583) fig.108; J. Stancliffe (991); E. Whitworth (1109); N. Penzer (823)

Plate 83. Five Dutch/Belgian case and/or case-gin bottles of different periods and capacities. Bottles (2) to (4) are named a 'lummel' (Dutch).

(1) Vertically straight-sided body. c.1720-1750. H: 25.5 x 10 x 10cm. Cap: 1.93 litres. Wt: 860gr.

(2) c.1770-1800. H: 54cm. Cap: 11 litres. Wt: 4005gr.

(3) c.1750-1770. H: 37cm. Cap: 5.46litres. Wt: 2350gr.

(4) c.1770-1800. H: 36cm. Cap: 4 litres. Wt: 1440gr.

(5) Sealed: 'SIMON RYNBENDE & ZONEN – SCHIEDAM' c.1880. H: 14.5cm. Cap: 19cl. Wt: 260gr.

Bottles (1) to (4) have a blowpipe pontil scar, (5) has no pontil scar. Bottles produced in Holland and Belgium. (3) probably produced in North Germany.

The tapered case-gin bottle evolved from c.1750-1770 onwards from the vertically straight-sided narrow neck case bottle which was, from 1570 onwards, a common utility bottle for all applications (as we can see in Plates 192, 253 and 272).

Due to the world-wide increase of gin consumption from the 1770s onwards the demand for case bottles was enormous. The vertically straight-sided case bottles tended to stick when being withdrawn from the mould and were impaired at the internal mould surface. The use of a tapered dip mould solved this problem and thus the tapered case-gin bottle was born. From 1770 these bottles were blown the world over, although mainly in Holland and Belgium. See also Figures 14, 26(1) (London gin bottles) and Plate 208(4)

Refs: W. Klein (612, 613); A.J. van der Horst (512, 513); R. McNulty (735) fig.24

Plate 84. Three 'Dutch' case bottles. All with blowpipe pontil scar.
  (1) Sealed: 'VG&C' (Van Gent & Co., distiller in Schiedam, Holland). Black glass. Dip moulded. Blowpipe pontil scar (very rare). c.1800. H: 26cm. Cap: 96cl. Wt: 650gr.
  (2) With straight vertical sides (in Dutch 'lummel'). c.1720-1750. A common utility bottle and forerunner of the case-gin bottle. Light green forest glass colour. Produced in North Germany for the Dutch market. Dim: 29 x 10.5 x 10.5cm. Cap: 2.3 litres. Wt: 1215gr.
  (3) A common case-gin bottle (in Dutch 'kelderfles'). c.1780-1830. Black glass. Tapered body. H: 23.5cm. Cap: 86cl. Wt: 450gr.
Bottles (1) and (3) produced in Schiedam (Holland) and in Charleroi (Belgium).
Ref: W. Klein (612, 613)

132

Plate 85. Three 'Dutch' case gin bottles. All sealed: 'AVH:' (A. van Hoboken, Rotterdam).
Not to be confused with 'ÅVH' for A.I. van Hoytema, Culemborg, Holland. (1) and (2)
embossed: 'A. van Hoboken & Co – Rotterdam'. Gin distillers. No pontil scars. c.1860–
1880. Blob top lips.
  (1) H: 28cm. Cap: 160cl. Wt: 915gr.
  (2) H: 11.5cm. Cap: 12cl. Wt: 125gr.
  (3) Sealed: 'AVH' and blowpipe pontil scar (very rare). Flared lip. c.1800. H: 28cm. Cap:
     150cl. Wt: 935gr. Black glass ('zwart glas'/'verre noir').
Bottles blown in Schiedam (Holland) and in Charleroi (Belgium).
Refs: D. Pettit (833); R. McNulty 736) fig.113

133

Plate 86. A 'Dutch' case-gin bottle (in Dutch 'kelderfles'). Embossed 'COSMOPOLIET – J.J. MELCHERS W.Z. – SCHIEDAM'. There exist nine different embossings for 'Cosmopoliet' bottles of different capacities. c.1870. Glass colour: dark olive green. Blown in Schiedam (Holland) and the Charleroi (Belgium) area in a three-part mould (Ricketts). H: 24cm. Cap: 78cl. Wt: 565gr.
Ref: R. Green (448) p.36

Plate 87. A 'Dutch' case gin bottle (in Dutch 'kelderfles'). Embossed 'THE OLIVE TREE – JOHN L. LINNENBRINK – SCHIEDAM' and an olive tree. c.1870. Johannes Ludovicus Linnenbrink was a gin distiller in Schiedam (Holland) from 1863-1878. Blown in a Ricketts mould. No pontil scar. Blown in Holland or Belgium ('bouteille de Hollande'). Black glass. H: 23.5cm. Cap: 71cl. Wt: 540gr.
Refs: P. Vermeulen 'The Olive Tree' in the Clubblad *De Oude Flesch,* Nieuwegein (NL) No 56, 1993; R. Green (448) p.36

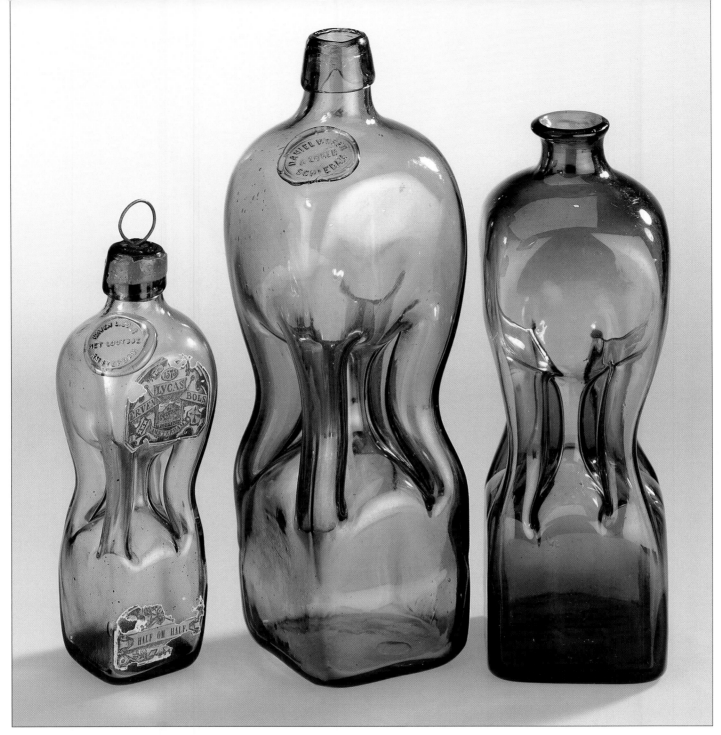

Plate 88. Three 'kuttrolf' case bottles in green glass (in Dutch 'kelderfles'). Used for gin and/or liqueur.

(1) Dutch sealed: 'ERVEN L. BOLS – HET LOOTSJE – AMSTERDAM'. c.1880-1920. No pontil scar. 18cm. Wt: 225gr. Remains of liqueur ('half om half') in the bottle.

2. Dutch sealed: 'DANIEL VISSER & ZONEN – SCHIEDAM'. c.1880-1920. No pontil scar. H: 26cm. Cap: 92cl. Wt: 585gr.

3. A mid-18th century 'kuttrolf' of North German or Scandinavian origin. Blowpipe pontil scar (very rare). See also Figure 13(No. 145). H: 25cm. Cap: 62cl. Wt: 550gr.

See also Plates 190(2), 205 and 298.

Refs: H. Henkes (489) pls.51.11 and 51.12 and photo Afb. 158 (painting from Jan Steen 1625-1679); R. McNulty (735) figs.28, 29

135

Plate 89. A Dutch or Belgian original 'case' or 'cellar' (in Dutch 'kelder') for storing or exporting case-gin bottles all over the world. This case contains twelve 'case' bottles, others sometimes fifteen. The bottles were packed in the case with straw or buckwheat husks. The name case-bottle originates from the 'case' in which they were packed and transported. All bottles have a blowpipe pontil scar. Dim. (case): 30 x 46 x 35cm. See also Plate 206.

Refs: H. Henkes (489) Photo afb. 150 on pp.236 and 387; B. Arendonk: 'Kelder' in Clubblad der Verzamelaarsklub *De Oude Flesch*, 4ᵉ Jaargang, No. 11, April 1982

Plate 90. A liqueur cellar for storing six case-gin bottles. In this case the gin bottles were used for liqueurs such as cognac, brandy, etc. Late 18th century. All blowpipe pontil scars. Dim. (cellar): 28.5 x 31.5 x 22cm.

Refs: H. Henkes (489) photo afb. 150 on pp.236 and 387; J. Bellanger (148) pl.p.289

Plate 91. A small 'Dutch' liqueur cellar (in Dutch 'likeurkeldertje') with four Bohemian made decanter bottles. The wooden cellar in Rococo style measures 23 x 19 x 19cm. The bottles are made in Bohemian crystal. Late 18th century. This type of small cellar or case was also very popular in Belgium and France.

Refs: A. Simon (979) pl.CVI (no 249); J. Bellanger (148) pl.p.412

Plate 92. Two 'Dutch' long neck 'horse hoof' (in Dutch 'paardenhoef') utility bottles. Black glass ('zwart glas', 'verre noir'). Blowpipe pontil scar. Most of these were produced in Belgium ('Bouteilles de Hollande') for the Dutch market. c.1750-1770.

(1) A small size 'horse hoof' (in old Dutch 'calcoentje') painted with coat of arms of Zeeland (left) and Friesland (right). The reverse painted with a portrait of a man. H: 16cm. Cap: 30cl. Wt: 390gr.

(2) A full size 'horse hoof' with a pouring lip and a (French) bottle label. Mostly used as a decanter bottle in pubs, pharmacies, households, etc. Bottle never seen with a seal. H: 24cm. Cap: 76cl. Wt: 755gr.

Refs: H. Henkes (489) pl.64.4 and fig.64.5; J. Stancliffe (991)

139

Plate 93. A 'Dutch' long neck 'horse hoof' ('paardenhoef') decanter or utility bottle c.1750–1770. Painted on the reverse in 'folk art' style with music players and on the front side with the proverb 'By Spel en Wyn past vroolyk en syn' (play, drink and be merry). Painting utility bottles was very popular in Holland in the 18th and 19th century. Dark olive green colour. Blowpipe pontil scar. H: 23cm. Ø: 14cm. Cap: 83cl. Wt: 730gr.
Ref: H. Henkes (489) pl.64.4

Plate 94. A small 'Dutch' long neck 'horse hoof' utility bottle. The old Dutch popular name is 'calcoentje'. A quarter-size bottle. c.1770–1800. Blowpipe pontil scar. Black glass ('zwart glas'). Painted in 'folk art' style with the portrait of 'ADRIAAN PAUW – HEER VAN HAEMSTEDE'. On the reverse the coat of arms of Zeeland, The Netherlands. H: 15cm. Ø: 9.2cm. Cap: 20cl. Wt: 245gr. Adriaen Pauw van Heemstede (1585–1653) represented Holland and West Friesland to negotiate with the Spanish the Peace of Münster, Westphalia, Germany (1648) when the Northern Netherlands were officially separated from the Southern Netherlands, now Belgium.

Plate 95. Two painted 'Dutch' utility bottles.
(1) A North German (Holstein) side-flattened bottle (in German: eine 'Blatte'). Forest green glass. c.1720-1730. A portrait on the front and a ship on the reverse. Dim: 22 x 19.5 x 14.3cm. Cap: 215cl. Wt: 990gr.
(2) A Dutch long neck 'horse hoof' decanter bottle. Portrait of 'ADRIAAN BANKERT' – Luitenant Admiraal van Zeeland'. On the reverse the coat of arms of South Holland. Black glass. Pouring lip. c.1750-1770. Blowpipe pontil scar. H:23cm. Cap: 80cl. Wt: 650gr.

Plate 96. A 'Dutch' half-cylindrical storage bottle (in Dutch 'lamsbout' – a leg of lamb). It stood with its flat rear side on shelves against the wall in pubs, etc. and was used for all types of liqueurs. Cold painted label 'Crème de Roses'. Dark green colour. Blowpipe pontil scar. c.1720-1760. Produced in one of the six 'Holländische Glashütten' (Dutch glasshouses) in Thuringia. The German name is 'eine halbrunde Bouteille' (a half round bottle). Dim: 43.5 x 13.6 x 12cm. Cap: 5.9 litres. Wt: 2280gr. See also Plates 97–100.

Refs: B.A. Arendonk (83) p.14; H. Kühnert (633) p.170; E. van Schoonenberghe (951) pl. p.2 for a similar bottle labelled 'Brandewijn'

Plate 97. Two 'Dutch' half cylindrical storage bottles ('lamsbout' or 'eine halbrunde Bouteille'). c.1720–1760. Early 19th century 'folk art' cold paintings. Dark grass green colour. Blowpipe pontil scars. Produced in Thuringia, Germany. Dim: 44.7 x 19.5 x 11.5cm. Cap: about 5.9 litres. See also Plate 96.

Ref: E. van Schoonenberghe (951) pl.p.2 for another painted item

Plate 98. A 'Dutch' half-cylindrical storage bottle (in Dutch 'lamsbout', in German 'eine halbrunde Bouteille'). c.1720-1760.

Folk art cold painting depicting the Protestant English King (1689-1702) and Dutch Prince William III of Orange (1650-1702) dressed as a field marshal after the Battle of the (River) Boyne (July 1690), Northern Ireland, where he defeated the Roman Catholic James II (1633-1701), King of England (1685-1688) and Ireland (1689-1690) in his attempt to regain the English Crown.

Dark grass green colour, blowpipe pontil scar and made in Thuringia, Germany for the Dutch market. Dim: 44 x 19.5 x 12cm. Cap: about 5.9 litres. See also Plates 64.1, 64.2 and 96.

Refs: E. van Schoonenberghe (951) pl.p.2 for a similar painted bottle type; Het Koninklijk Penningkabinet, Leiden, The Netherlands; Het Koninklijk Huis Archief, Den Haag, The Netherlands

Plate 99. A 'Dutch' half cylindrical storage bottle ('lamsbout' or 'eine halbrunde Bouteille'). c.1720-1760. Folk art painting depicting 'The violin player in front of the inn' (1673 reproduced from Adriaen van Ostade (Haarlem 1610-1684)). Signed 'A.v. Ostade' and monogram 'A.F.'. Dim: 45 x 20.5 x 13cm. Cap: about 5.9 litres. See also Plate 96.
Ref: E. van Schoonenberghe (951) pl.2 for another painted item

Plate 100. A 'Dutch' half cylindrical storage bottle ('lamsbout' or 'eine halbrunde Bouteille'). c.1720–1760. Folk art painting depicting 'The cutting of the stone' (het snijden van de kei) reproduced from Jan Steen (Leiden 1626–1679). Signed 'J. Steen' and monogram 'A.F.'. Dim: 46 x 19.5 x 12.5cm. Cap: about 5.9 litres. See also Plate 96.

Refs: H. Henkes (489), afb. 158 for a similar subject from J. Steen 'Het snijden van de kei'; E. van Schoonenberghe (951) pl.2 for another painted item

Plate 101. Two side-flattened onions. Dark grass green colour. German bottles (in German: eine 'Blatte') made for the Dutch market. Both bottles have a blowpipe pontil scar.

    (1)   A storage bottle. Painted with the coat of arms of Friesland (left) and South Holland (right). c.1720. Dim: 38.5 x 32 x 24cm. Cap: 10.2 litres. Wt: 4060gr.

    (2)   A small bottle. c.1730–1750. Dim: 11.5 x 8 x 4.5cm. Cap: 12cl. Wt: 140gr.

Plate 102. A squat cylindrical storage bottle, c.1720-1730. Coat of arms of Zeeland (left) and South Holland (right). Bottle made for the Dutch market. Dark grass green colour. Blowpipe pontil scar. H: 26cm. Ø: 20cm. Cap: 3.47 litres. Wt: 1300gr.

Plate 103. A 'Dutch' globular storage bottle ('ballonfles') c.1750-1770. Cold painted label. 'CITROENLIMONADE' (lemon drink). It was very common in Holland to paint the intended contents on storage bottles. Examples from other known bottles are: 'Triple Sec', 'Anisette' (Anise), 'Dubbele Anisette' (Double Anise), 'Citroen' (Lemon), 'Abrikoos' (Apricot), 'Dubbele Pepermunt' (Double Peppermint), 'Zilverwater' (Silverwater), 'Guldewater' (Goldwater), 'Dubbel Water' (Double Water), 'Perzik' (Peach), 'Volmaakte Liefde' (Perfect Love), 'Crème de Cacao' (Cream of Cocoa), 'Crème de Roses' (Cream of Roses), 'Bruidstranen' (Hippocras), 'Curacou' (Curaçao) 'Beste Curacou' (Best Curaçao), 'Nagelwater' (Clove Brandy), 'Schillen' (Peel), 'Roschalen' (Raw Peel), 'Jamaica Rum', 'Frambose' (Raspberry Liqueur), 'Half om Half' (Half and Half), 'Cardemon' (Cardamon) and 'Brandewijn' (Brandy). H: 32.5cm. Ø: 26cm. Cap: 7 litres. Wt: 2340 gr. See also Plates 104, 105, 108, 109 and 270(1).

Plate 104. A 'Dutch' globular storage bottle, flattened at the rear ('ballonfles'). Cold painted label 'Cardemon' (Cardamon). Pouring lip. Dark olive green colour. Blowpipe pontil scar. c.1750-1770. Dutch or Belgian origin. (1) Front view. (2) Side view. H: 28cm. Ø: 18cm. Cap: 3.9 litres. Wt: 1100gr. See also Plates 103, 105 and 270(1).

Plate 105. A 'Dutch' globular storage bottle ('ballonfles'). Labelled: 'Magorum'. Used in pharmacies or chemists' shops. The painting 'The Apothecary' from Willem van Mieris (Leiden 1662-1747) pictures several labelled globular storage bottles standing on the shelves. Apart from pharmaceuticals the same bottles were used for storing liqueurs, vinegar, oils, etc. c.1770. H: 22cm. Ø: 19cm. Cap: 2.9 litres. Wt: 1125gr. See also Plates 103, 104 and 270(1).
Refs: H: McKearin (733) p.23, pl.7; G. Kallinich (590) pl.304

Plate 106. A 'Dutch' globular storage bottle ('ballonfles') with a folk art painting of a sea battle. Early 18th century. Dark olive green colour. Blowpipe pontil scar. Pouring lip. H: 30cm. Ø: 25cm. Cap: 7.2 litres. Wt: 2230gr.

Plate 107. A 'Dutch' globular storage bottle ('ballonfles'). On the front a folk art painting depicting a sea battle, on the reverse the coat of arms of Zeeland. Pouring lip. c.1730–1750. Blowpipe pontil scar. H: 23cm. Ø: 18cm. Cap: 2.14 litres. Wt: 1380gr.

Plate 108. A 'Dutch' globular storage bottle depicting a 19th century folk art painting of a sea battle. The text reads: 'A°1644 – Vierdaagschen Zeeslag – A°1644' (the four day sea battle). The painting refers to the four day sea battle (11-14 June 1666) in the English Channel near Dunkirk, France between the English and Dutch fleets during the second Anglo-Dutch war. The date '1644' on the bottle seems to be a mistake by the painter. Bottle date c.1750-1770. Dark olive green glass colour. Blowpipe pontil scar. H: 36cm. Ø: 28cm. Cap: 11 litres. Wt: 3.2kg. See also Plates 103 and 109.

Plate 109. A 'Dutch' globular storage bottle depicting a late 19th century folk art painting of sailing ships. Dark olive green colour. Blowpipe pontil scar, c.1750–1770. H: 29.5cm. Ø: 23cm. Cap: 4.27 litres. Wt: 2020gr. See also Plates 103 and 108.

Plate 110. A 'Dutch' wide mouth onion ('wijdmond'). On the front a folk art painting of a skater in a Dutch landscape, on the reverse a coat of arms consisting of a castle surmounted by a helmet. Dark olive green colour. Blowpipe pontil scar. c.1800. H: 22.5cm. Ø: 15.3cm. Cap: 1.64 litres. Wt: 800gr. See also Plates 111, 284 and 285.
Ref: R. McNulty (736) figs.78, 79

Plate 111. A 'Dutch' wide mouth onion ('wijdmond') picturing a typical Dutch landscape. Painted in folk art style. Dark olive green colour. Blowpipe pontil scar. c.1800. H: 21cm. Ø: 14cm. Cap: 1.24 litres. Wt: 775gr. See also Plates 110, 284 and 285. Ref: R. McNulty (736) figs.78, 79

Plate 112. A 'Dutch' cylindrical storage bottle with a 19th century folk art painting of 'The Village of Blarikum' (near Hilversum, Holland). This bottle was mostly used in pharmacies. c.1800–1820. Dark olive green glass. Blowpipe pontil scar. H: 30cm. Ø: 14cm. Cap: 3.6 litres. Wt: 1500gr. See also Plates 268(1) and 268(2).

Plate 113. Three Dutch/Belgian/German/American spirits flasks. All late 18th–early 19th century. Glass tipped pontil scars.
    (1) Deep amethyst colour, L.15.5cm. Cap: 30cl. Wt: 138gr.
    (2) Deep amethyst colour and diamond pattern. H: 19cm. Cap: 45cl. Wt: 228gr.
    (3) Cobalt blue with vertical rib pattern. L.16cm. Cap: 50cl. Wt: 212gr.
Ref: T. Dexel (326) pl.323

Plate 114. Three patinated utility bottles. All c.1770. Belgium and Holland. Blowpipe pontil scars.
(1)   H: 25cm. Ø: 12cm. Cap: 90cl. Wt: 830gr.
(2)   H: 17cm. Ø: 5cm. Cap: 12cl. Wt: 182gr.
(3)   H: 29cm. Ø: 8.5cm. Cap: 74cl. Wt: 670gr.

Plate 115. An excavated glass seal from a broken gold patinated bottle. On the seal the North Netherlands lion rampant of the Seven United Provinces which formed the 'Republic of the United Netherlands' after the Treaty of Münster, Germany in 1648. Most of the nine remaining Southern Provinces became what is now Belgium.

On the seal are a glass goblet and the initials '**E** – **I**' for **E**lias **I**ungling, glassmaker at the glasshouses of Kletkamp, Güldenstein, Grünhaus and Lammershagen in Holstein (North Germany). Many 'Dutch' bottles were blown in Schleswig-Holstein for the Dutch market in the 17th century. Seal. c.1680. Seal die Ø:. 48mm. See also Plate 116.

Refs: L. Minard-Van Hoorebeke (752) pl.36, lot 1427 figures a giant globular bottle (about 40cm high) bearing this seal; H-J. Kruse (630) Typus B17 and pls.KMP 10 and 214; H. Henkes (489) p.295 (fig.2.68) and (380) fig.2.61

Plate 116. A collection of late 17th century (c.1665-1700) glass seals from broken bottles produced in Holstein (North Germany) for the 'Dutch market'. There are about 120 different 17th century Holstein seals excavated in Holland and they provide evidence that Holland was a bottle importing country at that time. Almost none of these seals turns up in Belgium, which was itself a very important bottle making country, exporting hundreds of thousands of bottles to Holland and France.

All the seals pictured were excavated in Holland and have a forest green glass colour, sometimes with a bluish tone. The seals are patinated. Notice the differences from the English seals. See also Plates 61, 64.1, 64.2, 115 and 214.

Row left from top to bottom etc.

(1) A 'raspberry prunt' seal (in German: 'eine Beerennuppe') which is usually used to ornament rummers. Plate 316 shows such a seal on the shoulder of a broken bottle. Die Ø: 32mm.

(2) Seal picturing a flying fish etc., the coat of arms of the Earl von Brockdorf who produced these bottles in his own glasshouse in Kletkamp. Die Ø: 42mm. This seal is photographed upside down.

(3) Seal depicting an ostrich holding a horseshoe in its beak, symbolising obstinacy. The initial '**C** – **S**' are those of **C**aspar **S**trecker, glassmaker at the glasshouses of Perdoel, Bossee and Langwedel. Die. Ø: 42mm.

(4) Seal depicting a parrot and the initials '**V** – **H**' for **V**alentin **H**off, glassmaker at the glasshouse of Seedorf. Die Ø: 44mm.

(5) Seal picturing the Dutch Lion. Produced at the glasshouses Bossee and Schönhorst Die. Ø: 48mm.

6. Seal depicting Bacchus, the god of wine, riding a horse. He holds a drinking beaker in his left hand. Seal produced at the glasshouse of Seedorf. Die. Ø: 48mm.

7. Seal depicting an angel (in German: 'ein Engel') between the initials '**EH** – **GL**' of **E**ngel**H**art **G**vnde**L**ach, glassmaker at the glasshouse of Lammershagen. Die. Ø: 36mm.

8. Bacchus, the god of wine, sitting on a tun. Text: **'PRVFT DE WIEN EN REIS WEL'** (taste the wine and travel well). Made at the glasshouses of Bossee, Wittenberg and Langwedel. Die. Ø: 52mm.

9. Seal depicting the Norwegian Lion and '**C5**' surmounted by a King's Crown referring to **C**hristian **V** (1670-1699), at that time King of Denmark and Norway. Bottles produced at the glasshouses of Wittenberg and Lammershagen. Die. Ø: 46mm. See also Plate 196(1).

Refs: H-J Kruse (630); H. Henkes (489) §60 and (490); R. McNulty (736); K-H. Poser (847), Abb. 14

III
BELGIUM
(Supplement)

During the 16th-19th centuries Belgium was the most important maker of utility bottles and vials on the European Continent, exporting annually, during certain periods, hundreds of thousands bottles and vials to Holland, France (Champagne and Burgundy areas) and Germany (Aachen, Cologne). For bottles produced for these markets see Plates 62-116 (Holland and Belgium), 139-187 (France), 188-243 (Germany) and 244-329 (Miscellaneous: Europe and America).

This part of the book (Plates 117-138) shows Belgian utility bottles made mainly for the internal market. Some of these bottle types, however, were exported all over the world, particularly to England, filled with the famous mineral water of Spa, a town south of the city of Liège, Belgium.

The Belgian glass historian R. Chambon (242, p.137) stated that 'about 1764, the yearly total amount of bottles produced on the whole Belgian territory is estimated at least at 1,500,000 bottles...vials not included'.

Due to the production of so many bottles at very competitive prices by the hundreds of Belgian glasshouses (more than 200!) very few foreign made bottles were imported. See also 'Holland and Belgium' (Plates 62-116) and 'Miscellaneous: Europe and America' (Plates 244-329).

Plate 117. A very rare kidney-shaped utility bottle. South Belgium (Hainault) or North-east France (Lorraine). c.1550-1620. No string rim! Flattened down folded-in lip. Olive green colour. Blowpipe pontil scar. For protection of the very thin glass (less than 1mm), the bottle was covered with leather ('a leather bottle') or wicker ('a wicker bottle'). Dumbrell and Baker figure a similar 'leather bottle' presented to Sir **T**hos. **L**eigh in 1600 by the City of London. The leather is 'embossed' with **'STL – 1600'** and a 'Tudor Rose'. The Musée de la Chartreuse in Douai, France possesses a similar bottle engraved and dated '1608'. Bottle type common in France in the 15th-16th century. Dim: 14.5 x 15 x 7cm. Cap: 47cl. Wt: 216gr. See also Plate 118 and Figure 8.

Refs: R. Dumbrell (346) p.143, fig.i; O. Baker (116) p.59, fig.24; H. Henkes (489) fig.51.13

Plate 118.

(1) A giant side-flattened kidney shaped storage bottle. Belgium. c.1580-1630. Olive green glass. Blowpipe pontil scar. Originally covered with leather or wicker. Flattened down folded-in lip. Note that pre-1630 bottles do not have a string rim. Bottle figured in 'The Quack' from Jan van der Velde II (Rotterdam 1593-Enkhuizen 1641). The bottle was used for storing beer, wine, liqueur, oil, vinegar, etc. See also Plate 117 and Figure 10. Dim: 35.5 x 45 x 23cm. Cap: 16 litre!. Wt: 3.9kg.

(2) A small North German side-flattened onion ('Plattflasche'). Forest green colour. c.1750. Blowpipe pontil scar. Dim: 9.5 x 7.5 x 5.5cm. Cap: 14cl. Wt: 115gr.

Refs: H. Henkes (489) Afb. 159 (pp.239 and 391); J. Kottman (627) p.37

Plate 119. Three late 16th/early 17th century bottles/vials. Excavated. Blowpipe pontil scars.

   (1) Belgium. H: 8.9cm. Ø: 8cm. Light yellowish green forest glass.
   (2) Belgium. H: 12.3cm. Ø: 5.5cm. Light yellowish green forest glass.
   (3) A North German vial in light greenish forest glass to show the difference with the yellowish green forest glass. H: 9.5cm. Ø: 4cm.
Refs: T. Dexel (336) pl.251; H. Henkes (489) p.330, pl.66.20 and pp.239, 289, pl.156

Plate 120. An early Belgian 'English style' onion bottle. Sealed with coat of arms. c.1680–1700. Dark grass green colour. Sand pontil scar. H: 19cm. Cap: 104cl. Wt: 940gr. A similar bottle dated '1697' is in the Provincial Museum Sterckshof, Antwerp-Deurne, Belgium.
Refs: H. Henkes (489) pl.59.10; R. Chambon (242) Planche T

Plate 121. Three Belgian 'mallets' ('potfles') used for beer, wine, liqueur and all other wet wares. Olive green colours.

    (1) c.1720-1750. Blowpipe pontil scar. H: 19cm. Cap: 88cl. Wt: 590gr.

    (2) c.1710-1730. Disc pontil scar. Excavated. Patinated. H: 22cm. Cap: 107cl. Wt: 940gr.

    (3) A Bruges 'pot-bottle' ('potfles'). Named not because the bottle has the shape of a pot, but because it has the capacity of a 'Bruges Pot' which is 112.96cl, a liquid measure used in the city of Bruges in the early 18th century. One 'Bruges Pot' contains two 'Bruges Pints'. One 'Pint' = 56.48cl. Bottle c.1730-1740. Olive green colour. Blowpipe pontil scar. H: 21.2cm. Ø: 13.3cm. Cap: 109cl. Wt: 760gr. See also Plate 126(2) for a half Bruges pot-bottle

Refs: A. Baar (108) pp.12, 13; R. Chambon (242) Planche T

Plate 122. A Belgian mallet ('potfles'). Sealed with a fish and capitals 'NIP', said to have been the property of the Fish Sellers Company in the city of Ghent. c.1730–1740. Disc pontil scar. Excavated in Leiden, Holland. Brown patination. H: 20.5cm. Cap: 100cl. (1 Pot). Wt: 795gr. A similar bottle sealed: **'OLV – KD'** (**O**nze-**L**ieve-**V**rouw **K**erk-**D**endermonde) is in the Oudheidkundig Museum of Dendermonde, Belgium.

Refs: H. Henkes (490) figs.6.05 and (489) par.60, figs.6.04-6.06.; A. Baar (108) pp.12-13; S. van den Berghe (150) pl.p.278

Plate 123. Four Belgian utility bottles of different shapes and/or capacities.

(1) c.1730–1750. Dark olive green. Glass tipped pontil scar. H: 21cm. Ø: 12.5cm. Cap: 105cl. Wt: 940gr.

(2) c.1730–1750. Half-size. Dark grass green. Glass tipped pontil scar. H: 16.5cm. Ø: 10.5cm. Cap: 58cl. Wt: 590gr.

(3) c.1730–1750. Dark grass green. Blowpipe pontil scar. H: 22cm. Ø: 13cm. Cap: 111cl. Wt: 1060gr.

(4) c.1680–1710. Grass green. Glass tipped pontil scar. Excavated. H: 20.5cm. Ø: 14.5cm. Cap: 133cl. Wt: 925gr.

Refs: A. Baar (108) pp.12-13; R. Chambon (242) Planche T; R. McNulty (735) fig.42, no. 8 for (4)

Plate 124. A Belgian utility bottle used for 'beer, wine, brandy and all other liquid wares' ('bier, wyn, brantwyn en alle andere natte waren'). c.1730-1750. Pewter gauge ring embossed with the capitals 'L.D.W.' and an indecipherable city or town letter ('I' for Ieper or 'T'?). Gauge rings were used to guarantee the minimum capacity of a bottle sold in a city or town. Everybody who wanted to sell liquid wares in a city or town had to gauge his bottles by the inspector of weights and measures recognised by that city/town, hence the city emblem and the inspector's initials on the gauge ring. The presence of a gauge ring under the string rim was proof to the buyer that the capacity of the bottle was correct and that he had not been cheated. Many Flemish and Dutch cities or towns had their own local measures and gauge rings, for example Ghent (from 1708), Brugge (from 1714), Maastricht (from 1722), Rotterdam (from 1730), Blanckenberge, Ieper, Rijsel, Menen, Charleroi, Schiedam, Arnhem and ST. B.A.E.F.S (Saint-Baefs Abbey in Ghent). The gauge ring is not related to a special bottle type, only to the capacity of the bottle.

Dark yellow olive green colour. c.1730-1750. Glass tipped pontil scar. Pouring lip. H: 21cm. Ø: 12.5cm. Cap: 97cl. Wt: 814gr. See also Plates 135 and 173-175.

Refs: H. Henkes (489) pp.298-299; S. Van den Berghe (150) pp.235, 280; R. McNulty (736) fig.75; M. Reidel (873) p.29, top row centre

Plate 125. A half-size Belgian utility bottle. c.1750. Sealed with a coat of arms. Compared with England, sealed bottles are very difficult to find in Belgium. Blowpipe pontil scar. Olive green colour. H: 19cm. Ø: 10.5cm. Cap: 65cl. Wt: 462gr.
Refs: A. Baar (108), pp.12-13; S. Van den Berghe (150) pp.235 and 280

Plate 126. Four Belgian utility bottles of different shapes and capacities. All colours named 'black glass' ('zwart glas', 'verre noir').

    (1) c.1740–1760. Olive green. Glass tipped pontil scar which has an opaque turquoise blue colour because 'glassgall' was used to make the pontil. H: 23cm. Ø: 13cm. Cap: 90cl. Wt: 818gr.

    (2) c.1730–1740. A half-size bottle ('halve Brugse potfles'). Olive green. Blowpipe pontil scar. H: 17cm. Ø: 11.5cm. Cap: 59cl. (½ Brugse pot = 1 Pinte = 56cl). Wt: 510gr. See also Plate 121(3) for a full size Bruges pot-bottle.

    (3) c.1740–1760. Clear olive green (wood firing). Blowpipe pontil scar. H: 24cm. Ø: 12cm. Cap: 101cl. Wt: 840gr.

    (4) c.1760–1780. Dark olive green. Opaque turquoise blue glass tipped pontil scar (glassgall). H: 24.5cm. Ø: 10cm. Cap: 76cl. Wt: 660gr.

Refs: A. Baar (108) pp.12-13; R. Chambon (242) Planche T; S. Van den Berghe (150) p.235 for (3)

Plate 127. Three Belgian cylindrical utility bottles. Black glass.
   (1) A mallet c.1780–1830. Glass tipped pontil scar. H: 23.5cm. Ø: 11.8cm. Cap: 88cl. Wt: 815gr.
   (2) c.1780–1830. No pontil scar. H: 26.5cm. Ø: 11cm. Cap: 90cl. Wt: 826gr.
   (3) c.1730–1780. Blowpipe pontil scar. H: 26.4cm. Ø: 12.4cm. Cap: 128.5cl (about 1 'Pot Liègois'). Wt: 885gr.
Refs: A. Baar (108) pp.12–13; R. Chambon (242) Planche T

Plate 128.

(1) An early Belgian cylindrical utility bottle in 'Burgundy' style. Sealed with a merchant's mark based on the rune 'four' symbol. Initials. 'M.I.' Yellowish olive green. Sand pontil scar. c.1760-1770. H: 26cm. Cap: 88cl. Wt: 790gr. See also Plates 61(4)(5)(6) for more rune 'four' merchant seals. A similar bottle sealed 'NIZET' is in the Provinciaal Museum Sterckshof, Deurne, Antwerp, Belgium. Made at the Nizet glasshouse in Liège, Belgium.

(2) An early Belgian cylindrical utility bottle in 'Bordeaux' style. Sealed with an unknown coat of arms. c.1760-1770. Yellowish olive green colour (wood firing). Disc pontil scar. H: 26cm. Cap: 75cl. Wt: 670gr.

Refs for bottle (1): R. Chambon (242), Planche T; G. Wills (1117) pl.12 for a '1698' rune "four" merchant seal; F.A. Girling (431) p.113 for a '1710' dated rune "four" merchant seal; H. Henkes (489) Afb. 194 and figs.2.40-2.41; S. Ruggles-Brise (920) p.167; A. Baar (108) pp.12-13

Plate 129. Two Belgian cylindrical utility bottles used for Burgundy wine. Black glass.

(1) Sealed. 'Société de Dison'. Dison is a village near the town of Verviers, Belgium. c.1780. A similar sealed bottle is in the Provinciaal Museum Sterckshof, Antwerp-Deurne. Another similar bottle sealed: 'M – Verviers' and labelled 'Bouteille à Bourgogne de la Loge Les Philadelpes en 1810' is in the same museum. H: 26cm. Ø: 10cm. Cap: 82cl. Wt: 670gr. Glass tipped pontil scar.

(2) A 'bouteille voleuse' (a cheat bottle). c.1880. No pontil scar. Push-up: 20cm. H: 26cm. Ø: 10cm. Cap: 78cl. (without push up: 98cl.). Wt: 810gr. The capacity of this bottle is 78cl. but when filled with red wine, it gives the impression of containing 98cl.

Refs: Provinciaal Museum Sterckshof Antwerp-Deurne for (1); E. Leitherer (668) pl.p.32 for (2); T. Dexel (326) pl. 298 for (2)

Plate 130. A Belgian 'lady's leg neck' utility bottle, in this example used for Constantia wine. Sealed: 'HAUT CONSTANCE – S.VAN REENEN – CAP DE BONNE ESPÉRANCE'. Sebastiaan Van Reenen owned the 'High Constantia' vineyards at the Cape of Good Hope, South Africa, from 1821. Black glass. Blown in the Charleroi area. Blowpipe pontil scar. H: 23cm. Cap: 35cl. Wt: 420gr. See also Plates 79–82.
Refs: W. Van den Bossche (187); G. Abrahams (2)

Plate 131A. A Belgian utility bottle, in this example for wine. Sealed on the left with the coat of arms of the noble Ghent 'Goethals' family and another seal on the right reading 'INDOCUS GOETHALS – 1650'. Bottlemaking date c.1750. A Jubilee bottle probably made to commemorate the 100th birthday of Jonkheer Judocus Goethals who was the counsellor of Charles II, King of Spain and The Spanish Netherlands (from 1665 until 1700). Goethals died 12 January 1712 and is buried in the church of 'Sint Maarten' in Akkergem, Ghent. A black glass bottle. Probably blown in a Charleroi glasshouse. Blowpipe pontil scar. H: 22cm. Ø: 13.5cm. Cap: 97cl. Wt: 726gr. For details see Plates 131B and 131C. For a similar bottle see Plate 132.

Refs: R. Chambon (242) p.111, note (2); L. Minard – Van Hoorebeke (752) p.151, lot 1425; M. Laine: *Généalogie de la Maison de Goethals,* Paris, 1838, p.65; Personal communications of Graaf J.L. Goethals de Mude de Nieuwland, Belgium

Plate 131B (side view of Plate 131A from the right). Detail of the seal: 'INDOCUS GOETHALS – 1650'. Seal Ø: 32/42mm. The seal die used was a fired clay die (Ø: 32mm) similar to that shown in Plate 317. c.1750! Bottle antedated. There is a spelling mistake in the Christian name which should be written 'IUDOCUS' and pronounced 'JUDOCUS'. This sort of spelling mistake occurs frequently on bottle seals. See e.g. Plate 25.3.

Plate 131C (side view of Plate 131A from the left). Detail of the coat of arms of nobleman Jonkheer Judocus Goethals (1650-1712) of Ghent, Belgium. His arms bear on a scutum the busts of three women, the whole surmounted by a helmet and a blackamoor who holds three roses in his right hand. The Goethals device is 'IN ALS GOET' ('In alles goed' – 'Good in all things'). This coat of arms is at variance with that of the noble Goethals family as illustrated in the *Armorial Général de la Noblesse Belge* from Baron de Ryckman de Betz, 1957, p.209. Seal Ø: 20/24mm. See also Plates 131A, 131B and 132.

Plate 132. A Belgian utility bottle used in this example for wine. Sealed 'INDOCUS GOETHALS – 1650' (right) and the coat of arms of the Goethals family Ghent (left). 'INDOCUS GOETHALS' has to be pronounced 'Judocus Goethals'. A Jubilee bottle. c.1750. Black glass. Blowpipe pontil scar. H: 20cm. Ø: 14cm. Cap: 99cl. Wt: 770gr. Of note is the great similarity among capacities of the 'Goethals' bottles (97cl) (refer to Plates 131A, 131B and 131C). A masterpiece in glass-blowing. Two seals on a bottle is extremely rare.
Refs: R. Chambon (242) p.111, note (2); L. Minard-Van Hoorebeke (752) p.151, lot 1425

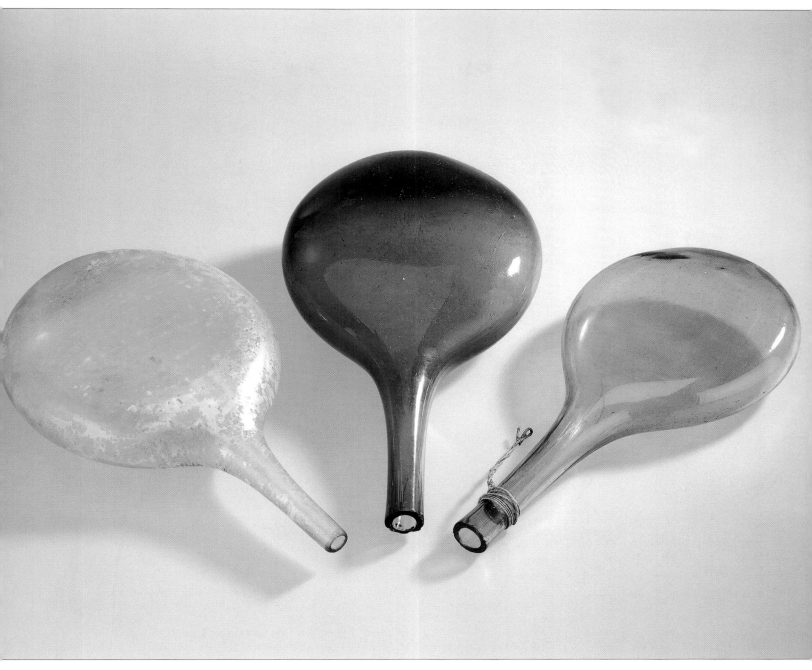

Plate 133. Three Belgian flattened ovoid-shaped bottles mainly used for containing mineral water from Spa, a town near Liège. They represent the different periods of use. The bottles were originally wickered. No pontil scars. The glass colours betray wood firing for melting the glass.

(1) Second half 17th century. Flat round ovoid shape, light yellowish colour. Dim: 27 x 16.5 x 7cm. Cap: 101cl. Wt: 432gr (lightweight).

(2) 1700-1740. Flat ovoid shape. Dark olive green colour. Dim: 30 x 16 x 7cm. Cap: 99cl. Wt: 600gr.

(3) 1740-1780. Flat ovoid shape. Yellowish olive green colour. Dim: 28 x 14 x 4cm. Cap: 54cl. Wt: 385gr.

Of note is that these bottles were not only used for containing Spa mineral water but also water from Chevron, Géronstère, Nivezé and other places south of Liège, Belgium.

Refs: H. Henkes (489) §59.17-59.20; A. Baar (108); L.M. Crismer (283-285); M.R.A. Vroom: *A Modest Message,* Interbook Schiedam, 1980. Painting 317 for bottle (1)

Plate 134. The only two existing different bottle styles in the 18th century used for mineral water from 'Spa' ('eauwe de Spa'), a town and watering place about 30km south-east of Liège, Belgium. Both types were always wickered and exported all over the world, e.g. to pharmacies and 'coffee-houses' in England in the 18th century. After consumption of the mineral water the bottles were mainly used as decanters in pharmacies or for serving wine at the table. In Belgium, particularly around Spa and Liège, they mostly featured as a serving bottle in a 'support' on the table, the support being of wood, marble or slate. Both types of bottle trace their origin to Italy in the 16th and early 17th century. In the 17th and 18th century the 'bouteilles à eauwe de Spa' were blown in the glasshouses of Francesco Savonetti in Brussels (c.1653), Henri Bonhomme in Liège (from 1650 onwards) and Grandchamps in Amblève (Verrerie d'Amblève, c.1727), Belgium.

   (1) Ovoid Spa bottle (popular between 1700-1830), c.1720-1740. Opaque turquoise blue glass tipped pontil scar. Dark olive green colour (coal firing). Dim: 25.5 x 15.2 x 9.5cm. Cap: 114cl. Wt: 675gr.

   (2) Flattened ovoid Spa bottle, c.1740-1780. Light yellowish olive green colour (wood firing). Dim: 37 x 18 x 5cm. Cap: 92cl. Wt: 685gr.

Refs: A. De Thiers (321); R. Chambon (242) Planche. T; L.M. Crismer (283) pl. p.34; A. Baar (109); H. Henkes (489), §59.17-59.20; R. McNulty (735), fig.31-34; E. Leitherer (668), pl. p.61; The National Portrait Gallery, London: 'Portrait of the Earl of Lincoln and the Duke of Newcastle at the Kit Cat Club, London' by Sir Godfrey Kneller, c.1721 for bottle (2); Musée du Louvre, Paris: 'The young wine taster' by Philippe Mercier (1689-1760) for bottle (1); Gemäldegalerie Alter Meister, Dresden: 'A drinking Bacchant boy' by Guido Reni, Italy (1575-1642) for bottle (1); Staatlichen Kunstsammlungen Dresden, Albertinum, Grünes Gewölbe display a flattened Spa bottle type in a metal support, dated 1574.

Plate 135. Three Belgian flattened ovoid shaped bottles of different capacities for containing mineral water from Spa and, occasionally, wine. c.1740-1780. Light olive green colour. These 'bouteilles à eauwe de Spa' (Spa bottles) mostly have no pontil scar. M. Reidel (873) pictures a flat ovoid 'Spa bottle' with a pewter gauge ring embossed MAESTRICHT and the five pointed Star of the city of Maastricht, The Netherlands. A second similar bottle exists. Both have a rigaree string rim. The gauge ring proves that the bottle has been gauged by the Maastricht Inspector of Weights and Measures to guarantee its minimum liquid capacity for selling **wine** in it in the city, as stated in the 'Reglement voor de Wyn-koopers', 1722. Flat Spa bottles never have glass seals.

    (1) Dim: 28 x 14 x 4cm. Cap: 54cl. Wt: 385gr.
    (2) Dim: 34.5 x 16 x 4.5cm. Cap: 74cl. Wt: 550gr.
    (3) Dim: 37 x 18 x 5cm. Cap: 92cl. Wt: 685gr.

See also Plate 124.

Refs: M. Reidel (873) pl. p.29, top row centre; 'Reglement Voor de Wyn-koopers ontrent de maete van haere Bouteilles, van den 16. September 1722', Stadsarchief Maastricht

Plate 136A. Three extremely rare Belgian ovoid-shaped bottles of different capacities for containing the famous mineral water of Spa ('Bouteilles à eauwe de Spa'). Sealed with the coat of arms of Georges-Louis de Berghes, Prince-Bishop of the Bishopric Principality of Liège (1724-1743) surmounted with a prince crown and surrounded with the name 'POUHON IN SPA' (for export). The arms of the Prince Bishop in the centre are also the coat of arms of the town of Spa, an important watering place in the Ardennes about 30km south-east of Liège, Belgium. 'Pouhon' is the name of a water source in the town of Spa. From 1580 the water was sold all over the world and the word 'Spa' became a synonym for all 'mineral waters' (namely 'a Spa') and for many watering places such as Leamington Spa, Bolton Spa, Holt Spa, in England. In the 18th century this 'eauwe de Spa' was named 'German Spa' or 'German Spaw' because at that time the Principality of Liège was a vassal of the German Empire.

From 1621 until 1724 the 'bouteilles à eauwe de Spa' (Spa bottles) were sealed with green wax on the 'Cap of Leather' or on the cork. Red wax was used after 1743. Glass seals appeared only between 1724 and 1743. The reason for sealing was to prevent fraud with this 'medicinal' water and as proof that this was true mineral water coming from the town of Spa and not from its neighbours and competitors in Chevron, Géronstère, Nivezé etc. who used the same bottles and tried to sell their water under the respected name 'Spa'. The Englishman Henry Eyre, who was the 'Purveyor for Mineral Water for her Majesty', imported 'German Spaw' and 'Pyrmont Water' (from Pyrmont, Germany) in the 1730s-1750s. (See Plates 61(1), 199A and 199B.) These sealed bottles were always wickered with straw, free blown and of yellowish olive green colour due to wood firing. They were in use between 1724 and 1743. Characteristics of the bottles (anti-clockwise from top):

(1) Small-size. Dim: 21 x 12.5 x 8cm. Cap: 72cl. Wt: 404gr.
(2) Full-size. Dim: 21.5 x 13 x 9cm. Cap: 90cl. Wt: 460gr.
(3) Over-size. Dim: 28.5 x 15.5 x 10.5cm. Cap: 130cl. Wt: 625gr.

See also Plates 61(1), 197-199, 133-135, 137 and 138.

Refs: G. Dugardin (345); L.M. Crismer (283, 284); A. Baar (108); R. Morgan (762) pls.p.90; R. Dumbrell (346) p.228; D. Westcott (1096) p.10, lots 8 and 9; R. Chambon (242) Planche T; H. Eyre (366)

Plate 136B. Detail of Plate 136A.

Plate 137. A Belgian ovoid shape bottle used for containing mineral water of Spa, Chevron, Nivezé, Géronstère and other places. c.1730. In order to lower the cost price of the bottles the Belgian glasshouses used slag in the batch (slag being a waste product from blast furnace operations in the local steel industry). The result is an opaque turquoise blue coloured bottle which originates from the glassgall (see Glossary) in the glass melt. No pontil scar. Dark olive green colour. Dim. 27 x 15.5 x 10.5cm. Cap. 134cl. Wt. 630gr.
Ref: F. Pholien (838) p.109, note 1

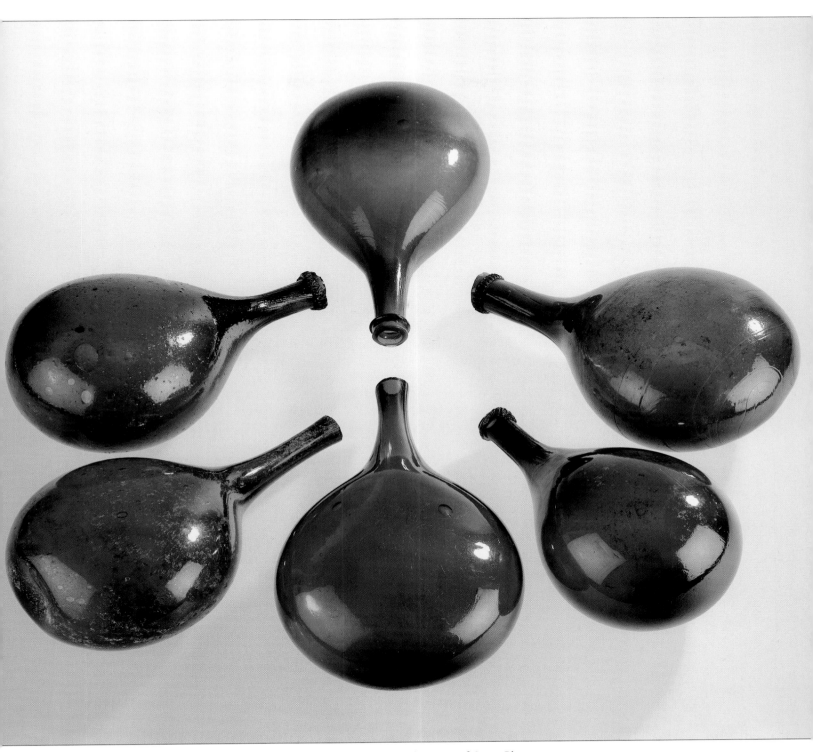

Plate 138. A collection of six ovoid Belgian bottles for mineral water of Spa, Chevron, Nivezé, Géronstère and other places. All c.1690–1760. No pontil scars.
Capacities: 90–135cl.

IV
FRANCE–ITALY–SPAIN
AND PORTUGAL

In the 17th to 19th centuries, Italy, Spain and Portugal were not wine-exporting countries although France was. In general their wines were not suitable for long term storage and were considered as ordinary daily drinks lacking prestige. Most of the Italian wines were below mediocrity and were consumed in making artificial claret or burgundy wines.

Spanish monarchs were always anxious to give every encouragement to the cultivation of the vine, so bad for health (drunkenness, etc). Mostly wine was brought from the cask to the table in a stoneware pitcher and there was less need to use glass bottles. Sometimes bottles used as decanters turn up in clear or light coloured glass. Wines (Sherry, Sack, Malaga, Madeira, Port) were exported in barrels and bottled in the countries of destination, such as England, Belgium, Holland and Germany, who used their own bottles. Italy, Spain and Portugal had no need to produce bottles for storing and/or transporting wine on a large scale.

French wines were prestigious and suitable for keeping for many years.

Finally, notice in this chapter the strikingly different colours of the bottles produced in the different regions.

See also Plates 244–329 (Miscellaneous: Europe and America).

Plate 145. A French long neck 'flowerpot'-shaped utility bottle called a 'Calvados bottle'. c.1730. Mainly used to contain Calvados brandy (an apple brandy) and cider (an apple wine under pressure, hence the thick-walled bottle). Dark grass green colour. Blowpipe pontil scar. A typical Normandy bottle. Seal unknown. H: 30cm. Cap: 93cl. Wt: 1100gr. See also Plates 144(2), 146(1) and 146(3).

Ref: R. Butler (228) col.pl.15 shows a still life with a similar bottle filled with red wine; S. Ruggles-Brise (920) pl.2, top row left; T. Dexel (326) pl.297

Plate 146. Three French long neck 'flowerpot' shaped utility bottles. Their colours all referred to as black ('verre noir').

    (1) c.1770-1800. A 'Calvados bottle' used for Calvados brandy and cider in Normandy. Grass green colour. Blowpipe pontil scar. The double string rim is necessary when used for cider for tying the cork under pressure. H: 34cm. Cap: 96cl. Wt: 930gr. See also Plates 144(2) and 145.

    (2) A snuff tobacco storage bottle with a pewter screw closure and cork to maintain the humidity of the tobacco. Also used as a storage bottle, e.g. for brandy. c.1800. Dark olive green colour. Disc pontil scar. H: 41cm. Wt: 2460gr. See also Plate 147(1).

    (3) A decanter bottle, Normandy. c.1730. Dark olive green colour. Blowpipe pontil scar. H: 39cm. Cap: 244cl. Wt: 1800gr.

Ref: T. Dexel (326) pl.297 for bottle (1)

Plate 147. Three French 'flowerpot'-shaped storage bottles. All c.1800.
  (1) A snuff tobacco and storage bottle with pewter screw closure and cork. 'Verre noir'.
      Disc pontil scar. H: 43cm. Cap: 7 litres. Wt: 2880gr. See also Plate 146(2).
  (2) A storage bottle with original contents (cherries and brandy). Embossed on the upper
      string rim with 'VERRERIE DE FOUGÈRES/ILLE-ET-VILLAINE'. Clear glass.
      Blowpipe pontil scar. H: 25.5cm.
  (3) A wide mouth storage bottle. 'Verre noir'. Disc pontil scar. H: 30.3cm. Cap: 164cl.
      Wt: 980gr.
Ref: T. Dexel (326) pl.306 for bottle (3)

Plate 148. Four French utility bottles. All blowpipe pontil scars.
  (1) A small-size flattened 'chestnut' shape. c.1780–1800. In general used for containing the French brandy 'Armagnac'. 'Verre noir'. Blowpipe pontil scar. Probably produced at the 'Verrerie arlésienne de Trinquetaille' (1782-1793), Arles (Rhône Delta), South France. Dim: 17.5 x 11.5 x 6cm.
  (2) An over-size flattened 'chestnut' shape. c.1780–1800. Similar to (1). A storage bottle (Armagnac). Dim: 34 x 24 x 12cm. See also Plate 277(2) and 307(2).
  (3) A cone-shaped storage bottle. c.1800. Flanged lip. Mainly used in pharmacies. H: 33.5cm.
  (4) A short neck flowerpot storage bottle. c.1730. 'Verre noir'. H: 31cm.
Ref: J. Bellanger (148) pl.p.284 left for bottles (1)(2)

Plate 149. Five French utility bottles for containing wine, oil or other liquids; mostly small sized.

(1) Sealed with a monogram surmounted by a Crown and surrounded by the words: 'CHATEAU MARGAUX'. The earliest known sealed Margaux wine bottle. c.1800. Blowpipe pontil scar. Olive green colour. H: 24cm. Cap: 40cl. Wt: 290gr. See also Plates 266(2) and 266(3) for later types.

(2) Sealed: 'HUILE D'OLIVE SURFINE CLARIFIÉE – JAURETTE & CASTAIRS'. A bottle containing olive oil. c.1800. Blowpipe pontil scar. Olive green colour. H: 27.3cm. Cap: 58cl. Wt: 400gr. This bottle seal proves that the same bottle types were used for wine, oil, vinegar, etc. Many of these bottles were exported to the U.S.A. See also Plate 152.

(3) Sealed with a 'rune' monogram, 'CD' (intertwined). c.1820. Red amber colour. Glass tipped pontil scar. Possibly also of German or Danish origin. H: 22.2cm. Cap: 41cl. Wt: 370gr. See also Plate 263(3).

(4) A full-size wine bottle sealed: 'CHATEAU LAFITE – 1874 – GRAND VIN'. Olive green colour. Made in a semi-automatic machine. No pontil scar. H: 30cm. Cap: 78cl. Wt: 640gr. The earliest sealed Lafite wine bottle known is dated '1864'.

(5) A half-size wine bottle sealed: 'CHATEAU LAFITE – 1874 – GRAND VIN'. Olive green colour. Made in a semi-automatic machine. No pontil scar. Note the very large seal. H: 24cm. Cap: 40cl. Wt. 410gr. The earliest sealed Lafite wine bottle known is dated '1864'.

Ref: D.L. Murschell (772) pp.65–72 for bottle (2)

Plate 150. Four French cylindrical utility bottles. Early 19th century. Black glass ('verre noir').

(1) A small-size 'Bordeaux' type cylindrical bottle. Sealed: 'SIROP DE LAMOUROUX A PARIS'. c.1780-1820. André Lamouroux was an apothecary in Paris. Blowpipe pontil scar. H: 18.5cm. Cap: 22cl. Wt: 305gr. See also Plate 263(1).

(2) A half-size 'Burgundy' type cylindrical bottle. Sealed: '½ LITRE'. c.1840. Bare iron pontil scar. H: 25cm. Cap: 44cl. Wt: 610gr. Notice the difference between the indicated capacity (50cl) and the measured capacity (44cl.)! Possibly also a 'Belgian' bottle.

(3) A full-size 'Burgundy' type cylindrical bottle. Sealed: 'LITRE'. c.1820. Blowpipe pontil scar. H: 29cm. Cap: 96cl. Wt: 865gr. The French 'litre' was introduced by law on 7 April 1793 and in practice from 1809 onwards. In Belgium the dates are 21 August 1816 (law) and 1820 (in practice). This bottle might also be a 'Belgian' bottle.

4. A half-size 'champenoise' style bottle. Sealed: 'RSC' in English style. c.1800. Blowpipe pontil scar. H: 21cm. Cap: 43cl. Wt: 500gr. See also Plate 151(2).

Refs: J. Bellanger (148) pl.p.275 left for bottle (4); T. Dexel (326) pl.305 bottom row left for bottle (3)

Plate 151. Two French dated cylindrical utility bottles of great historical importance. Black glass ('verre noir').

(1) Sealed: 'CHATEAU CHALON – 1864'. A bottle for containing yellowish wine from East France. This bottle has no pontil scar, despite still having been mouth blown in a mould. A snap-case (or 'un sabot') was used from c.1840 and was still in use in 1864. H: 24.5cm. Cap: 63.5cl. Wt: 915gr.

(2) Sealed: 'JOHANNOT – LITRE – 1840'. Bare iron pontil scar. This bottle shows that in Europe the use of the blowpipe pontil had been abandoned by c.1830-1840 and replaced by the bare iron pontil; this information is important for dating bottles. H: 31cm. Cap: 93cl. (1 litre - 100cl). Wt: 770gr. Possibly also a 'Belgian' bottle. See also Plates 150(2) and 150(3).

Plate 152. Three French utility bottles for mineral water and/or wine. All in 'verre noir'.
  (1) Sealed: 'EAU SULFUREUSE D'ENGHIEN – D.G.P.' (sulphurous water from Enghien). c.1780-1800. Blowpipe pontil scar. H: 24cm. Ø: 9cm. Cap: 58cl. Wt: 760gr. See also Plate 149(2).
  (2) Sealed: 'CHATEAU LAFITE – WEMYSS CASTLE – 1893' (Wemyss Castle is in Scotland). A 'Jeroboam' bottle (6 standard Bordeaux wine bottles). Machine-made in 1893. H: 38cm. Ø: 16.5cm. Cap: 4.42litres. Wt: 2450gr. See also Plate 153.
  (3) Sealed with an unknown coat of arms. c.1780-1800. Blowpipe pontil scar. French or Belgian. H: 26cm. Ø: 8.5cm. Cap: 64cl. Wt: 780gr.

Plate 153. Four French utility bottles of different capacities. Slightly tapered cylindrical bodies. All c.1800-1820 with pontil scar.
  (1) A mini-size bottle used for medicines, liqueur, etc. H: 14cm. Ø: 5.5cm. Cap: 12cl. Wt: 218gr. Blowpipe pontil scar. Also produced in Belgium.
  (2) A 'Jeroboam' bottle (4 standard Burgundy or Champagne bottles). Blowpipe pontil scar. H: 39cm. Ø: 13.5cm. Cap: 315cl. Wt: 1750gr.
  (3) A 'Salmanazar' bottle (12 standard Burgundy or Champagne bottles). Disc pontil scar. H: 54cm. Ø: 21.5cm. Cap: 9 litres. Wt: 2810gr.
  (4) A 'Magnum' bottle (2 standard Bordeaux, Burgundy or Champagne bottles). Blowpipe pontil scar. H: 31cm. Ø: 12cm. Cap: 185cl. Wt: 600gr. Large-size bottles today are those which contain multiples of the normal standard bottle size (75cl in Bordeaux, 78cl in Champagne and Burgundy). The names given to bottles of different capacities vary depending on the area in France, as listed right.

CAPACITY (litre)	BORDEAUX	BURGUNDY/CHAMPAGNE
1 bottle (0.75/0.78)	Standard	Standard
2 bottles (1.5/1.56)	Magnum	Magnum
3 bottles (2.25/2.34)	Marie-Jeanne	–
4 bottles (3/3.12)	Double Magnum	Jeroboam
6 bottles (4.5/4.68)	Jeroboam	Rehoboam
8 bottles (6/6.24)	Imperial	Methuselah
12 bottles (−/9.36)	–	Salmanazar
16 bottles (−/12.48)	–	Balthazar
20 bottles (−/15.60)	–	Nebuchadnezzar

These large-sized bottles were not only used for containing wine or champagne but also for storing vinegar, olive oil and all other liquid wares. They were produced initially in the 'Verrerie arlésienne de Trinquetaille' (1782-1798), Arles (Rhône Delta), South France, but later on most French and Belgian bottle makers produced them.

Refs: J. Bellanger (148) pl.p.333 for bottle (3); T. Dexel (326) pl.300 for bottle (3); J. Robinson (895) pp.141, 142

Plate 154. Three thin-walled low weight utility bottles. Original wicker protections are missing. Anti-clockwise from left:

    (1) A demijohn (une 'dame-jeanne'). Used as a storage bottle for all liquids. Red amber colour. c.1840. French Jura area and Flühli area (Switzerland). No pontil. H: 43cm. Ø: 42cm. Cap: c.30 litres! Wt: 4.3kg.

    (2) A flask. Dark yellowish brown, a typical colour ('verre noir') for the Vosges and Lorraine area (North-east France). c.1720-1750. Glass tipped pontil scar. L: 26cm. Cap: 82cl. Wt: 300gr.

    (3) A storage bottle. Yellowish brown. A typical colour for the Black Forest area. c.1840. No pontil scar, although mouth blown. H: 29cm. Ø: 22cm. Cap: 4.3 litres. Wt: 915gr.

See also Plate 273.

Ref: H. Horat (511) pl.43

Plate 155. A very unusual sealed utility bottle. France, c.1870. Each of the five seals depicts an eagle surmounted by an emperor's crown which is the coat of arms of the French Emperor, Napoleon I (1769-1821). Mouth blown bottle, blowpipe pontil scar. The lip and the 'modern' olive green colour suggest a production date c.1860-1870. This bottle seems to be a commemorative bottle made during the government of the later French Emperor Napoleon III (1808-1873). H: 37.5cm. Cap: 80cl. Wt: 1420gr. (a very heavy bottle).

Ref: R. Morgan (762) p.54 pictures a seven-sealed bottle; p.93 for 'Napoleon Brandy'

Plate 156. A French (Central France) round octagonal storage or preserving jar (un 'bocal') for fruit, vegetables, chemist wares, etc. c.1800. Yellowish olive green colour. Blowpipe pontil scar. Blown in a two-part wooden mould. H: 30.5cm. Ø: 16/17cm. Cap: 5 litres. Wt: 1540gr.

Plate 157. A French or possibly American square storage or preserving jar (un 'bocal'). c.1780–1800. Amethyst colour. Blowpipe pontil scar. Dim: 20 x 9.5 x 9.5cm. Cap: 1.46 litres. Wt: 510gr.

Plate 158.
(1) A French (Nivernais or the Mageride forest, Auvergne) brandy bottle in the shape of a barrel. Blue glass with a polychrome decoration in Venetian style. Glass-tipped pontil scar. Early 18th century. Dim: 8 x 11.5 x 6.5cm. Cap: 23cl. Wt: 134gr.
(2) A French storing barrel embossed: 'VERRERIES – JB – CANNES' (Cannes, Southeast France). c.1880-1920. Cobalt blue colour. No pontil scar. Used for storing brandy, liqueur, wine, beer, syrup or for blending and fining liquids. H: 39cm. Cap: 10.7 litres. Wt: 2690gr.
Refs: J. Bellanger (148) p.246 for (1); Farrow & Jackson (31) pp.136-138 for (2); M. Reinartz (874) pl.1626 for (2)

Plate 159.

(1) (2) Two French preserving jars, sealed 'PRUNES D'ENTE – FAU & HOFFMAN – BORDEAUX' (prunes). Aquamarine colour. Disc pontil scars. c.1830. (1) H: 27cm. Ø: 13cm. Cap:2.8 litres; (2) H: 19.5cm. Ø: 8.8cm. Cap: 104cl.

(3) A French (Provence) shepherd drinking flask, mostly wickered. c.1840. Flattened rear side. Disc pontil scar. H: 18.5cm. Cap: 31cl. These flasks can be up to 35cm high. See also Plate 182(3) for an earlier flask.

Refs: J. Bellanger (148), pls.p.381 for bottle (3); T. Dexel (326) pl.330 for bottle (3)

Plate 160. A Southern French utility bottle sealed 'FRONTIGNAN – 1847' and with a bunch of grapes. This bottle contained the south French 'Muscat de Frontignan' wine, the most important of the Languedoc's four Muscats. (Frontignan is a wine village on the Mediterranean Sea near Montpellier.) The bottle is in a colourless glass to enable a better visual check on the colour and quality of the clear to gold coloured sweet Muscat wine.
Bottle '1847', swirled with 20 ribs. Disc pontil scar. H: 31cm. Cap: 77cl. Wt: 435gr.
Ref: J. Robinson (895) p.410

211

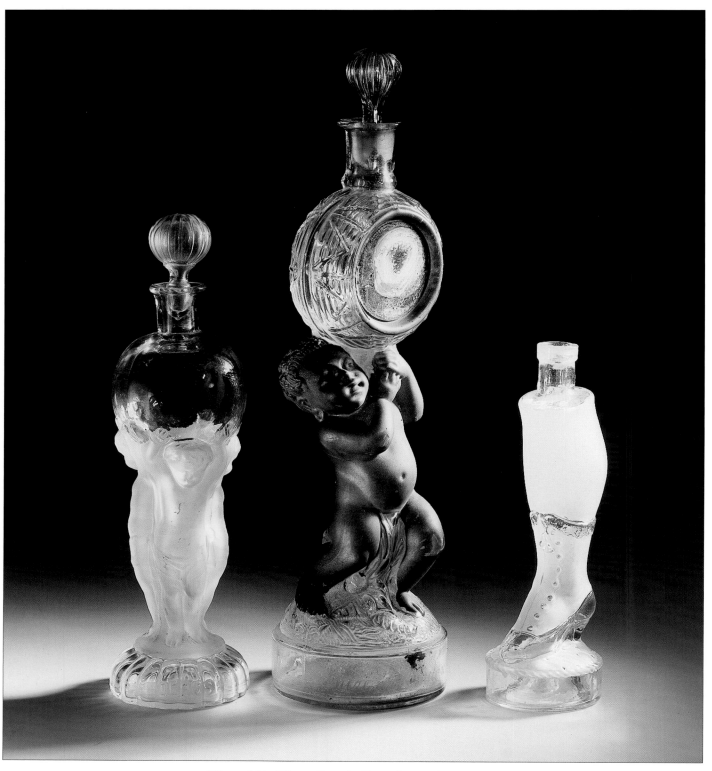

Plate 161. Three French 'figural' or 'character' bottles. c.1880. Blowpipe pontil scar. Produced first at the 'Verreries de Clichy' and later at many other places in France. Used as liqueur bottles. More than 900 different figural bottles are registered.

    (1) H: 30cm. Cap: 50cl. Wt: 490gr.

    (2) H: 40cm. Cap: 102cl. Wt: 700gr.

    (3) H: 22.5cm. Cap: 25cl. Wt: 240gr.

Ref: O.D. Wearin (1088)

Plate 162. A French ring-shaped 'gourde' (drinking flask). c.1740. Pinched hole through the centre. Clear glass with greyish tone. The flask is decorated with two rigarees, eighteen raspberry prunts and sixteen medallions each showing a mask. In Roman times, glass medallions on bottles and jugs often depicted a Gorgon's head (such as Medusa) and served the drinker 'as a protection means against misfortune and evil spirits'. Glass-tipped pontil scar. Dim: 17 x 15 x 7cm. Cap: 60cl. Wt: 750gr. See also Plate 179.
Ref: J. Bellanger (148) pp.377–380

Plate 163. Six French perfume and/or snuff tobacco bottles. Glass-tipped pontil scars. Clockwise from left:

(1) Snuff bottle – Normandy. c.1750-1800. Still filled with snuff. Turquoise blue opaline glass. L: 6.2cm. Wt: 40gr. See also Plates 304(1) and 305(1).

(4) Snuff bottle. c.1800. Bordeaux blue colour. L. 9.2cm. Ø: 7.2cm. Wt: 100gr. See also Plates 304(1) and 305(1).

(2), (3), (5), (6) Four perfume bottles attributed to the 'Verreries Royales du Duché d'Orléans' (1662-1754) from glassmaker Bernard Perrot (Bernardo Perroto: Altare 1619-Orléans 1709). Sometimes these bottles were also used for containing snuff tobacco or as a sand hour (by connecting two bottles together using their closures). Bottles blown in a two-part mould with embossings. Embossed bottles mostly appear in the late 18th century. These perfume bottles also exist in the green colour.

(2) Honey amber colour (a rare colour in the 17th century). c.1680. On the front side embossed with a double-headed eagle surmounted with an emperor's crown, representing the Hapsburger Austrian-Hungarian joint monarchy. To B. Dragesco (342) these bottles were made for those 'German' students from The Netherlands, Germany and Switzerland who finished their law studies at the University of Orléans. The reverse of this bottle is embossed with three 'coeurs-de-lis' (hearts with a fleur-de-lis), the coat of arms of the city of Orléans. L: 8.5cm. Wt: 60gr.

(3) Honey amber colour. c.1680. On the front embossed with the Potence Cross of the Crutched Friars surmounted by a crown, the coat of arms of the village of Olivet which is a parish of Orléans, and the home of glassmaker Bernard Perrot; on the reverse a lion rampant surmounted by a crown. Perrot's crest also bears a lion. L: 8.3cm. Wt: 35gr.

(5) Cobalt blue colour c.1680. On the front three fleur-de-lis surmounted by a king's crown, the coat of arms of the French crown (Les Armes de France) such as for King Louis XIV (1638-1715), le 'Roi Soleil' (the 'Sun King'); on the reverse embossed with three 'coeurs-de-lis' (hearts with a fleur-de-lis), the coat of arms of the City of Orléans depicting its device: 'Hoc vernant lilia corde' ('through this heart the lilies bloom'). Similar to (6). These blue bottles were also produced in Normandy in the late 18th century. L: 8cm. Wt: 50gr.

(6) Clear glass, c.1680. On the front the coat of arms of the City of Orléans and on the reverse the coat of arms of the French monarchy. Similar to (5). Still filled with snuff tobacco. L: 9.3cm. Wt: 55gr.

Refs: B. Dragesco (342) pp.42-46 for (2)(3)(5) and (6); J. Bellanger (148) p.332 for (2)(3)(5) and (6); H. Henkes (489) Afb. 215

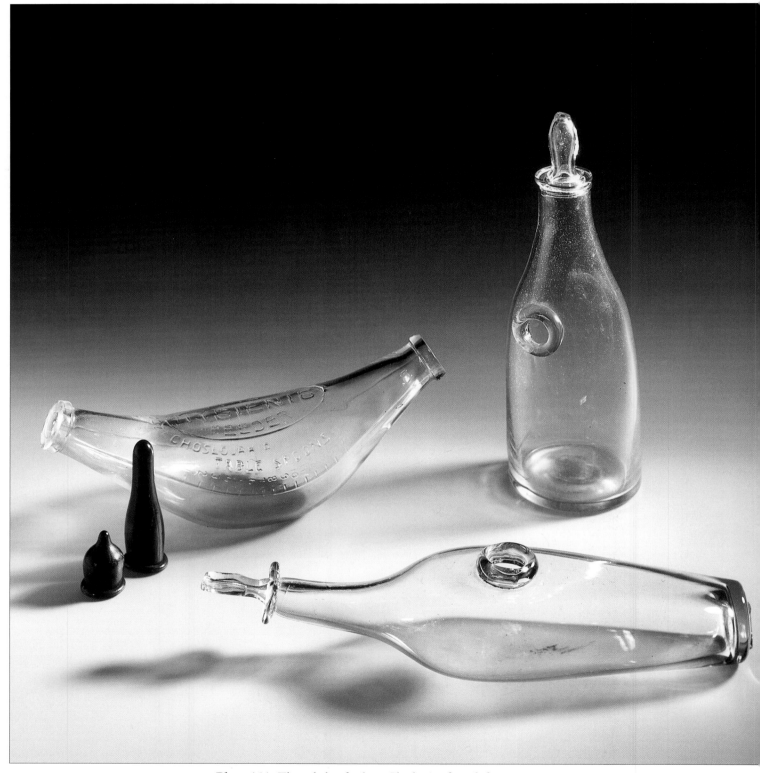

Plate 164. Three baby-feeders. Clockwise from left.
  (1) 'The hygienic feeder', Czechoslovakia, early 20th century. L: 21cm.
  (2) H: 19.5cm. French, c.1820–1850. Glass-tipped pontil scar.
  (3) L: 25cm. French, c.1820–1850. Glass-tipped pontil scar. The French name is 'un biberon-limande'.
Ref: D. Ostrander (814)

Plate 165. A collection of French/Belgian dolls' house miniature bottles. Late 18th century.
H: 3.4–5.5cm.
Ref: Haags Gemeente Museum (51)

Plate 166. A French storage bottle with a wax doll mounted inside. c.1850. H (with stopper): 20.4cm. Ø: 7.6cm.
Ref: G. Kallinich (590) pls.399 and 430

Plate 167. A French/Belgian liqueur cellar (une 'cave à liqueur') containing two bottles. c.1770. Bottles blown in Bohemia by the German half-post method for the French/ Belgian market. Colourless Bohemian crystal. Glass tipped pontil scars. Dim: 29.5 x 14.5 x 9.5cm (cellar). Dim: 25 x 7.4 x 5.5cm. (bottles). Cap: 60cl.
Ref: J. Bellanger (148) pp.289 and 412; A. Simon (979) pl.CVI (no.249)

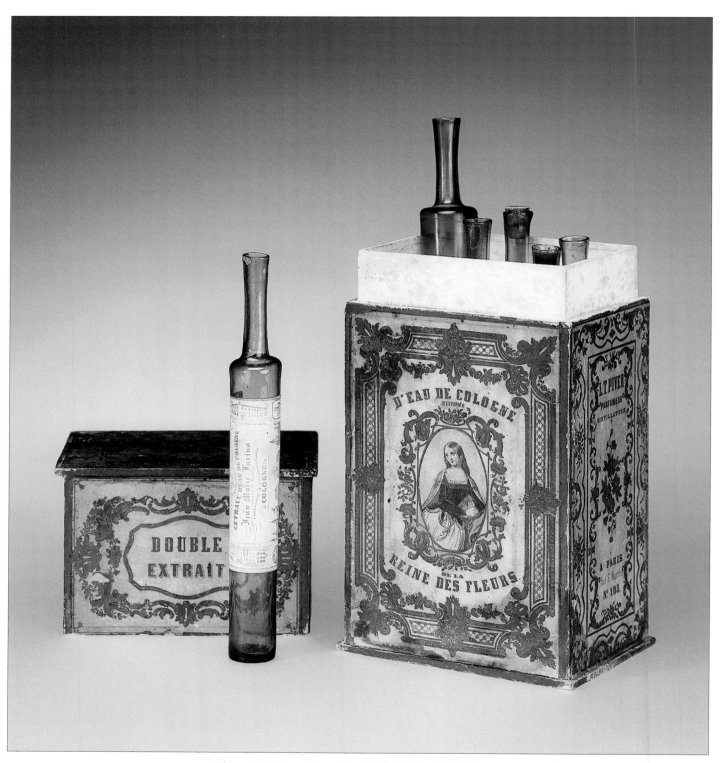

Plate 168. Six cologne bottles in their original box. c.1840. Sold by 'L.T. Piver, parfumeur, distillateur à Paris, Rue St. Martin, N° 103'. Dim: 31.3 x 14.3 x 10.2cm. The labels on the bottles read 'EXTRAIT D'EAU DE COLOGNE de Jean Marie Farina – Fournisseur de plusieurs Cours à COLOGNE s/R'. Johann Maria Farina (1685–1766) was the inventor of eau de cologne. Bottles in light green glass. Pontilled. H: 23.5cm. Ø: 3cm. Cap: 12cl. This bottle type was used for many other applications such as for containing balsam, oil, 'Haarlemmer Olie', medicines, liqueur such as Rosolio etc. See Plate 301.
Refs: E. Launert (655) pp.35-38, figs.25 and 26; E. Ferrari (369) pls.p.74

Plate 169. A 15th century French (Languedoc) pear-shaped common utility bottle. Sometimes used as a urinal. Wide-mouth. Flanged, folded-in lip. Light blue-green colour. ('verre bleu' or 'verre fougère'). Glass-tipped pontil scar. H: 12.5cm. Ø: 9cm. Cap: 36cl. Wt: 106gr. (lightweight).
Refs: F. Nagel (54) pl.1291 and col.pl.62; D. Foy (408) pl.374 p.XXIX; G. Kallinich (590) pl.p.23

Plate 170. A French 'shaft and globe' utility bottle. c.1660. Blue-green colour ('verre bleu' or 'verre fougère'). Produced in one of the many 'verreries de la Grésigne' in Castelnau-de-Montmirail, Languedoc, South-west France. The Grésigne forest, nearly 5,000 hectares, was an important glassmaking area in the 15th-18th centuries because of the abundance of wood (fuel) and fern. Burnt fern contains a lot of potash, a basic ingredient for producing glass with its typical 'blue-green' colour, hence the name 'verre bleu' or 'verre fougère'. Note the similarity of this bottle to the Belgian/Dutch 'shaft and globe' (Plates 62 and 63). H: 22.5cm. Ø: 13cm. Cap: 89cl. Wt: 530gr.
Refs: B. Klesse: Sammlung Helfried Krug, Part II, Rudolf Habelt Verlag, Bonn, 1973, pl.456; J. Bellanger (148) pl.p.166; C. Lapointe (645) p.20, fig.5

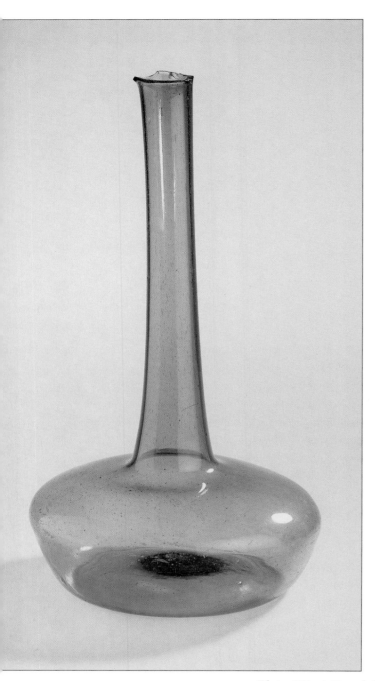

Plate 171. A French long-neck utility bottle. Produced between 1680 and 1770. Blue-green colour ('verre bleu'). Blowpipe pontil scar. Grésigne Forest, Languedoc, South-west France. H: 29.3cm. Ø: 16.1cm. Cap: 105cl. Wt: 330gr. This bottle type was mainly used for serving wine. The shape of the body increases the cooling effect of the bottle in a wine cooler. A still life of the Spanish painter Luis Melendez dated 1770 (Museo del Prado, Madrid) pictures this bottle standing in a wine cooler. The long neck prevents getting wet hands when serving. This bottle type was also produced in Spain and Italy and used in pharmacies. See Plate 172.
Ref: C. Lapointe (645) p.18, fig.3

Plate 172. A Southern French or Italian long-neck utility bottle. c.1780-1830. The lens-shaped body enhances the cooling of the wine when standing in a wine cooler. Light greenish glass. Mouth blown. No pontil scar. Mainly a decanter bottle (see Plate 171). H: 29cm. Ø: 22.3cm. Cap: 216cl. Wt: 425gr.
Refs: F. Nagel (54) pl.1282 and col.pl. 63; A.E. Theuerkauff-Liederwald (1021) Pls.511 and 516-518

Plate 173. A French (Grésigne, Languedoc) wine or walnut oil measuring bottle called 'une mesure à vin' or 'une mesure à huile'. c.1680-1720. Used to measure the right capacity of wine and nut-oil sold in public houses. Some 'mesures' are provided with an official gauge ring around the middle of the neck. This item possessed a metal gauging-plate (lost) stuck on the seal. The funnel-shaped mouth facilitates filling the 'mesure' with wine or walnut oil, then an expensive household oil in the south of France. In principle 'mesures' were used to measure the right quantity of any liquid to be sold independent of the shape of the 'mesure'. J. Barrelet (133) Planche XLVII, top left, illustrates a round octagonal 'wine-style' narrow neck utility bottle provided with a metal gauge ring used as a 'mesure'.

The dark blue-green colour ('verre bleu', 'verre fougère') refers to the Grésigne forest glasshouses between Montauban and Albi, about 50km north of Toulouse. Glass-tipped pontil scar. H: 22cm. Ø: 15cm. Cap: 107cl. Wt: 555gr. See also Plates 174 and 175.

Refs: J. Bellanger (148) p.406 (top row); J. Barrelet (133) Planche XLVII, top left

Plate 174. A French (Grésigne, Languedoc) round hexagonal wine or walnut oil measuring bottle ('une mesure à vin', 'une mesure à huile'). c.1710-1730. Metal gauge ring around the neck is missing. Sealed: 'P', the initial of the owner (a pub, merchant, etc). This type of measure exists also as a square or round octagonal shape and was probably used to measure any liquid to be sold, not only wine or oil as is believed in France. Verre fougère ('fern-glass'). Glass-tipped pontil scar. H: 24cm. Ø: 11.5/12.5cm. Cap: 135cl. Wt: 770gr. See also Plates 173 and 175.

Refs: J. Bellanger (148) pls.pp.166 and 406 (top row); J. Barrelet (133) pl.XLVII top row left

Plate 175. Three French (Grésigne, Languedoc) measuring bottles mainly used for measuring wine (une 'mesure à vin') and/or walnut oil (une 'mesure à huile'). c.1710-1730. Blue-green colour. The measure in the centre possesses its original metal gauge ring (damaged) which presents a small vertical 'level' gauge-lip to certify the correct guaranteed capacity. The gauge rings were sealed by an official inspector of weights and measures of the city where the wine or walnut oil was sold. At that time, as in many other cities or towns on the European Continent, each city/town in France had its own weights and measures standards. It seems to be logical that the 'mesures' were not only used to measure a quantity of wine or oil but any liquid to be sold and that the shape of the 'mesure' is independent of what had to be measured, as was the case in Belgium and Holland. (1) H: 16.3cm. Cap: 42cl. (2) H: 28cm. Cap: 230cl. (3) H: 24cm. Cap: 128cl.
Refs: J. Bellanger (148) p.406 (top row); J. Barrelet (133) pl.XLVIII top row right

Plate 176.

   (1) An Italian liquid 'measure' ('misure'). Early 19th century. Light green colour. A pewter gauge embossed '24' guarantees the measured capacity. Disc pontil scar. H: 21.8cm. Cap: 93cl. (to the gauge).

   (2) A South French (Grésigne, Languedoc) 'jar' with its original cork, c.1750. Blue green colour. Glass tipped pontil scar. H: 24cm. Cap: 235cl. The flared lip facilitates the tying of a leather cloth with string as a closure.

   (3) A South French (Grésigne, Languedoc) 'jar' mainly used for preserving capers. Verre bleu. These also exists in smoky brown glass and in a square shape. Disc pontil scar. H: 25cm. Cap: 58cl.

Refs: E. Ferrari (369) pl.p.90 for a measure (1); J. Alyluia (10) p.18, fig.7 for J.B. Chardin's painting 'A jar of apricots' (1750-1760) in the Art Gallery of Ontario, Toronto (2); J. Harris (465) pl.pp.138-140 for (3); J. Bellanger (148) p.167 top row centre for (3)

Plate 177. Three French (Grésigne, Languedoc) utility bottles in blue green colour, c.1760-1800. Pontil scars. Mainly used in pharmacies or chemists' shops.

    (1) A 'decanter' bottle (une 'burette') H: 22cm.

    (2) A 'shaft and globe' decanter. H: 22.5cm. Cap: 157cl.

    (3) A cylindrical short neck bottle. H: 23cm. Cap: 158cl.

Ref: J Barrelet (133) Planche XLVII, bottom row left for (1)

Plate 178. A French (Grésigne, Languedoc) utility bottle in blue green colour. c.1730. Sealed with three fleurs-de-lis surmounted by a crown, the coat of arms of the French crown (kings, from Louis XIV (1638-1715)). A triple capacity bottle (une 'Marie-Jeanne') H: 28.5cm. Cap: 226cl. (3 x 75 = 225cl) Wt: 1000gr. Disc pontil scar. See also Plate 181(2) for a magnum size and Figure 21 for the seal.
Ref: J. Bellanger (148) p.165, pl. left

Plate 179. A French (Grésigne, Languedoc) ring-shaped drinking flask (une 'gourde'). c.1720-1730. The pinched hole through the centre greatly improves the gripping of the flask. Verre bleu. Glass-tipped pontil scar. H: 18cm. Cap: 74cl. Wt: 305gr. See also Plate 162.
Ref: J. Bellanger (148) pp.377-380

Plate 180. A French (Grésigne, Languedoc) storage bottle. c.1740–1780. Blue-green colour. Glass-tipped pontil scar. Labelled 'AQUA HYSSOPI'. Used in pharmacies. H: 36cm. Ø: 12.5/16cm. Cap: 4.8 litres. Wt: 1070gr.

Plate 181. Three French (Grésigne, Languedoc) utility bottles in 'verre bleu'. All pontilled.
  (1) A 'demijohn' (une 'dame-jeanne'). c.1820-1850. H: 50cm. Ø: 32/35cm. Cap: 29
    litres. Wicker protection missing. A storage bottle.
  (2) A magnum. c.1730. H: 26cm. Cap: 1.37 litres. Wt: 630gr. See also Plate 178 for a
    'Marie Jeanne'.
  (3) A 'demijohn' (une 'dame-jeanne'). c.1650-1700. H: 49cm. Ø: 26/29cm. Cap: 18.5
    litres. Wicker protection missing. A storage bottle.
Ref: J. Bellanger (148) p.165, pl. left

Plate 182.

(1) A square utility bottle with a white opaque glass thread on the flared lip. c.1740–1780. South France and Italy. Blue green colour. Blowpipe pontil scar. Dim: 25 x 11.4 x 11.4cm. Cap: 245cl. Wt: 685gr.

(2) A French (Grésigne) 'demijohn' storage bottle in 'verre bleu'. c.1730–1750. Blowpipe pontil scar. H: 37cm. Cap: 6.5 litres. Wt: 1430gr.

(3) A rare and early shepherd flask or baby feeder. A linen wick was introduced through the hole on the top of the bottle and milk or liquid was sucked out of the flask. Bacterial infections stopped the use of this system which was replaced by a glass nipple. H: 16.7cm. Cap: 50cl. See also Plate 159(3).

Ref: E. Ferrari (369) pl.p.62 bottle (1); F. Nagel (54) pl.1304 bottle (2); J. Bellanger (148) pl.p.381 bottle (3); personal communication C. Laydu (3)

Plate 187. A Spanish flask. Body with pinched centre and decorated with rigarees. c.1750.
Green colour. Blowpipe pontil scar. H: 20.7cm. Cap: 36cl. Wt: 650gr. This bottle type was
also produced in Norway (1790-1830) in a dark green colour.
Ref: F. Nagel (54) pl.1411; A. Berntsen (156) Plansje XXII, item 313

V
GERMANY – ALPINE COUNTRIES
and SCANDINAVIA

Agreat variety of 'styles' and 'weights' of bottles were made in the different regions of this part of Europe.

In general, during the 17th to 19th centuries in North and Central Germany, bottles were thick-walled (2-5mm) and strong (due to the local availability of large quantities of raw glass materials and fuel) and of olive green, grass green or forest green colour. They were very useful for transporting and containing wine, beer, oil, liqueur, etc. Many of these (empty) bottles were exported to Holland, Denmark and South Sweden.

In South Germany, South Bohemia and the Alpine countries bottles were mostly thin-walled (1-2mm) and blown by the 'German half-post' method. Many of these bottles were 'brandy-flasks' ('Branntweinflaschen') in clear or colourful (blue, honey amber, green, etc.) glass for daily private use.

From the late 17th until the late 19th century, German bottlemakers emigrated to Scandinavia where they also produced 'German-style' bottles. Bohemia, reputed for its glassmaking, did not produce 'black-glass' bottles such as in North and Central Germany, England, Belgium, Holland, France, etc.

See also Plates 62-116 ('Holland and Belgium') and 244-329 (Miscellaneous: Europe and America).

Plate 188.

(1) The lower part of a German (Rhine-Main area) 'double-cone upset' bottle as shown in Plate 189. Used as a drinking beaker. Light green forest glass. 16th and early 17th century. Excavated at Worms, Germany. Restored. Blowpipe pontil scar. H: 4.7cm. Ø: 7 and 6cm. (oval section). Cap: 6cl. Wt: 40gr.

(2) An early German (Rhine-Main area) 'double-cone upset' bottle. Light green forest glass. 15th and 16th century. Excavated at Worms. Restored. Blowpipe pontil scar. H: 18cm. Ø: 11cm. Cap: 37cl. Wt: 225gr. The height may vary from 9cm up to 26cm and this bottle was a common utility bottle used for wine, spirits, medicines, oils, etc. Similar bottle types dated 13th–15th century were excavated in Eastern Europe (Bulgaria, Hungary, Serbia). See also Plate 247(1) and Figure 29.

Refs: H.E. Henkes (489), p.48, par. 12, Afb. 35; E. Baumgartner (144), items 46, 115, 376 and 377; F. Rademacher (846), Tafel 16d

Plate 189. A German (Rhine-Main area) 'double-cone upset' bottle of later type than Plate 188(2). Light olive green forest glass. 16th and early 17th century. Excavated in Worms, Germany. Restored. Blowpipe pontil scar. H: 12.5cm. Ø: 6.8cm. Cap: 13cl. Wt: 82gr. Similar bottles were produced at the Zirof glasshouse (1627-1631) in the Spessart forests (Hesse). See also Plate 247 and Figure 29.

Refs: E. Tochtermann (1037), p.27, Abb. 4; F. Rademacher (846), Tafel 16 a-c; E. Baumgartner (145), pl.527

Plate 190.

(1) A German pear-shaped utility bottle. Light greenish forest glass ('Waldglas'). 15th century. Excavated in the Rhine-Main area. Restored. Blowpipe pontil scar. H: 19.4cm. Ø: 9.5cm. Cap: 55cl. Wt: 232gr. See also Plate 247 and Figure 29.

(2) A German 'Kuttrolf' drinking bottle. Sometimes used as a urinal. Light greenish forest glass. Excavated in the Rhine-Main area. 15th century. Blowpipe pontil scar. H: 18cm. Ø: 11cm. Cap: 62cl. Wt: 158gr. See also Plates 205, 298 and Figure 7.

(3) A German pear-shaped utility bottle. Light bluish green forest glass. Excavated in Bingen, Germany. Restored. Blowpipe pontil scar. 15th and early 16th century. H: 13cm. Ø: 5.5cm. Cap: 9cl. Wt: 72gr.

Refs: F. Rademacher (846), Tafel 14b for (1); R. Chambon (242), Planche H for a 'Kuttrolf' shown on a miniature, dated 1253; E. Baumgartner (145), pls.384 and 526; H. Henkes (489), Afb. 51 and 77.

Plate 191. A German (Rhine-Main area) double bottle blown by the German half-post method. Colourless 'cristallo' glass with brownish tone. First quarter 16th century. Original glass foot replaced by a pewter foot in the 18th century. Exceptional in this colour and condition. Bohemia is the most likely production place for this bottle. Coloured items were produced in the Rhine-Main area. Dim: 22 x 10.5 x 5.5cm. Cap: 24cl. Wt: 278gr.

Ref: E. Baumgartner (145), pls.535 and 536 for a similar bottle in a dark grass bluish colour, displayed in the Hessisches Landesmuseum, Darmstadt, Inv. Nr. Kg 55:33

Plate 192. A German square 'case' bottle in clear greenish blue forest glass (Waldglas) with pewter screw closure. Between 1570 and 1640. This bottle was a common utility bottle in Germany, Holland and Belgium. Many were also produced in Bohemia and in Belgium by the Colinet Glasshouses. Blowpipe pontil scar. See also Plates 83-87, 253, 272 and Figure 39. Dim: 30 x 10.5 x 10.5cm. Wt: 870gr. Cap: 2.55 litres. This bottle type is the forerunner of the case-gin bottle (1750-1770).

Refs: A. von Saldern (930) fig.51 for a '1572' dated item; T. Dexel (326) fig.270 for a sealed item; R. McNulty (735) figs.14 and 18 (paintings); A. Colinet (260) fig.55 ('boutelle quarrée diste allemande'); H. Henkes (489) Afb. 153 (painting by Jan Steen, 1661)

Plate 193.

(1) A North German (Holstein) decanter bottle in light greenish forest glass, c.1670. Excavated in Holland. Restored. Blowpipe pontil scar. Pouring lip. H: 15.5cm. Ø: 9.7cm. Cap: 38cl. Wt: 255gr.

(2) A German (Hesse) or Belgian decanter bottle in yellowish olive green glass, c.1670. Excavated in Holland. Glass-tipped pontil scar. H: 14.5cm. Ø: 10cm. Cap: 36cl. Wt: 255gr.

Ref: K-H. Poser (847), p.28, item No. 8; R. McNulty (736), fig.76.

Plate 194. Two North–German (Holstein) decanter bottles in light greenish forest glass. Both with blowpipe pontil scar. Bottles also exported to Holland in the 17th century.

   (1) H: 12cm. Cap: 28cl. Wt: 295gr. c.1670

   (2) H: 27cm. Cap: 3.46 litres Wt: 1035gr. c.1670.

See also Plate 193.

Ref: K-H. Poser (847) p.28, item no. 8; R. McNulty (736), fig.76

Plate 195. An early North German (Schleswig–Holstein) 'shaft and globe', dated c.1660–1670. Dark grass green colour. Blowpipe pontil scar. H: 21.5cm. Cap: 108cl. Wt: 850gr.

Plate 196. Two early North German (Holstein) utility bottles. Dark grass green colour. Both with blowpipe pontil scar.
- (1) H: 28cm. Ø: 26cm. Cap: 5.44 litres. Wt: 2.5kg. Produced in the glasshouses of Wittenberg and Lammershagen in Holstein. Dated c.1690.
- (2) H: 14.6cm. Ø: 11.5cm. Cap: 54cl. Wt: 395gr. Produced in the glasshouse of Wittenberg, Holstein. Some of these bottles possess a seal with numbers from 1–36 under a king's crown. According to K-H. Poser they were used in pharmacies to help identify their contents when stored in a rows. Dated c.1700–1720.

Refs: H-J. Kruse (630) p.75, Typus B10 for a similar bottle as (1) sealed with 'C5' (King Christian V from Denmark and the Norwegian lion under a king's crown). Seal illust. pl.116(9). This sealed bottle is displayed at the Gruuthuse Museum in Bruges, Belgium; H. Henkes (489, 490) §5, fig. 5.01–5.03 for bottle (2)

Plate 197. The earliest known German (Weser river area) mineral water bottle sealed with the eight-pointed Waldeck Star and the English text 'PIERMONT WATER'. Pyrmont was the capital of Waldeck (Germany) and was an important exporter of mineral water to England between 1690 and 1720. The seal is the earliest known 'glass' seal in the world mentioning the contents of the bottle. Yellowish olive green glass, c.1690–1720. Bottle excavated in England. Brownish patination. Blowpipe pontil scar. H: 23.5cm. Cap: 1.9 litres. Wt: 690gr. See also Plates 136, 198 and 199.
Refs: I.N. Hume (548) fig.5(24) and fig.8; A. Lilge (679) p.65

Plate 198. A German (Weser river area) common utility bottle in this case used for mineral water. Sealed with the coat of arms of the Principality of Waldeck-Pyrmont and the English text 'PYRMONT WATER'. Made for the English market, c.1720-1735. Dark olive green glass colour. H: 26cm. Cap: 1.75 litres. Wt: 745gr. H.G. Stephan (56), Abb. 45 shows a bottle of the same type sealed with 'G-3Q' under a crown and a date '1744'. See also Plates 136, 197 and 199.

Ref: R. Morgan (762) p.92 for a similar bottle displayed in the Victoria and Albert Museum, London; R. Dumbrell (346) p.229; A. Lilge (679) p.65

Plate 199A (see detail of seal on Plate 199B). A very rare German (Weser river area) common utility bottle in this case used for exporting Pyrmont Mineral Water from Pyrmont, Germany to England. c.1730–1755. Light grass green forest glass. Blowpipe pontil scar. H: 23cm. Cap: 1.4 litres. Wt: 590gr. This bottle was found in a Wiltshire, England river bed in 1981. See also Plates 136, 197 and 198.

Plate 199B (detail of Plate 199A). Seal with the coat of arms of the Principality of Waldeck–Pyrmont (Germany) surrounded by the English text and names 'PYRMONT WAT. – IH REISENER & H. EYRE'. The coat of arms comprises six different coats of arms surmounted by a prince's crown. From left to right, from top to bottom:

In the 1st and 9th quarter the cross ancrée from Pyrmont
In the 2nd and 8th quarter the three shields from Rappolstein
In the 3rd and 7th quarter the three eagles' heads from Hoheneck
In the 4th quarter the lion rampant from Tonna
In the 5th quarter the eight-pointed star from Waldeck
In the 6th quarter the lion rampant of Geroldseck.

Iohann Heinrich Reisener and his brother Ulrich, both of Bremen, Germany, were merchants for Pyrmont mineral water in the 1730s to 1750s. They exported the Pyrmont water to Henry Eyre, a mineral water merchant and 'Purveyor for Mineral Waters to Her Majesty' in England in the 1730s and later. H. Eyre also imported the Belgian mineral water from the town of Spa known as 'German Spaw' because the Bishopric Principality of Liège was at that time vassal of the German empire. In this 'Account of the Mineral Waters of SPA…' H. Eyre (366, p.33) also specifies that: 'All the Pyrmont Water sold at my warehouses will be sealed on the top of the cap of Leather, with the annexed Impression…' (a lower leg with a spur). Dated Nov. 19. 1732. Seal Ø: 48mm. A variant of the seal with the same coat of arms as shown reads 'PYRMONT.W^R – IH REISENER & H. EYRE'. See also Plates 61.1, 136A and 136B.

Refs: H. Eyre (366); R. Dumbrell (346) pp.218 and 229; L.M. Crismer (283) p.40 for the same private seal of H. Eyre used on the Belgian Spa Mineral Water bottles; A. Lilge (679) pp.65-76

Plate 200. A North German so-called 'Dutch onion' used for wine, beer, pharmaceuticals, etc. Sealed with a crown above a monogram 'M'. Sealed 'Dutch onions' are very rare. Light green glass colour. Dated 1720-1730. The shape is copied from their English counterparts as, for example, the 'Robert-Smith – 1710' bottle (Plate 11). Hundreds of thousands of these bottles were blown in Schleswig-Holstein, Hesse, Mecklenburg, Thuringia and Belgium for the Dutch market.

The bottle shape was in use at least for 100 years. A sealed, dated '1804' onion is known. The Braunschweigisches Landesmuseum possesses a similar bottle with the monogram 'L.R.' of Duke Ludwig Rudolf (1731-1735) of Brunswick. Blowpipe pontil scar. H: 19cm. Cap: 90cl. Wt: 840gr. Ø: 15cm. See also Plates 74, 75 and 258.
Refs: T. Dexel (326) p.233, photo 281; J. Koch (621) Abb. 25

Plate 201. A rectangular common utility bottle, Baltic Sea area (Sweden, North Germany…). Light green forest glass, sometimes stored in a 'cellar' or 'case' of 3, 4, 6, 9, 12, or 15 bottles to be used as a spirit decanter bottle. Sealed 'IHH' and dated '1740'. 'IHH' are the initials of the glasshouse or the owner of the bottle. Blowpipe pontil scar. Dim: 24.8 x 13.2 x 6.1cm. Cap: 103cl. Wt: 599gr. See also Plates 33 (English dated '1740' seal), 202(2) and 214(2).

Ref: K-H. Poser (847), book cover pl., p.40, Abb. 34, Nr. 46 and p.70, Tafel 12, Nr. 46

Plate 202. Three North German utility bottles in light greenish forest glass, all with blowpipe pontil scars.

(1) A side-flattened onion ('Blatte' or 'Plattflasche'). c.1750. Dim: 14.1 x 10.5 x 7.5cm. Cap: 32.5cl. Wt: 300gr.

(2) A rectangular wide mouth bottle. c.1740. Brandenburg. Dim: 23 x 14 x 6cm. Cap: 124cl. Wt: 975gr. See also Plate 201.

(3) A flask, c.1760. Dim: 16.5 x 12.5 x 6cm. Cap: 44cl. Wt: 310gr.

Plate 203.
   (1) A North German storage/utility bottle in light green forest glass, c.1770. Blowpipe
          pontil scar. Dim: 42 x 31 x 21cm. Cap: 11.6 litres. Wt: 2.88kg.
   (2) A North German utility flask (spirits, etc) in greenish forest glass. c.1750, Blowpipe
          pontil scar. Dim: 14 x 12.5 x 6cm. Cap: 40cl. Wt: 355gr.
Ref: F. Nagel (54) lot 1360 for (1)

Plate 204.

    (1) An Alpine (Austria) utility bottle used for storage. Made by the German half-post method. Funnel-shaped lip for ease of filling or pouring from the bottle. Dated c.1800–1830. Light green glass. Square with concave chamfers. Blowpipe pontil scar. Dim: 38.5 x 19.3 x 19.3cm. Cap: 8.7 litres. Wt: 1.99kg.

    (2) A North German small side-flattened bottle ('Blatte' or 'Plattflasche'). Light olive green glass. Wide mouth. Dim: 9.3 x 8 x 5cm. Cap: 14cl. Wt: 85gr.

Ref: F. Nagel (54) lot 1317 (1); R. McNulty (736) fig.80B (2); M. Reidel (873) p.33, bottom row (1)

Plate 205. A pinched waisted rectangular 'case' bottle (Kuttrolf) with six tubes and a blank seal. Strong green-aquamarine colour. Baltic Sea area, North Germany and Poland. c.1750–1770. Blowpipe pontil scar. H: 30cm. Cap: 2.1 litres. Wt: 1.46kg.

Blank seals were not uncommon in the 18th century on the European Continent. Diamonds were used to inscribe the owner's name or other things. See also Plates 208(3), 210(1) and 258(3). The six tubes in the bottle arise by blowing out a rectangular bottle immediately followed by suction through the blowpipe so that the body centre collapses. Collapsing a very flat rectangular bottle (or bottle-neck) develops two tubes (see Plates 190.2 and 298), a square shape develops five tubes (see Plate 88) and a triangular shape develops four tubes (see Plate 298).

Plate 206. A Danziger Goldwater liqueur 'case' or 'cellar' for storing and/or exporting case-bottles all over the world. Made in North-east Germany, Poland and the Baltic Sea area. c.1770, The bottles are sealed with a salmon surmounted by a hexagram and the initials 'I.W.L.'.

The salmon (in German 'Der Lachs') is the trade mark of the distillery 'Der Lachs' or 'Der Danziger Lachs', at that time situated in the Breitgasse, No. 52, in Danzig and still existing now in Nörten Hartenberg, Poland, formerly Germany. In 1711 Isaac Witwe Ling (the widow of Isaac Ling) was one of the owners of this 'salmon liqueur' (in German 'Lachs Likör') distillery.

For religious or mystical reasons, the liqueur also contains many small flakes of gold, hence its alternative name 'Danziger Goldwater' (in German 'Danziger Goldwasser'). The hexagram symbolises protection of the drinker against demonic spirits (certainly a good thing after drinking too much liqueur). This hexagram is still seen today in North-east Germany and Poland, used as a trade mark on many sign-boards outside pubs serving spirits. This 'Star of David' should not be confused with the Jewish.

Danziger Goldwater, a sweet liqueur with a very similar taste or flavour to 'Elixir d'Anvers', a liqueur from Antwerp, Belgium, was brought to Danzig from Lier near Antwerp by the Fleming Ambrosius Vermeulen in 1598.

Dim. (bottle left): 17.5 x 8.1 x 7.3cm. Cap: 70cl. Wt: 535gr. Dim (case) 23 x 25 x 22cm. All bottles have a blowpipe pontil scar. See also Figures 13(No.143), 14, 26(1) and Plates 89, 207 and 208.
Refs: R. Morgan (762) p.88; K. Humbsch (536)

Plate 207A. A 'Danziger Goldwater' liqueur bottle with a double seal (see Plate 207B for detail). Olive green colour. c.1770. Blowpipe pontil scar. Dim: 18 x 8.5 x 7.5cm. Cap: 72cl. Wt: 535gr.

Plate 207B. Detail of the unusual double sealed 'Danziger Goldwater' bottle shown in Plate 207A. For description see Plate 206.
Ref: R. Morgan (762) p.88; p.55 shows an English mallet with a double seal

Plate 208. A collection of nearly square and rectangular case bottles (in Danish: 'cantin flasker') for liqueur, brandy or gin. Bottles made and mainly used in the countries around the Baltic Sea, such as the Scandinavian countries, the Baltic States, Finland, Russia, Poland and North Germany.

(1) Unsealed. c.1770. Dim: 19 x 8 x 6cm. Cap: 58cl. Wt: 400gr. Blowpipe pontil scar.

(2) Sealed 'J.J. KEILER-6,2'. c.1830. Dim: 20 x 7.6 x 6.3cm. Cap: 58cl. Wt: 580gr. Blown in a Ricketts mould. No pontil scar because of the use of a 'snap case'.

(3) Bottle with a 'blank' seal ready for inscribing the name of the distiller or the owner with a diamond. c.1770. Dim: 19 x 8.3 x 7cm. Cap: 75cl. Wt: 590gr. Blowpipe pontil scar. For more 'blank' seals see Plates 205, 210(1), and 258(3).

(4) A 'London-gin' case bottle sealed 'LONDON' surmounted by a noble crown; the initials 'C E' beneath may be those of Carl-Philip von Essen, director of the glasshouse of Gorodyonka (1764-1771), Estonia. Light green forest glass. Blowpipe pontil scar. Dim: 18.5 x 9 x 8cm. Cap: 88cl. (⅔ Russian Stop). Wt: 420gr. See also Figures 13(No.143), 14, 26(1) and Plates 83-91 (Dutch case-gins).

(5) Sealed with a hexagram, a salmon and the initials, I.W.L. (Isaac Witwe Ling). Used for 'Danziger Goldwasser' liqueur. Also exported to England. c.1850. Dim: 18.5 x 9 x 8.2cm. Caps. 95cl. Wt: 595gr. Blowpipe pontil scar. See also Plates 206, 207.

Ref: R. Morgan (762) p.88; M. Roosma (903); A. Polak (843).

Plate 209A.

(1) A German (Lower Saxony) quarter-size utility bottle sealed with the lion rampant from Hesse and the text '**GL. FABR. Z. OBERENKIRCHEN**' (**GL**AS **FABR**IK **Z**U **OBERENKIRCHEN**). Obernkirchen was a part of Hesse until 1933. Bottle blown in a two-part wooden mould. The deep olive green colour (black glass) betrays the use of coal for melting the glass. c.1820. Blowpipe pontil scar H: 17cm. Cap: 23cl. (about ½ hessicher Schoppen). Wt: 400gr. See also Plates 214 and 217.

(2) A German (Lower Saxony/Hanover) half-size utility bottle locally named a 'Georg-Rex-Bouteille'. Sealed '**GR**' for **G**eorge III – **R**ex, King of Hanover and England (1760-1820). '**GR**' was inscribed to prove that the bottle was made by a Hanoverian

glasshouse. The name of the glasshouse and owner are mentioned around 'GR' on the seal as '**H-D-M-ERB-GL-FAB-A-SÜNTEL**' ('**H**ermann **D**ietrich **M**eyers **Erb**en **Gl**as**fab**rik **a**m Kleinen **Süntel**'). Sometimes the capacity of the bottle is indicated on the seal. Dating between 1778 and 1788. Blown in a two-part wooden mould. The light olive green glass colour betrays the use of wood for firing the melting furnace. Blowpipe pontil scar. H: 19.5cm. Cap: 44cl. (½ hannoverscher Quart = 48.6cl.) Wt: 445gr. See also Plate 214(1).

(3) A German (Lower Saxony/Hanover) three-quarter-size utility bottle. Sealed with the 'Saxony Horse', the initials '**ST**' of the glasshouse **St**einkrug am Deister and the capacity of the bottle '¾' (¾ Hanoverian quart = 72.7cl). H: 22.5cm. Cap: 71.5cl. Wt: 555gr. Dating between 1824 and 1840. Yellow olive green colour. Blown in a wooden two-part mould. Blowpipe pontil scar. The Hanoverian Law of 13 December 1824 compelled the glasshouses to seal their bottles in this way to avoid fraud with the capacity. The bottles (1) (2) and (3) look much older (first half 18th century) than they are in reality (late 18th to early 19th century). See also Plates 214(5) and 214(8).

Refs: H-D. Kreft (629); W. Van den Bossche (188); J. Koch (621); C. Sauermilch (937); K-H. Poser (847), items 173, 174 and 175

Plate 209B. Detail of the seal on bottle Plate 209A(1). See also Plate 217.

Plate 210. Two North German bottles used for beer, wine, pharmacy, etc.

(1) Prussia. Dark olive green colour with a blank seal. c.1780. Blowpipe pontil scar. H: 35cm. Cap: 95cl. (¾ Berliner Quart = 88cl). Wt: 710gr. See also Plates 205, 208(3) and 258(3).

(2) Brandenburg. Light forest glass green colour with a Prussian Eagle crest, the name of the glasshouse 'MARIENWALDE – F' (in former days Brandenburg, now in Poland) and the capacity of the bottle '¾ BERLINER QUART'. c.1810. Blowpipe pontil scar. H: 34cm. Cap: 80cl. (¾ Berliner Quart = 88cl). Wt: 555gr. The Marienwalde glasshouse worked from 1602-1824. This bottle shape exists with a dated seal 'GB-CHORIN – 1737' and occurs also in Spain in the 18th century in a blue-green colour.

Ref: G .& K. Friese (418), pp.62-65, Tafel 4; K-H. Poser (847) p.108, item no. 269

Plate 211. A North German bottle for snuff tobacco. Sealed 'FEINER RAPPÉ' – 'SCHABBEHARD & COMPAGN: IN BREMEN'. Dark olive green colour. c.1800–1820. Blowpipe pontil scar. Dim: 22 x 7.8 x 6.6cm. Cap: 77.5cl. Wt: 555gr.

Ref: E. Leitherer (668), p.121 for a similar snuff tobacco bottle, unsealed but with an original label from J. Schürer, Würzburg

Plate 212. Three large utility storage bottles and a small bottle for reference.

(1) Black Forest (Germany) area, c.1820-1850. Blowpipe pontil scar. H: 33cm. Ø: 19cm. Cap: 6.8 litres.

(2) Black Forest (Germany) area, c.1820-1850. H: 51cm. Ø: 24.5cm. Cap: 16 litres. Wt: 1950gr. Blowpipe pontil scar.

(3) A small side-flattened bottle for reference. Dim: 9.3 x 8 x 5cm. Cap: 14cl. Wt: 85gr. See Plate 204(2)

(4) An Austrian round octagonal bottle in aquamarine colour. c.1820-1850. H: 38cm. Ø: 21cm. Cap: 8.5 litres. Blowpipe pontil scar.

See also Plate 273

Refs: F. Nagel (54) pl.1349 (2); M. Reinartz (847), p.62, pl.1625 (1) and (2); M. Reidel (873) p.31

Plate 213.

(1) A rectangular German utility bottle for storing liqueur. Two examples are known with the original label on the narrow side ('KUMMEL' and 'SPANISCHE BITTER LIKÖR'). The vertical ribs facilitate gripping the bottle when taken from the shelves. Blown by the German half-post method. Blowpipe pontil scar. c.1820-1840. Colourless glass with greyisyh/yellowish tone. Dim: 27.5 x 12 x 8cm. Cap: 176cl. Wt: 600gr.

(2) An Austrian utility bottle. Sealed with a '3' probably to indicate No 3. of a series. German half-post method. Aqua colour. Blowpipe pontil scar. c.1850-1880. H: 32cm. Cap: 5.1 litres. Wt: 990gr.

(3) A giant flat octagonal storage bottle for containing 'STARGARDER TROPFEN', a bitter liqueur. Sealed with the coat of arms of Stargard, a town in Pommern (at the time Germany, now Poland) and the text: 'GESETZ z. SCHUTZ d. WARENBEZ. v. 12 MAI 1894' (GESETZ ZUR SCHUTZ DER WARENBEZEICHNUNG VON 12 MAI 1894 – LAW FOR THE PROTECTION OF TRADEMARKS). The embossing on both narrow sides of the bottle reads: 'F.J. MAMPE – STARGARD I/POM.' (F.J. MAMPE – STARGARD IN POMMERN). The original label (missing) on the bottle reads: 'STARGARDER TROPFEN – FABRIK ZU STARGARD IN POMMERN – GEGRÜNDET 1835. GOLDENE MEDAILLEN 1907/BERLIN'. Mampe also had a distillery known as Carl Mampe in the Veteranenstrasse, 24 in Berlin where he produced spirits, liqueurs, essences, schnapps, brandies, bitters, liqueur essences and brandy essences. This bottle is the largest sealed bottle in the world. Machine made c.1900–1920. Dim. 57 x 21.5 x 16cm. Cap: 11 litres. Wt. 5.4kg. Seal Ø: 7.5cm. Die Ø: 6cm.

Refs: M. Reinartz (847) p.39, item 1510 for (1); M. Reidel (873) p.31, bottom row for (2); A. Schwiezer, personal communication for (3)

Plate 214. A collection of nine North German seals from broken bottles. All 18th or early 19th century. Excavated in North Germany. Patinated. Note the differences of the glass colours which may be considered the 'fingerprints' of each glasshouse. This plate also shows important differences between the practice of sealing bottles in North Germany and in England, such as the dimensions, the colours, the contents of what is pictured and the quality of the embossings. See also Plates 61, 115, 116 and 209.

Row left from top to bottom, etc..

(1) A seal with the initials '**GR**' intertwined with and surmounted by a king's crown – capacity indication '**3Q**' (**3** Hanoverian '**Q**uartieren' or 3 x 97.2cl. or 2.917 litres) and the initial '**B**' of the '**B**ramwaldhütte' glasshouse in Amt Münden, Lower Saxony, where the bottle was made between 1773 and 1780. Clear yellowish olive green glass colour (denoting wood firing). Die Ø: 24mm. In order to reduce the large unemployment in the Hanoverian glasshouses, utility bottles for beer, wine, brandy, vinegar, oil etc. produced in foreign countries (to be read as 'outside Hanover') and imported to the Hanover Country were imposed with a tax named '**Impost**', a contraction of the German words **Impo**rt and **St**euer (tax).

   To distinguish between the bottles produced in Hanover and those of the foreign countries, George III (1760-1820), King of England and Hanover, determined in a decree of 7 June 1773 that all the local (Hanoverian) made bottles had to be sealed with '**GR**', the initials for **G**eorge **R**ex (King George) and the name of the glasshouse. In this way everybody could identify that a bottle had been made in Hanover and thus was free of taxes. In this same decree of 1773 it was stipulated to indicate 'the correct capacity on each bottle'. In an attempt to obtain the correct capacity aimed for, the bottles were blown in a two-part wooden mould. In practice, however, many sealed '**GR**' bottles do not indicate the capacity at all. See Plate 209(2).

(2) Seal '**GRIMNITZ-1747**'. Bottle produced in 1747 by the glasshouse of 'Grimnitz' (1601-1792), Brandenburg. Clear forest green glass colour (wood firing). Die Ø: 25mm. In order to prevent fraudulent practice with the capacity of the bottle (when used for wine, beer, brandy, etc), the King of Prussia in Berlin in January 1739 ordered all the glasshouses to seal the bottles with the name of the glasshouse and the year of production. Many dated seals of glasshouses have been excavated. See also seals (3), (7), (9) and Plate 201.

(3) Seal showing the Prussian Eagle and the name of the Brandenburg glasshouse in '**ANNENWALDE**' (1755-1865) and dated '**1792**'. '**No 11**' identifies the glassmaker. The name of the glassmaker or his reference was often mentioned on the seal in order to count his daily production and to identify him (and the glasshouse) should anything have been wrong with the bottle or its capacity. Clear forest green glass colour (wood firing.) Ø: 25mm. See also seal (2).

(4) Seal made by the glasshouse in '**FRIEDRICHSTHAL**' (1790-1842), Brandenburg which produced mainly 'Berliner Quart' bottles. One Berliner Quart = 1.17 litres (between 1722 and 1816) or 1.145 litres (after 1816). The centre of the seal pictures a noble crown. Dark olive green glass colour. Ø: 20mm.

(5) Seal picturing a '**jumping horse**' and the initials '**H.U.**' of the glasshouse which made the bottle. c.1720-1740. In order to certify the capacity of a green bottle used for selling wine, brandy, beer, vinegar, oil and all other liquid ware in Hanover, George I (1714-1727), King of Great Britain and Hanover, issued on 3 February 1718 a decree that every bottle had to be sealed with the Saxon Horse (the 'Sachsenross' or 'Welfenross'), the coat of arms of Hanover and Brunswick. A similar law was issued in Hanover in 1824 stipulating that every bottle used for selling liquids had to be sealed with 'the sign of the horse', the capacity and the name of the glasshouse. The glass seal is of olive green colour. Ø: 22mm. See also seal (8) and Plate 209(3).

(6) Seal indicating the name of the glasshouse '**BEHLE**' (1800-1850), a place in Posener Land, in former days a part of North-east Germany, now Poland. The name **BEHLE** is surmounted with the crown of Count Poniatowski of the Countship Behle, West Prussia, now Poland. The capacity of the bottle is '**1Q**' (one 'Quartier'). Number '**4**'

refs to the glassmaker who made the bottle at the Behle glasshouse. Deep olive green colour. Ø: 24mm.

(7) Seal indicating '**CHORIN – 1747 – JW**'. Produced at the glasshouse in Chorin (1706-1772), Brandenburg, in 1747 by glassmaker **J**ohann **W**entzel. Clear forest green glass colour (wood firing) Die Ø: 25mm. See also seals (2) and (3) and Plate 317.

(8) Similar Hanoverian seal to (5) but with the initial '**W**' of the glasshouse which made the bottle. c.1824–1850.

(9) Seal depicting the Prussian Eagle, the name of the glasshouse '**ANNENWALDE**' (1755-1865), Brandenburg and its production date '**1792**'. '**No. 7**' refers to glassmaker number 7 out of the twelve working at the Annenwalde glasshouse making bottles. Dark olive green glass colour. Ø: 26mm. See also seals (2), (3) and (7).

Refs: K. Friese (418); W. Van den Bossche (188); J. Koch (621); C. Sauermilch (937)

Plate 215. A German (Hesse or Thuringia) side-flattened utility bottle ('Blatte'), Dark grass green colour. c.1720. Blowpipe pontil scar. Bottle found in the sea. Dim: 22 x 15.5 x 8cm. Cap: 85cl. Wt: 628gr.

Plate 216. Four typical German side-flattened common utility bottles ('Blatte' or 'Plattflasche') in dark olive green and light grass green colour. All c.1730–1770 and with blowpipe pontil scar.

(1) Dim: 19.5 x 19 x 8.5cm. Cap: 97cl. Wt: 580gr.

(2) Dim: 19.5 x 17.5 x 8cm. Cap: 75cl. Wt: 630gr. A sealed bottle dated '1739' is known.

(3) Dim: 18 x 19 x 8.5cm. Cap: 76cl. (1 English reputed quart = 76cl). Wt: 770gr. This bottle type turns up mostly in England, where is is called a 'boot bottle'. Produced in Germany for the English market.

(4) Dim: 11.5 x 9 x 7cm. Cap: 24cl. Wt: 175gr. North Germany.

See also Plate 278.

Ref: K-H. Poser (847) items 23-26

Plate 217. A German (Lower Saxony, North Hesse) side-flattened common utility bottle ('Plattflasche'). Sealed with a lion rampant surmounted with a crown. Below the lion a capital '**F**', probably the initial of the glasshouse or glassmaker (**F**leckenstein?). Light yellowish olive green colour (wood firing). Blown in a two-part wooden mould, c.1780. Blowpipe pontil scar. Dim: 23 x 15.5 x 8.5cm. Cap: 94cl. (1 Braunschweiger Quartier = 93.5cl; 1 Hanoverian Quart = 97.2cl). Wt: 640gr. See also Plates 209A(1), 209B and 283(3). For its English counterpart see Plate 41(2).

Refs: T. Dexel (326) pl.283; K-H. Poser (847) item 220 (p.38, Abb. 32 and p.100); A. von Rohr: *Lauensteiner Glas* (1701-1827) pp.22-24, Historisches Museum, Hannover, 1971

Plate 218. Three German (Franconia/Würzburg) 'Bocksbeutel' used for Steinwein. Dark red amber glass colour. The name 'Bocksbeutel' appears for the first time in the 1785 price list of the Gehlberger Glashütte (Thuringia). All items c.1860–1880 and with blowpipe pontil scars.

    (1) Dim: 14.5 x 12.2 x 9.2cm. Cap: 52cl (half-size). Wt: 375gr. See Plate 281(3) for a side view of this bottle.

    (2) Dim: 18.5 x 14 x 10.5cm. Cap: 103cl. Wt: 455gr.

    (3) Dim: 19 x 14.5 x 8.5cm. Cap:88cl. Wt: 600gr.

For further comments see Plate 220.

Refs: W. Stieda: *Thüringische Glashütten in der Vergangenheit,* Leipzig 1910, pp.83–85.; K-H. Poser (847) p.101 items 227 and 228; H. Jung (588); K. Schneider (948)

Plate 219. A typical Franconian 'Bocksbeutel' used for Steinwein (Frankenwein). Sealed 'BÜRGERSPITAL WÜRZBURG' and with a flying pigeon, the emblem of the Bürgerspital zum Heiligen Geist im Würzburg. Dark red amber colour. c.1840. Blowpipe pontil scar. Dim: 17 x 15 x 10cm. Cap: 100cl. Wt: 580gr. For further comments see Plate 220.

Ref: K-H. Poser (847) p.101, item 227; H. Jung (588); K. Schneider (948), pp.93–103

Plate 220. A German (Franconia/Würzburg) 'Bocksbeutel' used for Steinwein. Sealed 'BÜRGERSPITAL WÜRZBURG' and with a flying pigeon, symbolising the Holy Spirit. Dark red amber glass colour. c.1880. Blowpipe pontil scar. Probably produced by the 'Fürstlich Löwenstein-Wertheim-Rosenbergische Karlshütte zu Einsiedel im Spessart' (1807–1889). Dim: 19 x 14 x 9cm. Cap: 72cl. Wt: 700gr. See also Plates 218, 219, 281 and 282.
Refs: K-H. Poser (847), p.101 items 227 and 228; H. Jung (588); K. Schneider (948)

Plate 221. A South–German or Alpine (Flühli, Switzerland) area spirits bottle. Ovoid section with a flat rear side. Pewter screw closure. Engraved I.H.S. ('JESU HOMINI SALVATOR' or 'IN HOC SIGNO'). c.1730. Clear glass with brownish tone. Blown by the German half-post method. Blowpipe pontil scar. H: 22cm. See also Plate 223(1).

Refs: H. Horat (511), p.204, pls.277 and 278 for a similar '1758' dated example; J. Bellanger (148) p.348 for a similar '1721' dated example; F. Nagel (54) lot 704 col. photo 39 for an amber bottle dated '1720'

Plate 222. A German barrel–shaped spirits bottle. Clear glass. Mid–18th century. Blowpipe pontil scar. Dim: 13 x 16 x 9cm. Cap: 60cl. Wt: 384gr.
Refs: T. Dexel (326) p.272, photo 349; F. Nagel (54) lots 531–534 and col. photo 531

Plate 224. (*top*) Three North German (Lower Saxony, North Hesse) spirits flasks with cold enamelled 'peasant style' designs. All glass-tipped pontil scars and early 19th century.

    (1) With the emblem of a miller. On the reverse the saying: 'Vivat es Leben die Müller' ('Long live the miller'). H: 11.5cm. Cap: 20cl. Wt: 116gr.

    (2) With the emblem and tools of a wagonmaker. On the reverse the saying: 'Vivat der Wagner' ('Long live the wagonmaker'). H: 13cm. Cap: 28cl. Wt: 108gr.

    (3) With a flower. On the reverse the saying: 'Zum Vergnügen – 1834' ('For pleasure – 1834'). H: 16cm. Cap: 35cl. Wt: 218gr.

Refs: C.F. Lipp (683); F. Nagel (54) lots 739-741

Plate 223. (*left*) Three central European spirits flasks ('Branntweinflasche', 'Schnapsflasche'). Clockwise from top:

    (1) South Germany and Alpine area (Austria, Switzerland/Flühli…). Ovoid section flattened at the rear side. Cold painted in 'peasant style', two white doves on a heart surrounded by a medallion. Clear glass. Blown by the German half-post method. Glass-tipped pontil scar. Pewter screw closure. c.1750-1770. H: 18cm. Cap: 40cl. Wt: 226gr. See also Plate 221.

    (2) North Germany (Lower Saxony, North Hesse). Ovoid section flattened at the rear side with text. 'Ich muß meine Gänß verkaufen – Vivat 1775' (I have to sell my goose – Vivat 1775). On the front side, cold painted in 'peasant style', a fox selling four geese. Clear glass. Blowpipe pontil scar. H: 14.5cm. Cap: 22cl. Wt: 244gr.

    (3) North Germany (Lower Saxony, North Hesse). Round flat shape. On the front side a boot with shoe repairing tools; on the rear side a text: 'Es blühe unser löbliges Handwerck – 1827' ('That our praiseworthy handwork may flourish – 1827'). Clear glass. Glass tipped pontil scar. L: 14.5cm. Cap: 22cl. Wt: 244gr. This plate clearly shows the differences between North German and South German/Alpine/Bohemian flasks. The latter are in general provided with pewter screw closures (and folded-out lips) and are blown by the German half-post method.

Refs: A. von Saldern (930), Flask 129 for (1); F.C. Lipp (683) pl.VIII, d, for (1); item 96 (dated 1793) for (2) and item 197 for (3). P. 47 shows a good classification of 'Central European'

Plate 225A. Three central European spirits flasks ('Schnapsflaschen') cold painted in 'peasant style'. All glass tipped pontil scars.

(1) North Germany (Lower Saxony, North Hesse, Lauenstein). On the reverse the saying: 'Vivat innen rein muß Brandewein – 1801' (Vivat, inside must be brandy – 1801'). Ovoid horizontal section with flattened reverse side. H: 12cm. Cap: 20cl. Wt: 80gr.

(2) (3) Produced in Bohemia, Alpine lands, Central and South Germany, Alsace and exported to many European countries, c.1770. Dim: (2) 14.5 x 7.5 x 5.2cm. Cap: 36cl. Wt: 180gr. Half-post method. Bohemian crystal. Dim: (3) 13.5 x 6.4 x 4.2cm. Cap: 24cl. Wt: 122gr. Half-post method. Colourless with purple tone. See Plate 225B for the reverse side of flask (3).

Refs: F. Nagel (54) lot 735 for (1); C.F. Lipp (683) col.pl.XI; A. von Saldern (930) items 131-142; H. Horat (511) item 146

Plate 225B. Reverse side of flask (3) in Plate 225A. Saying: 'Zu Jesu sinn steht mir mein Sinn – Anno 1772' ('I long to be with Jesus'). It was very common in Central Europe to write proverbs, sayings, etc on flasks. The subjects concerned drinking, professions, religion, sex, erotica, love, friendship, history, flowers, etc.

Refs: W. Bernt, 'Sprüche auf alten Gläsern', Uban-Verlag, Freiburg i. Brg., 1928; F.C. Lipp (683)

Plate 226. Three spirits flasks, all glass–tipped pontil scar.
  (1) Flühli glass (Switzerland), c.1800. Honey colour. Dim: 12.5 x 5.7 x 3.6cm. Cap: 17cl. Wt: 116gr.
  (2) Alpine lands and South Bohemia, c.1750. Cobalt blue. Half-post method. Flowers on both sides. Dim: 12.9 x 6.3 x 4.9cm. Cap: 26cl. Wt: 170gr.
  (3) Hungary. Dark red amber. Early 19th century. H: 11.5cm. Cap: 16cl. Wt: 92gr.

Refs: H. Horat (511) pl.147 for (1); K-H. Poser (847) item 92 for (2); B. Borsos (185) pl.45 for (3)

Plate 227.

(1) A Central European (Alpine lands and South Bohemia) spirits flask in white opaline glass. Half-post method. Glass-tipped pontil scar. Dim: 12.2 x 6.9 x 5.2cm. Cap: 27.5cl. Wt: 180gr.

(2) An opaque white ('Beinglas') inkwell and/or sand sprinkler (perforated plate missing) with enamel decoration. South Germany (Black Forest) and Flühli (Switzerland). Glass tipped pontil scar. Dim: 5.8 x 5.5 x 5.5cm. Cap: 9cl. Wt: 100gr.

(3) An apothecary jar in white opaline glass. Germany. Late 18th century. H: 15.5cm. Cap: 18cl. Wt: 305gr.

(4) A barrel-shaped flask. Opaline glass with blue glass flecks. Half-post method. Glass tipped pontil scar. H: 17.5cm. Cap: 57cl. Wt: 215gr. Flühli glass (Switzerland).

Refs: W.E. Covill (270) fig.1075 for (2); H. Horat (511) figs.176 and 178 for (2), fig.172 for (4); A. von Saldern (930) figs.140 and 141 for (1); G. Kallinich (590) pl.190 for (3)

Plate 228. An Austrian (Tirol/Kramsach) spirits bottle named a 'Warzenflasche'. 17th century. Blue colour. Blown by the German half-post method. Blowpipe pontil scar. H: 15cm. Cap: 49cl. Wt: 225gr.

Ref: T. Dexel (326) pl.314

Plate 229. An Austrian (Tirol/Kramsach) brandy or spirits bottle. c.1700. Honey brown colour. Blown by the German half-post method. Blowpipe pontil scar. Dim: 20 x 8.5 x 6.5cm. Cap: 78cl. Wt: 355gr.

Refs: F. Nagel (54) lot 660, col. photo 41; T. Dexel (326) pl.317; M. Reidel (873) pp.46–48

Plate 230. An early 18th century Alpine pinched spirits bottle ('Nabelflasche'), 24-rib pattern, deep cobalt blue. Made by the German half-post method. Pewter screw closure. Blowpipe pontil scar. H: 17cm. Cap: 32cl. Wt: 176gr.
Ref: T. Dexel (326) pl.310

Plate 231. An early 18th century Alpine pinched spirits bottle ('Nabelflasche'), 24–rib pattern
swirled to right, light green. Made by the German half-post method. Pewter screw closure.
H: 21cm. Cap: 77cl. Wt: 336gr.
Ref: T. Dexel (326) pl.310

Plate 232. A German (Brandenburg, Saxony, Franconia) utility bottle of yellowish olive green forest glass with pewter screw closure ('Schraubflasche'). Dated between 1670 and 1720. Blowpipe pontil scar. Many of these bottles were cold painted with armorials or other decorations in the 16th–18th century. Dim: 16.5 x 9.5 x 8.5cm. Cap: 80cl. Wt: 630gr.
Ref: A. von Saldern (930) fig.139, for a '1694' dated example

Plate 233. A round hexagonal German (Potsdam) 'gold ruby' lead crystal glass bottle, c.1700. Used as a tea preserving bottle. Gold plated silver closure and flowers engraved on the top lid. Pontil scar ground away. Note the deep red colour with a purple tint which is characteristic of 'gold ruby' glass (see Glossary). This 'gold ruby' glass invented and first made by Johann Kunckel in 1679 colours the glass red throughout with a purple tone and is very expensive to produce because it requires pure gold. In her book *Sächsisches Glas,* pages 124–126, Gisela Haase refers to Johann Friedrich Böttger (1682-1719), the inventor of Meissen porcelain, who also invented in 1713 bottles and other glassware in 'Böttger ruby glass' which are produced from colourless flint crystal glass with a thin innerlay or overlay of ruby red glass to save gold. This 'Böttgerrubinglas' was first produced in 1713 at the Dresden Glasfabrique (1698-1762). H: 16cm. Cap: 80cl. Wt: 770gr. See also Plate 304(1) for a 'copper ruby red' snuff bottle and Plate 304(2) for a 'gold ruby' inkwell.

Refs: B. Klesse: *Veredelte Gläser aus Renaissance und Barock,* Wien 1987, item 140; W. Fetzer: *Johann Kunckel,* Berlin 1977, item 13

Plate 234. A Norwegian rectangular utility bottle with pewter screw closure. The top lid has a pewter mark, a crowned rose and the pewter maker's initials 'S.G.' at both sides of the rose. c.1770. Unusual green colour similar to Plate 289(3). Blowpipe pontil scar. Dim: 23.5 x 10 x 8.5cm. Cap: 1.22 litres. Wt: 1200gr.
Ref: J.H. Korshavn (625), p.120 for jar with similar colour

Plate 235. An Austrian (Steiermark) historical spirits flask, locally named 'Erzherzog Johann Flasche'. Embossed with **'E HERZOG IOHANN'** (**E**rzherzog Johann) and his portrait, a panther rampant surrounded by **'STEYERMARK'** (the coat of arms of Steiermark), agricultural tools surrounded by the date **'1840'** and other agricultural tools surmounted by the capitals **'D-B-V'** and surrounded by **'K.K. PRIV. GLASFAB.'** (**K**aiserliche und **K**önigliche **Priv**at-**Glasfab**rik). The bottle was produced in 1840 to commemorate Archduke Johann as founder of the Agricultural Society in Steiermark. Bottle blown at the K.K. Priv. Glasfabrik. Cobalt blue glass. Blowpipe pontil scar. Half-post method. Dim: 13.5 x 11.5 x 3.8cm. Cap: 29cl. Wt: 180gr.

Ref: Schloßmuseum Göbelsburg, Österreichisches Museum für Volkskunde, Wien 1975, Glass catalogue lot 101, col.photo X; F. Nagel (54), lot 686, col.photo 43

Plate 236. A South German (Black Forest area) spirits flask. On the reverse side embossed with a wild boar's head, a hunting horn, a shotgun and a deer catcher. Cobalt blue glass colour. Glass-tipped pontil scar. Dim: 14 x 11 x 3.5cm. Cap: 21cl. Wt: 220gr.
Ref: M. Reinartz (874) p.86, item 1793

Plate 237. A Latvian (Riga area) flask sealed 'RIGA BALSAM' for containing Riga Balsam, an aromatic oil used as a stomach bitter. The blacksmith Abraham Kunze possessed the Imperial privilege to be the sole producer of this balsam in Riga in 1804. Riga Balsam had existed since c.1635. The bottles, c.1820-1840, look older than they are. Some seals read 'RIGA BALSAM – 1834'. Green aquamarine colour. Blowpipe pontil scar. Produced in the Baltic states.

After consumption of the balsam, the illustrated flask was filled with smelling salts and a linen cloth. Dim: 13 x 8.8 x 2cm. Cap: about 9cl. Wt: 150gr. (full). See also Plates 238 and 257(5).

Ref: D.A. Wittop Koning: 'Riga Balsem' in the *Nederlands Pharmaceutisch Weekblad*, Nr. 109, pp. 603-605, 1974

Plate 238. Three Latvian (Riga area) Riga Balsam flasks. All c.1820–1840. Blowpipe pontil scar.
- (1) Dim: 10.5 x 7.5 x 2cm. Light green aquamarine colour.
- (2) Dim: 9.5 x 7 x 3cm. Aquamarine colour. Blank seal.
- (3) Dim: 10 x 7.5 x 2.5cm. Green aquamarine colour. Sealed: 'RIGA BALSAM – W'.

Flasks (1) and (2) are imitations of the original Riga Balsam flask (3) and as depicted in Plate 237. See also Plate 257(5).

Ref: D.A. Wittop Koning 'Riga balsem in Nederland', *Pharmaceutisch Weekblad,* No 109, pp.603–605, 1974

Plate 239.1.

(1) A Swedish bottle sealed '**LGB-A.G-1757**' which are the initials for **L**immareds **G**las **B**ruck (Limmared Glasshouse) where **A. G**iöbel was a glassmaker in 1757. Deep grass green colour. Blowpipe pontil scar. H: 23.5cm. Cap: 98cl. Wt: 490gr.

(2) A Swedish/Finnish mallet-shaped bottle sealed: '**MF**' surrounded by a wreath of leaves. c.1740. Clear grass green colour. Blowpipe pontil scar. Restored. H: 23.5cm. Cap: 86cl. Wt: 720gr.

Refs: H. Seitz (961) pp.170 and fig.38 for (1); H. Seitz (962) pp.114 and 115, Plansch 86A shows another Swedish bottle sealed 'LGB-1750' for (1).

Plate 239.2. A unique flat octagonal handled bottle sealed '**AF**' surmounted by a king's crown and dated '**1760**'. The seal represents the initials and crown of **A**dolph **F**rederick, King of Sweden (1751-1771) who originates from the House of Holstein-Gottorp, Schleswig-Holstein, now North Germany. The bottle was made at the 'Skånska glasbruket' glasshouse in Henrikstorp, South Sweden, which was active from 1691 until 1760. On 20 September 1691 the glasshouse obtained the 'Kongelige Privilegium' (Royal Privilege) to make 'buteljer, laboratorie – och vinglas…' (bottles, laboratory glass, wine glasses, etc.).

Most of the glassmakers were of German origin. Such royal seals have been found for every year from 1751, the year of coronation of the King, to 1760 when production at the glasshouse ceased.

The bottle is dark grass green colour. Blowpipe pontil scar. Blown in a dip mould. Dim: 17.5 x 9 x 6cm. Cap: 30.8cl (1 Kvart = ¼ Stop = 32.7cl). Wt: 387gr.

Ref: S.E. Noreen (790), p.135, illustrates a similar handled bottle made at Henrikstorp in clear glass, unsealed and engraved with the date '1752'

Plate 240. Three Danish cherry liqueur ('Kirsebær' liqueur) bottles with ribbon seals.
 (1) Sealed: 'IOH VON PEIN'. Johann von Pein was a liqueur maker in Altona,
     Hamburg, Germany in the 19th century. Altona was Danish until 1864. c.1840. Black
     glass. Blowpipe pontil scar. Unusually high capacity. H: 25cm. Cap: 71cl (¾ Danish
     Pott = 72.5cl). Wt: 640gr.
 (2) Sealed: 'C.E. KNUDSEN' Red amber colour. c.1840-1860. Sand pontil scar. H:
     22cm. Cap: 41.5cl. Wt: 390gr.
 (3) Sealed: 'P.F. HEERING'. Peter Fredericson Herring, Heering, Hering, Hearing,
     Herrink or Haering, founded his cherry distillery in Copenhagen in 1818 and it still
     exists. c.1818-1840. Black glass. Blowpipe pontil scar. H: 18.5cm. Cap: 31.5cl (⅓
     Danish Pott = 32.2cl). Wt: 385gr. See also Plate 266 (1).
Refs: D. Knight (619) mentions 26 different cherry cordial bottle seals or names; M. Schlüter (944) figs.416-419

Plate 241. A Norwegian decanter bottle sealed with a capital 'K', the initial for Casper **K**auffeldt (1773-1843) who was the owner of the Gjøvigs Glasværk (1807-1843), Norway. Cobalt blue glass bottle with opaque white spirals. c.1820. Blowpipe pontil scar. H: 19cm. Cap: 50cl. Wt: 238gr.
Ref: J.H. Korshavn (625) pp.60, 89-91

Plate 242. A Norwegian decorative decanter bottle ('Ziiratkarafler') probably made at the Gjøvig Glasvœrk (1807–1843), Norway. c.1830–1840. Colourless glass with greyish tone. Blowpipe pontil scar. H: 21.7cm. Cap: 91cl. Wt: 470gr. See also Plate 296(2).
Refs: J.H. Korshavn (625) p.133; A. Berntsen (156) Plansje X, item 48

Plate 243. A Swedish bottle with four seals inscribed '**BJ–ER**' and dated '**1850**'. Dark amber colour. Blowpipe pontil scar. H: 20.5cm. Cap: 147cl. Wt: 795gr.
Refs: H. Seitz (961) fig.8 and E. Steenberg (993) p.37 for similar bottles with four seals

VI
MISCELLANEOUS:
EUROPE AND AMERICA

This chapter deals with utility bottles, Codd–bottles, flasks, jars, inkwells and vials of several periods selected from different European countries and the United States in order to highlight their differences and similarities, for example in shape, glass colour, glass seal, capacity, weight, contents, technology, production area, protection means and applications.

To conclude, some bottle-seal dies and bottle related items such as corkscrews, corking tubes, bottle machines, etc. are illustrated (Plates 316-329).

Plate 244. Two handled ancient utility bottles. Roman period. Bluish green aquamarine colour. Their shape was very practical for being packed in wooden cases for transport.

(1) Rectangular shape. 2nd–3rd century A.D. Blowpipe pontil scar. Excavated from a tomb in France. Dim: 16 x 8.7 x 5cm. Cap: 38cl. Wt: 375gr.

(2) Square shape. 1st–3rd century A.D. Roman Empire. No pontil scar. Blown in a dip mould. Dim: 17.5 x 9 x 9cm. Cap: 78cl. Wt: 685gr.

Ref: C. Isings (556) Form 50 for (2) and Form 90 for (1)

Plate 245. A double ungentarium used to contain balm, scented ointment. Roman period. 3rd–4th century A.D. Green aquamarine colour. Excavated. Mediterranean area. The twin tubular bodies are fused together. Pontil scar. H: 17cm.

Plate 247. (top)
  (1) An ancient flask. 6th century. Syrian. Aquamarine colour. Glass tipped pontil scar. Note the glass reinforcing ring inside the thin-walled bottle. This system is also used later on German double cone bottles and pear-shaped bottles in the 15th-17th century. See also Plates 188, 189 and 190(1). Dim: 14.5 x 9 x 3.7cm. Cap: 18cl. Wt: 178gr.
  (2) An early Islamic (Persian) decanter bottle. 10th-12th century. Aquamarine colour. Excavated. Patinated. Glass-tipped pontil scar. H: 15cm. Ø: 7cm. Cap: 30cl. Wt: 108gr.
Ref: G. Loudmer (688), pl.616 for (2)

Plate 246. (left)
  (1) An ancient 'twins' decanter bottle. Roman period. Late 1st-2nd century. Excavated. Patinated. Greenish aqua colour. Glass tipped pontil scar. Used to contain two different liquids (oil and vinegar) at the same time. H: 17.5cm. Wt: 720gr.
  (2) A 'modern' multiple bottle with four separate compartments. c.1910. French Patent. Mouth blown bottle. Crystal glass. Pontil scar ground away. Used to be filled with four different coloured liqueurs such as Apricot Brandy (orange), White Curaçao, Parfait Amour (purple) and Crème de Menthe (green). H: 35cm (including glass stoppers). Wt: 1440gr.
Refs: S. Auth (103) p.103, pl.116 for (1); C. Isings (556) Form 14 for (1); French Patent No 397.261 (A. MEYER) from 4/05/1909 for (2)

Plate 248. A collection of 16th/17th century utility vials. Excavated in Holland. Mainly produced in Belgium and Germany, they appear in most European countries. Used for medicines, spirits, poisons, perfumes, pulverware. Often they were used as a drinking bottle in pubs and households. Sometimes these vials contained relics and were used as a religious attribute in the Catholic church. They were mostly closed with a cork or a stopper in wood, linen, paper, etc. Wax was commonly used to make the stoppers airtight and sometimes the stopper (cork) and wax were covered with a piece of leather, pig's bladder or parchment tied with a string around the lip of the vial. H: 6.3-11.2cm. Wt: 20-75gr. (thin walled).
Ref: H. Henkes (489), pl.66.20, Afb. 78 and 155

Plate 249. A collection of 16th-18th century free-blown utility vials. Excavated in Holland. In use in most West-European countries. The tallest vial (4) was mainly used as a sand hour-glass but sometimes also as a cupping-glass for drawing blood. These vials were mainly produced in Belgium and Germany. Pontil scars. H: 5-10.5cm. Wt: 12-108gr. See also Plate 248.
Ref: H. Henkes (489) pls.66.20, 66.28-66.30 and 67.26, Afb. 206 and 215

Plate 250. A collection of 16th–18th century utility vials. Excavated in Holland. They turn up in most North-west European countries. Mouth blown. Pontil scar. H: 6.8-9.2cm. Wt: 25-50gr. See also Plate 248.

Ref: H. Henkes (489) pl.66.20

Plate 251. A collection of 16th–18th century utility vials. Excavated in Holland. Popular in most North–west European countries but mainly produced in Belgium and Germany. Mouth blown. Pontil scar. H: 5–7.2cm. Wt: 14–20gr. See also Plate 248.
Ref: H. Henkes (489) pls.66.20–66.22

Plate 252. A collection of 16th–18th century utility vials. Mostly excavated in Holland, but they turn up in most North-west European countries. Vial (4) is of Spanish origin. Mouth blown. Pontil scar. H: 4–9cm. Wt: 6–60gr. See also Plate 248.
Ref: H. Henkes (489) pl.66.20

Plate 253. Four 'case' bottles used as common utility bottles. They are the forerunners of the 'Dutch' case gin bottles from c.1750 onwards. All with blowpipe pontil scars. Note the different colours for the different production periods and areas.

  (1) Belgium. c.1600. Probably from the Colinet glasshouses known as a 'boutelle quarrée diste Allemande' (a German square bottle). Clear yellowish forest glass. Dim: 13.6 x 6.5 x 6.5cm. Cap: 42cl. Wt: 175gr.
  (2) Belgium. c.1660. Yellowish forest glass. Pewter screw closure. Dim: 15.5 x 5.5 x 5.5cm. Cap: 29cl. Wt: 280gr.
  (3) Alpine countries. c.1720-1760. Blown by the German half-post method. Clear glass. Dim: 25.3 x 10.3 x 10.3cm. Cap: 207cl. Wt: 780gr.
  (4) Germany, Bohemia and Belgium. c.1570-1600. Light green forest glass with bluish tone. Dim: 17 x 5.7 x 6cm. Cap: 36cl. Wt: 245gr.

See also Figures 10, 39 and Plates 83-87, 192, 272.

Refs: A. Colinet (260) fig.55 for (1); F. Nagel (54) pls.705 and 1308 for (3); A. von Saldern (930) fig.51 shows a '1572' dated example for (2) and (4); H. Henkes (489) pl.51.1 for (1)

Plate 254. Two side-flattened onion bottles. Used for all applications. Excavated in Holland. Patination. Pontil scars.

(1) Belgium and North-east France. c.1630. Yellowish colourless glass. Extremely thin glass (0.3mm). Dim: 14.4 x 10.5 x 7.5cm. Wt: 140gr.

(2) A North German (Schleswig-Holstein) 'Blatte'. c.1720-1740. Light green forest glass with blue tone. H: 19 x 17 x 12cm. Cap: 1.26 litres. Wt: 725gr. At that time in Germany this bottle was called a 'Hamburger blatte Bouteille' (a flat bottle from Hamburg). Similar bottles are known with the coat of arms of Schleswig-Holstein-Gottorf and dated 1734 and 1739.

Plate 255. Four late 16th–early 17th century utility bottles. Very thin walled. Excavated in Holland. Patinated. All with blowpipe pontil scars.

  (1) Belgium and North-east France (Lorraine). c.1620-1630. Colourless with yellowish tone. H: 11.7cm. Wt: 135gr.

  (2) North-east France (La Vôge and Lorraine). c.1620-1630. Side-flattened. An important bottle, historically, for the bottle colour is 'verre noir' (black glass), a dark brown colour which is characteristic of the forest glass blown in the 'La Vôge' area such as Darney in the 15th-18th century. Dim: 16 x 11.2 x 7.2cm. Wt: 200gr.

  (3) Belgium. c.1580-1600. Round octagonal bottle. Colourless glass with yellowish tone ('Waldglas'). H: 15cm. Ø: 6/6.5cm.

  (4) Germany or Belgium. c.1630. Rectangular tapered shape. Colourless glass with greenish tone ('Waldglas'). Gold patinated. Wide mouth. Dim: 16.5 x 7.5 x 5.5cm (base). Cap: 44cl. Wt: 270gr.

Refs: G. Ladaique (637, 638) for (2); G. Rose-Villequey (904) for (2); H. Henkes (489) pls.51.6, 51.7 and Afb. 165 for (3)

Plate 256. Three utility bottles. Excavated and patinated.
  (1) A 'Dutch' onion, half-size. North German production, light green forest glass. c.1720–1730. Blowpipe pontil scar. H: 14.5cm. Ø: 12cm. Cap: 47cl. Wt: 430gr.
  (2) An English wide mouth mallet. c.1730–1740. Black glass. A 'magnum' storage/ preserving bottle. Sand pontil scar. H: 17cm. Ø: 16cm. Cap: 1.47 litres. Wt: 1090gr.
  (3) An English onion (a 'pancake'). c.1710–1720. Black glass. Sand pontil scar. H: 15.5cm. Ø: 15cm. Cap: 78cl. Wt: 974gr.

Plate 258. (top) Three unusual 'onion' utility bottles. Anti-clockwise from top:
  (1) A half-size 'Dutch' Belgian/German onion. Olive green. c.1730. Blowpipe pontil scar.
       H: 14.5cm. Ø: 12cm. Cap: 40cl. Wt: 495gr.
  (2) An English onion. c.1710-1720. Turquoise blue opaline glass (originated from using
       'glassgall'★). Sand pontil scar. H: 14cm. Ø: 15cm. Cap: 80cl. Wt: 920gr (a heavy bottle).
  (3) A 'Dutch' Belgian/German onion. c.1720-1750. Blank seal on the neck. Dark olive
       green colour. Blowpipe pontil scar. H: 18.5cm. Ø: 14cm. Cap: 82cl. Wt: 705gr.
See also Plates 11, 74, 200, 205 and 208(3).
★See Glossary

Plate 257. (left) Five European utility bottles. Clockwise from left to right:
  (1) A very rare 'shaft and bladder'. North-east France (Argonne). c.1670-1710. Dark grass
       green colour with bluish tone. Blowpipe pontil scar. A common utility bottle for
       containing wine, beer, liqueur, oil, and all other wet wares. The long neck suggests use as
       a decanter. H: 43cm. Cap: 2.25 litres. Wt: 1220gr. See also Plate 141.
  (2) An Austrian (Kramsach) mineral water bottle of conical shape. Early 19th century. Olive
       green colour with yellowish tone. Blowpipe pontil scar. H: 25cm. Cap: 84cl. Wt: 300gr
       (light weight). See also Plate 262(1).
  (3) A snuff tobacco preserving bottle, sometimes also used for containing powder wares such
       as spices. England. c.1800. Flat octagonal shape. Dark olive green colour. Sand pontil
       scar. H: 13.6cm. Cap: 26cl. Wt: 290gr. See also Plates 269(1), 287(1) and 305(2).
  (4) Flowerpot-shaped bottle in dark grass green colour. North Germany (Schleswig-
       Holstein). c.1700-1720. Blowpipe pontil scar. H: 14.6cm. Cap: 54cl. Wt: 395gr. See also
       Plate 196.
  (5) A round flat flask from Latvia (Riga area). c.1820-1840. Sealed: 'RIGA BALSAM', a
       stomach bitter. Clear grass green colour. Blowpipe pontil scar. Dim: 10.2 x 7.5 x 2.2cm.
       Cap: 9cl. See also Plates 237 and 238.

Plate 259. Two utility bottles mainly used for containing champagne. Blowpipe pontil scars.
  (1) North-east France (Argonne). c.1710–1720. Olive green colour (sometimes dark grass green). H: 24cm. Cap: 91cl. Wt: 690gr. A similar bottle was excavated at the glasshouse of 'Sommergrund' (till 1719) in the North Spessart forest (Germany).
  (2) Germany (Mecklenburg). c.1770. Olive green colour. Notice the flanged lip for tying the cork with a string. In the U.S.A. this bottle is known as a 'Lau Lau' bottle. H: 25cm. Cap: 80cl. Wt: 680gr.

Refs: Gemeente Den Haag: *Tussen koor en controle*, 1996, pl.p.54 for (1); *Glastechnische Berichte*, 49 (1976) No. 5, pp.126-129 for (1); Jean-François de Troy (1679-1752): 'Le déjeuner aux huîtres', painting c.1730, Musée de Rennes (France) for bottle (1); K-H. Poser (847) No. 154 for bottle (2)

Plate 260. Three European utility bottles. All blowpipe pontil scars.
    (1) North France. c.1720-1730. Grass green colour. H: 20cm. Ø: 12.2cm. Cap: 73cl. Wt: 670gr.
    (2) Denmark and Norway. c.1730-1750. Black glass. See Figure 13 (No.109). H: 21.5cm. Ø: 11.5cm. Cap: 93cl. Wt: 545gr.
    (3) A 'Dutch' bell-shaped mallet, probably made in North Germany (Mecklenburg). c.1740. Olive green colour. H: 22cm. Ø: 12cm. Cap: 83cl. Wt: 765gr.
Ref: M. Schlüter (944) pl.p.14, top left, for (2); W. Klein (613) fig.8 for (3)

Plate 261. Three utility bottles of different shapes. All blowpipe pontil scars.
- (1) Belgium or Germany. c.1750-1770. Cylindrical-conical shape. A similar bottle is known with a 'fish' on the seal (as in Plate 122). This bottle should not be confused with the bottle in Plate 262(1). H: 27cm. Ø: 11.5cm. Cap: 83cl. Wt: 630gr.
- (2) North Germany (Mecklenburg). c.1770. A long neck squat cylinder with a nearly flat bottom. H: 25.7cm. Ø: 11.3cm. Cap: 93cl. Wt: 515gr.
- (3) A German rectangular 'case' bottle with a short flared lip, designed for a pewter screw closure mounting. c.1720. Yellowish olive green colour. Dim: 23.2 x 9.4 x 8cm. Cap: 131cl. Wt: 755gr.

Plate 262. Three utility bottles of different shape and origin. Blowpipe pontil scars.

(1) Austria. c.1820-1840. A Kramsacher mineral water bottle of conical shape. Olive green colour. H: 25cm. Ø: 10.5cm. Cap: 84cl. Wt: 300gr. (light weight bottle). This bottle should not be confused with the one in Plate 261(1). See also Plate 257(2).

(2) North Germany. c.1770. A long neck squat cylindrical bottle. Grass green colour. H: 25cm. Ø: 11.8cm. Cap: 88cl. Wt: 700gr.

(3) Finland. c.1740-1760. A thin-walled squat cylindrical bottle. Light grass green colour. H: 23cm. Ø: 11.6cm. Cap: 113cl. Wt: 460gr.

Ref: J Seela (959) fig.37 for (3)

Plate 263. Three utility bottles of different capacity. Olive green colour. Blowpipe pontil scars.

(1) French c.1780-1820. Sealed: 'ELIXIR DE GUILLIE' around a 'G'. A cough mixture. H: 20.5cm. Ø: 7.5cm. Cap: 32cl. Wt: 500gr. See also Plate 150(1).

(2) A 'Dutch' Belgian long neck cylinder. c.1770. Sealed 'IHS – HOBRION WYN'. An Haut-Brion Bordeaux wine for the Dutch/Belgian market. IHS means 'IN HOC SIGNO' (In this sign) or 'JESU HOMINI SALVATOR' (Jesus Saviour of Humanity). H: 30cm. Ø: 8.5cm. Cap: 83cl. Wt: 840gr. See also Plates 79, 81 and 82.

(3) A French tapered cylinder, c.1800-1820. Sealed: 'Ht. SAUTERNE – JS&F – BORDEAUX' A common utility bottle used in this case for 'Haut Sauterne' Bordeaux wine. H: 24cm. Ø: 6cm. Cap: 34cl. Wt: 365gr. See also Plate 149(2) for an 'olive oil' bottle.

Plate 264. Two utility bottles with unusual positions for the seal. Both in black glass ('zwart glas'; 'verre noir').
(1) Belgium, c.1780-1820. Sealed: **'VH'**, the initials of '**V**an **H**avert', a wine merchant in Antwerp. Burgundy style bottle. Remains of red wine in the bottle. Glass–tipped pontil scar. H: 27.5cm. Ø: 9.4cm. Cap: 80cl. Wt: 700gr.
(2) England. Sealed: **'ST – 1822'**. Another bottle exists sealed: 'D' on the neck of the squat cylinder. Sheelah Ruggles-Brise (920) pictures a similar bottle with the seal 'ST – 1828' on the shoulder which is also an unusual place for an English seal. H: 26.7cm. Ø: 8.7cm. Cap: 78cl. Wt: 640gr.
Refs: E. Leitherer (668), pl.p.35 (top left) for (1); S. Ruggles-Brise (920) pl.3 (bottom row) for (2)

Plate 265. Three typical German wine-style bottles used in the 19th century for exclusively containing Mosel wine and/or Hock, a wine produced at Hochheim on the Main and commercially extended to Rhine wines. The term 'Hock' is the English pronounced abbreviation for 'Hochheim', a vineyard village south of Mannheim, Germany where the first Main-Rhinewine ('Hochheimerstein') exported to England came from.

In the 19th century the red amber and the green coloured bottles were both used for containing red and white Hock and Mosel wine. Today the red amber bottles are only used for containing white Rhine wine and the green coloured bottles for white Mosel wine.

Nowadays the term 'Hock' is used for all white wines from the whole of the Rhine area, in particular the Rheingau area.

(1) A German-style English made 'HOCK' bottle. c.1848. Sealed: **'OLD HOCK – 1648'** The date on the seal is the earliest antedated antique bottle known and refers to the wine year for Hock in 1648. A. Simon (974) gives the following reason for it:

> *In Germany, for instance, when a great tun was first laid down and filled with the wine of a particularly fine vintage, such as the vintage of 1648, it was 'refreshed' from time to time with wines of later good vintages, but it continued for years and years to be known as the '1648' tun. When some of the wine from that particular tun happened to be sold, after a hundred years or more, it was sold and bottled as '1648' wine, although the purchaser knew perfectly well that such was the date of the oldest wine in the blend but not a pure '1648' wine, which would have been no longer wine – and certainly unfit for consumption – had it not been for the wines of later vintages added from time to time. Thus it was that before the war one could still drink at Bremen and some of the old Hanseatic cities of Northern Germany, hocks of fabulous age in the hoary municipal cellars.'*

In Germany 1648 was declared a great wine year, most probably in celebration of the Peace Treaty of Münster, better known as the Peace of Westphalia, in 1648. In that year the Thirty Years War (1618-1648) between Germany, Sweden and France and the Eighty Years War (1568-1648) between the Spanish and The Netherlands came to an end. It seems logical to suppose that in 1848 wine of 1648 was bottled to commemorate the 200th anniversary of the Peace of Westphalia knowing that there was a small fraction of the original 'peace-wine' in the bottle.

The bottle illustrated has an 'English' green colour and is provided with a pouring lip. Bare-iron pontil scar. H: 24.5cm. Ø: 7.5cm. Cap: 57cl. Wt: 505gr.

2. A German Hock and/or Mosel wine bottle. Dated between 1821 and 1835. Sealed '**HR**' for Victor Amadeus (died 1835) who was Landgraf zu **H**essen-**R**otenburg (Earl of Hesse and Rotenburg), **H**erzog von **R**atibor (Duke of Ratibor, Silesia) and 'Fürst von Corvey' (Prince of Corvey, Westphalia). The bottle has a grass green colour and a blowpipe pontil scar. H: 31cm. Ø: 7.2cm. Cap: 68cl. Wt: 465gr.

3. A German Hock and/or Mosel wine bottle. c.1820–1840. Dark red amber colour. Blowpipe pontil scar. H: 32cm. Ø: 8.2cm. Cap: 82cl. Wt: 620gr.

Refs: R. Dumbrell (346) p.272 for (1); D. May (719) for (2) and (3); B. Hardy, personal communications; A. Simon (974) for (1)

Plate 266. Three ribbon-sealed utility bottles.

(1) Denmark. c.1840–1860. Sealed: 'P F HEERING', a distiller still producing cherry-liqueur in Copenhagen. Yellowish amber colour. Disc pontil scar. H: 19.5cm. Ø: 7.3cm. Cap: 34cl. (about ⅓ Danish Pot). Wt: 370gr. See also Plate 240.

(2) France. c.1858. Sealed 'MARGAUX BEL-AIR – MARQUIS DE POMMEREU' and on the ribbon seal (reverse) 'DÉFENDU D'EN LAISSER' (Forbidden to leave one drop). A claret named 'un Margaux-défendu' (a forbidden Margaux). No pontil scar. See also Plate 149(1). H: 30cm. Ø: 7.5cm. Cap: 78cl. Wt: 745gr. A very rare bottle.

(3) France. c.1858. Sealed: 'DÉFENDU D'EN LAISSER' (Forbidden to leave one drop) and on the reverse 'MARGAUX BEL-AIR – MARQUIS D'ALIGRE'. A claret named 'un Margaux défendu' (a forbidden Margaux). Blowpipe pontil scar. See also Plate 149(1). H: 30.5cm. Ø: 7.5cm. Cap: 75cl. Wt: 635gr. The Marquess of Aligre was owner of the Château of Bel-Air in Margaux (Gironde) France. During his life he did not want to sell his excellent wines. After his death the whole quantity of Margaux wine was sold without leaving any (défendu d'en laisser!) in the cellars. The wine was then bottled in about 3,000 bottles with the name of the original owner and an extra seal 'Défendu d'en laisser' (Forbidden to leave one drop). (It is not clear what the 'Marquis de Pommereu' bottle story is.)

Refs: D. Knight (619) for (1); *Le Monde Illustrée* (France), 25 September 1858, No. 76 de la 2ème Semaine; p.195 du *Courier de Paris,* 3ème Colonne for (2) and (3)

Plate 267. Four utility bottles, all 19th century.

(1) Sealed with the Castle of PRESLE (Belgium), the home of the Count d'Outremont. A half-size wine bottle. Red wine deposits. c.1860. No pontil scar. H: 20.5cm. Cap: 36cl. Wt: 370gr.

(2) Sealed with an unknown coat of arms. 'Burgundy' style bottle. Blowpipe pontil scar. c.1780-1800. France or Belgium. H: 28cm. Cap: 87cl. Wt: 680gr.

(3) Sealed with a 'bunch of grapes' and CHATEAU BERNON-MÉDOC'. The standard Bordeaux wine bottle. c.1870. No pontil scar. H: 29.8cm. Cap: 70cl. Wt: 714gr.

(4) Sealed with an old Slovenic Russian text. c.1820. Blowpipe pontil scar. Note the weight of this bottle compared with that of (1) for a nearly similar capacity. H: 27cm. Cap: 47cl. Wt: 928gr.

Plate 268.

  (1) A Dutch utility bottle used in this case in the pharmacies of the Dutch army/navy. c.1820. Sealed **'RYKSEIGENDOM'** (The property of the State). Dark olive green colour. Blowpipe pontil scar. H: 13cm. Ø: 6.9cm. Cap: 30cl. Wt: 280gr. This bottle type turns up in different dimensions and colours (aqua, amber, black) sealed or unsealed. See Plates 112 and 300(1)(2). For its English counterpart see Plate 268(2).

  (2) An English utility bottle mainly used for pharmaceutical applications. c.1800. Sealed **'GR'** for **G**eorge III – **R**ex, King of England and Hanover from 1760–1820. Bottles used in the British navy or army were owned by the Government and as such indicated by **'G.R.'**

      Some later bottles are sealed **'WR'** or **'VR'**, again indicating the property of the British State during the reigns of **W**illiam IV – **R**ex and **V**ictoria – **R**egina (1837-1902). There are about thirty-seven different **'GR'**, **'WR'** or **'VR'** seals known (with a crown, an anchor, etc.). Captain James Cook (1728-1779) discovered during his scientific expeditions to the Pacific (1768-1771) that none of the crew on his sailing ship H.M.S. *Endeavour* died from scurvy thanks to the drinking of **'LIME JUICE'**. These bottles contained mainly 'Lime Juice'. A similar bottle embossed 'Lime Juice' is known. Black glass. Sand pontil scar. H: 27cm. Ø: 11.5cm. Cap: 191cl. (about ½ gallon). Wt: 1150gr. For its Dutch counterparts see Plates 268(1) and 300(1)(2).

  (3) A French storage/preserving bottle used for preserving truffles. Sealed **'AR'** surrounded by **'CONSERVES de TRUFFLES garanties'** (Preserves of guaranteed truffles). These characteristic bottles were afterwards also used for preserving other foodstuffs. They are even known with original closure and label for containing 'Eau de Cologne'. Black glass. Bare iron pontil. c.1860. H: 25cm. Ø: 7.7cm. Cap: 41cl. Wt: 735gr.

Ref: W. Van den Bossche (188) for (1)(2); W.H. Klein (613) fig.20 for (1); P. Hanrahan (460) for (2); E. Leitherer (668) pl.p. 78, bottom row for (3); Musée du Parfum, Graz (France) displays 3 'truffle bottles' with original closure and labels: 'Eau de Cologne'

Plate 269. Three American utility bottles. c.1800-1820. Dark olive green colour.

   (1) A square storage bottle mainly used for snuff tobacco and spices. Blowpipe pontil scar. Dim: 12 x 6 x 6cm. Cap: 25cl. Wt: 300gr. See also Plates 257(3), 287(1) and 305(2).

   (2) A case bottle (a 'Maraschino' style bottle) used for oil, liqueur, medicines, etc. Glass-tipped pontil scar. Dim: 18 x 5.2 x 5.2cm. Cap: 37cl. Wt: 220gr.

   (3) A demijohn. Flowerpot-shaped. Sand pontil scar. Pouring lip. H: 44.5cm. Ø: 23/27cm. Cap: 11 litres. Wt: 1750gr.

Plate 270. Three storage utility bottles ('carboys'). Black glass.
  (1) A 'Dutch' globular bottle ('ballonfles') used for 'BERLINER KUMMEL' (Kümmel liqueur). c.1780–1820. Pouring lip. Blowpipe pontil scar. H: 28.7cm. Ø: 24cm. Cap: 6.4 litres. Wt: 1680gr. See also Plates 103–105.
  (2) An English cylindrical bottle. c.1800. With original stoppers. Sand pontil scar. Labelled: 'TR:BENZ:C'. H: 32cm. Ø: 16cm. Cap: 4.6 litres. Wt: 1670gr. Used in chemists' shops and pharmacies. See also Plate 60.
  (3) An English pear-shaped bottle. c.1770–1800. Labelled: 'TR. ZINGIB (tincture of Zingiberaceous). Disc pontil scar. H: 33cm. Ø: 25cm. Cap: 5.5 litres. Wt: 2240gr.
Ref: J.F. Crellin (277) fig. 25 for (2) and fig. 35 for (3)

Plate 271. Three utility bottles for storing liquids. Black glass.
  (1) England (Alloa glassworks). Sealed 'A.F. – 1828'. Sand pontil scar. H: 30cm. Ø: 21cm. Cap: 4.3 litres. Wt: 1535gr.
  (2) England for the American market. c.1800–1820. Sand pontil scar. H: 25.5cm. Ø: 18cm. Cap: 2.60 litres. Wt: 1070gr.
  (3) England. A side-flattened bladder. c.1780–1800. Sand pontil scar. Dim: 24.5 x 21 x 14cm. Cap: 3.20 litres. Wt: 1960gr. A very heavy bottle. See also Plate 283(2).

Plate 272. Three 'case' bottles of square shape for better transportation and storage. May be filled with any liquid.

    (1) England. c.1780-1800. Black glass. Sand pontil scar. Whittle marks. Dim: 28.5 x 14.5 x 14.5 cm. Cap: 4.2 litres. Wt: 2500gr.

    (2) England. c.1600. Greyish green forest glass. Pontil scar. Flattened down folded-in lip. Dim: 14.5 x 7.5 x 7.5cm. Cap: 58cl. Wt: 335gr.

    (3) England/France. c.1720-1730. Black glass. Blowpipe pontil scar. Slightly tapered. Dim: 31 x 10.5 x 10cm. Cap: 2.23 litres. Wt: 2250gr.

See also Plates 83-87, 192 and 253.

Plate 273.

   (1) A German (Black Forest) common storage bottle for vinegar, oil, wine, etc. c.1840–1860. With original wicker protection. Light green glass. Blowpipe pontil scar. H: 32cm. Cap: 5.5 litres.

   (2) A French (Alsace and Jura area) or Swiss (Flühli) storage bottle. c.1840–1860. Original wicker protection. No pontil scar. H: 32cm. Cap: 11 litres. Wt: 2140gr. The dark red amber colour ('verre noir') is typical of that area.

   (3) A German (Bavaria) utility bottle, mainly used for mineral water. Sometimes seen with remains of wine in it or labelled 'GIN'. Also used in pharmacies. Pouring lip. Bottle also exists in the (rare) blue colour. Blowpipe pontil scar. Yellowish olive green but mostly in dark olive green colour. Wicker protection missing. H: 28.6cm. Ø: 13.5cm. Cap: 2.3 litres. Wt: 780gr.

See also Plates 154 and 212.

Refs: M. Reinartz (874) fig. 1625 for (1); H. Horat (511) pl.43, for (1) (2); M. Reidel (873) p.27 for (3); K-H. Poser (847) no. 101 for (3)

Plate 274A. Four 'side-flattened onion' bottles of different capacities. Mainly produced in Belgium (Charleroi, Bruges) and Germany (Schleswig-Holstein, Mecklenburg, Hesse, Thuringia) for the 'Dutch' market. (1) (2) and (4) are storing bottles for liqueur, wine, pharmaceutical products, etc. All bottles are dark grass or dark olive green. Blowpipe pontil scar.

    (1) c.1720. Dim: 23 x 18 x 12cm. Cap: 1.82 litres. Wt: 1240gr. With pouring lip.

    (2) c.1760. Dim: 32 x 27 x 18cm. Cap: 5.7 litres. Wt: 2000gr. With pouring lip.

    (3) c.1740-1760. Dim: 11.5 x 8 x 4.4cm. Cap: 11.5cl. Wt: 140gr.

    (4) c.1720. Dim: 30 x 21 x 28cm. Cap: 6.1 litres. Wt: 2710gr.

Refs: Johann Michael Hambach, a painter active in Cologne (between 1672 and 1686) pictures a 'Blatte' in one of his still-lifes; K-H. Poser (847) p.38, Abb. 31, item 313 and p.46, Abb. 38, item 20; H. Henkes (489) pl.59.12; H. McKearin (733) pl.p.191 (bottom row) for (3).

Plate 274B. Side view of Plate 274A.

Plate 275A. Three 'side-flattened' onion utility bottles. In German 'eine Blatte' (a flat bottle). Black glass. Blowpipe pontil scar. Mainly produced in Belgium (Charleroi, Bruges) and Germany (Schleswig-Holstein, Mecklenburg, Hesse, Thuringia) for the 'Dutch' market. Used for storing/preserving liquids such as liqueur, wine, vinegar, pharmaceutical products, etc.

   (1) c.1720-1730. Dim: 18.5 x 17 x 10.5cm. Cap: 100cl. Wt: 750gr.

   (2) c.1740-1760. Dim: 11.5 x 8 x 4.4cm. Cap: 11.5cl. Wt: 140gr. A reference bottle as described for Plate 274A(3).

   (3) c.1730. Dim: 40.6 x 38 x 32cm. Cap: 19.4 litres. Wt: 5.5kg.

See also Plates 216 and 278(2).

Refs: K-H. Poser (847) p.38, Abb.31, items 25, 313 and p.46, Abb. 38 item 20; H. Henkes (489) pl.59.12

Plate 275B. Side view of Plate 275A (left).

Plate 276A. Four utility bottles of different capacities and shapes.

(1) America, Holland and Belgium. Side-flattened. c.1780-1820. Black glass. Blowpipe pontil scar. Dim: 29 x 20.5 x 14.5cm. Cap: 3.45 litres. Wt: 912gr. (light-weight).

(2) Holland, Belgium and Germany. Side-flattened onion. A reference bottle as described for Plate 274A (3).

(3) America and North Germany. A kidney-shaped 'demijohn' with ovoid horizontal section. c.1840. Sand pontil scar. Wicker protection missing. Dim: 41 x 40 x 22cm. Cap: 15 litres. Wt: 2730gr.

(4) England. A bladder. c.1740-1760. Disc pontil scar. Dim: 32 x 24 x 19cm. Cap: 3.9 litres. Wt: 2300gr. (heavy).

Refs: H. McKearin (733) pl.p.191 (bottom row) for (2) (3); R. Dumbrell (346) fig.99 for (4)

Plate 276B. Side view of Plate 276A (left).

Plate 277A. Three 'bladder-shaped' or 'flattened chestnut-shaped' utility bottles of different countries. Black glass.

    (1) England. c.1780. Sand pontil scar. Dim: 24 x 17 x 10cm. Cap: 1.32 litres. Wt: 945gr.

    (2) South France (Arles, Rhône delta). c.1780–1800. Mainly produced at the 'Verreries arlésiennes de Trinquetaille'. An 'Armagnac' style bottle used as a drinking bottle. Blowpipe pontil scar. Dim: 26.5 x 18.5 x 10.5cm. Cap: 1.92 litres. Wt: 950gr. See also Plates 148(1), 148(2) and 307(2).

    (3) America. c.1780–1820. Blowpipe pontil scar. Dim: 25 x 16 x 12.5cm. Cap: 1.70 litres. Wt: 500gr.

Refs: R. Dumbrell (346) fig.99 for (1); J. Bellanger (148) pl.p.284 for (2); H. McKearin (733) pl.p.191 (Top row) for (3)

Plate 277B. Side view of Plate 277A (left).

Plate 278. Three different shaped utility bottles. Black glass (coal firing).

(1) A North German side-flattened bottle (eine 'Blatte' or 'Plattflasche', in England a 'boot bottle') c.1750-1770. Blowpipe pontil scar. Dim: 18 x 19 x 18.5cm. Cap: 76cl. Wt: 770gr. Also pictured in Plate 216(3). For its yellowish olive green counterpart see Plate 279(2).

(2) A North German side-flattened bottle (eine 'Blatte' or 'Plattflasche'). c.1720-1730. Similar sealed bottles are known with the coat of arms of Schleswig-Holstein-Gottorf and dated 1734 and 1739. is known. Blowpipe pontil scar. Dim: 18.7 x 17 x 10.5cm. Cap: 100cl. Wt: 750gr. Also pictured in Plate 275(1).

(3) An English 'bladder' c.1730. Sand pontil scar. Dim: 17 x 15 x 12cm. Cap: 75cl. (one English reputed quart). Wt: 855gr.

Refs: R. Dumbrell (346) pls.49 and 56 for (1) and fig.94 for (3); K-H. Poser (847) items 19 and 25 for (2); *Glastechnische Berichte,* 49 (1976), No 5, pp.126-129 for (2)

Plate 279. Three unusual shaped utility bottles. Blowpipe pontil scars. Clockwise from left.
(1) A French wide-mouth bladder. c.1710-1730. Dark grass green colour. Dim: 30.8 x 14 x 11.5cm. Cap: 3.58 litres. Wt: 1050gr.
(2) A German (Lower Saxony) side-flattened bottle. c.1750-1770. Unusual yellowish olive green colour (woodfiring). Dim: 18 x 19 x 7.5cm. Cap: 81cl. Wt: 630gr. For 'black' counterparts see Plates 216(3) and 278(1).
(3) A North-German bottle, cylindrical with one side flattened. c.1720-1730. Developed to lie down to keep the cork wet. L: 18.2cm. Ø: 8cm. Cap: 46cl. Wt: 380gr.

Plate 280A. Four 'side-flattened onion' bottles (in German: 'Plattflaschen') of different capacities. Used as common utility bottles for storing or transporting liqueur, wine, beer, pharmaceutical products, etc.

 (1) Germany. c.1750. Black glass. Blowpipe pontil scar. Dim: 9.5 x 11 x 6.5cm. Cap: 25cl. Wt: 260gr.

 (2) Germany (Mecklenburg). c.1720-1730. Excavated in Holland. Olive green colour. Blowpipe pontil scar. Dim: 12.8 x 11 x 5.5cm. Cap: 25cl. Wt: 228gr.

 (3) America. Bottle named a 'demijohn'. c.1840. Olive green colour. Sand pontil scar. Wicker protection missing. Dim: 40 x 37 x 19cm. Cap: 15 litres. Wt: 2740gr.

 (4) North Germany (Schleswig-Holstein). c.1680. Grass green forest glass ('Waldglas'). Dim: 28 x 21 x 16cm. Cap: 3.1 litres. Wt: 1325gr.

Refs: R. Wendt (1092) pl.p.45 for (2); H. McKearin (733) pl.p. 191 (bottom row) for (2) and (3); K-H. Poser (847) item 313 in pl.31, p.38 and Tafel 60 p.118

Plate 280B. Side view of Plate 280A (left).

Plate 281. Three different utility bottles for different applications.

    (1) England. A Bristol blue decanter bottle. Slightly side-flattened. c.1800. Used as a spirits decanter. Glass-tipped pontil scar. Dim: 21 x 12.2 x 10.1cm. Cap: 82cl. Wt: 470gr.

    (2) America. A handled flattened chestnut bottle, c.1845. Yellowish amber. Sealed: 'AMBROSIAL – BM & E.A.W & C^{O}'. A whisky bottle from Ben.M. & Edw. A. Whitlock, 84 Frontstreet, New York in 1845. They were 'For Sale Retail by Druggists Everywhere'. Blowpipe pontil scar. Dim: 22.8 x 15.5 x 7cm. Cap: 92cl. Wt: 505gr.

    (3) Side view of a German (Franconia/Würzburg) 'Bocksbeutel' used for containing the famous Franconian Steinwein. c.1860-1880. Red amber colour, Blowpipe pontil scar. Dim: 14.5 x 12.2 x 9.2cm. Cap: 52cl. (½ size) Wt: 375gr. See Plate 218(1) for a front view of this bottle.

Refs: D.L. Murschell (772) p.47 and pl. for (2); K-H. Poser (679) 'Ein Bocksbeutel für Whisky' in *Glas-historische Notitzen,* Heft 4, Dec. 1989, pp.76-78; K. Schneider (948)

Plate 282. An American side-flattened handled bottle in the German 'Bocksbeutel' shape. c.1860. Sealed: 'VAN BEIL – CHESTNUT ST. – 1810-PHIL[A]'. This 'flat chestnut handled jug' was used in 1860 as a whisky bottle for dealer Henry Van Beil, 1810, Chestnut Street in Philadelphia (USA). The dark red amber bottle has been produced by Whitney Glass Works, Philadelphia. Note the similarity to the German 'Bocksbeutel' bottles mainly used for Steinwein. See Plates 218-220 and 281. Dim: 16.5 x 13.5 x 8cm. Cap: 79cl. Wt: 470gr.
Ref: D.L. Murschell (772) p.46; K. Schneider (948)

Plate 283. Three wide-mouth storage/preserving utility bottles from three different European countries.

   (1) Belgium. c.1720-1730. A straight-sided wide-mouth onion. Olive green colour. Blowpipe pontil scar. H: 12cm. Ø: 14cm. Cap: 85cl. Wt: 755gr.

   (2) England. c.1780-1800. A wide-mouth bladder with pouring lip. Black glass. Sand pontil scar. Dim: 21 x 18 x 14.5cm. Cap: 2.26 litres. Wt: 1100gr. See also Plate 271(3).

   (3) Germany (Lower Saxony). c.1780-1820. A wide-mouth side-flattened bottle. Yellowish olive green. Blown in a wooden two-part mould. Blowpipe pontil scar. Dim: 14.7 x 15 x 9cm. Cap: 94cl. Wt: 655gr. See also Plate 217.

Plate 284. Three wide-mouth utility bottles used for storing/preserving/decanting all liquid or powder wares. Used as flower vases, as decanters in households, pharmacies, etc. or as relic bottles in religious ceremonies. The bottle shape had existed since the 13th century and was mainly excavated and produced in the North-east of France, in areas such as 'Lorraine' and 'La Vôge'. The long neck makes it easier to grip the bottle when decanting liquids, for example, and the pouring lip prevents spillage during decanting.

(1) North-East France (La Vôge, Darney…). c.1650-1700. Typical yellowish amber colour ('verre noir') for the 'La Vôge' area such as Darney and Dompaire where the produced forest glass has been 'black' since at least the 15th century. H: 25.5cm. Ø: 13cm. Cap: 133cl. Wt: 495gr. (lightweight).

(2) A 'Dutch' (Belgian) wide-mouth onion (een 'wijdmond'.). c.1780-1820. Black glass ('zwart glas'). Blowpipe pontil scar. H: 22.5cm. Ø: 13cm. Cap: 82cl. Wt: 780gr.

(3) A French 'wide mouth onion'. c.1780-1830. Clear green glass. Disc pontil scar. H: 22.5cm. Ø: 17cm. Cap: 240cl. Wt: 668gr.

See also Plates 110, 111 and 285.

Refs: E. Baumgartner (145) pl.54 for a pre '1284' wide-mouth onion similar to (2); M.D. Waton (79) p.19 §5b and fig.2 nos. 12-14 and 17 for several 14th and 15th century wide-mouth onions as (2); G. Rose-Villequey (904); G. Ladaique (637, 638); R. McNulty (736) p.143, figs.77-79 for (2)

Plate 285. Three wide-mouth onions of different capacities. Black glass ('zwart glas', 'verre noir'). Disc pontil scars.

    (1) Holland/Belgium. c.1780–1820. A 'wijdmond' (wide-mouth). Pouring lip. H: 22.8cm. Ø: 16.5cm. Cap: 170cl. Wt: 1150gr.

    (2) Holland/Belgium. c.1780–1820. A 'wijdmond' (wide-mouth). Pouring lip. H: 16.7cm. Ø: 12.9cm. Cap: 78cl. Wt: 630gr.

    (3) France. c.1820–1830. A giant storage/preserving utility bottle. H: 28.3cm. Ø: 23.8cm. Cap: 6 litres. Wt: 2460gr.

See also Plates 110, 111 and 284.

Refs: R. McNulty (736) p.143, figs.77–79 for (1)(2); F. Nagel (54) pl.60 and col.pl.60 for (3)

Plate 286. Three wide-mouth case bottles. Used as a common utility bottle for storing/preserving and transporting liquids, powders, vegetables, fruit, etc. Mainly used in pharmacies, chemists' shops, etc. The tapered shape of these jars has been developed for fast blowing in a dip mould and for easy transportation in cases of 6, 9, or 12 jars. All with blowpipe pontil scars.

(1) Holland/Belgium. c.1770–1800. A giant jar in black glass ('zwart glas' or 'verre noir'). The Dutch name for this jar is 'wijemond celderfles' (wide-mouth case bottle). Dim: 31.5 x 9.5 x 9.5cm (base). Cap: 3 litres. Wt: 1670gr.

(2) North Germany. c.1770–1800. Forest green colour. Dim: 24 x 8.3 x 8.3cm (base). Cap: 167cl. Wt: 735gr.

(3) Holland/Belgium/Germany. c.1800–1820. Bluish aquamarine colour. Dim: 23 x 6.5 x 6.5cm (base). Cap: 114cl. Wt: 680gr.

See also Plates 83-87.

Ref: R. McNulty (735) p.106, fig.23

Plate 287. Four storage/preserving utility bottles or jars.

    (1) A 'Dutch' flat octagonal cacaobottle ('cacaofles') produced in England for the Dutch market. c.1840. Blown in a Ricketts mould. Sand pontil scar. Black glass. This bottle type is also used in England and the USA for preserving snuff tobacco, spices and other powder wares. See Plates 269(1) and 305(2).

    (2) A German (Upper Rhine area) or North-east French cylindrical jar. c.1780-1800. Dark red amber colour. Disc pontil scar. H: 23cm. Ø: 17.4cm. Cap: 4.6 litres. Wt: 1420gr.

    (3) A small French tapered cylindrical jar (un 'bocal'). c.1800-1830. Dark yellow olive green colour ('verre noir'). H: 19cm. Ø: 10cm. Cap: 110cl. Wt: 506gr. See also Plates 290(2) and 291(2).

    (4) An English round octagonal jar. c.1800-1830. Olive green colour. Sand pontil scar. H: 26cm. Ø: 13cm. Cap: 2.36 litres. Wt: 1200gr.

Refs: M. Reidel (873) pl.p.19 (middle row) for an original labelled ''Poeder Chocolade' from F. Korff in Amsterdam for (1); E. Leitherer (668) pl.p.77, bottom row for a 'cacaofles' with original label 'Cacao Suchard' (1); B. Arendonck (83) pl.CO1 for (1); J. Bellanger (148) pl. p.384 for (3)

348

Plate 288. Three common utility jars. Folded–out flat lips. c.1800.

(1) England. Black glass (coal firing). Disc pontil scar. H: 9.5cm. Ø: 14cm (base). Cap: 1.25 litres. Wt: 630gr.

(2) North Germany (Mecklenburg). Dark olive green colour. Mainly used in pharmacies. Blowpipe pontil scar. H: 7.5cm. Ø: 5.5cm. (base) Cap: 14cl. Wt: 125gr. See also Plate 290(1).

(3) North Germany (Mecklenburg). Light forest olive green colour (wood firing). Blowpipe pontil scar. H: 22.8cm. Ø: 14.5cm. Cap: 3.5 litres. Wt: 1280gr. See also Plate 290 (1).

Ref: K-H. Poser (847), item 303 (p.115) for (2); item 290 (p.113) and col.pl.10, p.16 for (3)

Plate 289. Three utility jars.

   (1) Baltic Sea area (Schleswig-Holstein, Sweden, Norway). c.1760. Illustrated in the 'Nøstetangen Catalogue' item No 164 (see Fig.13). Light forest glass green colour (wood firing). Blowpipe pontil scar. H: 15.6cm. Ø: 12.4cm. Cap: 1.35 litres. Wt: 812gr.

   (2) France. c.1820-1840. Light yellowish olive green colour. Disc pontil scar. H: 23cm. Ø: 21cm. Cap: 5 litres. Wt: 1375gr.

   (3) Norway. c.1800-1820. Unusual dark green colour with bluish tone, similar to Plate 234. Hadeland or Gjøvigs Glasshouse. H: 27.3cm. Cap: 2.9 litres (3 Pott). Wt: 876gr.

Ref: K-H. Poser (847) Abb. 41, item 292 for (1), item 293 for (2) and item 271 for (3); J.H. Korshavn (625) p.120 for a jar with a similar colour and shape

Plate 290. Three utility jars. Olive green colour.

  (1) North Germany (Mecklenburg). c.1800. Flowerpot shape. Blowpipe pontil scar. H: 19.1cm. Ø: 13.2cm. (base) Cap: 2.4 litres. Wt: 955gr. See also Plate 288(2) (3).

  (2) France. c.1800-1830. Cylindrical shape. Blowpipe pontil scar. H: 28.1cm. Ø: 14cm. Cap: 3.5 litres. Wt: 1470gr. See also Plates 287(3) and 291(2).

  (3) France. c.1800-1830. Square shape with flat chamfered corners. Disc pontil scar. Dim: 33.5 x 15.4 x 14.7cm. Cap: 4.9 litres. Wt: 2350gr.

Refs: K-H. Poser (847) item 289 and col.pl.10, p.16 for (1); J. Bellanger (148) pl.p.384 for (2)

Plate 291. Three cylindrical jars.
   (1) Belgium. c.1840. Blown in an 18-rib dip mould. Blue bottom and body, turquoise
       blue lip. Glass-tipped pontil scar. H: 22.2cm. Ø: 10cm. Cap: 110cl. Wt: 915gr.
   (2) France. c.1800–1830. Cylindrical shape. Dark olive green colour ('verre noir').
       Disc pontil scar. H: 22cm. Ø: 10.5cm. Cap: 140cl. Wt: 895gr. See also Plates 287(3) and
       290(2).
   (3) Germany (Upper Rhine) or North-east France. c.1840–1860. Red amber colour.
       Disc pontil scar. H: 23.7cm. Ø: 10cm. Cap: 115cl. Wt: 595gr.
Ref: J. Bellanger (148) pl.p.384 for (2)

Plate 292. Three utility bottles used for chemical or pharmaceutical applications.

(1) England. c.1820. Labelled: 'OXYM:SCILL' (Oximide:Scilla). Cobalt blue glass colour. Glass stopper. Glass-tipped pontil scar. These bottles contained all sorts of syrups. H: 23cm (with stopper). Ø: 9cm. Cap: 90cl. Wt: 412gr.

(2) France. c.1830–1850. Labelled under glass: 'VIOLA ODORATA' ('Gilliflower' or 'Fleurs de Violettes'). Original metal cap closure. Clear glass. Blowpipe pontil scar. H: 24.8cm. Ø: 11cm. Cap: 1.9 litres. Wt: 504gr.

(3) France. c.1830–1850. Labelled: 'COBALTUM'. Original metal cap closure. Clear glass. Glass-tipped pontil scar. H: 19.5cm. Ø: 8cm.

Refs: J.F. Crellin (277) figs. 61 and 62 for (1); G. Kallinich (590) pl.399 for (2) and pl.430 for (3)

Plate 293. Three utility bottles used for chemical or pharmaceutical applications.

(1) South-Germany/Alpine countries/Bohemia. c.1750. Cold painted. Labelled: 'ACID: SULPHURIC: CONC' (concentrated sulphuric acid) surmounted by a '13' engraved in the glass, number '13' in a series. Blown by the German half-post method. Clear glass with purple tone. A square case bottle. Dim: 18.5 x 9 x 9cm. Cap: 104cl. Wt: 600gr.

(2) South-west Germany (Black Forest area). c.1820-1840. Labelled: 'LIQUOR FERRI ARSENICAL'. Yellowish olive green colour. Disc pontil scar. A stoneware ball is used as a stopper. H: 22.6cm. Ø: 14.5cm. Cap: 257cl. Wt: 870gr.

(3) French, c.1880. Cold painted label: 'PULVIS VIOLAE ARV:' Cobalt blue glass. Sand pontil scar. Original metal cap closure. H: 24.6cm. Ø: 9.2cm.

Ref: G. Kallinich (590) pls.239 and 448 for (1), pl.241 for (2) and pl.430 for (3)

354

Plate 294. Two early 18th century decanter bottles. c.1730.

(1) England. Cruciform body. Lead glass. Exists also in purple colour (rare). Pontil scar ground away. Dim: 29 x 11.5 x 9.5cm. Cap: 81cl. Wt: 1315gr. (heavy weight).

(2) France (Normandy). Named a 'bonne femme' (a good woman). Blown in a 20-rib dip-mould. Clear glass with amethyst tone. Blowpipe pontil scar. H: 33.5cm. Ø: 12cm. Cap: 211cl. Wt: 2145gr. (light weight). For its Belgian counterpart see Plate 295(2). Note the serious differences in capacity and weight between (1) and (2).

Refs: A. Simon (979) pl.XCVIII item 244 (f) for (1); J. Bellanger (148) pl.p.279 for (2)

Plate 295.

   (1) South–west Germany (Black Forest area). c.1780. Double globular shape, an imitation of a calabash gourd. Blown in a 24–rib dip–mould by the German half–post method. Clear glass. Glass–tipped pontil scar. See also Plates 307 (1)(2) for similar technology. H: 17cm. Ø: 6.3/12cm. Cap: 75cl. Wt: 400gr.

   (2) Belgium (Liège). Named a 'bonne femme' (a good woman). c.1730. A decanter bottle. Clear glass. Blown in a 20–rib dip–mould. Glass–tipped pontil scar. H: 34.5cm. Ø: 13.8cm. Cap: 265cl. Wt: 545gr. For its French counterpart see Plate 294(2).

   (3) Alpine countries (Austria). c.1680. Flat octagonal shape. Clear glass bottle blown by the German half–post method. Glass–tipped pontil scar. Mainly used as a spirits bottle. Dim: 21 x 11.5 x 9.5cm. Cap: 142cl. Wt: 730gr.

Refs: T. Dexel (326) pl.260 for (1); Fl. Pholien (838) fig.44 for (2); F. Nagel (54) lot 1302 for (3)

Plate 296. Three decanter bottles. Glass–tipped pontil scar.

(1) England. c.1710-1725. Small-size handled onion in clear lead glass. H: 16.2cm. Ø: 11.2cm. Cap: 44cl. Wt: 830gr. See also Plates 12 and 38(3).

(2) Norway. c.1830-1840. A flat octagonal decanter ('Åttekantete buteljer med zirater') with rigarees and prunts. Clear glass with greyish tone. Dim: 25.2 x 11 x 7.5cm. Cap: 100cl. Wt: 555gr. Probably produced at Gjøvigs Glasvœrk (1807-1843). See also Plate 242.

(3) Alpine countries (Austria). c.1820-1840. A bladder-shaped decanter bottle with rigarees. Blown by the German half-post method. Aquamarine colour. Notice the funnel-shaped lip for better filling the bottle or drinking out of it. Dim: 22 x 18 x 13cm. Cap: 200cl. Wt: 716gr.

Refs: A. Simon (979) pl.XCVIII, item 244(c) for (1); J.H. Korshavn (625) Plansje XVII, item 40 and pl.p.132 for (2); T. Dexel (326) pl.265 for (3); F. Nagel (54) pl.1410 for (3)

Plate 297.

    (1) A French (Lower Normandy) spirits flask. c.1780. Clear glass with 'combed' loop decoration in opaque white enamel ('latticino'). Glass-tipped pontil scar. H: 16.1cm. Ø: 7.8cm. Cap: 20cl. Wt: 150gr.

    (2) A Bohemian tea preserving bottle. c.1760-1780. A flat octagonal bottle in Bohemian crystal. Hand-blown glass screw stopper (rare). The front and reverse side figure a bowman. Wheel engraved. Pontil scar ground away. This bottle is mentioned in a Bohemian price list for the Dutch market (Amsterdam, 15 December 1769) and is described as a 'Theeflasche mit Glasschraube, geschnitten' (a tea-bottle with a glass-screw, engraved). Dim: 11.9 x 5.4 x 3.9cm. Cap: 9cl. Wt: 254gr.

Refs: J. Bellanger (148) pl.p.37 for (1); E. Schebek (942) p.226 for (2)

Plate 298. A German or English kuttrolf, used as a drinking bottle. The lower neck part has four tubes, the upper part two. During drinking air enters through the tubes into the bottle and facilitates drinking. Clear glass. H: 27cm. Cap: 32cl. (filled to the brim). Wt: 350gr. See also Plates 88, 190(2) and 205.

Refs: H. Henkes (489) pp.116, 117 and photo Afb. 77 (painting from J. Ratgeb c.1510); J. Bellanger (148) pl.p.175

Plate 299. A Belgian decanter of c.1820 with a model of the Crucifixion assembled inside. An example of a popular form of folk-art in Continental Europe, mainly Germany, during the 19th and early 20th century. Subjects included religion, ships and professions such as miners at work. Clear crystal glass. Mouth blown hollow glass stopper. Glass-tipped pontil scar. H: 37.5cm. Ø: 13.5cm.
Ref: Otto Fitz (380)

Plate 300. Three utility bottles mainly used for pharmaceutical applications.

   (1) A mini-size Dutch medicine bottle. c.1820. Sealed: 'RYKSEIGENDOM' (property of the State). Used in pharmacies of the Dutch navy/army. Green-aquamarine colour. Glass-tipped pontil scar. This bottle (vial) is the smallest sealed pontilled bottle known in the world. H: 7.2cm. Ø: 3.8cm. Cap: 4.5cl. Wt: 80gr. See also Plates 112, 268(1) and 300(2).

   (2) A Dutch medicine bottle. c.1820. Sealed: 'RYKSEIGENDOM' (property of the State). Aquamarine colour. Glass-tipped pontil scar. H: 12.3cm. Ø: 6.8cm. Cap: 28cl. Wt: 216gr. Similar to Plates 268(1) and 300(1). See Plate 268(2) for its English counterpart.

   (3) A German onion-shaped utility bottle. c.1720. Greenish aquamarine colour. Blowpipe pontil scar. A small-size bottle used for medicines, spirits and many other liquids. H: 10.5cm. Ø: 7.8cm. Cap: 17cl. Wt: 95gr.

Refs: W.H. Klein (613) fig.20 for (1)(2); W. Van den Bossche (188) pl.18 for (1)(2); T. Dexel (326) pl.256 for (3)

Plate 301. Four utility bottles used for a wide range of applications such as perfume, balsam, stomach-bitters, oil, smelling salts, medicines, etc.

(1) A Dutch 'Haarlemmer Olie' vial. c.1850-1880. 'Haarlemmer oil' has been produced and sold from 1696 until today, first by Claes Tilly (died 1734) and later by Claes De Koning Tilly from Haarlem (Holland). This 'Medicamentum Gratia Probatum' was well known as a medicine against many ailments such as diseases of the stomach, liver, lungs, pain, headaches, ulcers, blue flecks, sprains, internal injuries, fever, cough, worms, heart complaints, 'English disease' (whatever that might be!) etc. Clear yellowish coloured bottle. Glass-tipped pontil scar. H: 8cm. Ø: 17mm. Cap: 15ml. Wt: 10gr.

(2) A German vial c.1850. Label: 'Balsam-Apotheke zum Aescu... des Franz Fichtner in...'. Yellowish colour. Glass-tipped pontil scar. H: 14.5cm. Ø: 17mm. Cap: 25ml. Wt: 20gr.

(3) A long tubular utility bottle used in this case for containing 'eau de Cologne'. c.1840. Appears in Holland, Belgium, France and Germany. Label: 'EXTRAIT D'EAU DE COLOGNE de Jean Marie Farina – Fournisseur de Plusieurs Cours à Cologne s/R'. This bottle type was also used for 'Haarlemmer Olie'. H: 23.5cm. Ø: 3cm. Cap: 12cl. Pontil scar. See also Figure 10 and Plate 168.

(4) A French round octagonal utility bottle. c.1840-1860. Aquamarine colour. Pontil scar. H: 22cm. Cap: 10cl. Wt: 120gr.

Refs: Directions for use of the 'Haarlemmer Olie', edited by C. De Koning Tilly, 1749, Haarlem, Holland for (1)(3); E. Ferrari (369) pl.p.74 for (2)(3); J. Bellanger (148), pl.p.285 for (4); H. Henkes (489) pls.66.20 and 66.25 for (1)(3); E. Launert (655) pp.35–38 for (3)

Plate 302. Three inkwells.

   (1) America. Between 1815-1840. Blown in a three-part mould. Applied disc on top. Dark olive amber colour. Blown at Coventry Glassworks, Connecticut, USA. Blowpipe pontil scar. Pattern GII-16A (Covill (270)). H: 4.2cm. Ø: 6cm. Cap: 4cl. Wt: 154gr.

   (2) England. c.1840. Black glass. Glass-tipped pontil scar. Applied disc on top. H: 9cm. Ø: 11.4cm. Cap: 5cl. Wt: 395gr.

   (3) Austria. c.1860-1880. Cobalt blue. Glass-tipped pontil scar. Originally packed three together in a straw package. H: 8cm. Ø: 7.7cm. Cap: 18cl. Wt: 112gr. See also Plate 303(2).

Ref: W. Covill (270) fig.1182 for (1)

Plate 303. Three inkwells.

(1) France, c.1830–1860. Embossed: 'ENCRE DE LA GRANDE VERTU – … SAUX' and 'L.G.'. Blown in a two-part mould. Black glass. Sand pontil scar. A similar inkwell is known embossed 'BERTINGUOIT'. p H: 5cm. Ø: 6.5cm. Cap: 6cl. Wt: 78gr.

(2) Austria. c.1860–1880. Cobalt blue. Round hexagonal shape. Glass-tipped pontil scar. H: 6.8cm. Ø: 4/4.6cm. Cap: 5cl. Wt: 46gr. See also Plate 302(3).

(3) America. c.1840. Aqua colour. Blowpipe pontil scar. H: 2.5cm. Ø: 4cm. Cap: 2cl. Wt: 40gr. Original cork box (7.8 x 7.8 x 4cm).

Ref: W. Covill (270) fig.1056 for (3)

Plate 304.

    (1) A Chinese snuff tobacco bottle, c.1780–1800. Copper ruby red glass colour named 'Oxblood red' (in French 'Sang de boeuf'). Mouth blown. Pontil scar ground away. Dim: 6.5 x 5.2 x 3cm. See also Plates 163 (1)(4) and 305(1).

    (2) A French fountain inkwell ('tea kettle' type). c.1800–1825. Gold ruby red glass colour with purple tone, a very rare unrecorded colour for an inkwell. Gold decorated. Gold plated closure. Works as a syphon. H: 6cm. Ø: 7.6/5.1cm. Cap: 15cl. Wt: 210gr. See also Plate 233 for another gold ruby coloured bottle.

Ref: W. Covill (270) fig.1240 for (2)

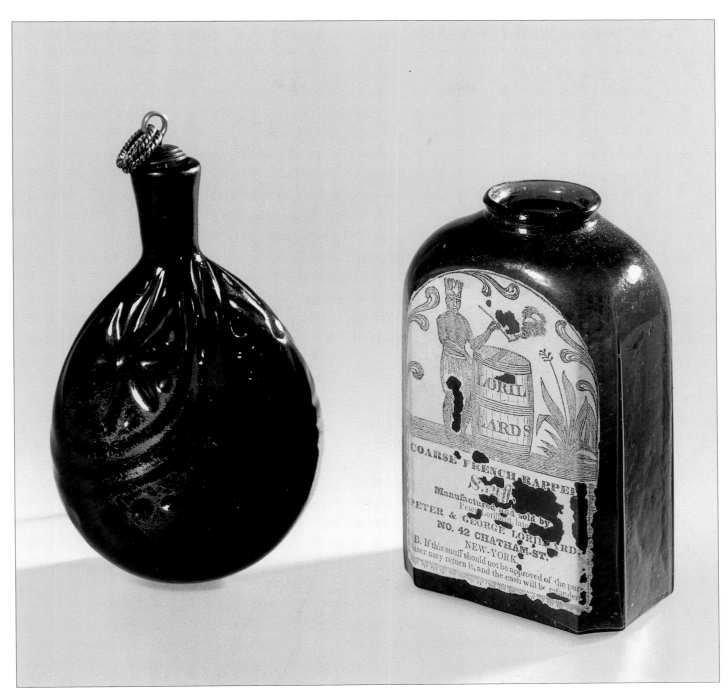

Plate 305.

    (1) A German (Bavarian Forest) or South Bohemian pocket snuff tobacco bottle. c.1780–1820. Dark amber colour. Glass-tipped pontil scar. Dim: 11.5 x 7.3 x 2.5cm. Wt: 114gr. See also Plate 163(1)(4) and 304(1).

    (2) An American utility bottle used for storing snuff tobacco. c.1830–1840. Flat octagonal shape. Label: 'LORILLARDS COARSE FRENCH RAPPEE – SNUFF – Manufactured and sold by Peter Lorillard, later Peter & George Lorillard, No 42 Chatham St. New York'. Dark grass green colour. Dim: 10.5 x 6.8 x 4.4cm. Cap: 22cl. Wt: 166gr. This bottle type is also used for preserving spices and other powder ware such as tea or cacao. A similar bottle is labelled: 'This Package Contains ¼lb. Whole Mixed Spices – The People's Tea – Spice and Baking Powder Co – Cincinnati – Ohio'. See also Plates 269(1) and 287(1).

Ref: H. Schaefer (938–940) for (1); H. McKearin (733) pl.p.277 (bottom row) for (2)

367

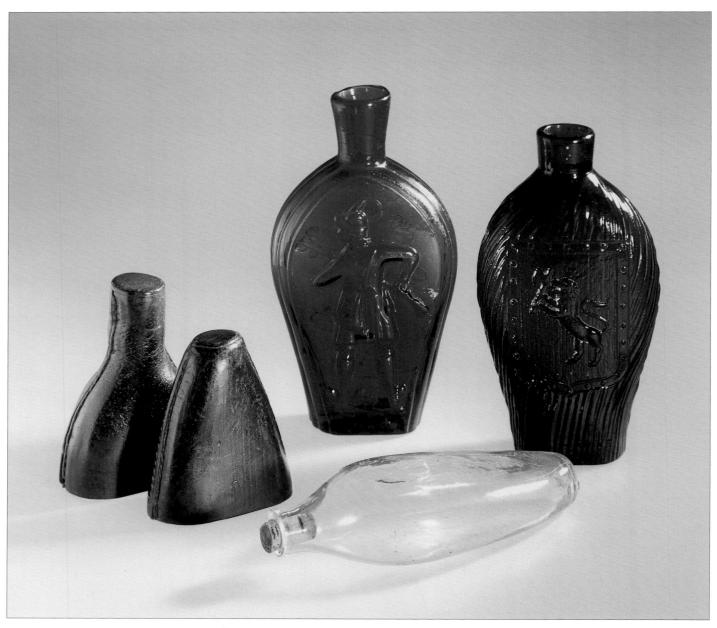

Plate 306. Three spirits flasks. Glass-tipped pontil scars. Clockwise from bottom:
  (1) England. c.1820-1850. With original leather cover to protect the thin glass. Covering glass bottles with leather, straw, reed, wood, cord, etc. has always been very common from Roman times until the early 20th century. Dim: 15.5 x 6.6 x 3.2cm. Cap: 16cl. Wt: 120gr.
  (2) Scandinavia. c.1840-1880. Cobalt blue colour. Embossed on the front with a hunter and on the reverse with a vine figuring bunches of grapes and vine leaves. Dim: 17.3cm x 9.5cm x 3cm. Cap: 23.5cl. Wt: 315gr.
  (3) Norway. c.1840-1880. Cobalt blue colour. Blown in a 54-rib dip-mould. Embossed with a lion rampant holding an axe in his claws surmounted by a crown, the coat of arms of Norway. In Norway this flask is called a 'Jaktflasker', a 'Lommeflasker' or a 'Løveflasker' (a hunting flask, a pocket flask or a lion-flask).
  B. Berntsen (156) pictures a flat round flask with the same coat of arms. The flasks were produced in clear, blue, green and amber colour and were very popular in the Scandinavian countries. Dim: 16.3 x 8.8 x 3.6cm. Cap: 24cl. Wt: 310gr.
Ref: B. Berntsens (156) Plansje XXXIV items 298, 557, 577 and Plansje XXXVI item 110 for (3)

Plate 307. Four spirits flasks.

(1) Germany (Black Forest area). c.1780-1830. Hobnail patterned. Clear glass. Glass-tipped pontil scar. Blown by the German half-post method. Dim: 12.5 x 11 x 5cm. Cap: 28cl. Wt: 235gr. See also Plate 295(1) for the same technology.

(2) Germany (Black Forest area). c.1780-1830. Amber colour. Broken rib pattern swirled to the right. Blown by the German half-post method. Glass-tipped pontil scar. Dim: 11.8 x 10.3 x 4.2cm. Cap: 20cl. Wt: 195gr. See also Plate 295(1) for the application of the same technology.

(3) South France (Rhône delta). c.1780-1800. An 'Armagnac' spirits bottle. 'Verre noir'. Blowpipe pontil scar. Dim: 17.8 x 13.5 x 4.5cm. Cap: 47cl. Wt: 400gr. See also Plates 148 (1)(2) and 277 (2).

(4) Germany/Belgium/Holland/America. c.1770-1800. A Stiegel-type flask with a 20-diamond pattern. Deep amethyst colour. Glass-tipped pontil scar. Dim: 14.8 x 10 x 5.5cm. Cap: 42cl. Wt: 115gr. Several flasks are provided with 'bottle tickets' showing that the contents might have been anything.

Refs: M. Reinartz (874) pl.1486 for (1); K-H. Poser (847) p.80, Tafel 22, item 97 for (1); J. Bellanger (148) pl.p.284 for (3); H. McKearin (733) pl.p.317 for (2) and pl.p.337 for (4)

Plate 308. Three different flasks.

(1) England. c.1820. A 'twins' flask made by fusing two flasks together immediately after being blown. Rigaree decoration. Glass-tipped pontil scar. Dim: 22 x 10 x 6cm. Cap: 14 and 16cl. Wt: 445gr.

(2) Belgium (Liège). c.1730-1750. Embossed with a 16-diamond pattern. Disc pontil scar. Clear glass. Dim: 18 x 8 x 5.5cm. Cap: 35cl. Wt: 286gr.

(3) South-west France (Grésigne Forest, Languedoc). c.1730. Blue-green colour ('verre bleu' or 'verre fougère'). Dim: 24 x 12.5 x 6.5cm. Cap: 84cl. Wt: 502gr. This flask was wickered and provided with a cord to carry it on the body when travelling, etc.

Plate 309. Three American spirits flasks.
  (1) A 'Pitkin' flask. c.1780–1810. A 36-rib pattern swirled to the right. Blown by the German half-post method. Light green colour. Blowpipe pontil scar. Dim: 13.5 x 8.6 x 5.2cm. Cap: 26cl. Wt: 140gr. See also Figure 38.
  (2) A 'chestnut' flask. c.1780–1820. Light yellowish olive green colour. Disc pontil scar. A common bottle. Dim: 14.2 x 9.6 x 6.5cm. Cap: 29cl. Wt: 155gr.
  (3) A 'Pitkin-type' flask. c.1800–1820. Medium emerald green colour. Embossed with a 16 broken rib pattern swirled to the right. Blown in the German half-post method. Pontil scar. Dim: 13.6 x 12 x 4.5cm. Cap: 36cl. Wt: 220gr.

Ref: H. McKearin (733) pl.p.315 (bottom row right) for (1), pl.p.191 (top row) for (2) and pl.p.317 (middle row right) for (3)

Plate 310. Three American spirits flasks. Olive amber colour. Blowpipe pontil scars.

(1) A 'Sunburst' flask. c.1815-1841. Embossed: 'KEEN – P&W'. Produced at the 'Keene-Marlboro-Street-Glassworks', Keene, New Hampshire (1815-1841). Flask classified by H. McKearin (733) in Groupe III-7. Dim: 14.5 x 8 x 5cm. Cap: 29cl. Wt: 220gr.

(2) An 'American Eagle' flask. c.1846-1860. Both sides embossed with the American Eagle. Attributed to the Granite Glassworks, Mill Village, Stoddard, New Hampshire (1846-1860). Flask classified by H. McKearin (733) in Groupe II-78. Dim: 18.5 x 10.5 x 5.6cm. Cap: 50cl. Wt: 305gr.

(3) A 'Cornucopia' flask. c.1813-1849. Embossed on the front with a cornucopia, the horn of plenty, coiled to left and filled with produce. The reverse shows an urn with six bars and filled with produce. The paper label informs us of the contents of the flask: 'FRENCH BRANDY from LEE & OSGOOD, DRUGGISTS and APOTHECARIES, 148 Main Street, NORWICH, CONN.' The flask is attributed to the 'Keene-Marlboro-Street-Glassworks', Keene, New Hampshire (1815-1841) and also to the Coventry Glassworks, Coventry, Connecticut (1813-1849). It is classified by H. McKearin (733) in Groupe III-7. Dim: 13.5 x 9.5 x 5cm. Cap: 26cl. Wt: 220gr.

Embossed flasks were very popular in 19th century America. Helen McKearin (733) has classified them in fifteen groups: Portrait flasks (GI), American Eagle flasks (GII), Cornucopia flasks (GIII), Masonic flasks (GIV), Railroad flasks (GV), Baltimore Monument flasks (GVI), Cabin bottles (GVII), Sunburst flasks (GVIII), Scroll flasks (Violin or Scroll) (GIX), Miscellaneous flasks (GX), Pike's Peak flasks (GXI), Shield and Clasped Hands flasks (GXII), Pictorial flasks (GXIII), Traveller's Companion flasks (GXIV) and finally the Lettered flasks (GXV).

Ref: H. McKearin (733)

Plate 311.

(1) An American 'violin' or 'scroll' spirits flask. c.1845–1855. Embossed on both sides with scrolls, a large fleur-de-lis, a medium eight-pointed star and a tiny pearl. Probably produced by the Pittsburg Flint Glass Works in Pittsburg, Pennsylvania (1802–1882). Aquamarine colour. Blowpipe pontil scar. Classified by H. McKearin (733) in Groupe IX-37. Dim: 14.7 x 10.2 x 5.2cm. Cap: 25cl. Wt: 195gr.

(2) An American handled whisky bottle. c.1855–1870. Vertical rib pattern. Amber colour. Blowpipe pontil scar. Sometimes sealed as, for example, with 'STAR WHISKEY – W.B. CROWELL JR. – NEW YORK'. H: 20.5cm. Ø: 11cm. Cap: 71cl. Wt: 585gr.

(3) An American conical eight panelled ink bottle (an 'umbrella' ink). c.1840–1855. Deep yellowish amber. Glass-tipped pontil scar. Labelled: 'Bradford's Fine Blue Black Writing Fluid! Rindge, N.H.' Thought to be blown at the Stoddard Glass Works, New Hampshire. H: 6.5cm. Ø: 5.8/6.2cm. Cap: 4cl. Wt: 85gr.

Ref: H. McKearin (733) p.626 for (1) and col.pl.XV for (2); W. Covill (270) fig.131 for (3)

Plate 312. A Dutch rare coloured dumpy 'ball-stoppered' aerated liquid bottle, today named a 'Codd Patent 4' bottle relating to Codd's fourth British Patent No 2621 of 3 Sept. 1872. The front of the bottle is embossed with a girl pouring water out of two pitchers. The rear is embossed 'DE SNELLE SPRONG – TEGELEN'. This 'Codd' bottle (in Dutch 'knikkerfles') was made between 1889 and 1950. Emerald green colour. H: 19cm. Ø: 7.8cm. Cap: 26.5cl. Wt: 690gr.

Hiram Codd (1838-1887) of Camberwell, London was the manufacturer and inventor of a most popular bottle for aerated liquids such as mineral water, soda water, lemonade, etc. In the neck of a bottle are formed two inclined projecting ridges, one on each side, and the lower part of the neck is contracted. A glass marble, captive inside the neck, seals the bottle by the gas pressure of the aerated liquid holding the marble up against a rubber washer just inside the rim. The bottle is filled whilst upside down. After the inside gas pressure is formed, the bottle is turned upright and the marble held up. When the marble is pushed in to open the bottle, it rolls down the projecting ridges until it is stopped by the contraction. It is then allowed to roll to the opposite side of the ridges which prevent it from returning when the bottle is inclined for pouring the liquid. The pushing on the marble was done with a Codd bottle opener (Plates 313(1) and 315(3)).

In his British Patent No 3448 of 1874 Hiram Codd claims an **earthenware (clay) 'Codd-bottle'.** It never turned up until today.

From the late 19th to the mid-20th century Codd bottles were very popular all over Europe. See also Figure 43 and Plates 314(1)(2).

Refs: R. Harrison (468), front cover and p.137; E. Fletcher (385); P. Douglas (339); R. Dunn (348); British Patents

Plate 313. Four European 'Codd' bottles and an opener. Between 1889–1950.

  (1) A 'Codd' bottle opener. The glass marble was pushed down by the peg protruding inside the turned wood opener. See also Plate 315(3).

  (2) Germany. Emerald glass colour. Dumpy shape. Embossed: 'GLASHÜTTENWERK OLDENBURG/Gr.– No 4 – HS & C°'. In Germany this Codd is named a 'Knickerflasche'. H: 19.3cm. Ø: 7.3cm. Cap: 31cl. Wt: 600gr.

  (3) Belgium. Dark amber. Embossed (front): 'CH. ANTOIN VERHULPEN – IN DEN GROOTEN BAK – MECHELEN'; (back): 'MADE IN ENGLAND – JULES SAMSON – LIEGE'. H: 21.7cm. Ø: 6cm. Cap: 24.5cl. Wt: 580gr.

  (4) France. Clear amber. Embossed: 'GRILLON & Cie'. H: 30cm. Ø: 6.6cm. Cap: 52.5cl. Wt: 815gr.

  (5) Germany. Dark green. Embossed (front). 'BRAUSELIMONADE'; (back) 'F. WIEHE'. H: 18.5cm. Ø: 6.5cm. Cap: 26.5cl. Wt: 445gr.

See also Plate 312 for more information on Hiram Codd.

Plate 314. Four European 'Codd' bottles. Between 1889-1950.

    (1) England. Clear glass with a lip in blue glass. Embossed (front): 'W. WRIGHT – MINERAL WATER MANUFACT. – LONG EATON'; (back): 'RELIANCE PATENT – SOLE MAKER – DAN RYLANDS – BARNSLEY'. Dan Rylands' British Patent No 1811 of 8 February 1886 claims that 'internal projections are made in the bottle-neck to prevent the ball from rolling into the mouth while pouring and also other projections at right-angles to the former to prevent the ball from jamming the rotating brush used in cleaning the bottle'. In order to identify the bottle-maker, Dan Rylands introduced in 1889 blue, amber or green 'coloured lips' as a new style of marking bottles. By this means a mineral water manufacturer could detect his bottles at a considerable distance when still in the crate. The 'coloured lips' forced other Codd-bottle makers to produce their bottles in amber, blue, brown, black or green glass for the same reason of identification. See also Plate 314(2). H: 19cm. Ø: 5.4cm. Cap: 20.8cl. Wt: 332gr.

    (2) England. Clear glass with lip in amber glass. Embossed (front): 'THIS BOTTLE IS THE PROPERTY OF R. WHITE – CAMBERWELL – NO DEPOSIT CHARGED'. The back reads: 'RYLANDS PATENT – SOLE MAKER – RYLANDS – BARNSLEY/BUYING OR SELLING THIS BOTTLE IS ILLEGAL'. See also Plate 314(1). H: 18.5cm. Ø: 5.4cm. Cap: 17.8cl. Wt: 392gr.

    (3) France. Clear amber. Embossed. 'FRIT FRERES – SARLAT'. H: 20.5cm. Ø: 6.2cm. Cap: 27cl. Wt: 524gr.

    (4) Belgium/England. Dark amber. Embossed 'J. BAKER – ANVERS/BRUXELLES – DEPOSE – JB – TRADE MARK'. H: 21.5cm. Ø: 5.8cm. Cap: 23cl. Wt: 565gr.

See also Plate 312 for more information on Hiram Codd.

Refs: E. Fletcher (385); British Patents

Plate 315. Three European 'Codd' bottles. Between 1889–1950.
(1) England. Rare coloured dark cobalt blue. Embossed (front):'J.W. – S.H. [intertwined] – THE RYLANDS – 4 – BARNSLEY'; (back): 'J. WADSWORTH – ST. IVES – HUNTS'.. The neck of the Codd is embossed with 'LEMON', the contents of the bottle (rare). H: 18.7cm. Ø: 5.7cm. Cap: 20cl. Wt: 410gr.
(2) Hungary. Deep cobalt blue. Round twelve-sided. Embossed: 'ÖZV. WINKLER SANDOR NE – ERZSEBET – SZIKVIZGYARA – ARADON. H: 24.2cm. Ø: 6.5cm. Cap: 33cl. Wt: 640gr.
(3) France. Clear blue bottle with green marble. Embossed: 'DAMADE – VIVIER/ CORBIE – SOMME'. The top of the 'Codd' shows a Codd opener as pictured in Plate 313(1).
See also Plate 312 for more information on Hiram Codd.

Plate 316.

  (1) A German (Spessart) early 17th century fired clay die for pressing 'raspberry prunts' on rummers and bottles. Prunts were often impressed to give a semblance of fruit. Die Ø: 21mm. L: 45mm. Collection H. van Vliet, Amsterdam.

  (2) A 'raspberry prunt' seal (in German: eine 'Beerennuppe') on the shoulder of a broken bottle excavated in Holland. 'Raspberry prunt' seals are only used for decorating the bottle. Bottle made in North Germany (Holstein) c.1665–1700 and has a typical clear green forest glass colour. Die. Ø: 26mm. H: 13cm. See also Plate 116(1).

Refs: E. Tochterman (1037) p.50, Abb. 14 for (1); F. Nagel (54), Lot 222 for (1)

Plate 317. A German (Brandenburg) die with handle made in fired clay for pressing the initials **'KK'** of a private person on the seal of a bottle. Excavated at the Waldglashütte (forest glass house) Chorin II (1747–1772).

This type of die was used for producing small amounts (200–300) of bottles for private persons, pharmacists, etc., because it was relatively cheap compared with a bronze or brass die. Note also that stoneware dies never produce such a clear seal as metal dies. Die Ø: 24mm. L: 5cm. See also Plate 214(7)

Ref: K. Friese (418) Tafel 3

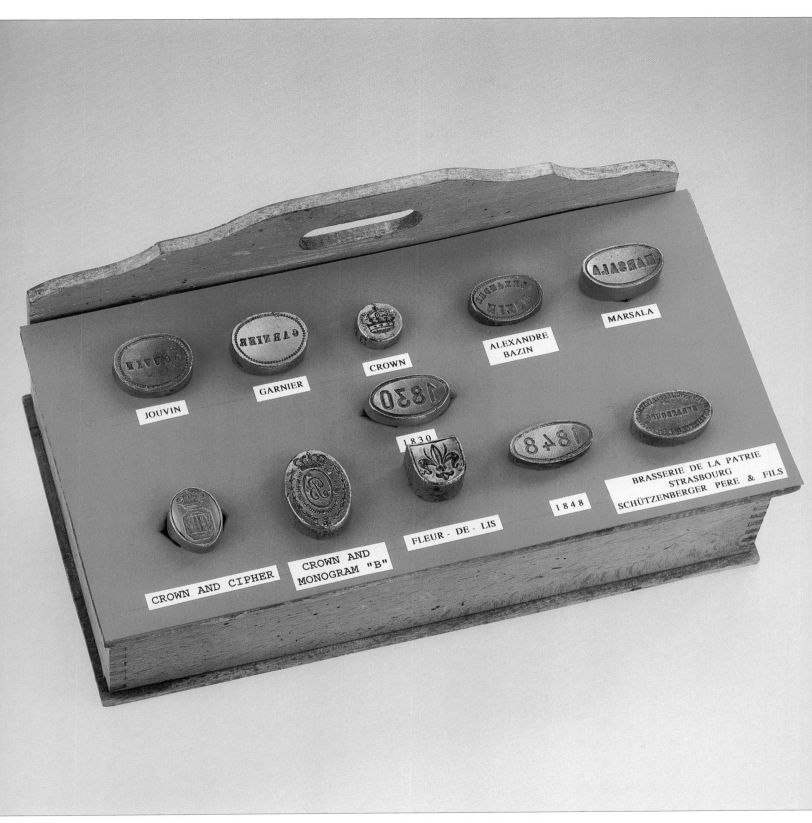

JOUVIN

GARNIER

CROWN

1830

ALEXANDRE
BAZIN

MARSALA

CROWN AND CIPHER

CROWN AND
MONOGRAM "B"

FLEUR - DE - LIS

1848

BRASSERIE DE LA PATRIE
STRASBOURG
SCHÜTZENBERGER PERE & FILS

Plate 318. A box showing eleven French bronze or brass dies for pressing glass seals on bottles. Their wooden handles are missing. From c.1700 onwards until 1848. Dim: (box) 9 x 32 x 17cm. See also Figure 28 and Plates 316, 317, 319 and 320.
Ref: T. Fogelberg (394) p.196 shows four similar dies

Plate 319. Three English brass dies to impress wax seals on bottles and jars. Private names, shipping marks, dates, figures, initial letters or names of wines, brandies, etc. may be engraved on the dies. c.1880. Die Ø: 26mm (1), 32mm (2) and (3). See also Plates 318 and 320.
Ref: Farrow & Jackson (31) p.148

Plate 320. An English brass die with an ebony handle for impressing 'PORT' on the wax seal of a port wine bottle. c.1880. Die. Ø: 14mm. L: 8cm. See also Plate 319.
Ref: Farrow & Jackson (31) p.148

Plate 321. Two French hand corking tubes, the first in a wooden body, the second in a brass body. The cork is put into the body and then pushed into the bottle with the handle. These corking tubes were very popular in the 19th century in most European countries. L: (1) 28cm, (2) 25cm (in closed position).
Ref: Farrow & Jackson (31), p.13

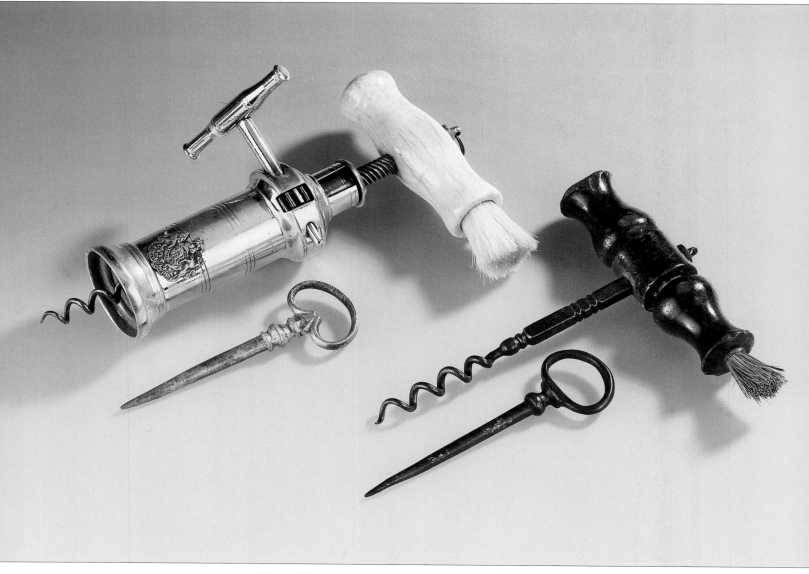

Plate 322.

(1) An English 'rack and pinion' King's corkscrew with a Thomason type bronze barrel and an applied coat of arms. Late 18th/first half 19th century. L.18cm.

(2) (4) Two late 17th-early 18th century Dutch cork extractors in the form of a prong. After being inserted obliquely into the cork the prong is pivoted and extracts the cork. Many 17th-18th century bottles are damaged (chipped) at the lip or string rim, due to levering out the cork with the prong. Notice the deformations at the top of each prong. L: (2) 10cm. (bronze), (4) 10.5cm. (iron).

(3) A simple English 'T' corkscrew. Turned wooden handle with brush and wire helix. The brush served as a bottle-mouth cleaner. Late 19th century. L: 14cm.

Refs: B.M. Watney (1081); P. de Sanctis (935)

Plate 323. An English syphon-action bottle filling machine. c.1890-1900. Used for filling bottles with wines, spirits, delicate liqueurs, beer, etc. This four syphon was used as on a strong beer bottling machine. The beer was poured from a tun in the syphon reservoir and when a bottle was put on the filling machine the beer started to flow into the bottle by syphon action. Dim: 60 x 50 x 40cm.

Ref: W. Chester-Master (20); Farrow & Jackson (31) figured on p.27, no.3

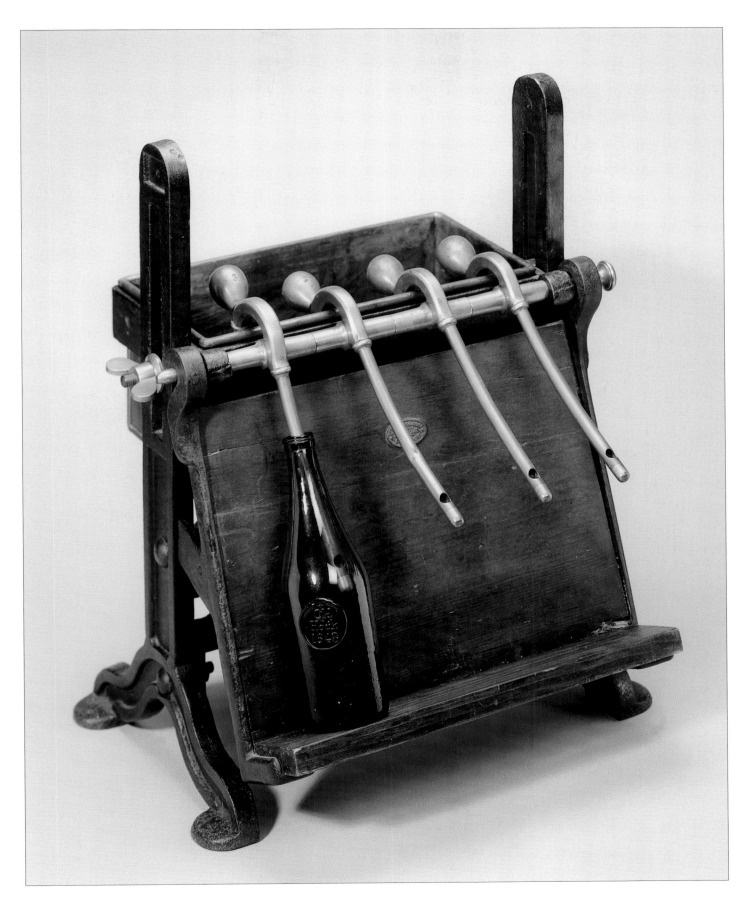

386

Plate 325. (top) An English 'trade token'. The *Shorter Oxford English Dictionary on Historical Principles* (1973) defines a token as 'a stamped piece of metal, issued as a medium of exchange by a private person or company, who engage to take it back at its normal value, giving goods or legal currency for it' (since 1598). The merchant who used this token as private change embossed his references and wishes on both sides of the token.

The front shows a squat cylindrical utility bottle surrounded by the motto: 'MORE TRADE AND FEWER TAXES'. The reverse pictures a standing woman with an anchor – symbol of hope (on lower taxes) – surrounded by the motto 'PROSPERITY TO OLD ENGLAND'. The copper token has a diameter of 29mm. and is dated c.1780.

Tokens were also popular in Holland (Friesland), Norway and Germany (Saxony) from the late 16th century.

Plate 324. (left) A bottle washing apparatus, hand revolving type. France, Belgium, Holland, England. c.1880-1920. H: 80cm. Ø: 30cm.
Ref: Farrow & Jackson (31) figured on p.30

Plate 326. A 17th century Dutch delft blue wall tile picturing an innkeeper (in Dutch: 'herbergier') carrying bottles. Dim: 13 x 13cm.

Plate 327. A French decorative faience wall plate depicting ten Burgundy wine bottles standing on the table. The text reads: 'Falon, Maître de Vin: au Français invétéré, le bon vin est assuré' (Falon, Winemaster: to the French inveterate drinker, the good wine is assured) and 'J'suis pris d'la! J'suis poitrinaire (I am congested. I am consumptive). Dated. c.1840. Plate Ø: 24cm.

Plate 328. A Dutch polychrome faience statue depicting a Bacchus boy sitting on a tun containing red (in old Dutch: 'root') wine and dated '1776'. The bottom of the statue is marked with the initials **PAK** for **P**ieter **A**driaensz. **K**ocks, a Dutch faience maker whose initials were still in use after his death (first quarter 18th century). H: 13.5cm.

Plate 329. A Belgian polychrome statue made of terracotta and showing a man selling filled bottles. c.1830. H: 69cm.

GLOSSARY OF BOTTLEMAKING TERMS

Alloa Glassworks: A glasshouse at Alloa, Scotland, making mainly black glass bottles of unusual shapes and often decorated with rigarees and/or white or coloured flecks in Nailsea style. See Plate 51.

ancient glass bottle: Pre-Roman and ancient Roman glass bottles. See Plates 244 and 245.

annealing: The process of slowly cooling a completed bottle in an auxiliary part of the glass furnace or in a separate annealing furnace. This is an integral part of glassmaking because if a hot glass bottle is allowed to cool too quickly it will be highly strained by the time it reaches room temperature; indeed, it may break as it cools.

antique glass bottle: Frequently used to mean bottles more than 100 years old.

applied colour labelling: A method of decorating by applying glass of low melting temperature to a bottle through a metal screen and then baking it in a muffle furnace. See Plate 293(3).

base: The bottom of a bottle.

batch: The raw materials, properly proportioned and mixed, for delivery to the glass furnace.

Beinglas: Bone glass. The German term for milk glass. See Plate 227(2).

bitters: A patent or proprietary medicine containing alcohol.

black glass: (1) A popular term for a glass bottle colour of dark green, dark brown or any other colour that is so dark as to appear almost black.
(2) A bottle term used since the 16th century for dark brown or dark green glass resulting from the inclusion of oxides of iron, manganese and sulphur combined with the use of a reducing furnace atmosphere (e.g. from coal, peat…).
When increasing the melting temperature and the residence time the colour changes from brown to olive-green and light green. Black glass was first made in Lorraine, North-east France, and Southern Belgium in the early 16th century, where it was called 'verre noir'. It became very popular in England from 1615 onwards; later the process was sometimes adapted for use with blast furnace slag in those regions producing the latter. See Figure 31.

blank: (1) A parison or preliminary shape from which a finished article is formed, or mould for producing same.
(2) Any article of glass on which subsequent forming or finishing is required.

blank mould: The mould which first shapes the glass in the manufacture of hollow ware.

Blatte: See Hamburger Blatte.

blister: An imperfection; a relatively large bubble or gaseous inclusion in the glass bottle.

block: A wooden dipper-like device cut out on one side and used during free blowing to give symmetrical form to a bottle in its early stages.

blow mould: The mould in which a blown glass article is finally shaped.

blow-and-blow process: The process of forming hollow ware in which both the preliminary and final shapes are formed by air pressure. See Figure 44.

blowing iron: See 'blowpipe' and Figure 37.

blown glass: Glassware shaped by air pressure, as by mouth blowing or by compressed air.

blowpipe: An iron tube, usually up to 1.7m long, for mouth blowing glass. Blowpipes have a conical mouthpiece at one end; the other end is thickened for gathering and retaining the molten glass. The tube is about 2-2.5cm in diameter and sometimes has tubular wooden grips at positions where the glassblower must hold it. See Figure 37.

Bocksbeutel (German): A bottle of a side-flattened, spherical body and a short neck, traditionally used for Steinwein from the Franconian wine region (Würzburg) of Germany. Bottle term in use since 1785. See Plates 219 and 220.

Bohemian crystal: A term used for colourless glass with a slight yellow tone, obtained by adding Bohemian chalk to the glass instead of lead. Bohemian chalk contains a high amount of zinc and other elements, such as lead and cadmium. The glass has a high refractive index and is particularly brilliant, like 'lead crystal' glass. See also 'crystal' and Plate 91.

bone-ash: Ashes of calcined bones, used as an opacifier in making opaque white glass, milk glass, and opaline.

bonne femme: The French name for a colourless, cylindrical, optically blown decanting bottle made at Liège (Belgium) in the early 18th century. See Plate 295(2).

bottle glass: A naturally coloured, dark greenish or brownish glass used for making early glass bottles.

capacity: The volume of liquid a bottle holds when it is filled to the brim. This represents the maximum capacity of the bottle. The functional capacity is always less than the brimful capacity. It should be stressed that this is the liquid capacity of a bottle. Powdered substances may have been sold by weight.

carboy: A large bottle normally holding five to fifty litres of liquid. See Plates 59 and 154.

case bottle: A bottle with a square cross section, sometimes widening from base to shoulder, with a short neck and indented base, and usually in dark green glass. See Plates 192, 206 and 253.

case-gin bottle: A case bottle used for containing gin. See Figure 14 and Plate 85.

cased glass: Glassware whose surface layer has a different composition from that of the main glass body.

casing: The application of a layer of glass on glass of contrasting colour. The glassblower either gathers a layer over another gather, or inflates a gob of hot glass inside a pre-formed blank of another colour. The two components adhere and are inflated together until they have the desired form. See also 'flashing'.

chestnut flask: A free-blown and semi-flattened flask. See Plate 281(2).

chill mark: A wrinkled surface condition on glassware resulting from uneven contact in the mould prior to forming.

clear glass: Colourless, transparent glass.

closure: A device, such as a cork, cap, or stopper, used to seal a bottle.

Codd bottle: A type of bottle for effervescent soft drinks that had a rubber washer in the neck and a loose glass ball (like a marble) that was forced against the washer by pressure when a bottle was full and sealed the contents. To release the pressure and permit pouring, a wooden dowel was used. The invention is attributed to Hiram Codd, c.1872. See Figure 43 and Plate 312.

cold painting: Application of paint or gilding to finished glass bottles.

container: Container is the general term applied to glass bottles and jars. Generally a bottle has a small mouth, but may have a comparatively wide mouth, and a long well-defined neck. A jar has a wider mouth, the diameter of which approaches that of the body, and usually has a very short neck.

copper ruby: Deep red glass coloured by the addition of copper oxide to the batch; in France called 'sang de boeuf' (ox-blood). This red colour should not be confused with 'gold ruby' (see below), which has a deep red colour with a light purple tint. See Plate 304(1).

crackled: Glassware, the surface of which has been intentionally cracked by water immersion and partially healed by reheating before final shaping.

crizzle: An imperfection in the form of a multitude of fine surface fractures.

crown cork: A metal cap with cork liner used on soda and beer bottles.

crystal: A term for (colourless) lead glass which has a high refractive index and which is particularly brilliant. See also 'Bohemian crystal'.

cucurbit: A glass bottle, used with an alembic, to contain a liquid that is to be distilled.

cullet: (1) Waste or broken glass, usually suitable as an addition to raw batch.
(2) Foreign cullet – cullet from an outside source.

(3) Domestic cullet (factory cullet) – cullet from within the plant.
(4) The portion of a glass article which will later be cut off and discarded or remelted.

cure: A patent or proprietary medicine sold as an all-purpose remedy.

decanter bottle: A type of glass bottle that preceded the decanter and was used for bringing wine to the table from the cask. See Plate 49.

decolorizing: The process of making glass clear by the addition of manganese, selenium, or arsenic to the batch.

demijohn: A large bottle normally holding five to fifty litres of liquid. See Plates 59 and 154.

dip mould: A one-piece mould open at the top to facilitate removal of the expanded gather of glass. See Figures 37 and 39.

dip-moulded and expanded: Glass that is blown into a small one-piece dip mould in order to give it a pattern. It is removed from the mould, blown, and expanded, with the design being expanded as well.

double bottle: A bottle that is divided internally into two separate compartments each with its own mouth or spout. See Plate 246.

double-cone bottle: A glass bottle in the form of an inverted, truncated cone with a flat base, on the rim of which appears to be superimposed another conically-shaped bottle tapering upward to form a slender neck. The rim of the upper cone projects slightly over the lower cone, in an overhanging fashion. They were made in Germany (Rhine-Main area) in the 15th-17th centuries. The German name is 'Doppelkonisch gestauchte Flasche'. See Plate 188(2).

embossed: Raised letters and symbols created on the glass through use of full-size moulds, either blown, pressed, or machine-made. This was the most common form of marking on bottles in the 18th, 19th and 20th centuries. See Plate 86.

empontilling: The process of attaching a metal rod to the bottom of a bottle to hold it while finishing the upper portion of the bottle. See Figure 46.

figural bottle: A moulded bottle in the form of a person or any of a variety of objects. See Plate 161.

fire-polished: By re-exposing glass bottles to sufficient heat the glass surface can be made smooth, glossy and sharp edges rounded. For lips, this results in the top of the lip being rounded and slightly thickened. See Figure 37.

flashing: The application of a very thin layer of glass of one colour over a layer of contrasting colour. This is achieved by dipping a gather of hot glass into a crucible containing hot glass of the second colour. See also 'casing'.

flask: Originally designed as a travelling bottle, in section it has one or two flattened sides and approaches an oval. Vertically, flasks come in a variety of shapes or decoration, e.g. violin, scroll, and horseshoe. See Plate 310.

forest glass: Glass made in the forest glasshouses of Europe in the late Middle Ages and the early modern period. Most forest glass was fluxed with potash derived from the wood with which the furnaces were fuelled. It is green, blue, yellow or brown because of iron impurities in the sand from which it is made. The German term for forest glass is 'Waldglas'. See also 'verre fougère'.

forming: The shaping of hot glass.

free-blown: Glass formed by blowing and hand and tool manipulation alone, without the aid of a mould. See also 'offhand glass' and Figure 37.

French blue-green (verre bleu, verre fougère): A term used to describe a group of bottles produced in South-west France in the 17th and 18th centuries. The glass is characterized by its colour, a distinctive blue-green. See also 'verre fougère' and Plate 173.

fusion: See 'melting'.

gather: (1) The mass of molten glass picked up by the glassmaker on the punty or blowing iron.
(2) To get glass from a pot or tank on the pipe or punty.

German half-post: An old technique of blowing 'ribbed', 'fluted', 'swirled' or 'columned' patterns on glass bottles which became very popular in Germany from the 15th century.

The dip moulds utilized by this method were about one-third the size of the finished object, with perpendicular ridges or grooves cut into its inner walls. The first gather or 'post' was formed into a parison and allowed to chill harder than usual. This was redipped to cover it with a second coating of the hot glass. If the second gather did not extend the full length of the parison, it was called a 'half post'. (The resulting ridge of such a specimen is very apparent near the neck of the bottle.) After securing the second gather, the parison was quickly lowered into the mould and inflated so that its sides pressed against the ribs of the mould. After removal from the open mould, the bottle can be further inflated and shaped by the off-hand methods. The ribbed design impressed by the dip-mould will remain on the surface of the bottle.

The method was very popular in the Alpine regions of Europe, namely Austria, South Germany and Switzerland, and also became very popular in America from the late 18th century onwards. See also 'Pitkin flasks', 'half-post' and Figure 38.

glass: An inorganic product of fusion which has cooled to a rigid condition without crystallizing. Glass is typically hard and brittle and has a conchoidal fracture. It may be colourless or coloured, and transparent to opaque. Masses or bodies of glass may be made coloured, translucent, or opaque by the presence of dissolved, amorphous, or crystalline material.

glass seals: Applied glass blobs on the body or shoulder of a bottle are marked by pressing a small clay or metal die with a design on to the hot glass. The inscriptions on the seals may apply to individuals, to kings, or to specific products. Seals were most frequently used on bottles and are more common on bottles dating between 1650-1850. See Figure 26.

glassblower's chair: A workbench with long arms and extended seat specially designed for a glassblower to use in his work. See Figure 37.

glass-blowing: The shaping of hot glass by air pressure.

glassgall: A turquoise blue opaque sulphate salt of sodium (Na_2SO_4). A normal glass dissolves up to 5% Na_2SO_4 as sodium silicate (Na_2SiO_3), but if the content is above 5% the excess sodium sulphate swims on the molten glass surface and is opaque turquoise blue in colour, whereas the melt for bottle production is mainly black (olive brown or olive green).

This turquoise colour sometimes appears on the surface of a black bottle, also when blast furnace slag is used in the batch.

Gall is often used to make the pontil, mostly in Belgium. The German name is 'Glasgalle' or 'Glasspeck'; in French 'la graisse du verre'. See Plate 36.

glory hole: An opening exposing the hot interior of a furnace used to reheat the ware in hand-working. See Figure 37.

gob: (1) A portion of hot glass delivered by a feeder.
(2) A portion of hot glass gathered on a punty or pipe.

gold ruby: Deep red glass coloured by the addition of gold chloride to the batch. After producing the bottle it is cooled and looks greyish, but when reheated a deep red colour with a purple tint develops. The method was developed by Johann Kunckel shortly before 1679 at the Drewitz Glasshouse, Potsdam, near Berlin. The German term is 'Goldrubinglas'. See also 'copper ruby' and Plate 233.

half-post method: A process of moulding an object by which a gather ('post') is dipped again into the pot so as to be covered half-way ('half-post'), and thus is thicker on the lower half. See also 'German half-post method' and Figure 38.

Hamburger Blatte: a German side-flattened onion bottle first mentioned in the Thuringian glassmakers' price-list 'Glas-Taxa' (858) from 1735-1737 as 'Hamburger blatte Bouteille' (a Hamburg flat bottle). See Plate 254(2).

hand-blown: Glass formed by blowing and manipulation, with the use of moulds. See Figure 37.

hard glass: (1) A glass of exceptionally high viscosity at elevated temperatures.
(2) A glass of high softening point.
(3) Commonly refers to a glass difficult to melt.
(4) A glass hard to scratch.

historical flask: A flask embossed with portraits, emblems, symbols, or inscriptions. See Plate 310.

iridescence: The quality of being iridescent; the interchange of colours as in the rainbow, mother-of-pearl, etc.; a play of glittering and changing colours. See also 'patination' and Plate 47.

iridescent: Displaying colours like those of the rainbow, etc.; glittering or flashing with interchanging colours. This term should not be used to describe patination. See Plate 47.

jar: A deep wide-mouthed utilitarian bottle for holding a variety of substances. See Plate 290.

kick-up: A concavity in the base of a bottle, where it has been pushed in by a tool. The provision of a kick reduces its capacity. See Figure 37.

kuttrolf: A bottle with one long, narrow neck or with the neck or body divided into two or more tubes. The 'kuttrolf', which has Roman antecedents, was produced by German glassworkers in the later Middle Ages. See Plates 190(2) and 298.

label under glass bottle: A bottle with the label stuck on the inside of the bottle or jar to protect the label against damage from outside. See Plate 292(2).

lampworking: Forming glass articles from tubing and cane by heating in a gas flame.

lead glass: Glass containing a substantial proportion of lead oxide (PbO).

lehr (leer): A long, tunnel-shaped oven for annealing glass by continuous passage.

lime: CaO, or a mixture of CaO and MgO.

limestone: Either calcitic limestone ($CaCO_3$) or dolomitic limestone ($CaCO_3$-$MgCO_3$).

lip: The lip is the upper part of the bottle next to the mouth.

marble bottle: See 'Codd bottle', Figure 43 and Plate 312.

marver: (1) A flat plate on which a hand gather of glass is rolled, shaped, and cooled. See Figure 37.
(2) Also the process of doing same.

measuring bottle: In French 'une mesure'. A bottle whose liquid capacity is of specified quantity. Some are of polygonal or circular section with a high neck and a funnel-shaped mouth and were made in a blue-green colour in South-west France (Languedoc) in the 17th and 18th century, for measuring wine and oil. See Plate 175.

melting: The thermal process by which the charge is completely converted into molten glass free from undissolved batch.

milk glass: Opaque white glass. See Plate 227(2).

mould: (1) A metal, ceramic, or wooden form with an interior design in which a gather of glass was expanded to give it shape and/or decoration. See Figures 40 and 41.
(2) A form used for shaping molten glass. Some moulds (e.g. dip moulds) impart a pattern to the parison, which is then withdrawn, and blown and tooled to the desired shape and size; other moulds are used to give the object its final form.

mould blowing: Blowing a parison of hot glass in a mould. The glass is forced against the inner surfaces of the mould and assumes its shape.

mould-blown: Glass formed in whole or in part by the use of moulds.

mould marks: Raised lines or ridges left on the body of a piece of mould-blown glass. The marks are created when the hot glass is forced out of the interstices between parts of the mould by the pressure of blowing or pressing. See Plate 209.A.

moulded glass: Glass which is formed in a mould, as distinct from cast, rolled, drawn, or offhand ware.

mouth: The opening at the top of the bottle. 'Mouth' may also be used in a general way as in 'wide-mouthed' or 'narrow-mouthed' bottle or jar.

multiple bottle: A bottle that is divided internally into separate compartments, each with its own mouth or spout. See Plate 246.

Nailsea glass bottles: Black glass bottles with white or coloured flecks thereon, first produced at the Nailsea glasshouse near Bristol, England, in the late 18th century. Glass bottles of the Nailsea type are now mostly attributed to unidentified glassworks other than the Nailsea glasshouse. See Plate 50.

nipt-diamond-waies: A style of network decoration on glassware, somewhat in the form of diamonds, made from applied or mould-blown glass threads pincered together at regular alternate intervals (hence 'nipped diamond-wise'). The term was used by George Ravenscroft in his price list of 1677. See Plate 67.

offhand glass: Glass produced by the offhand process.

offhand process: The process of forming glassware by a glassblower, working without the aid of moulds.

opal glass: A translucent white glass. Seen by transmitted light it shows brownish or reddish tones. See Plate 227(3).

opaline: A slightly translucent type of glass, opacified with ashes of calcined bones and coloured with metallic oxides, usually pastel hues but sometimes whitish like (but less dense than) opaque white glass and sometimes of strong colours (e.g. dark blue) or black. See Plate 227(1).

opaque white glass: A type of opacified glass that has the appearance of white porcelain. The Italian term is 'lattimo'; the German 'Milchglas'; the French 'blanc de lait'. See Plate 227(2).

open pot: A glass-melting pot, open to the flames and gases of combustion in the furnace.

overlay: A method of decorating glass objects by applying several layers of glass, often in different colours. See Plate 233.

oxidizing agent: A compound which decomposes during the melting of fining stages supplying oxygen to other batch chemicals.

parison: A preliminary shape or blank from which a glass article is to be formed. See Figure 44.

parison mould: See 'blank mould'. See Figure 44.

parting line: Line or seam on glassware resulting from the joint of two mould parts.

patination: Coloured layered crust that is produced by decomposition of the glass (weathering) and is quite distinct from the unaffected glass itself. Patination should be regarded as a natural process of decomposition of glass buried in the ground or in water. The presence of patination (or its absence) is no guarantee of age. Some bottle glass is more prone to decomposition and some environments tend to accelerate the process. See also 'iridescence' and Plate 254.

pictorial flask: A flask bearing a purely decorative motif.

pinched: Hot glass nipped together by tools.

Pitkin flasks: Small bottles of green glass made by pattern-moulding a second gather of glass over a first layer (half-post method). Originally made in the United States at the Pitkin factory in East Manchester, Connecticut. See also 'German half-post' and 'half-post'. See Figure 38.

pocket-flask: A flat flask made to be carried on the person, usually in the hip pocket. See Plate 306(1).

poison bottle: A type of glass bottle used for containing poisons. See Plate 248.

pontil or punty: The pontil is a long iron rod attached to the base or bottom of a bottle that is still hot to hold the bottle while the lip, rim, or mouth is being formed. When the pontil is detached from the bottle there is a scar left on the base, called a pontil mark. Five different empontilling methods have been identified based on the distinct pontil marks left on the bases of glass objects. They are glass-tipped pontil, sand pontil, blowpipe pontil, disc pontil, and the bare iron pontil. See also 'pontil mark' and Figures 45-48.

pontil mark: The scar or mark left on the base of glassware after the removal of the pontil. Different types of empontilling techniques leave different types of pontil marks. The type and size of the mark may be useful in determining country of origin. See also 'pontil' and Figures 45-48.

pontil mark diameter: The outer diameter of the pontil mark.

pontil scar: The scar of rough glass (generally circular) left on the finished bottle bottom after removal of the pontil. See Figures 47 and 48.

pot: A one-piece refractory container for molten glass.
Open pot: a pot wherein the glass surface is not protected from the furnace atmosphere.
Closed pot: a pot having a crown protecting the glass from the furnace atmosphere.

pot furnace: A furnace for melting glass in pots. See Figures 32 and 35.

potash: Potassium carbonate (K_2CO_3). It is, as the alternative to soda, the alkali ingredient of glass. It was obtained in early Germany and Bohemia by burning beechwood, oak, or certain other timber (see 'Waldglas') and in France by burning fern and bracken (see 'verre fougère'). The process was to leach the wood ashes, evaporate the lye, and calcine the residue.

potassium-lime glass: A glass containing three major compounds in varying proportions: silica, potash, and lime. Forest glass is a common type of potassium-lime glass.

press-and-blow process: A process of glass manufacture in which the parison is pressed and subsequently blown to form the final shape. See Figure 44.

pressed glass: Glassware formed by mechanical pressure between a mould and a plunger, without blowing.

prunts: Small lumps of glass that are added to a bottle's surface as decoration. They can be shaped like berries, pointed cones, etc. See Plate 162.

punty: (1) A gathering iron of solid cross section.
(2) A device to which ware is attached for holding during fire polishing or finishing. See also 'pontil' and Figure 46.

purple glass: Glass coloured purple by the use of oxide of manganese.

push-up: When the basal indentation of a bottle is deep, it is referred to as a push-up or a kick-up. See Plate 129.

push-up mark: Mark or marks left by tools used to form the push-up on the bottom of a bottle. These marks occur as impressions, raised areas, or areas with iron oxide or other deposits.

raw batch: A glass charge without cullet.

raw cullet: A glass charge made totally of cullet.

reducing agent: A chemical which, at high temperatures, lowers the state of oxidation of other batch chemicals.

rigaree: A narrow ribbon of glass, marked off by ladder-rung type indentation, applied by tooling to form an ornamental feature on a bottle. See Plate 54.

sabot: See 'snap-case' and Figures 36 and 46.

scent bottle: A small bottle for perfume, sometimes called a 'perfume bottle'. The French term is 'flacon'; the German term is 'Flakon'. See Plate 163.

seam: Mark on glass surface resulting from the joint of matching mould parts. See Plate 217.

seed: An extremely small gaseous inclusion in glass.

settle mark: See 'chill mark'.

shaft and globe bottle: An early (1630-1700) European glass bottle of bulbous body and a long tapering neck, thick-walled and mostly in black glass, used as a decanting bottle or for storing beer, wine, oil, vinegar, spirits, powders, etc. The term shaft and globe was first used in 1929 by W.A. Thorpe in *A History of English and Irish glasses,* p.318. In the 17th century this bottle type was simply referred to as a 'bottle'. See Figures 2 and 3 and Plates 2, 62 and 139.

silica glass: Vitreous SiO_2; quartz glass; pure SiO_2 glass.

smoked: A term applied to the discolouring of glass in a reducing flame.

snap: A device for gripping a piece of formed glass for fire polishing and finishing. See Figure 46.

snap case: Variously called spring 'snap' and 'sabot', the tool is defined as a four-pronged clip attached to an iron rod, a closely fitting case of wrought iron mounted on a long handle from which only the neck of the bottle is allowed to project, etc. Some time between 1840 and 1860 the snap case came into use which held the bottle while its mouth was being formed without leaving a pontil mark. See Figures 36 and 46.

snuff bottle: A small vial for powdered tobacco, or snuff. See Plate 305(1).

soda: Na_2O. Loosely, a carbonate of sodium.

soda-lime glass: The most common form of glass. It contains three major compounds in varying proportions, but usually silica, soda and lime.

strain cracks: Fissures in the body of a bottle caused by internal strain resulting from inadequate annealing and/or thermal shock.

stress: Any condition of tension or compression existing within the glass, particularly due to incomplete annealing, temperature gradient, or inhomogeneity.

string rim: A rim of glass applied near the top of the neck; used for retaining the string which held the cork in place and for reinforcing the lip necessary for bottles where the cork was flush with the top of the bottle. See Plate 136B.

sun-coloured glass: Glass containing manganese that has reacted to the ultraviolet rays of the sun by turning purple or amethyst.

target ball: A glass ball designed to be shot at by sportsmen.

tea kettle ink bottle: A side-spouted ink bottle. See Plate 304(2).

torpedo bottle: A soda or mineral water bottle with a torpedo-shaped bottom.

translucent: Glass that allows a small amount of light to pass through it but which does not permit clear visibility or transparency.

transparent: Having the quality of transmitting light without diffusion so that objects behind can be distinctly seen.

turn mould: A process by which a blown bottle is spun in the mould before removal to erase seam markings.

umbrella ink bottle: A conical eight-sided ink bottle. See Plate 311(3).

utility bottle: It is a very broadly applied term as it is used for everything from the shaft and globe versions of the 17th century to the short-necked, onion-shaped bottles of the early 18th century and the cylindrical versions that started to be produced in the mid-18th century and continue in use to the present.

vacuum-and-blow process: A bottle-manufacturing process whereby molten glass is preformed by vacuum and subsequently blown. See Figure 44.

verre fougère: Literally, fern glass. A type of blue-green glass produced in France, the alkali ingredient of which was provided by potash made from burnt bracken (fern). This type of glass was produced in forest areas where this source of potash was readily available, such as the Languedoc in South-west France. See also 'Waldglas' and 'French blue-green'. See Plate 173.

vial: A small bottle for holding liquid medicines, pills, etc. The term generally implies use for medicinal purposes. See Plate 248.

Waldglas: See also 'forest glass' and 'verre fougère'. Literally, forest glass. A type of glass (greenish, yellowish, bluish or brownish) produced in the glasshouses (Waldglashütten) in the forests of Belgium, Central Europe and North-east France during the Middle Ages and later; the alkali ingredient of such glass was provided by potash from the ashes of burnt beechwood and other woods.

water-worn: Bottles that have become cloudy (matt) and whose surfaces are worn, through exposure to water or water and sand.

weathering: Changes on the surface structure of glass caused by chemical reaction with the environment. Weathering usually involves the leaching of alkali from the glass by water, leaving behind siliceous weathering products that are often laminar and coloured.

wetting off: Marking the neck of a bottle with a ring of water, so that it can be easily broken away from the blowpipe to which it was affixed during the process of blowing.

whittle marks: Rough marks of a dimpled or wavy nature on the surface of a blown bottle, caused by blowing the bottle in an insufficiently heated mould. See Plate 272(1).

verre fougère: Literally, fern glass. A type of blue-green glass produced in France, the alkali ingredient of which was provided by potash made from burnt bracken (fern). This type of glass was produced in forest areas where this source of potash was readily available, such as the Languedoc in South-west France. See also 'Waldglas' and 'French blue-green'.

vial: A small bottle for holding liquid medicines, pills, etc. The term generally implies use for medicinal purposes.

Waldglas: See also 'forest glass' and 'verre fougère'. Literally, forest glass. A type of glass (greenish, yellowish, bluish or brownish) produced in the glasshouses (Waldglashütten) in the forests of Belgium, Central Europe and North-east France during the Middle Ages and later; the alkali ingredient of such glass was provided by potash from the ashes of burnt beechwood and other woods.

water-worn: Bottles that have become cloudy (matt) and whose surfaces are worn, through exposure to water or water and sand.

weathering: Changes on the surface structure of glass caused by chemical reaction with the environment. Weathering usually involves the leaching of alkali from the glass by water, leaving behind siliceous weathering products that are often laminar and coloured.

wetting off: Marking the neck of a bottle with a ring of water, so that it can be easily broken away from the blowpipe to which it was affixed during the process of blowing.

whittle marks: Rough marks of a dimpled or wavy nature on the surface of a blown bottle, caused by blowing the bottle in an insufficiently heated mould. See Plate 272(1).

WORLD-WIDE BIBLIOGRAPHY
OF GLASS BOTTLES

Author's note

The bibliography specifically concerns books and articles on glass utility bottles published world-wide and in many languages.

The cited literature relates to bottles for all applications, such as bottles for wine, beer, spirits, vinegar, oil, mineral water, medicines, perfumes, poisons and all other liquids or powders (snuff tobacco, spices, etc.).

Decanters, flasks, preserving and storage jars, pharmaceutical bottles, stoneware bottles, etc. are also included to complete the list.

In addition the bibliography encompasses books and articles on bottle-making technology and ancient glass bottles.

In order to give a complete picture of the field of antique and modern bottle collecting, the bibliography mentions important sales catalogues and relevant books on bottle-related articles, such as corkscrews, bottle closures, bottle tickets or labels, bottle cleaning methods, pharmacy, bottle filling machinery, beer and wine drinking, etc.

The books and articles in this bibliography have been alphabetically listed by author and title with the aim of providing a guide for all those interested in collecting and studying antique glass bottles from all over the world.

Sources without an author's name, such as museum and auction house catalogues, are listed under ANONYMOUS.

Abbreviations of periodical titles most referred to

A	*Antiques*
AC	*Antique Collector*
ADCG	*Antique Dealers and Collectors' Guide*
A.I.H.V. Verre	*Association Internationale pour l'Histoire du*
AP	*Apollo*
CJGS	*Journal of Glass Studies* (Corning Museum of Glass, New York)
CL	*Country Life*
CONN	*Connoisseur*
GC	*Papers of the Circle of Glass Collectors* (Glass Circle). London (duplicated typescripts)
ILN	*Illustrated London News*

AALTO, Risto

1   '*Suomalainen Lasipullo*'. *Suomen lasimuseon tutkimusjulkaisu – The Bulletin of the Finish Glass Museum. Lasitutkimuksia – Glass Research IX (1995).* Publ. by Suomen Lasimuseo, The Finnish Glass Museum, Tehtaankatu 23, 11910 Riihimäki, Finland. ©1995.

ABRAHAMS, Gabeba

2   '*Seventeenth and Eighteenth Century Glass Bottles excavated from Fort De Goede Hoop, Cape Town*'. In 'Annals of the South African Cultural History Museum', Vol 1, No.1, Nov 1987; Cape Town.

ADAMS, John P.

3   '*Bottle Collecting in New England*' - *A Guide to Digging, Identification, and Pricing.* New Hampshire Publishing Company, Somersworth, New Hampshire, 1969.

4   '*Bottle Collecting in America*'. New Hampshire Publishing Company, Somersworth, ©1971.

5   '*Third Bottle Book*'. *A Guide to Collecting and Pricing Antique Bottles.* Publ. by New Hampshire Publishing Company, Somersworth, 1972.

ADRIAENSENS, Anne-Mie

6   '*Drinken en Klinken*'. Publ. by the Provinciaal Museum Sterckshof, Antwerpen-Deurne, Belgium.

AGEE, Bill

7   '*Collecting the Cures*'. ©1969 William D. Agree. Printed by Texian Press, Waco, Texas.

8   '*Collecting All Cures*'. ©1973 William D. Agee, Waco, Texas.

ALFORD, B.W.E.

9   '*The flint and bottle glass industry in the early nineteenth century [Phoenix Glassworks, Bristol]*'. In Business History, 10 Jun 1968, p.12-21.

ALYLUIA, Jeanne

10   '*Eighteenth-Century Container Glass from the Roma Site, Prince Edward Island*'. In 'History and Archaeology 45'. National Historic Parks and Sites Branch, Parks Canada, Environment Canada, 1981.

ANDERBJÖRK, J.E.

11   '*Flaskor och buteljer. Några anteckningar om glastillverkningen i äldre tider*'. Publ. Svensk bryggeritidskrift. 6:1952.

ANDERSON, Will

12   '*The Beer Book - An Illustrated Guide to American Breweriana*'. The Pyne Press, Princeton; ©1973.

ANDREWS, David

13   '*Antique Bottles of Rhode Island*'. Publ. by Little Rhody Bottle Club, Cranston, RI 02910, 1996.

ANDRIAN-WERBURG, Bettina von

14   '*Gebrauchsglas (1800-1945)*'. ©1993 Staatliche Museen Kassel und Autorin.

ANONYMOUS

15   '*400 Jaar Gebruiksflessen*'. Exhibition 1-7 t/m 30-9-1983; Nationaal Glasmuseum, Lingedijk 28, Leerdam. In samenwerking met Verzamelaarsklub 'De Oude Flesch'

16 **'650 Jahre Bürgerspital zum Heiligen Geist Würzburg'**. Publ. by the Bürgerspital Würzburg, Würzburg, Germany, 1969.

17 **'2000 Jahre Weinkultur an Mosel-Saar-Ruwer'**. *Denkmäler und Zeugnisse zur Geschichte von Weinanbau, Weinhandel, Weingenuß*. Rheinisches Landesmuseum Trier, 1987.

18 **'3000 Ans de Parfumerie'**. *Parfums, Savons, Fards et Cosmétiques, de l'Antiquité à nos jours*. Exposition organisée à l'occasion de l'Année du Patrimoine, et de la tenue du VIIIe Congrès Mondial des Huiles Essentielles, 22 juillet-22 octobre 1980. Musée d'Art et d'Histoire, Grasse, France.

19 **'Åbo Stads Historiska Museum'**. *Årsskrift 34-35, 1970-1971*. Polytypos, Åbo, 1971.

20 **'Aerated Water Machinery'**. *Catalogue*. Publ. by William Chester-Master, Fairford, Glos., England; 1893.

21 **'American Historical Flasks & Bottles'**. *The Collection of the late H. Bradford Richmond*. Auction Catalogue. Public Sale by Auction, 15 Oct 1938. American Art Association, Anderson Galleries, Inc., New York, USA.

22 **'A Remarkable Gathering of Stiegel, Wistarberg, Jersey, Three-Section-Mold and Other Rare Early American Glass, Belonging to the Widely Known Connoisseur Mr. Herbert Lawton of Boston'**. Auction Catalogue. Public Sale – 1-2 Feb 1923. American Art Galleries, New York City, USA.

23 **'Aus alten Apotheken'** - *Sammlung Roese*. Ausstellung im Museum Hameln vom 24.5. bis zum 13.8.1995. Herausgegeben vom Museum Hameln 1995®

24 **'Autour du Parfum - du XVIe au XIXe siècle'**. Exposition du 31 mai au 15 sept. 1985, avec la collaboration des parfums Guy Laroche. Mai 1985. Edité par Sagec 'Le Louvre des Antiquaires'.

25 **'Baltimore Bottle Book'**. *Being an annotated list of 150 years of the Collector Bottles of Baltimore City and Baltimore County, 1840-1990*. Publ. by The Baltimore Antique Bottle Club, Inc., Baltimore, 1998.

26 **'Bierflaschen, Weinflaschen, Gebrauchsglas'**. *Auktion 211; Versteigerung 26. März 1988*. Waltraud Boltz, Kunstauktionshaus Bayreuth, 8580 Bayreuth.

27 **'Bottle Collector's Treasury'**. *A collection of information about Classic and Common Bottles*. E.G. Warman Publishing, Inc., Uniontown, PA. Jan 1972.

28 **'Bottles of every Description – "Diamond I" Products'**. General Catalogue "A". Publ. by Illinois Glass Company, Alton, Illinois, USA. Undated, c.1920.

29 **'Catalogue - Ancient Glass - Formerly the Kofler-Truniger Collection'**. Christie, Manson & Woods Ltd., London, 5-6 Mar 1985.

30 **'Catalogue - Ancient Glass'**. Sotheby's, London, 16-19 Nov 1987.

31 **'Catalogue: Farrow & Jackson, Limited; Wine and Spirit Merchants'** *and General Engineers; manufacturers of Iron Wine Bins, Cellar and Bar Fittings, Bottle Wax, Taps, &c., Mineral Water and Beer Carbonating Machinery; Brewers' & Bottlers' Requisites; American Iced Drinks and Bar Appliances*. Catalogue of Nov 1989. First publ. by Farrow & Jackson Limited 1898. Reprinted by Richard Dennis, The Old Chapel, Shepton Beauchamp, Somerset TA19 OLE, 1997.

32 **'Catalogue - Important Ancient Glass, from the Collection formed by the British Rail Pension Fund'**. Sotheby's, London, 24 Nov 1997.

33 **'Catalogue of English and Continental Glass and A Collection of Sealed Wine Bottles'**. *The Property of Mr. and Mrs. G.B. Slater and Other Owners*. Sales Catalogue; Auction 2 Dec 1968: Sotheby & Co, London.

34 **'Catalogue of English and Continental Glass and Paperweights'**. Sotheby's, London, 13 Jly 1987.

35 **'Catalogue of English and Continental Glass and Paperweights'**. Christie's London, 23 May 1989.

36 **'Catalogue of English, Continental Glass and Paperweights'**. Sotheby Parke Bernet & Co., London, 18 Jly 1983.

37 **'Catalogue of Fine Chinese Snuff Bottles'**. Sotheby's, London, 23 Mar 1988.

38 **'Catalogue of Fine Chinese Snuff Bottles'**. Sotheby's, Hong Kong, 28 Oct 1992.

39 **'Catalogue of Fine Chinese Snuff Bottles'**. Sotheby's Hong Kong Ltd., 28 Apr 1993.

40 **'Catalogue of Fine Chinese Snuff Bottles'**. Sotheby's, New York, 12 Oct 1993.

41 **'Catalogue of Fine Objects of Vertu and Portrait Miniatures including a Collection of Scent-Bottles'**. Christie, Manson & Woods Ltd., London, 8 Dec 1982.

42 **'Catalogue of Important Chinese Snuff Bottles from the Collection of Eric Young, Part IV'**. Sotheby's Hong Kong Ltd., 28 Oct 1993.

43 **'Catalogue of Important Chinese Snuff Bottles - from the Kardos Collection'**. Sotheby's, New York, 1 Jly 1985.

44 **'Catalogue of The E.S. Blaisse Collection of Glasses, Bottles and Objects concerning liqueurs and their history and Fine Wines'**. Christie's Amsterdam B.V., Amsterdam, 25 May 1982.

45 **'Catalogue of The Krug Collection of Glass - Parts I-IV'**. Auction, 7 Jly 1981, by Sotheby Parke Bernet & Co.

46 **'Catalogue - The Benzian Collection of Ancient and Islamic Glass'**. Sotheby's, London, 7 Jly 1994.

47 **'Catalogue - The Constable-Maxwell Collection of Ancient Glass'**. Sotheby Parke Bernet & Co., London, 4-5 Jun 1979.

48 **'De Ontwikkeling der Nederlandsche Flesschenindustrie'**. In 'Tijdschrift voor Economische Geographie'. Uitgevers: Mouton & Co. 's-Gravenhage 1914, p.1-9.

49 *'De Sint–Pietersabdij te Gent. Het rijke leven van zieke monniken. Twee afvalputten uit de infirmerie 1600-1780'; p.47-56, 106-108, 119-121, Gent, 1985. (On bottles excavated in Gent/Belgium).

50 *'Early American Bottles and Flasks, and Other Rare American Glass Collected by the Late Alfred B. Maclay'*. Sales Catalogue; Auction 7 Mar 1945: Parke-Bernet Galleries, Inc., New York.

51 *'Een rondgang door het poppenhuis - A guide to the dolls'house'*. 2e Herziene druk 1977 Haags Gemeentemuseum.

52 *'Encyclopédie, ou dictionnaire raisonné des sciences, des arts et des métiers. . . par Diderot: Recueil de planches, sur les sciences, les arts libéraux, et les arts mécaniques, avec leur explication'*. 1751/1772. "Verrerie en bouteilles chauffée en charbon de Terre". In Briasson, Paris. 10 Vols., Vol.10.

53 *'Essen und Trinken in alter Zeit'*. *(Sonderausstellung aus der Reihe 'Was man sonst nicht sieht', 8. November 1991 - 12. Januar 1992).* ©1991 Mainfränkisches Museum Würzburg.

54 *'Europäisches Formglas 15.-19. Jahrhundert sowie Emailglas und Farbglas'*. 'Sammlung Uwe Friedleben'. Auktion 5. Oktober 1990. Stuttgarter Kunstauktionshaus Dr. Fritz Nagel, 7000 Stuttgart 1.

55 *'Flaschen und Behälter'* - *Zur Geschichte des industriellen Markenartikels im 19. Jahrhundert.* Deutsches Museum; Ausstellung vom 15. Dezember 1983 bis 24. Februar 1984.

56 *'Glasherstellung in Nienburg - 100 Jahre Wilhelmshütte 1891-1991'*. Ausstellung im Museum Nienburg/Weser, 16. Februar bis 1. September 1991. Herausgeber: ©Museum Nienburg, Nienburg/Weser 1991.

57 *'Glass: a handbook for the study of glass vessels of all periods and countries and a guide to the Museum collection, by W.B. Honey'*. Victoria and Albert Museum. HMSO, 1946, 241p.

58 *'Glass Collections in Museums in the United States and Canada'*. The Corning Museum of Glass and The American National Committee of the International Association of the History of Glass. Corning, New York - 1982.

59 *'Glassware/1880, Whitall, Tatum and Co.'*. Catalogue reprint Princeton, NJ: Pyne, 1971 (Bottles, chemical and pharmaceutical glass).

60 *'H&R Duftatlas, Damen-Noten, Herren-Noten'*. *Duftlandschaft des internationalen Marktes.* Glöss Verlag, Hamburg, 1991.

61 *'Harvest 2nd Fruit Jar Finders'*. *Price Guide.* ©1970 Harvest Publishing Co., Milwaukee, Wisconsin.

62 *'La Verrerie ancienne - aux Musées Royaux d'Art et d'Histoire'*, *Bruxelles.* Museum catalogue - untitled.

63 *'Maurice Marinot, Exceptionnel ensemble de 59 oeuvres de la collection Alain Lesieutre - dont la vente aux enchères publiques aura lieu le mercredi 14 décembre 1994 à 20 h 30)'*. Sales catalogue Auction House: Drouot Montaigne

64 *'Nybyn Lasiruukin Vaiheita'*. Pohjois - Pohjanmaan Museo - Oulu, 1981.

65 *'Poids & Mesures du Languedoc et des Provinces Voisines'*. Musée Paul-Dupuy, Toulouse, 1953.

66 *'Répertoire international des Musées et Collections du Verre'* - *'International Repertory of Glass Museums and Glass Collections'*. Ed. Comité International de l'ICOM pour les Musées et Collections du Verre, Liège, Musée du Verre, 1966.

67 *'Research on San Francisco Whiskey Bottles'*. ©1967 Bev and Joe Silva.

68 *'The Bertrand Bottles, a study of 19th century glass and ceramic containers'*. Washington, D.C.: GPO, 1974.

69 *'The Cow & Gate Babyfeeding Collection'*. Catalogue of an exhibition held at the Monica Britton Museum, Frenchay Hospital, Bristol, England, from 12 Apr 1999 until 31 Mar 2000.

70 *'The English Glass Bottle through the Ages'*. *Catalogue.* The County Museum, Truro, Cornwall, 1 Jly30 Sept 1976.

71 *'The Guide To Collecting Fruit Jars; Fruit Jar Annual. Vol.I, 1996'*. ©1995. Publ. Jerry McCann.

72 *'The Guide To Collecting Fruit Jars; Fruit Jar Annual. Vol.2, 1997'*. ©1996. Publ. Jerry McCann.

73 *'The Guide to Collecting Fruit Jars, Fruit Jar Annual; Vol 3 - 1998'*. Jerry McCann, Chicago. 1998.

74 *'The Late Hiram Norcross Collection of Chestnut Bottles'*. Exhibition. Apr-Sept 1966. Memphis: Brooks Memorial Art Gallery, 1966.

75 *'The Official Price Guide to Bottles Old & New'*. *From the Editors of the House of Collectibles.* ©1986 Random House, Inc.; publ. by The House of Collectibles, New York.

76 *'The Ontario Pop Bottlers List (1931-1965)'*. Iron Gate Publishing Co., Sarnia, Ontario, Canada. ©1994.

77 *'Trois millénaires d'art verrier à travers les collections publiques et privées de Belgique'*. Musée Curtius, Liège, 1958.

78 *'Una Farmacia Preindustriale in Valdelsa'*. *La Spezieria e lo spedale di Santa Fina nella città di San Gimignano, Secc. XIV-XVIII.* Publ. by Città di San Gimignano 1981.

79 *'Verrerie de l'Est de la France, XIIIe - XVIIIe siècles'*. *Fabrication - Consommation.* Revue archéologique de l'Est et du centre-Est neuvième supplément, Dijon, 1990.

80 *'Vitrum - Le Verre en Bourgogne'*. Ville d'Autun (Musée Rolin) & Ville de Dijon (Musée Archéologique; 1990, S.A. Typoffset Impressions, 71400 Autun.

81 *'Wem der geprant wein nutz sey oder schad... - Zur Kulturgeschichte des Branntweins'*. Katalog zur Eröffnungsausstellung des Wilhelm-Fabry-Museums der Stadt Hilden/Historische Kornbrennerei. ©Wilhelm-Fabry-Museum der Stadt Hilden, 1989.

APUZZO, Robert

82 **'Bottles of Old New York – A Pictorial Guide to Early New York City Bottles (1680-1925)'**. ©1994 Robert Apuzzo. Publ. by R&L Publishing, New York.

ARENDONK, Bert A.

83 **'De Flessenloods'**. Namen en Kenmerken van gebruiksflessen. "De Oude Flesch" Terheijden, Netherlands, Mar 1989.

ARMSTRONG, David &
METZGER ARMSTRONG, Elizabeth

84 **'The Great American Medicine Show'**. ©1991. Publ. by Prentice Hall, New York, NY 10023.

ARNOLD, Ken

85 **'A History In Bottles And Stoneware'**. 1852-1930. Publ. Bendigo, Vic., Australia.

86 **'Australian Preserving & Storage Jars – pre 1920'**. Printed by D.G. Walker Pty. Ltd., Bendigo, Vic.; Publ. 1983.

87 **'Bottle Collectors' Guide'**. Printed in Australia by D.G. Walker Pty Ltd., Kangaroo Flat. 1997.

88 **'Collecting Australian Found Bottles'**. Part One. Publ. Bendigo, Vic., Australia.

89 **'Collecting Australian Found Bottles'**. Part Two. Publ. Bendigo, Vic., Australia.

90 **'Eucalyptus Oil'**. *(A Sad Scene)*. Eucy bottle identification & price guide. Crown Castleton Publishers, Golden Square, Vic. 3555, Australia, 1998.

91 **'Old bottles – Identification & Valuation Guide'**. Crown Castleton Publishers, Golden Square, Vic., Australia. ©1993.

92 **'Old Bottles'**. Publ. by Crown Castleton Publishers, Golden Square, Vic. 3555, Australia, 1996.

ARNOULD, A. & others

93 **'Les Routes de la Treille'**. ©1990, Didier Hatier, Bruxelles.

ASH, Douglas

94 **'How to identify English drinking glasses and decanters, 1680-1830'**. Bell, 1962, 200p.

ASHFORD, Roger

95 **'English glass decanters'**. In A., Jly 1981, p.26-8.

ASHTON, Robert J.

96 **'The Bottle Collector's Price List for Embossed, Ink, and pontil-scarred bottles'**. New York: Exposition Pr, 1972.

ASHURST, Denis

97 **'The History of South Yorkshire Glass'**. ©Denis Ashurst. Publ. by J.R. Collis Publications, Sheffield, England.

ASKEY, Derek

98 **'Stoneware Bottles from Bellarmines to Ginger Beers 1500-1949'**. ©1981 Derek Askey. Publ. by Bowman Graphics, Brighton.

99 **'Stoneware Bottles from Bellarmines to Ginger Beers 1500-1949'**. ©1981, 1998 Derek Askey. Second updated hard-back ed. Jly 1998. Publ. by: BBR Publishing, Elsecar Heritage Centre, Nr Barnsley, South Yorkshire, UK.

100 **'Sussex bottle collectors guide'**. Brighton (Sx.), Kensington Press, 1976, 120p.

AU HANG

101 **'The Au Hang Collection of Chinese Snuff Bottles'**. ©1993; Publ. by Jihu Jingshe, Scarborough Ontario, Canada.

AUSTEN, Ferol

102 **'Poor Man's Guide to Bottle Collecting'**. ©1971 New Hampshire Publishing Co., U.S.A.

AUTH, Susan H.

103 **'Ancient Glass at the Newark Museum'**. Publ. by the Newark Museum, with assistance from The Ford Foundation and The National Endowment for the Arts, 1976.

AVERY, Constance & CEMBURA, Al

104 **'Garnier Bottles'**. *Identification and Price Guide*. ©1970 Constance Avery and Al Cembura. Distributed by Al Cembura, Berkeley, Calif.

105 **'Luxardo Bottles'**. *Figurals, Decanters. Identification and Price Guide*. ©1968 Al Cembura and Constance Avery. Publ. by Metropolitan Printing, Portland, Oregon.

AVERY, Constance/Leslie & CEMBURA, Al

106 **'Bischoff Kord and Kamotsuru Bottles'** – *Identification and Price Guide*. ©1969 Constance Avery and Al Cembura. Publ. by Avery and Cembura.

AYERS, James C.

107 **'Pepsi : Cola Bottles – Collectors Guide'**. ©1995; RJM Enterprises, Mount Airy, NC.

BAAR, Armand

108 **'A Propos des Bouteilles Armoriées Liègeoises'**. Undated; publ. c.1920.

BABYLON, Philip

109 **'Schatten uit Brugse Apotheken'**. Brugge, Nov 1998. © K.B.A.V. – Brugge Sint-Andries, Belgium.

BACON, Elizabeth M.

110 **'How Glass Bottles Are Made'**. *The Story of the Oldest Manufacturing Industry in America*. Whitall Tatum Company, Millville, New Jersey & New York, N.Y., USA. 1935.

BACON, John

111 **'Bottle-decanters and bottles'**. In GC, no.6.

112 **'Bottle-decanters and bottles'** In AP, Jly-Dec 1939, p.13-15.

113 **'Decanters, 1677-1750 and 1745-1800'**. In GC, nos.41 and 42.

BADDERS, Veldon

114 **'The Collector's Guide to Inkwells, Identification & Values'**. ©1995, Veldon Badders. Collector Books, Paducah, Kentucky.

BAILEY, Shirley R.

115 **'Bottle Town'**. ©1968 Shirley R. Bailey, Millville, N.J.

BAKER, Oliver

116 **'Black Jacks and Leather Bottells'** – *Being some account of Leather Drinking Vessels in England and incidentally of other Ancient Vessels*. Ed. J. Burrow & Co., Ltd., Cheltenham Spa, London. ©1921.

401

BAKER, Vernon G.
117   *'Carillo's statistical study of English wine bottles: some comments and further consideration'*. In Papers: Conference on Historic Site Archaeology, 1976, 11, 1977, p.111-13.

BALDWIN, Joseph K.
118   *'A Collector's Guide to Patent and Proprietary Medicine Bottles of the Nineteenth Century'*. Publ. by Thomas Nelson Inc., Nashville/New York; 1973.

BALL, Joanne Dubbs & TOREM, Dorothy Hehl
119   *'Commercial Fragrance Bottles'*. Schiffer Publishing Ltd., Atglen, PA; 1993.

BALLOU, Hazel & ALLEY, Kaylen
120   *'The Beginners Book – Collecting Jars and Bottels for Fun and Money'*. © 8-66 Hazel Ballou, Fort Scott, Kansas.

BANISTER, Judith
121   *'Relics of a gentlemanly vice: cut-glass, decanters of the eighteenth and nineteenth centuries'*. In ADCG, Jun 1961, p.34-6

BANKS, Fay
122   *'Seals from the Three Tuns Tavern, Oxford'*. In 'British Bottle Review, Elsecar (GB) 1994, No.64.

123   *'Wine Drinking in Oxford 1640-1850 – A Story revealed by Tavern, Inn, College and Other Bottles'*. *With a catalogue of bottles and seals from the collection in the Ashmolean Museum.* ©1997 F. Banks. Publ. by Archaeopress, Oxford.

BARBER, Edwin Atlee
124   *'American Glassware, Old and New'*. *A sketch of the glass industry in the United States, and manual for collectors of historical bottles.* Philadelphia: Patterson & White, 1900; Philadelphia: D. McKay, 1900; reprint as Old American Bottles. Fort Davis, Tx: Frontier Pr, 1974.

125   *'Old American Bottles'* - *A Sketch of the Glass Industry in the United States and Manual for Collectors of Historical Bottles, and Old Glass.* ©1900. Frontier Book Co., Publisher, Fort Davis, Texas.

BARCLAY, John C.
126   *'The Canadian Fruit Jar Report'*. ©1977 John C. Barclay, Ontario, Canada.

BARNETT, R.E.
127   *'Western Whiskey Bottles'*. ©1991 R.E. Barnett, Lakeview, Oregon. Printed by Maverick Publications, Inc., Bend, Oregon.

128   *'Western Whiskey Bottles'*. ©1997 R.E. Barnett, Lakeview, Oregon. Printed by Maverick Publications, Inc., Bend, Oregon.

BAROSA, Santos
129   *'Museu Santos Barosa', 1º Volume Fundaçâo'*. Publ. by Santos Barosa – Vidros, Marinha Grande, Portugal. Undated.

130   *'Museu Santos Barosa', 2º Volume O Fabrico de Garrafas no Séc. XVIII'*. Publ. by Santos Barosa – Vidros, Marinha Grande, Portugal. Undated.

131   *'Museu Santos Barosa', 3º Volume Fabrico de Garrafas em 1995'*. Bottle Production in 1995. Publ. by Santos Barosa – Vidros, Marinha Grande, Portugal. Undated.

132   *'Museu Santos Barosa', 4º Volume Fabricação do Vidro no Séc. XIX'*. Glass Manufacturing in the XIXth Century. Publ. by Santos Barosa – Vidros, Marinha Grande, Portugal. Undated.

BARRELET, James
133   *'La Verrerie en France de l'époque Gallo-Romaine à nos jours'*. Librairie Larousse - Paris-VIᵉ. ©1953.

134   *'Quelques points d'histoire à propos de la bouteille en verre'*. In Saint-Gobain Verre Creux, No.10, p.4-7, Nov 1958.

BARRERA, Jorge
135   *'La verrerie des fouilles de la cour Napoléon du Louvre'*. P.365-377 in 'Annales du 12ᵉ Congrès de l'Association Internationale pour l'Histoire du Verre'; Vienne - Wien, 26-31 août 1991; ©1993 - A.I.H.V. - Amsterdam.

BARTHOLOMEW, Ed.
136   *'1001 Bitters Bottles'*. Bartholomew House, Publisher, Fort Davis, Texas, 1970.

137   *'1200 Old Medicine Bottles'*. Frontier Book Company, Publisher, Fort Davis, Texas; 1971.

138   *'1250 Bitters Bottles'*. Bartholomew House, Publisher, Fort Davis, Texas. 1971.

BATEMAN, Bill & SCHAEFFER, Randy
139   *'Coca-Cola Collectibles'*. *The new compact study guide and identifier.* Publ. by Chartwell Books, Edison, NJ, USA. ©1996.

BATES, Virginia T. & CHAMBERLAIN, Beverly
140   *'Antique Bottle Finds in New England'*. Peterborough, N.H.; Noone House, 1968.

BATTENBERG, Christoph
141   *'Die Sammlung der Siegelstempel im Kestner-Museum Hannover'*. Herausgeber: Landeshauptstadt Hannover, Kestner-Museum. ©1985 Kestner-Museum, Hannover, Germany.

BAUER, H. & MILLACH, W.
142   *'Danzigs Handel in Vergangenheit und Gegenwart'*. Danzig, Poland, 1925.

BAUER, Ingolf
143   *'Glas – zum Gebrauch'*. Katalog zur gleichnamigen Ausstellung des Bayerischen Nationalmuseums, München, 27. September 1996 bis 19. Januar 1997. ©1996 Bayerisches Nationalmuseum, München und Verlag Gerd Hatje, Ostfildern-Ruit.

BAUMGARTNER, Erwin
144   *'Glas des späten Mittelalters'*. *Die Sammlung Karl Amendt.* Kunstmuseum Düsseldorf, 22. März bis 31. Mai 1987.

BAUMGARTNER, Erwin & KRUEGER, Ingeborg
145   *'Phönix aus Sand und Asche'*. *Glas des Mittelalters.* ©1988 Klinkhardt & Biermann Verlagsbuchhandlung GmbH, München.

BEAUDET, Pierre R.
146   *'Bottle Glass from a Privy at Fort George Military Reserve, Ontario'*. In 'History and Archaeology 45'. National Historic Parks and Sites Branch, Parks Canada, Environment Canada, 1981.

BECK, Doreen
147   *'The Book of Bottle Collecting'*. ©1973: The Hamlyn Publishing Group Ltd., London, New York, Sydney, Toronto, Feltham, Middlesex, England; 96p.

BELLANGER, Jacqueline
148   *'Verre d'Usage et de Prestige'*. *France 1500-1800*. Les Editions de l'Amateur - Paris, 1988.

BENNETT, Raymond
149   *'Collecting for pleasure'*. Bodley Head, 1969. Contents include: Decanters, p.68-71.

BERGHE, S. van den
150   *'Van Rank tot Drank'*. Editor: Algemene Spaar- en Lijfrentekas (A.S.L.K.), Brussel, 1990.

BERGMEISTER, Astrid
151   *'Mindestens haltbar bis .....'*. *Konservieren und Bevorraten in Glasgefäßen*. Schriften Band 20. Landschaftsverband Westfalen – Lippe, Westfälisches Industriemuseum. Klartext-Verlag, Essen, Germany. ©1998.

BERGUIST, Steve
152   *'Antique Bottles of Rhode Island'*. Publ. by The Little Rody Bottle Club, Cranston, RI 02910, USA, 1998.

BERKOW, Nancy Pratt
153   *'The Award Guide to Collecting Bottles'*. ©1973 Nancy Pratt Berkow. Publi. by Award Books, 235 East 45th Street, New York.

BERLIN, Froma
154   *'Ship decanters called Rodneys. . .'*. In Collectors Weekly, 11 Apr 1972, p.15.

BERNTSEN, Arnstein
155   *'En Samling Norsk Glass'*. Bredo H. Berntsens samlervirksomhet. Gyldendal Norsk Forlag, Oslo 1962.

156   *'En Samling Norsk Glass'*. Bredo H. Berntsens samlervirksomhet. Reprinted by Bjørn Ringstrøms Antikvariat, Oslo 1986.

BERNTSON, Buster & EKMAN, Per
157   *'Scandinavian corkscrews'*. Tryckeriförlaget, Täby, Sweden, 1994.

BERRY, F.
158   *'Dated English wine bottles'*. In CL, 30 Mar 1935.

BESEKER, W.J.
159   *'Glass Labels for Bottles'*. Stationers Patent Office, London 1854.

BETTS, William
160   *'Manufacturing, Stoppering, and Covering Bottles, Jars, Pots, &c.'*. British Patent No. 10449 (William Betts) from 1844 (Photostat).

BEZBORODOV, M.A.
161   *'Chemie und Technologie der antiken und mittelalterlichen Gläser'*. Verlag Philipp von Zabern, Mainz ©1975.

BIGNALL, R.G.
162   *'Label decanters'*. In AC, Apr 1957, p.66-7.

BIMSON, Mavis
163   *'Ring "Pontil Marks" and the Empontiling of a Group of seventh-Century Anglo-Saxon Glass'*. In CJGS, Vol.22, p.9-11, 1980.

BIRAM, R.S.
164   *'The Introduction of the Owens Machine in Europe'*. Publ. in the Journal of the Society of Glass Technology, Vol. 42, p. 194-454, 1958.

BIRD, Douglas & Marion
165   *North American Fruit Jar Index'*. Orillia, Ont.: Authors, 1968.

BIRD, Douglas, Marion, & CORKE, Charles
166   *'A Century of Antique Canadian Glass Fruit Jars'*. Lond., Ont.: 1970.

167   *'A Century of Antique Canadian Glass Fruit Jars'*. Publ. by Douglas Bird, London, Ontario, Canada: 30 Jan 1971.

BIRINGUCCIO, Vannoccio
168   *'De la Pirotechnia' (1540)*. Facsimile dell'edizione originale. Editione Il Polifolo, Milano, 1977.

BIRINGUCCIO, Vannoccio
169   *'La Pirotechnia'*. Trans. and ed. C.S. Smith and M.T. Gnudi. New York, American Institute of Mining and Metallurgical Engineers, 1942.

BLAIR, Dorothy
170   *'A History of Glass in Japan'*. Publ. by Kodansha International/USA, Ltd., New York. ©1973.

BLAKEMAN, Alan
171   *'A Collectors Guide - Ginger Beers'*. *Ginger Beers, Stone Stouts, Herb Beer, Ale & Porter* with *Price Guide*. ©1998. BBR Publishing, Elsecar Heritage Centre, Nr Barnsley, South Yorkshire, UK.

172   *'A Collectors Guide - Inks - Pottery & Glass Ink Bottles, with Price Guide'*. ©1996 Alan Blakeman. BBR Publishing, Barnsley, S. Yorks.

173   *'Antique Bottles Collectors Encyclopaedia'*. *Vol.1*. ©1995, Alan Blakeman. BBR Publishing, Barnsley, S.Yorks.

BLAKEMAN, Alan & SMITH, Mike
174   *'British Bottle Collectors Price Guide and Directory - 1983'*. ©1983 Alan Blakeman and Mike Smith. Publ. by British Bottle Review, Nr.Barnsley, S.Yorks.

BLASI, Betty
175   *'A Bit About Balsams'*. *A Chapter in the History of Nineteenth Century Medicine*. ©1974 Mrs. Eugene J. Blasi, Sr., Louisville, Kentucky. Printed by Farley-Goepper Printing Company, Louisville, Kentucky.

BLASI, Gene
176   *Louisville's Early Medicine bottles'*. Louisville, Ky; 1992.

BLENCH, Brian J.R.
177   *'Two unusual chip-engraved bottles'*. In Scott. Glass Soc. Newsletter, no.5, Jun 1982, p.5-6.

BLUMENSTEIN, Lynn

178 *'Bottle Rush U.S.A.'* ©1966 Old Time Bottle
Publishing Company, Salem, Oregon.

179 *'Old Time Bottles'. (Found in the Ghost Towns)*. ©Dec
1963 Lynn Blumenstein. Printed by Adolphson's
Printing Co., Salem, Oregon.

180 *'Old Time Bottles - Found in the Ghost Towns'*.
©1963-1966 Lynn Blumenstein. Publ. by Old Time
Bottle Publishing Co., Salem, Oregon. Revised 1971.

181 *'Redigging The West - for Old Time Bottles'*. ©1965
Old Time Bottle Publishing Company, Salem, Oregon. USA.

BOND, Ralph

182 *'Fruit Jar Patent Book'*. 200 US-patents Nᵒˢ 9,989 to
94,452. Publ. in 1970.

BONTEMPS, Georges

183 *'Guide du Verrier: traité historique et pratique de la
fabrication des verres, cristaux, vitraux'*. 1868, Librairie
du dictionnaire des arts et manufactures, Paris

BORDIGNON, Carla

184 *'Profumi Mignon - Miniature Perfume Bottles'*. ©1986
BE-MA Editrice, Milano.

BORSOS, Béla

185 *'Glassmaking in Old Hungary'*. ©1963 Corvina Press,
Budapest.

BORTON, Warren

186 *'Wyoming Bottles'*. *Historical Bottles of Wyoming 1868-
1910*. ©1988. Reprinted 1999.

BOSSCHE, Willy van den

187 *'Beschrijving der Constantiawijnflessen'*. (Illustrated
evolution of 10 different Constantia winebottle shapes
in Holland and Belgium) in the Klubblad van de
Verzamelaarsklub "De Oude Flesch", No.21, Oct
1984, Nieuwegein, The Netherlands

188 *'Glassiegel mit königlichen Monogrammen'* (Glass-seals with
Royal Monograms). Publ. in Der Glasfreund, p.2-21, Heft
10, Mar 1998, Verlag Lenover Neustrelitz, Neustrelitz.

BOTTLEMEN, The 'Ole'

189 *'Antique Bottles Collectors Encyclopaedia'*. *Vol.1*.
B.B.R. Publishing, Barnsley, S. Yorks. Undated

BOWMAN, Glinda

190 *'Miniature Perfume Bottles'*. ©1994 Glinda Bowman.
Schiffer Publishing Ltd., Atglen, PA.

191 *'More Miniature Perfume Bottles'*. ©1996 Glinda
Bowman. Schiffer Publishing Ltd., Atglen, PA.

BOYNE, William

192 *'Tokens – Issued in the Seventeenth Century in
England, Wales, and Ireland, by Corporations,
Merchants, Tradesmen, etc.'*. 630 p. ©1858. John
Russell Smith, 36, Soho Square, London, UK.

BOYNE, William & WILLIAMSON, George

193 *'Trade Tokens – Issued in the Seventeenth Century in
England, Wales, and Ireland, by Corporations, Merchants,
Tradesmen, etc.'*. *A New and Revised Edition of William
Boyne's Work, by George C. Williamson. 2 Volumes, 1584 p.*
©Reprinted 1970. Burt Franklin, New York, N.Y., USA.

BOYNTON, Beatrice White

194 *'A Very Amateur Guide to Antique Bottle Collecting'*.
Caldwell, Idaho: Caxton Printers, 1965.

BRANNON, P.A. (Editor)

195 *'Catalogue of Bottle finds'*. Montgomery, Ala. In 'Glass
Collectors Mimeograph Series' No. 1-10. 1937-38.

BRANTLEY, William F.

196 *'A Collector's Guide to Ball Jars'*. Rosemary Humbert
Martin, Publ. Muncie, Indiana; 1975.

BRASSINNE, J.

197 *'Supports de bouteilles à eau de Spa, XVIIᵉ et XVIIIᵉ
siècles'*. *Collections E. Brahy-Prost et J. Brassinne*. In
'Chronique Archéologique du Pays de Liège', t. VII,
1912, p.12-18. (Belgium).

BRAY, Charles

198 *'Dictionary of Glass, Materials and Techniques'*. ©1995
Charles Bray. Publ. by A&C Black, London, 1996.

BRAZEAL, Frances

199 *'Old Bottles Sketched and Catalogued'*. Clovis, Cal.:
Clovis Printing, 1964.

BREMEN, Walther

200 *'Die Reliquiengläser des Diözesanmuseums in
Rottenburg am Neckar'*. Kunstverein der Diözese
Rottenburg am Neckar, 1967.

BRESSIE, Wesley & Ruby

201 *'101 Ghost Town Relics'*. *How to Display - Price Guide*.
Rev. sec. ed. publ. by Old Time Bottle Publishing
Company, Salem, Oregon 97301. Undated

202 *'Ghost Town Bottle Price Guide'*. Eagle Point, Ore.:
1964.

203 *'Ghost Town Bottle Price Guide'*. 3rd ed. - Feb. 1965;
News-Journal Print Shop, Yreka, Calif.

204 *'Ghost Town Relics; how to display, price guide'*.
Yreka, Cal.: Nolan's News-Journal, printer, 1967.

205 *'Relic Trails to Treasure; the American price guide'*.
Salem, Ore.: Old Time Bottle Publishing, 1970.

BRIMBLE, John

206 *'Glass bottles and stone jars: items in the Black Country
Society's Collection'*. In Blackcountryman, 8, 1975,
p.49-50.

BROADBENT, Michael

207 *'The Great Vintage Wine Book II'*. ©1991 Michael
Broadbent 1991 (Text). Publ. by Mitchell Beazley,
London, in association with Christie's Wine
Publications.

BRODY, Alexander

208 *'Old Wine into Old Bottles'*. A Collector's
Commonplace Book. Hong Kong: C.A., 1993.

BROOKS, John A.

209 *'Questioning Collector III: Glass stoppers and handles'*.
In ADCG, Jun 1978, p.126-8.

BRUNHAMMER, Yvonne

210 *'Baccarat', 'Les Flacons à Parfum', 'The Perfume
Bottles'*. Compagnie des Cristalleries de Baccarat,
Henri Addor & Associés Paris, 1993.

DRALLE, Robert

343 *'Die Glasfabrikation'. 2 Volumes.* München und Berlin, Druck und Verlag von R. Oldenbourg, 1911.

344 *Die Glasfabrikation' (Making bottles and jars). Zweite gänzlich umgearbeitete und verbesserte Auflage. 2 Volumes.* Publ. by Dr. Gustav Keppeler. 1926 – München und Berlin, Druck und Verlag von R. Oldenbourg. Germany.

DUGARDIN, Gaston

345 *'Histoire du Commerce des Eaux de Spa'.* Edited in Liège (Belgium), 1940 by Vaillant.

DUMBRELL, Roger

346 *'Understanding Antique Wine Bottles'.* Publ. by the Antique Collectors' Club, Suffolk; ©1983; 338p.

DUNCAN, George Sang

347 *'A bibliography of glass (from the earliest records to 1940). . . edited [with supplement] by Violet Dimbleby. Subject index by Frank Newby'.* Dawsons, for the Society of Glass Technology, 1960, 552p. An annotated list of 15,752 items covering the whole field of glass.

DUNN, Russell & June

348 *'Codd. The Man and The Bottle'.* ©1987 Russell and June Dunn, Whittlesea.

DUNSMUIR, Richard

349 *'Old and rare English wine bottles'.* In AC, Aug 1976, p.28-31.

DURFLINGER, Roger L.

350 *'Poison Bottles'. Collector's Guide.* ©1975 Maverick Publications, Bend, Oregon.

EASTIN, June

351 *'Bottles West – Their History and current Values'.* Publ. 1969, The Old Bottle Exchange, Bend, Oregon.

EDGINGTON, John H. & HAMMOND, Charles R.

352 *'Emhart Glass and The Story of Glass Packaging'.* Publ. by Emhart Glass SA, Cham., Switzerland. Undated.

353 *'Emhart Glass and The Story of Glass Packaging'.* Publ. by Epworth (U.K.), 1996.

EDWARDS, Jack M.

354 *'A Collectors Guide to the Whiskeys That Were'.* ©1967 Jack M. Edwards, King City, Calif.

EIKELBERNER, George & AGADJANIAN, Serge

355 *'American Glass Candy Containers'.* Priv. publ. by Serge Agadjanian, Belle Mead, NJ, USA. First printing 1967. ©1967.

356 *'More American Glass Candy Containers'.* (Revised, Updated and Publ. by Adele L. Bowden) Priv. publ. by Serge Agadjanian, Belle Mead, NJ, USA. ©1970.

357 *'The Compleat American Glass Candy Containers Handbook'.* ©1986. Bowden Publishing Co., Mentor, Ohio, USA.

EISEN, Gustavus A.

358 *'Glass – Its Origin, History, Chronology, Technique and Classification to the Sixteenth Century'. Vol.I and II.* William Edwin Rudge, New York; 1927.

ELLIOTT, Rex R.

359 *'Hawaiian Bottles of Long Ago'.* ©1971 Rex R. Elliott. Publ. by Hawaiian Service, Inc., Honolulu, Hawaii.

EMERSON, Edward R.

360 *'Beverages Past & Present, Vol. I and Vol. II'.* New York; G.P. Putman's Sons, 1908.

EMHART GLASS SA.

361 *'The Emhart Book of Punt Marks'.* Punt Marks are used by glass container manufacturers to identify the products they produce. Usually the embossed symbols are on the base or near the base of the container. Publ. by Emhart Glass SA, CH-6330 Cham, Switzerland, 1996.

ENGEN, Luc

362 *'Het Glas in België van de oorsprong tot heden'.* Mercatorfonds – Antwerp, Belgium, 1989.

363 *'Le Verre en Belgique des origines à nos jours'.* Fonds Mercator – Antwerp, Belgium, 1989.

ENGLISH, S.

364 *'The Ashley Bottle Machine'* – A Historical Note in the Journal of the Society of Glass Technology, Vol. 7, p. 324-334, 1923.

ESWARIN, Rudy

365 *'Tags and tickets [bottle labels engraved on glass]'.* In Wine Tidings, Mar. 1982, p.7-9.

EYRE, Henry, Purveyor for Mineral Waters to Her Majesty

366 *'An Account of the Mineral Waters of Spa, Commonly called the German Spaw'.* London: Printed for J. Roberts in Warwick-Lane; 1733.

FADELY, Don

367 *'Hair Raising Stories'.* 1992.

FERLAY, John

368 *'Market favours glass wine bottles [recent prices]'.* In ADCG, Feb 1969, p.89.

FERRARI, Elisabetta Barbolini

369 *'Viaggio tra vetri e cristalli nel Ducato Estense'.* ©1993 by studio Lobo, Correggio RE.

FERRARO, Pat & Bob

370 *'A Bottle Collector's Book'.* ©1966 Pat and Bob Ferraro. Printed by Western Printing & Publishing Co., Sparks, Nevada.

371 *'The Past in Glass'.* ©1964 Pat and Bob Ferraro. Printing by Western Printing & Publishing Co., Sparks, Nevada.

FERSON, Regis R.

372 *'Yesterday's Milk Glass Today'.* 1981.

FETZER, Wolfgang

373 *'Pharmazie, Historisches aus Museen und Sammlungen der DDR'.* ©VEB Deutscher Verlag für Grundstoffindustrie, Leipzich 1983.

FIELD, Anne E.

374 *'On the Trail of Stoddard Glass'.* ©1975 Anne E. Field.

FIKE, Richard E.

375 *'Guide to Old Bottles, Contents and Prices; illustrations and advertisements to over 250 bottles, plus additional*

current price guide'. 2 Vol. ©1966 Richard E. Fike, Ogden, Utah: 1966.

376 *'Guide to Old Bottles, Contents and Prices'*. *Vol.II.* ©1967 Richard E. Fike, Curator Pioneer Arizona Museum, Phoenix, Arizona.

377 *'Handbook for the Bottle-ologist; over 1000 bottles listed including a background and description of those found in the Great Basin'*. ©1965 Richard E. Fike, Ogden, Utah: 1965.

378 *'The Bottle book: a comprehensive guide to historic, embossed medicine bottles'*. Salt Lake City: Gibbs M. Smith Inc. - Smith Books, 1987.

FILDES, Valerie A.

379 *'Breasts, Bottles and Babies'*. *A History of Infant Feeding.* Edinburgh University Press, Edinburgh (UK). ©1986.

FITZ, Otto & HUBER, Peter

380 *'Bergmännische Geduldflaschen'*. *Inhalt und Verbreitung bergmännischer Eingerichte aus dem Gebiet der ehemaligen österreichisch-ungarischen Monarchie und aus deutschen Bergbaurevieren. Mit einem Bestandskatalog.* Im Selbstverlag des österreichischen Museums für Volkskunde. Wien, Austria. 1995.

FITZ, Stephan & LEITHERER, Eugen

381 *'Flaschen und Behälter. Zur Geschichte des industriellen Markenartikels im 19. Jahrhundert'*. (Ausstellungskatalog). München 1983, m.Abb.

FLETCHER, Edward

382 *'A Bottle Collectors' Guide'* - *European Seals, Case Gins and Bitters.* ©1976, Edward Fletcher. Publ. by Latimer New Dimensions Limited, London.

383 *'Antique Bottles in Colour'*. ©1976 Blandford Press Ltd., Poole, Dorset.

384 *'Bottle Collecting - Finding, Collecting and Displaying Antique Bottles'*. ©1972 Edward Fletcher. Publ. by Blandford Press Ltd., Poole, Dorset; 96p.

385 *'Edward Fletcher's Non-Dating Price Guide to Bottles, Pipes and Dolls' Heads'*. ©1976 Edward Fletcher. Publ. by Blandford Press Ltd., Poole, Dorset.

386 *'Ginger Beer, Collector's Manual'*. ©1974. Edward Fletcher. Bottles & Relics Publications, Braintree, Essex, UK.

387 *'International Bottle Collectors' Guide'*. ©1975 Edward Fletcher. Publ. by Blandford Press Ltd., Poole, Dorset.

388 *'Marble Bottles and Other Closures - a History'*. ©1974, Black Notley, Braintree, Essex

389 *'Undiscovered Bottle Dumps - Essex & Kent Edition, where & how to find them with a GPS'*. London, 1998(?)

390 *'Where To Dig Up Antiques'*. ©1976 Southern Collectors Publications, Southampton, England.

FLETCHER, Johnnie W.

391 *'A Collectors Guide to Kansas Bottles (1854-1915)'*. 1994.

392 *'Oklahoma Drug Store Bottles'*. Printed by Moore Printing Co., Inc., Moore, Okla; 1991.

FLIPPO, K.F.

393 *'Van Glashut tot Glasfabriek'*. De Delftse flessenfabriek en enige generaties glasblazers in de jaren 1798-1926. Publ. by Driebergen (NL), 1994.

FOGELBERG, Torbjörn

394 *'Värmländska glasbruk II - Liljedals glasbruk'*. Editor: Småskrifter Uitgivna av Värmlands Museum 14, Karlstad 1979.

FONTAN, Geneviève

395 *'Cote générale des échantillons de parfums'*. Editions Fontan & Barnouin,31400 Toulouse. ©Editions Fontan & Barnouin pour la version française, 1996.

396 *'L'Argus des échantillons de parfum'*. Collection Jean-Marie Martin-Hattemberg. ©1992, Editions Milan.

397 *'Les échantillons modernes'* - *La cote internationale des échantillons de parfum 1995-1996.* 1995, 813 édition F&B, 31000 Toulouse.

FORD, John

398 *'Ford cameo glass decanter'*. In CONN, May-Aug. 1925, p.97-8.

FOSSING, Poul

399 *'Glass Vessels before Glass-Blowing'*. Ejnar Munksgaard, Copenhagen, 1940.

FOSTER, John Morrill

400 *'Old Bottle Foster and His Glass-Making Descendants'*. ©1972. Keefer Printing Company, Fort Wayne, Indiana.

FOSTER, Kate

401 *'Scent Bottles'*. Connoisseur and M. Joseph, 1966 (Connoisseur monograph). Glass, p.33-44.

FOUNTAIN, John C. & COLCLEASER, Donald E.

402 *'Dictionary of Soda & Mineral Water Bottles'*. ©1968 'Ole Empty Bottle House, Publishing Company', Amador City, Calif.

403 *'Dictionary of Spirits and Whiskey Bottles'*. ©1969 'Ole Empty Bottle House, Publishing Company', Amador City, Calif.

FOWLER, Ron

404 *'Washington Sodas'*, *the illustrated history of Washington's soft drink industry.* Dolphin Point Writing Works, Publishers, Seattle; ©1986.

FOY, Danièle

405 *'De la Verrerie Forestière à la Verrerie Industrielle du Milieu du XVIIIe Siècle aux Années 1920'*. Publ. by Association Française pour l'Archéologie du Verre. Aix-en-Provence 1998.

406 *'Le verre médiéval et son artisanat en France méditerranéenne'*. Editions du Centre National de la Recherche Scientifique, 75700 Paris, 1989.

FOY, Danièle & SENNEQUIER, Geneviève

407 *'Ateliers de Verriers de l'Antiquité à la période Pré-Industrielle'*. Edit. Association française pour l'Archéologie du Verre, Actes des 4èmes Rencontres, Rouen 24-25 novembre 1989; Rouen 1991.

408 *'A travers Le Verre - du moyen âge à la renaisance'*. ©1989. Edited by Danièle Foy, Chargée de recherche

au C.N.R.S., Laboratoire d'Archéologie Médiévale Méditerranéenne, E.R.A. 6 du C.R.A., Aix-en-Provence & Geneviève Sennequier, Conservateur aux Musées Départementaux de la Seine-Maritime, Rouen.

FRANCIS, Alan David
409 *'The Wine Trade'*. 1972. Adam & Charles Black, London.

FRANKL, Beatrice
410 *'Parfum-Flacons – Miniaturen, Flacons und Großfactisen'*. Battenberg. ©1994 Weltbild Verlag GmbH Augsburg.

FRANSEN, Hans
411 *'Groot Constantia, a description of its architecture, its history and collection'*. Cape Town, 1972.

FRASER, Robert B.
412 *'The South Carolina Dispensary Bottle'*. n.p.: 1969.

FREEMAN, Dr. Larry
413 *'Grand Old American Bottles'*. *Descriptive listings of Glass Bottle Types from Colonial Times to the Present. Lavishly Illustrated, Encyclopedic.* ©1964. Century House, Watkins Glen, N.Y.

414 *'Medicine Showman and His Bottles'*. Century House, Watkins Glen, N.Y. 1957.

FREEMAN, Graydon La Verne
415 *'Bitters Bottles, by James H. Thompson (pseud.)'*. Watkins Glen, NY: Century, 1947.

416 *'The Medicine Showman'*. Watkins Glen, NY: Century, 1949, 1957.

FREMERSDORF, F.
417 *'Die Denkmäler des römischen Köln'*. Vol.III (1958)-Vol.IX (1984), Verlag der Löwe, Köln. (On Roman glass and bottles in the "Römisch-Germanische Museum", (Cologne).

FRIESE, Gerrit† & Karin
418 *'Glashütten in Brandenburg'*. *(Die Geschichte der Glashütten vom 16. bis zum 20. Jahrhundert mit einem 'Katalog ihrer Marken' und 16 Farbtafeln).* Herausgegeben mit Fördermitteln des Ministeriums für Wissenschaft, Forschung und Kultur des Landes Brandenburg vom Stadt- und Kreismuseum Eberswalde-Finow, 1992.

FROTHINGHAM, Alice Wilson
419 *'Spanish Glass'*. Faber and Faber, London. Undated.

GABORIT, Jean-Yves
420 *'Parfums'*, *Prestige et haute couture.* Office du Livre, Fribourg, Suisse. ©1985.

GAI, Antonella Sveva
421 *'Die Verwendung von Glasgefässen für die Auf-bewahrung von Reliquien'*. *Die Glassammlung des Diözesanmuseums Rottenburg am Neckar.* P.383-395 in 'Annales du 12e Congrès de l'Association Internationale pour l'Histoire du Verre'; Vienne - Wien, 26-31 août 1991; ©1993 - A.I.H.V. - Amsterdam.

GARDNER, Charles B. & EDWARDS, J. Edmund
422 *'Collector's Price Guide to Historical Bottles & Flasks'*. ©1970 J. Edmund Edwards. Publ. by John Edwards, Publisher, Stratford, Conn.

GARNIER, Ëdouard
423 *'Histoire de La Verrerie et de L'Emaillerie'*. Alfred Mame et Fils, Editeurs, Tours, 1886.

GAUDE, Werner
424 *'Die alte Apotheke'*. *Eine tausendjährige Kulturgeschichte.(2. Auflage).* Deutscher Apotheker Verlag Stuttgart 1986.

GAUPP, Charles
425 *'Georgian decanters'*. In ADCG, Apr 1958, p.24-6.

GAYNOR, Suzanne
426 *'French Enameled Glass of the Renaissance'*. In CJGS, Vol.33, p.42-81, 1991.

GEFFKEN PULLIN, Anne
427 *'Glass, Signatures, Trademarks and Trade Names, from the seventeenth to the twentieth century'*. ©1986. Radnor, Pennsylvania 19089

GELDER, Dr.H.E. van & JANSEN, Dr. Beatrice
428 *'Glas in Nederlandse Musea'* ©1969, W. de Haan, Bussum; N.V. Standaard Boekhandel, Antwerpen.

GIEGERICH, W. & TRIER, W.
429 *'Glasmaschinen'*; *Aufbau und Betrieb der Maschinen zur Formgebung des heißen Glases.* Springer-Verlag, Berlin/Göttingen/Heidelberg, 1964.

430 *Glassmachines'* (for making bottles and jars). English translation of the original book 'Glasmaschinen'. Springer-Verlag, Berlin, 1964.

GIRLING, F.A.
431 *'English Merchants' Marks'*. *A field survey of marks made by Merchants and Tradesmen in England between 1400 and 1700.* Oxford University Press, New York, Toronto, London, 1964; Contents include: Bottle seals, p.112-14..

GIULIAN, Bertrand B.
432 *'Corkscrews of the Eighteenth Century'*. White Space Publishing, 1995.

GIVELET, J.
433 *'Le verre, la verrerie et les bouteilles champenoises'*. In 'Verres Réfract.', vol.34, no.6, nov-dec 1980.

GLASS MANUFACTURERS' FEDERATION
434 *'Glass Containers'*. Publ. by the Glass Manufacturers' Federation, London, UK. Undated, c1962.

GLATZ, Regula
435 *'Hohlglasfunde der Region Biel'* - *Zur Glasproduktion im Jura.* Staatlicher Lehrmittelverlag Bern 1991.

GLOVER, Brian
436 *'The World Encyclopedia of Beer'*. Publ. in 1997 by Lorenz Books, London, UK.

GODFREY, Eleanor S.
437 *'Specialized Glassware: Bottles, Hour-Glasses, Mirrors, and Scientific Wares'*. In 'The Development of English Glassmaking 1560-1640', Chapter X, p. 224-258. The University of North Carolina Press, Chapel Hill, 1975.

438 *'The Development of English Glassmaking, 1560-1640'*. Unpublished Ph.D. thesis, Univ. of Chicago, 1957.

439 *'The Development of English Glassmaking 1560-1640'*.

The University of North Carolina Press, Chapel Hill, 1975.

GOODELL, Donald
440 *'The American Bottle Collector's Price Guide'. To Historical Flasks, Pontils, Bitters, Mineral Waters, Inks & Sodas*. ©1973 The Charles E. Tuttle Company, Inc. of Rutland, Vermont & Tokyo, Japan.

GORDON, L.
441 *'Wine Containers Through the Ages'*. The Decanter.

GRACI, David
442 *'American Stoneware Bottles' - A History and Study*. Calem Publishing Co., South Hadley, Mass.; ©1995.

GREAT BRITAIN, Parliament, Sessional Papers. No.94
443 *'Report from the Select Committee of the House of Lords, appointed to consider the Petition of the Directors of the Chamber of Commerce and Manufactures, established by Royal Charter in the City of Glasgow, taking Notice of the Bill, intituled, "An Act for Ascertaining and Establishing Uniformity of Weights and Measures"....'*. 1824.

GREAT BRITAIN, Parliament, Sessional Papers, No.356
444 *'Report of the Commissioners appointed to consider the Steps to be Taken for restoration of the Standards of Weight and Measure'*. 1842. H.M.S.O. London.

GREAT BRITAIN, Patent Office
445 *'A.D. 1821, No. 4623, Glass Bottles. Ricketts' Specification'*. 1857. Eyre & Spottiswoode. London.
446 *'Manufacturing, Stoppering, and Covering Bottles, Jars, Pots etc. Betts and Stocker's Specification, No.10, 449'*. 1844. Eyre & Spottiswoode. London.

GREEN, C.G.
447 *'Cleaning Methods - A Dump Diggers Guide'*. ©1977, Southern Collectors Publications, Southampton, England.

GREEN, Roger
448 *'A Treasury of British Bottles'*. 1982. Old Bottles & Treasure Hunting, Bridgenorth, Shropshire.
449 *'Bottle Collecting, Comprehensive Price Guide'*. © Roger Green. First publ. 1977. Reprinted 1978. Publ. by Old Bottles and Treasure Hunting, Bridgenorth, Salop.

GREWENIG, Meinrad Maria
450 *'Mysterium Wein'* - Die Götter, der Wein und die Kunst. Historisches Museum der Pfalz Speyer 1996, Verlag Gerd Hatje.

GUEST, Gary
451 *'Brewers & Bottlers'. A catalog of Brooklyn Beer Bottles; includes: neighboring Queens Nassau & Suffolk Counties* ©1991. Priv. publ./U.S.A.
452 *'New York City Beer Bottles'; Brewers & Bottlers (1837-1950)*. ©1994, U.S.A. Priv. printed.

GYÜRKY, Katalin H.
453 *'Gläser in mittelalterlichen Ungarn'*. Die wissenschaftliche Werkstatt des historischen Museums der Stadt Budapest 3., Budapest, 1991.

HAANSTRA, Bert
454 *'Glas'*. (A videofilm in Dutch of the original film produced in 1958 on the industrial production of bottles). N.V. Vereenigde Glasfabrieken Leerdam/Schiedam/Maastricht, 1995.

HAHN, Gerhard
455 *'Die Geschichte der Glasindustrie im Schaumburger Land'*. Diplom-Arbeit. Ausgefertigt im Seminar für Wirtschaftsgeschichte an der Universität Köln, 1953.

HAMMER, S.C.
456 *'Den norske flaskeindustri. Et bidrag til dens historie gjennem århundrer'*. Utg. av AS. Moss glassverk. Oslo 1931.

HAMPTON, David
457 *'Collecting Bottles'*. ©1987. Printed by The C.Y. Services, Nottingham, England.

HAN, Dr. Verena
458 *'Le Verre aux Balkans pendant la Domination Ottomane (XVIe - XVIIe siècles)'*. P.257-279 in 'Annales du 9e Congrès International d'Etude Historique du Verre'; Nancy (France), 22-28 mai 1983. Editions du Centre de Publications de l'A.I.H.V., Liège, 1985.
459 *'The Origin and Style of Medieval Glass Found in the Central Balkans'*. In CJGS, Vol. XVII, 1975, p. 114-126.

HANRAHAN, Paul
460 *'Bottle Seals from Canadian Historic Sites'*. In 'Canadian Bottle & Stoneware Collector', No.10, Oct 1994, p.25-39.
461 *'Bottles in the Place Royale Collection'*. Publ. by the National Museum of Man in 'Material History Bulletin - Bulletin d'histoire de la culture matérielle - No.6, p.52-73. Ottawa, Fall, 1978.
462 *'Old Bottles with British Guyana Commercial Markings'*. Publ. by the Walter Roth Museum, Georgetown, Guyana, in 'Journal of Archaeology and Anthropology' 7, 1990.
463 *'The CS/Ostrich Wine Bottle'*. Publ. by the Walter Roth Museum, Georgetown, Guyana, 1993 in 'Journal of Archaeology and Anthropology 9, 1993; p.35-39.
464 *'Wine Bottles of New France'*. Publ. in 'Canadian Collector', Jan/Feb 1980; p.36-39.

HARRIS, Jane E.
465 *'Eighteenth-Century French Blue-Green Bottles from the Fortress of Louisbourg, Nova Scotia'*. In 'History and Archaeology' No.29, p.83-149. National Historic Parks and Sites Branch, Parks Canada, Environment Canada, 1979.

HARRISON, Don
466 *'Old Tyme Bottles'*. ©1973, Don Harrison. Printed by Precise Instant Printing, Vancouver, B.C.

HARRISON, Elmer J.
467 *'Modern Bottle Collector's Catalog'*. Distr. Elmer J. Harrison. Cheyenne, Wyoming; ©1971.

HARRISON, Russell

468 *'Mineral Waters and Closures'* - *An Illustrated Guide to Internal Stopper Variations.* Printed by Quintrells, Trenant Industrial Estate, Wadebridge, Cornwall; 1993

HARTMANN, Carolus

469 *'Glasmarken Lexikon 1600-1945'*. *Signaturen, Fabrik- und Handelsmarken.* Arnoldsche – Stuttgart, Dec 1997.

HARTSHORNE, Albert

470 *'Antique drinking glasses. A pictorial history of glass drinking vessels'*. New York, Brussel & Brussel, 1967, 490p., illus. A facsimile reprint of Old English glasses with new title-page.

471 *'Old English glasses: an account of glass drinking vessels in England, from early times to the end of the eighteenth century. With introductory notices, original documents, etc.'*. Edward Arnold, 1897, 490p., illus. This book marks the beginning of glass literature (excluding technology) in England. Contents include: transcripts of State Papers, Patent Rolls, Ravenscroft's Patent (1674), p.454-6.

HASLAM, Jeremy

472 *'Oxford Taverns and the Cellars of All Souls in the 17th and 18th Centuries'*. 1969. Oxoniensia, Vol.34, p.45-77. Oxford.

473 *'Sealed bottles from All Souls College'*. In Oxoniensia, XXV (1970), p.27-33.

HASTIN, Bud

474 *'Avon Bottle Collector Encyclopedia™'*. The Official Guide For Avon Bottle Collectors. 11th ed. Publ. by Bud Hastin, Fort Lauderdale, ©1988.

HAUDICQUER DE BLANCOURT

475 *'L'Art de la Verrerie'*. 2 Vol., Claude Jombert, Paris, 1718.

HAYDN, Joseph & VINCENT, Benjamin

476 *'Haydn's Dictionary of Dates and Universal Information relating to all Ages and Nations'*. Twenty-Fourth Edition, containing the History of the World to the Summer of 1906. London: Ward, Lock & Co., Ltd., 1906.

HAYNES, E.

477 *'Some Ravenscroft jugs [decanter jugs and pitchers]'*. In CONN, Jly-Dec 1941, p.175-9. Includes a chart of styles and locations.

HAZEL-ATLAS GLASS COMPANY

478 *'Glassware for Packers and Preservers'*. Hundreds of various jars and bottles illustrated. Sales catalogue. Publ. by Hazel-Atlas Glass Company, Wheeling, West Virginia, 1930.

HEACOCK, William

479 *'Encyclopedia of Victorian Colored Pattern Glass, Book 6 - Oil Cruets from A to Z'*. ©1981, Antique Publications, Inc., Marietta, Ohio.

HECKLER, Norman C.

480 *'American Bottles in the Charles B. Gardner Collection'*. Publ. by Robert W. Skinner Inc., Bolton, Mass., 1975.

481 *'The Bill & Leah Pollard Collection of Premier Baltimore Flasks, Pattern Molded Flasks and Rare Bottles'*. Unreserved Public Auction, Saturday 16 March 1996 at 11:00 a.m. Norman C. Heckler & Company, Woodstock Valley, Connecticut 06282.

482 *'The Edmund & Jayne Blaske Collection of American Historical Flasks'*. *Public Auction May 1983.* ©1983 by R.W. Skinner, Bolton, Masss.

483 *'The Edmund & Jayne Blaske Collection: Part II'*. *Sept. 1983.* ©1983 by R.W. Skinner, Bolton, Mass.

HECKROODT, R.O. & SAITOWITZ, S.J.

484 *'Characterization of bottles manufactured at the Cape Glass Company, Glencairn, circa 1904'*. South African archaeological bulletin 40: 94-99, 1985.

HEDGES, A.A.C.

485 *'Bottles and Bottle Collecting'*. Shire Publications Ltd. Undated.

HELLIWELL, Anthony

486 *'Meat and similar Extract Bottles'*. ©1995. Publ. 1995 by Anthony Helliwell, Beeston, Nottingam.

487 *'Meat and similar Extract Bottles'*. Second ed. May 1996 publ. by Anthony Helliwell, Beeston, Nottingam.

HENKES, Harold E.

488 *'Flaschensiegel des 17. und 18. Jhs. aus niederländischem Boden'*. P.405-410 in 'Annales du 12e Congrès de l'Association Internationale pour l'Histoire du Verre'; Vienne – Wien, 26-31 août 1991; ©1993 - A.I.H.V. - Amsterdam.

489 *'Glas zonder Glans'*. *Vijf eeuwen gebruiksglas uit de bodem van de Lage Landen 1300-1800. 'Glass without Gloss'. Utility glass from five centuries excavated in the Low Countries 1300-1800.* Rotterdam papers 9. ©1994, Coördinatie Commissie van Advies inzake Archeologisch Onderzoek binnen het Resort Rotterdam.

490 *'Glaszegels uit Nederlandse bodem'*. Publ. in Westerheem, Orgaan van de Archeologische Werkgemeenschap voor Nederland (AWN), Schagen. Jaargang 39, No.6, p.234-252, Dec 1990.

HENNESSY, F.

491 *'Our humble servant, the bottle'*. In Chambers Jnl., Apr. 1937, p.283-4.

HENNEZEL D'ORNOIS, J.M.F. de

492 *'Gentilhommes verriers de la Haute-Picardie'*. Nogent-le-Ratvov, Charles-Fontaine, 1933.

HENRIVAUX, Jules

493 *'Fabrication Mécanique des Bouteilles'*. In 'La Nature'. Vol.37, 1909, p.392-395. Masson et Cie., Editeurs, Paris.

494 *'La Verrerie au XXe Siècle'*. Librairie des Sciences et de l'Industrie, Paris 1911.

HENRIVAUX, M.J.

495 *'Le Verre et le Cristal'*. P. Vicq-Dunod et Cie., Editeurs, Paris 1897.

HERMANN-LACHAPELLE & GLOVER, CH.
496 *'Des Boissons Gazeuses, aux points de vue Alimentaire, Hygiénique et Industriel'*. *Guide Pratique du Fabricant & du Consommateur*. Paris, France, 1867.

HERR, J.A.
497 *'The Ontario Soda Water Bottle Collector's Index and Price Guide'*. *Vol.II for Ontario Series*. Canada West Publishing Company, St.Thomas, Ontario.

HETTINGER, Theodor
498 *'Arbeitsbedingungen in der Glasindustrie'* - *Band IV - Flaschen- und Behälterglasherstellung*. Aus dem Fachgebiet Arbeitssicherheitstechnik einschl. Ergonomie der Bergischen Universität – Gesamthochschule Wuppertal. Leiter: Prof. Dr. med. habil. Th. Hettinger, 1987.

HINTON, David A.
499 *'A glass bottle seal from Oxford'*. In Oxoniensia, 32, 1967, p.10-12.

500 *'Hiram Codd's bottles [Letters discussing early aerated liquid bottles]'*. In CL, 1964; Jly, p.247; Sept, p.579; Oct, p.845; Dec, p.1718. Bottles of this type were patented by Codd in 1875.

HODGES, Elizabeth
501 *'The Story of Glass; bottles and containers through the ages'*. New York: Sterling Publishing Co., Inc., ©1960.

HODKIN, F.W. & COUSEN, A.
502 *'A Textbook of Glass Technology'* (*Bottle-making machines*). Constable & Company Ltd., London, 1925.

HOLINER, Richard
503 *'Collecting Barber Bottles'*- *Pictorial Price Guide with History*. Collector Books, Paducah. ©1986 Richard Holiner.

HOLL-GYÜRKY, Katalin
504 *'The Use of Glass in Medieval Hungary'*. In CJGS, Vol.28, p.70-81, 1986.

HOLLINGWORTH, Jane
505 *'Collecting Decanters'*. Studio vista, Christie's South Kensington Collectors Series, London; 1980; 128 p.

HOLST, Jim
506 *'Pontiled Medicines'*. Third ed. ©1995 Jim Holst, 1008 27th Av. SE, Apt. B. Minneapolis, MN 55414.

HÖLTL, Georg
507 *'Das Böhmische Glas - 1700-1950'*. *Volumes I-II*. Passauer Glasmuseum – Passau, 1995.

HONEY, W.B.
508 *'Glass'*. *A Handbook for the Study of Glass Vessels of all Periods and Countries & a Guide to the Museum Collection*. Victoria and Albert Museum. London: Publ. under the authority of the Ministry of Education: 1946.

HOOVER, Herbert Clark & Lou Henry
509 *Georgius Agricola: 'De re Metallica'*. *Translated from the first Latin Edition of 1556 with Biographical Introduction, Annotations and Appendices upon the Development of Mining Methods, Metallurgical Processes, Geology, Mineralogy & Mining Law from the earliest times to the 16th Century*. Dover Publications, Inc., New York; 1950.

HORAT, Heinz
510 *'Der Glasschmelzofen des Priesters Theophilus'*. Verlag Paul Haupt Bern und Stuttgart, ©1991.

511 *'Flühli-Glas'*. Verlag Paul Haupt Bern und Stuttgart, 1986.

HORST, A.J. van der
512 *'Wijnflessen afkomstig uit een V.O.C.-schip'*. Review: 'Antiek', mei 1986, 20ste jaargang no.10, p.640-643.

513 *'Wijnflessen uit scheepswrakken uit de zeventiende en achttiende eeuw'*. Review: 'Antiek', dec 1991, 26ste jaargang no.5, p.233-250.

HOTCHKISS, John F. & CASSIDY, Joan H.
514 *'Bottle Collecting'*. *Manual with Prices*. ©1972. Publi. by Hotchkiss House, Inc., Pittsford, N.Y.

515 *'The New and Revised Bottle Collecting Manual with Prices'*. Rochester, NY: Hotchkiss, Hawthorne, 1972.

HOUDOY, J.
516 *'Verreries à la Façon de Venise'* - *La Fabrication Flamande d'après des documents inédits'*. ©1878, Bruxelles.

HOUGHTON, John
517 *'List of glasshouses in operation in England in 1696'*. In Elville, E.M. English table glass. Country Life, 1951, p.77.

HOWE, John
518 *'A Whiskeyana Guide - Antique Whiskey Bottles'*. ©1967 John Howe. Publ.by John Howe, San Jose, Calif.

HUDIG, Ferrand W.
519 *'Das Glas'*. Mit besonderer Berücksichtigung der Sammlung im 'Nederlandsch Museum voor Geschiedenis en Kunst' in Amsterdam. Abhandlung zur Erlangung der Doctorwürde der philosophischen Fakultät I der Universität Zürich. Im Selbstverlag des Verfassers, Amsterdam, Wien 1923.

HUDSON, J. Paul
520 *'Seventeenth-century glass wine bottles and seals excavated at Jamestown'*. In CJGS, 1961, p.78-89.

HUGGINS, Phillip Kenneth
521 *'The South Carolina Dispensary: a bottle collectors Atlas and history of the system'*. Lexington, SC: Sandlapper Pr, 1971.

522 *'The South Carolina Dispensary'*. *A Bottle Collector's Atlas and History of the System*. ©1997. Publ. by Sandlapper Publishing Co., Inc., Orangeburg, South Carolina, USA.

HUGHES, George Bernard
523 *'Decanters for the admiral's table'*. In CL, Oct 1960, p.722-3.

524 *'Discovered in the cellars [bottles]'*. In CL, June 1955, p.1575-6.

525 *'English, Scottish and Irish table glass. From the sixteenth century to 1820'*. Batsford, 1956, 410p. Contents include: Serving bottles, ... squares and carafes, p.257-83.

526 *'Label decanters of Georgian times'*. In CL, Apr 1961, p.764-5.

527 *'Old English decanters'*. In AP, Jly-Dec 1943, p.137-40.

528 *'Old English decanters'*. In ADCG, June 1948, p.40-2.

529 *'Old English decanters and their labels'*. In A, 1929, p.475-80; and in Old Furniture, 1929, p.227-33; and in Chambers's Jnl., Sept 1937, p.667-8.

530 *'Rodney decanters'*. In ADCG, Jly 1974, p.63-5.

531 *'Square bottles for sundry uses [spirit decanters, medicine bottles, etc.]'*. In CL. May 1963, p.1007, 1009.

532 *'The hey-day of Irish decanters'*. In CL, Aug 1964, p.510-11.

533 *'When Wine was Bought by the Butt'*. CL, Apr 1969.

HUGHES, Therle

534 *'Decanters and Glasses'*. Country Life Books, London, 1982; 128p.

HULME, E. Wyndham

535 *'Sir Kenelm Digby and the green glass manufacture'*. In Notes & Queries, 8th Series VIII (1895), p.67.

HUMBSCH, Kristian

536 *'Christliche und magisch-okkulte Symbole auf Glasmarken'*. (The meaning of symbols on glass seals). Verlag Lenover Neustrelitz, Neustrelitz, Germany, 1998.

HUME, Ivor Noël

537 *'A century of London glass bottles, 1580-1680'*. In Connoisseur Year Book, 1956, p.98-103.

538 *'All the Best Rubbish'*. ©1974. Harper & Row, Publishers, New York, N.Y., USA.

539 *'A lyttle bottell: charm of apothecaries phials'*. In ADCG, Oct 1954, p.32.

540 *'A seventeenth-century Virginian's seal: detective story in glass'*. In A, Sept 1957, p.44-5.

541 *'Bottled treasure from the Goodwins'*. In CL, Feb 1955, p.570-1. Eighteenth-century ale bottles washed up at Sandwich, Kent.

542 *'Collection of glass from Port Royal, Jamaica'*. In Historical Archaeology, 1968, p.5-34.

543 *'English glass wine bottles'*. In AP, Jan-June 1956, p.155-6.

544 *'Glass in Colonial Williamsburg's Archaeological Collections'*. Publ. by The Colonial Williamsburg Foundation, Williamsburg, Virginia. 1969.

545 *'Medieval bottles from London'*. In CONN, Jan-June 1957, p.104-8

546 *'Neglected glass [apothecary and medicine bottles]'*. In CL, Sept 1954, p.716-17.

547 *'Relics from the Wine Trade's own church'*. In Wine and Spirit Trade Record, Feb 1958, p.158-64.

548 *'The glass wine bottle in Colonial Virginia'*. In CJGS, 1961, p.91-118.

549 *'To corking and wiring'*. In Wine and Spirit Trade Record, June 1958, p.772-6.

550 *'Wine bottle treasures'*. In Wine and Spirit Trade Record, 1956, p.288-94; 580-6; 868-70; 1010-18.

551 *'Wine relics from the colonies [bottles]'*. In Wine and Spirit Trade Record, Aug 1952, p.1052-8.

HUNTER, Frederick William

552 *'Stiegel Glass'*. Dover Publications, Inc. New York, 1950.

HUTCHINSON, Francis

553 *'Patents for Invention, Abridgements of Specifications, Class 125 Stoppering and Bottling, 1855-1930'*. Publ. priv. for the I.C.C.A. 1983.

IELATI, P.C.

554 *'Old Mining Towns and Old Bottles'*. Publ. 1964.

INTERNATIONAL COMMISSION ON GLASS

555 *'English, French and German dictionary of glass making'*. Classified with indices. Charleroi, 1965, 233p.

ISINGS, Clasina

556 *'Roman Glass from dated finds'*. Groningen/Djakarta, 1957.

JACOBS, E.

557 *'Tussen koor en controle'*. Opgravingen op het terrein van de Algemene Rekenkamer aan het Lange Voorhout. VOM-reeks 1996 No.3, Gemeente Den Haag, Dienst Stadsbeheer, Afd. Archeologie.

JAMES, D.

558 *'Drug, Perfume & Chemical Bottles 1902'*. Compilation from the Whitehall Tatum Company's catalog of 1902. Compiled and publ. by D. James, 1967, printed by The Copy Center, USA.

JÁNOS, Hunyadi

559 *'A Natural Purgative Water Drawn from Saxlehner's Bitter-Water Springs near Budapest'* - 'The sovran'st thing on earth'. Firm of Andreas Saxlehner, Budapest. 1898.

JASCHKE, Brigitte

560 *'Glasherstellung'*. *Produkte - Technik - Organisation*. Deutsches Museum, München, 1986.

JEAN, Morin (or Morin-Jean)

561 *'La Verrerie en Gaule sous l'Empire Romain'*. Paris, Société de Propagation des Livres d'Art, 1922-1923.

JENSEN, Al

562 *'Old Owl Drug Bottles and Others'*. Mountain View, Cal.: Author, 1967, 1968.

JENSEN, Al & Margaret

563 *'Old Owl Drug Bottles & Others'*. ©1967 Al & Margaret Jensen, Mountain View, Calif.

JOHNSON, Tom

564 *'The Story of Berry Bros. & Rudd - Wine and Spirit Merchants'*. Priv. publ., London, by Berry Brothers. Undated.

JONES, David

565 *'One Hundred Thirsty Years, Sydney's aerated water manufacturers from 1830 to 1930'*. ©Sept. 1979 David Jones. Printed by Reliance Press, Deniliquin, NSW.

JONES, John Lemuel

566 *'Soda and Mineral Water Bottles'*. *(Over 2000 Varieties), Price Guide*. ©1972 J.L. Jones. Publ. by Palmetto Enterprises, Greer, S.C.

JONES, May

567 **'The Bottle Trail'**. *Vols (1-9), 1961-1968.* ©1961. Printed by Chalfant Press, Inc., Bishop, Calif., and by Southwest Offset, Inc., Hereford, Texas.

568 **'The Bottle Trail'**. *Vol.3.* ©1963. Printed by Southwest Offset, Inc., Hereford, Texas.

569 **'The Bottle Trail'**. *Vol.4.* ©1964. Printed by Southwest Offset, Inc., Hereford, Texas.

570 **'The Bottle Trail'**. *Vol.5.* ©1965. Printed by Southwest Offset, Inc., Hereford, Texas.

571 **'The Bottle Trail'**. *Vol.6.* ©1966. Printed by Southwest Offset, Inc., Hereford, Texas.

572 **'The Bottle Trail'**. *Vol.7.* ©1967. Printed by Southwest Offset, Inc., Hereford, Texas.

573 **'The Bottle Trail'**. *Vol.8.* ©1967. Printed by Southwest Offset, Inc., Hereford, Texas.

574 **'The Bottle Trail'**. *Vol.9.* ©1968. Printed by Southwest Offset, Inc., Hereford, Texas.

JONES, Michael

575 **'Time, Gentlemen, Please!'**. *Early Brewery Posters in the Public Record Office.* PRO Publications, Kew, Surrey, ©1997.

JONES, Olive R.

576 **'Catalogue of the Glass Bottles and Other Miscellaneous Glassware Excavated at Coteau du Lac, Quebec'**. 1975. Manuscript on file, National Historic Parks and Sites Branch, Environment Canada – Parks, Ottawa.

577 **'Commercial Foods, 1740-1820'**. In 'Historical Archaeology', 1993, 27(2):25-41. Ottawa, Canada.

578 **'Cylindrical English Wine and Beer Bottles 1735-1850'**. Studies in Archaeology, Architecture and History. National Historic Parks and Sites Branch, Environment Canada – Parks. ©Minister of Supply and Services Canada 1986.

579 **'Glass Bottle Push-Ups and Pontil Marks'**. 1971. Historical Archaeology, Vol.5, p.62-73. Lansing, Mich.

580 **'Les bouteilles à vin et à bière cylindriques anglaises 1735-1850'**. Etudes en archéologie architecture et histoire. Lieux et parcs historiques nationaux, environnement Canada – Parcs. ©Ministre des Approvisionnements et Services Canada 1986.

581 **'The contribution of the Ricketts' mould to the manu-facture of the English 'wine' bottle, 1820-1850'**. In CJGS, 1983, Vol.25, p.167-77. Corning, N.Y.

JONES, Olive R. & SMITH, E. Ann

582 **'Glass of the British Military, ca. 1755-1820'**. 1985. Environment Canada – Parks, Ottawa. Studies in Archaeology, Architecture and History.

JONES, Olive R. & SULLIVAN, Catherine

583 **'The Parks Canada Glass Glossary for the description of containers, tableware, flat glass, and closures'**. National Historic Parks and Sites, Canadian Parks Service, Environment Canada. ©1989.

JONES-NORTH, Jacquelyne Y.

584 **'Commercial Perfume Bottles'**. Schiffer Publishing Ltd., West Chester, Pennsylvania.

585 **Czechoslovakian Perfume Bottles and Boudoir Accessories'**. ©1990 Antique Publications, Marietta, Ohio.

586 **'Perfume, Cologne and Scent Bottles'**. Schiffer Publishing Ltd., Atglen, PA. ©1986.

JOUVET, Jean

587 **'Giorgio Morandi'** - *Ölbilder, Aquarelle, Zeichnungen, Radierungen.* ©1982 Diogenes Verlag AG Zürich.

JUNG, Hermann

588 **'3000 Jahre Bocksbeutel – Der Siegeszug einer Weinflasche'**. ©1970 Stütz Verlag Würzburg.

KAHNT, Helmut, und KNORR, Bernd

589 **'Alte Masse, Münzen und Gewichte'**. Leipzig 1986.

KALLINICH, Günter

590 **'Schöne alte Apotheken'**. Verlag Georg D.W. Callwey München, ©1975.

KALNEIN, Wend Graf

591 **'Das Wein Gefäss'**. Ariel Verlag, Frankfurt am Main, Germany. Undated.

KÄMPFER, Fritz

592 **'Beakers – Tankards – Goblets'**. ©1978 by Edition Leipzig.

KAUFFMAN, Donald M. & June

593 **'Dig Those Crazy Bottles; a handbook of pioneer bottles'**. Cheyenne, Wyo.: 1966.

KENDRICK, Grace

594 **'The Antique Bottle Collector'**. ©1971. Harcourt Brace Jovanovich, New York and London.

595 **'The Antique Bottle Collector'**. *Secrets revealed to date and evaluate old bottles.* Third ed. ©1966 Grace Kendrick, Fallon, Nevada.

596 **'The Antique Bottle Collector'**. *Secrets revealed to date and evaluate bottles of the 19th century'.* Sparks, Nev.: Western Printing, 1963, 1964. Price Supplement. 1965, 3rd ed. with Price Supplement. 1966.

597 **'The Mouth-Blown Bottle'**. ©1968, Grace Kendrick, Fallon, Nevada.

KENYON, G.H.

598 **'Glass industry of the Weald'**. Leicester University Press, 1967, 231p.

KETCHUM Jr., William C.

599 **'A Treasury of American Bottles'**. ©1975. Publ. The Bobbs-Merrill Company, Inc., Indianapolis/New York.

600 **'Collecting Bottles for Fun & Profit'**. Publ. by HP Books, Inc., Tucson, Az. ©1985.

KILLING, Margarete

601 **'Die Glasmacherkunst in Hessen'** - *Ein Beitrag zur Gewerbe- und Kunstgeschichte der deutschen Renaissance.* 1927, Verlag von N.G. Elwert, Marburg.

KIMBLEBY, V. & TURNER, W.E.S.

602 **'Durability of Bottles – Some experiments on the effects of humidity on the weathering of bottle glass'**. In 'J. Soc. Glass Tech., <u>23</u>, 98, p.242-52.

KINCADE, Steve

603 **'Early American Bottles and Glass'**. Clovis, Cal.: Clovis Printing, 1964.

KING, W.

604 *'Flämisches Glas und seine Beziehungen zum englischen Glas [The relationship between Flemish and English glass]'*. In Pantheon (Munich), Apr 1931, p.158-60, with English translation.

KIPPERS, Marjan

605 *'Een kloos die goed geblazen werd. Technologische en sociaal-economische factoren in de glas-industrie te Leerdam 1899-1938'*. Doctoraalscriptie Economische en Sociaalgeschiedenis, Vrije Universiteit Amsterdam, 1987.

KISA, Anton

606 *'Das Glas im Altertume'*. Volumes I-III. Leipzich, Verlag von Karl W. Hiersemann, 1908

607 *' Die antiken Glaeser der Frau Maria vom Rath zu Koeln'*. Bonn, Druck von Carl Georgi, 1899.

KISTEMAKER, R.E.

608 *'Bier! - Geschiedenis van een volksdrank'*. De Bataafsche Leeuw, Amsterdam 1994.

KJELLBERG, Sven T.

609 *'Kulturen en Årsbok 1953'*. Publ. in Lund, 1954.

KLAMKIN, Marian

610 *'The Collector's Book of Bottles'*. Flasks, bitters, medicines, inks, fruit jars, etc. New York: Dodd, Mead, ©1971.

KLAMKIN, Marian & GARDNER, Charles B.

611 *'American Glass Bottles'*. ©1977. Publ. Wallace-Homestead Book Co., Des Moines, Iowa.

KLEIN, W.H.A.

612 *'Antieke gebruiksflessen in Suriname'*. Reprint: uit: 'Nieuwe West-Indische Gids, Jrg. 45, 1966'. Editor: Martinus Nijhoff, 's-Gravenhage.

613 *'Antieke gebruiksflessen in Suriname - Antique bottles in Surinam'*. 1974. Surinam Museum Foundation, Stichting Surinaams Museum, Paramaribo (Suriname).

KLEINER, Robert

614 *'Chinese Snuff Bottles'*. Publ. by Oxford University Press (Hong Kong) Ltd., Quarry Bay, Hong Kong. ©1994.

615 *'Chinese Snuff Bottles'* - In the Collection of Mary and George Bloch. Publ. to accompany an exhibition at the British Museum, 20 Jun-15 Oct 1995.

KLEINFELDT, Kay

616 *'Georgian decanters'*. In Ray, Cyril, ed. The complete imbiber, 5. Vista Books 1962, p.155-60.

KLESSE, Brigitte &
REINEKING-VON BOCK, Gisela

617 *'Glas'*. Kunstgewerbemuseum der Stadt Köln, Köln 1973.

KLINT, David K.

618 *'Colorado Historical Bottles & Etc., 1859-1915'*. ©1976 by Antique Bottle Collectors of Colorado, Inc.

KNIGHT, David

619 *'Cherry Cordials in the Danish West Indies'*. Publ. by 'Antique Bottle & Glass Collector', East Greenville, PA, USA, July, 1992; p.36-37.

KOCH, Jens

620 *'Braunschweiger Brauersiegel des 17. bis 19. Jahrhunderts'*. Glasmarken früher braunschweigischer Bierflaschen. Schriftenreihe der IG-Glassiegel Peine, Peine 1998.

621 *'Glassiegel mit königlichen Monogrammen'* - Hoheitszeichen englischer und hannoverscher Gebrauchsflaschen. Schriftenreihe der IG-Glassiegel Peine, Peine 1995. Herausgeber: Jens Koch, Edemissen. ©1995 - P-age-press.

KOLTHOFF, Benedict

622 *'Glass Terminology: a German-English Glossary'*. G.B. van Goor Zonen's Publishing Co., Ltd., The Hague, Holland; 1967.

KOPISTO, Sirkka

623 *'Lasia-Suomen kansallismuseon kokoelmista'*. (Glass in the National Museum of Finland). Helsinki, 1978.

KORFF, Friedrich-Wilhelm

624 *'Die Kugel- oder Knickerflasche, ihre Herstellung und Verwendung'*. 1978. In Schaumburger Heimat 9 (1978), p.71-98.

KORSHAVN, Jan Håvar

625 *'Norske empire glass'*. Gjøviks Glasvoerk 1807-1843. Gjøvik Historielag 1994

KOSLER, Rainer

626 *'Gebrauchsflaschen aus Glas'* - Form und Technik. ©1991 - ck press, Ismaning.

KOTTMAN, J.

627 *'Flessen, Glazen en een Tazza'*. 1991. Rijksdienst voor het Oudheidkundig Bodemonderzoek, Amersfoort, Holland. Overdruk nr. 394.

628 *'Glas'*. 1990. Rijksdienst voor het Oudheidkundig Bodemonderzoek, Amersfoort, Holland. Overdruk nr. 382.

KREFT, Hans Dieter

629 *'Streifzug durch die Geschichte der Glashütten am Kleinen Süntel'*. In Der Söltjer, Heft 18, Bad Münder 1993 S.49-57.

KRUSE, Hans-Joachim

630 *'Holsteinische Glassiegel'*. In Plöner Glasforschungen, Vol.1, 1992. Edited by: Verein zur Förderung und Pflege des Kreisheimatmuseums in Plön e.V.

KUHN, Rudy

631 *'Poison Bottle Workbook'*. USA, undated.

632 *'Poison Bottle Workbook II'*. USA, undated.

KÜHNERT, Herbert

633 *'Urkundenbuch zur thüringischen Glashüttengeschichte - und Aufsätze zur thüringischen Glashüttengeschichte'*. Franz Steiner Verlag GmbH, Wiesbaden, 1973.

KUNCKEL, Johannis

634 *'Ars Vitraria Experimentalis, oder Vollkommene Glasmacher-Kunst'*. Gedruckt bei Christoph Günthern, Frankfurt/Leipzig, 1679.

KUNST & ANTIQUITÄTEN

635 *'Glück und Glas'*- Zur Kulturgeschichte des Spessartglases. Kunst & Antiquitäten - München, 1984.

KÜRTZ, Jutta
636 'Aus Kanne, Fass und Buddel'. Lübbeck, 1986.
LADAIQUE, Gabriel
637 'Deux Siècles de Travail Verrier dans la Vôge (1448-1636)' - Historique du grand verre; Les Techniques verrières de la Vôge; Les Familles de Gentilshommes verrier - Thèse pour le Doctorat de troisième cycle présentée à la Faculté des Lettres et des Sciences Humaines de l'Université de Nancy. Nancy, Oct 1970.
638 'Les Verriers de la Vôge (1390-1636)'. Archéologie et Travail Verriers; l'Age d'Or des Verrières; l'Exode et les Fondations Entreprises à l'Etranger. Thèse pour le doctorat de troisième cycle. Nancy, May 1973.
LAGHI, Anna
639 'Vetri da Farmacia'. Publ. Octavo, Franco Cantini Editore, Firenze, 1998.
LAMM, Carl Johan
640 'Mittelalterliche Gläser und Steinschnittarbeiten aus dem nahen Osten'. (Glasses of the Middle Ages and cut stone-work from the near East), 2 Vols, Berlin, 1929-1930. (L.M.B.).
LANE, Lyman & Sally, & PAPPAS, Joan
641 'A Rare Collection of Keene & Stoddard Glass'. ©1970 Lymand and Sally Lane and Joan Pappas.
LANMON, Dwight & PALMER, Arlene
642 'The "B. Johnson" Case Bottles'. In CJGS, Vol.XVIII, p.56-57, 1976.
LANS, Nathalie
643 'Schiedam Jeneververleden - Een wandeling door de tijd'. Druk: Tijl Offset Zwolle
LAPOINTE, Camille
644 'Le verre des latrines de la maison Perthuis'. Les collections archéologiques de la place Royale. Dossier 52. Febr.1981, Ministère des Affaires culturelles, Direction générale du Patrimoine, Ottawa, Canada.
645 'Le verre et les terres cuites communes de la maison Perthuis à la Place-Royale'. Les Publications du Québec. 1997; Bibliothèque nationale du Québec; ©Gouvernement du Québec, 1997.
LARWOOD, Jacob & HOTTEN, John Camden
646 'English Inn Signs'. Being a Revised and Modernized Version of History of Signboards. ©1951, 1985 Blaketon Hall Limited, Exeter, UK.
647 'The History of Signboards, From the Earliest Times to the Present Day'. Seventh ed. ©1866. Chatto and Windus, Publishers, London.
LASTOVICA, Ethleen
648 'Bottles & Bygones' - A guide for South African collectors. Don Nelson, Cape Town; ©1982.
LASTOVICA, E. & A
649 'South African stoneware ginger beer bottles'. Cape Town: 1990.
LATHAM, R.
650 'Taverns, Inns and Eating-Houses'. In 'The Diary (1660-1669) of Samuel Pepys', Vol.X from X Vol., S.416-431, London, 1983.

LATIMER, Tirza True
651 'The Perfume Atomizer - An Object with Atmosphere'. Schiffer Publishing Ltd., West Chester, Pennsylvania; ©1991.
LAUNERT, Edmund
652 'Perfume and Pomanders - Scent and Scent Bottles'. From the Schwarzkopf Collection and European Museums. ©1987 Potterton Books Ltd. First publ. 1985 by Georg D.W. Callwey GmbH & Co., Munich under the title: "Parfüm und Flakons".
653 'Scent bottles'. In The Glass Circle 1, 1972, p.58-64.
654 'Scent & Scent Bottles'. Pts. 1 & 2. In ADCG, Aug 1971, p.64-9; Sept p.62-8.
655 'Scent & Scent Bottles'. Barrie & Jenkins, London, 1974, 176p., illus. (some col.).
LAUNERT, Edmund, joint author see also
GODFREY, A. and LAUNERT, Edmund
LAURIOUX, Bruno
656 'Tafelfreuden im Mittelalter'. Kulturgeschichte des Essens und Trinkens in Bildern und Dokumenten. Belser Verlag, Stuttgart Zürich. ©1992 by Belser AG für Verlagsgeschäfte & Co. KG, Stuttgart und Zürich.
LAWRENCE, Grace & TEAL, Gretchen
657 'Worldwide Bottles'. Balboa, Canal Zone, 1983.
LAZARUS, Peter
658 'The story of decanters'. Pts. 1 & 2. In ADCG, Feb 1971, p.66-71; Mar 1971, p.72-6.
LECHNER, Mildred & Ralph
659 'The World of Salt Shakers'. ©Ralph Lechner, Bill Schroeder, 1976. Collector Books, Box 3009, Paducah, Kentucky 42001.
LECOCQ, Maurice
660 'Variaties op een Stoop'. Nationaal Jenevermuseum, Hasselt, België, ©1991.
LEEDS, E. Thurlow
661 'Glass bottles of the Crown Tavern, Oxford'. In Oxoniensia, v.14, 1949, p.87-9.
662 'On the dating of glass wine bottles of the Stuart period'. In The Antiquary, v.50, 1914, p.285-90.
663 'Seventeenth- and eighteenth-century wine bottles of Oxford taverns'. In Oxoniensia, v.6, 1941, p.44.
LEFEBVRE, E.
664 'Histoire d'une Bouteille'. Librairie Hachette, Paris, 1886.
LEFKOWITH, Christie Mayer
665 'Design des Luxus: Parfum-Flakons' - Guide für Sammler und Liebhaber. Mit einem Lexikon der Designer, Couturiers, Parfümeure und Hersteller. Verlag Christian Brandstätter, Wien. ©1994.
666 'The Art of Perfume - Discovering and Collecting Perfume Bottles'. Thames and Hudson, London. ©1994.
LEHMANN, Fritz
667 'Les verreries suisses'. Lausanne 1940.

LEITHERER, Eugen & WICHMANS, Hans

668 *'Reiz und Hülle-Gestalte Warenverpackungen des 19. und 20. Jahrhunderts'*. Birkhauser Verlag, Stuttgart, 1987.

LENNEP, J. van & GOUW, J. ter

669 *'Uithangtekens, Gevelstenen en Opschriften'*. Publ. N.V. Foresta, Groningen, The Netherlands. Undated, c.1950.

LERK, James Andrew

670 *'Bottles in Australian Collections'*. ©1971 James A. Lerk, Bendigo.

671 *'Bottles in Collection'*. Bendigo, Victoria, Australia: Author, 1971.

LEWIS, M.

672 *'Vintage bottles'*. In Art & Antiques, 23 Aug 1975.

LEYBOURNE, Jr., Douglas M.

673 *'The Collector's Guide to Old Fruit Jars'*. No.7. Publ. by Douglas M. Leybourne, Jr., ©1993.

674 *'The Collector's Guide to Old Fruit Jars'*. No.8. Publ. by Douglas M. Leybourne, Jr., ©1997.

LI, Raymond

675 *'A Glossary of Chinese Snuff Bottle Rebus'*: *Re-Discovering the Hidden Internal Beauty in Snuff Bottles.* Nine Dragons, Hong Kong 1976.

676 *'Snuff Bottle Terminology, Chinese and English Equivalents'*. Part I, Glass, Agate, Quartz. Publ. by Nine Dragons, Hong Kong. ©1981.

677 *'The Medicine-Snuff Bottle Connection'*. *Chinese Miniature Containers: A Dual Role.* Hong Kong: Nine Dragons, 1979.

LIEF, Alfred

678 *'A Close-up of Closures; history and progress'*. New York: Glas Container Manufacturers Institute, 1965. (Bottle seals).

LILGE, Andreas

679 *'Bad Pyrmont - Tal der sprudelnden Quellen - Zur Geschichte der Pyrmonter Heil- und Mineralquellen'*. *(Texte und Materialien zur Sonderausstellung im Museum im Schloß Bad Pyrmont vom 18. Juni - 13. September 1992).* Schriftenreihe des Museums im Schloß Bad Pyrmont Nr. 21. ©1992.

LIMMARED

680 *'Limmared 1740-1940'*. Utg. av AB Fredrik Brusewitz. Ulricehamn 1940.

LINCOLN, Gerald David

681 *'Antique Blob Top Bottles'*; *Central and Southern New England.* ©1970 Gerald David Lincoln, Marlboro, Mass.

LINDEN, Robert A

682 *'The Classification of Violin Shaped Bottles'*. *(Including Bottles in the Shape of Banjos).* Second ed, 1999. ©December 1994, National Bottle Museum, USA.

LIPP, Franz Carl

683 *'Bemalte Gläser'* - *Volkstümliche Bildwelt auf altem Glas - Geschichte und Technik.* ©1974. Verlag Georg D.W. Callwey, München.

LITHERLAND, Gordon

684 *'Bottle collecting price guide'*. Burton-upon-Trent, MAB Publishing, 1977, 96p.

LÖBER, Hans

685 *'Die erste Kartell-Liste der deutschen Glasindustrie (Glas-Taxa 1735/37)'*. In 'Glastechnische Berichte', Frankfurt a.M, 45. Jahrg., Heft 12, p.568-575.

686 *'Guttrolfe, Formgebung und Herstellungstechnik'*. In 'Glastechnische Berichte', Frankfurt (Dec 1966), p.539-548.

LONDON: Patent Office

687 *'Subject list of works on the silicate industries [ceramics and glass]'*. London, 1914.

LOUDMER, Maître Guy

688 *'Ancient and Islamic Glass'*. *Catalogue.* Auction at Hotel Drouot, Paris, 3 and 4 Jun 1985.

LUTZ, Dietrich

689 *'Vor dem großen Brand'*. *Archäologie zu Füßen des Heidelberger Schlosses.* 1992. Landesdenkmalamt Baden-Württemberg.

MACLEOD, Catriona

690 *'The land we live in: a toast on Cork decanters'*. In Cork Hist. & Arch. Soc., 1978, p.59-65, Cork Glass Co. 1783-1818.

MAGAZINES

691 *'Antique Bottle & Glass Collector,* 102 Jefferson St, P.O. Box 180, East Greenville, PA, USA.

692 *'Australian Antique Bottles & Collectables'*. Publ. by Crown Castleton Publishers, P.O. Box 235, Golden Square, Vic. 3555, Australia.

693 *'Bottles & Extras'*. Editor: Dave Hinson, 2842 El Sol Drive, Lancaster, CA 93535, USA. Publ. by the Federation of Historical Bottle Collectors.

694 *' "BBR", (British Bottle Review)'*. Elsecar Heritage Centre, Nr Barnsley, S Yorks, UK.

695 *'De Oude Flesch'*, *Klubblad van de verzamelaarsklub.* Anjerhof 8, 3434 HR Nieuwegein, The Netherlands.

696 *'Der Glasfreund'*, *Zeitschrift für Glassammler.* Verlag Lenover Neustrelitz, Postfach 15 28, 17225 Neustrelitz, Germany.

697 *'Glas - Historische Notizen'*. *Heft 1 (1989) - Heft 10 (1992).* Herausgeber: Karl-Heinz Poser, Neumünster, Germany.

MANSELL, Sir Robert

698 *'Patent from the 22nd May 1623 relating to the 'Manufacture of Glass with Fuel, not being Timber or Wood'*.

MANSFELD, J. van

699 *'Recueil de Verres, Grès, etc., dessinés d'après les tableaux de l'école flamande et hollandaise, du XVIe et du XVIIe Siècle, et les pièces originales conservées dans les musées publics et les collections particulières'*. Brussels, 1880.

MANUSCRIPTS (Photostats)

700 *'An Act for the ascertaining the Measures for retailing

Ale and Beer'. CAP. XV, Anno 11 & 12 Gul. III, C. 15, S.274-277, 24th June A.D.1700, House of Lords Records Office, London.

701 **'Bill of Parliament for Glass Bottles'**. 'Draft of an Act to confirm the (John Colnett) invention and manufacture of glass bottles and for preventing of frauds and abuses in the making and public vending thereof', London, House of Lords Record Office, Historical Manuscript, 10th April 1662, Page 164b.

MARCUS, Ad.
702 **'Les Verreries du Comté de Bitche - Essai historique (XVᵉ - XVIIIᵉ Siècles)'**. Imprimerie Berger-Levrault et Cie. Nancy. ©1887.

MARIACHER, Giovanni
703 **'La Scoperta di due Bottiglie Veneziane del Secolo XV'**. In CJGS, Vol.VI, p.70-74, 1964.

MARKEL, Stephen
704 **'Indian and "Indianate" Glass Vessels in the Los Angeles County Museum of Art'**. In CJGS, Vol.33, p.82-95, 1991.

MARKOTA, Peck & Audie
705 **'A Look at California Hutchinson Type Soda Bottles'**. Printed by Kinko's Copy Center, Sacramento, Ca., USA. 1999.

706 **'Western Blob Top Soda and Mineral Water Bottles'**. ©1971. Printed by Ántique and Hobby Publishing Company', Amador City, Ca.

707 **'Western Blob Top Soda and Mineral Water Bottles'**. ©1993 Peck and Audie Markota, Sacramento, CA. Printed by Kinko's Copy Center, Sacramento, CA.

MARKS, Jay
708 **'The Idaho Bottle Book'**. Mar 1996.

MARTIN, Byron & Vicky
709 **'Here's to Beers - Blob Top Beer Bottles 1880-1910'**. ©1973 Byron & Vicky Martin.

MARTIN, L. & PACKHAM, Colin
710 **'Deadly delights: early [glass] poison Bottles'**. In Art & Antiques Weekly, 17 Jun 1978, p.18-20.

MARTIN, Milward W.
711 **'Twelve Full Ounces'**. ©1969 Milward W. Martin (sec. ed.). Publ. simultaneously in Canada by Holt, Rinehart and Winston of Canada, Limited.

MASSART, Daniel
712 **'Verreries et verriers du Centre (de 1764 à nos jours)'**. Editors: Publications du 'Cercle d'Histoire' et de Folklore 'Henri Guillemin', La Louvière. Haine-Saint-Pierre, Belgium, 1983.

MATHEW, N.
713 **'Decanters'**. In AC, Apr 1977, p.56-60.

MATTHEWS, Leslie G.
714 **'The Antiques of Perfume'**. G. Bell & Sons, London. 1973.

MATTHEWS, Robert T.
715 **'A Collection of Old Glass Candy Containers'**. Publ. by author, Glenelg, Maryland, 1966.

MAURACH, H.
716 **'Glasschmelzöfen in alter Zeit'**. In 'Glastechnische Berichte', Frankfurt a.M., (Aug 1934), 12.Jahrg., Heft 8, p.266-274.

MAUST, Don
717 **'Bottle and Glass Handbook'**. *A History of Bottles showing their various styles, types and uses from ancient times to the present.* ©1956 E.G. Warman Publishing Co., Uniontown, Penna. Bottle Digger's Library, 197-?

MAY, Degenhard
718 **'Aspekte der Massenproduktion von Flaschen um 1900 am Beispiel der Kreuznacher Glashütte'**. P.459-470 in 'Annales du 11ᵉ Congrès de l'Association Internationale pour l'Histoire du Verre'; Bâle, 29 août - 3 septembre 1988; ©1990 - A.I.H.V. - Amsterdam.

719 **'Zur Entwicklung der Weinflasche im 19. Jh. am Beispiel des südwestdeutschen Raums'**. P.529-540 in 'Annales du 12ᵉ Congrès de l'Association Internationale pour l'Histoire du Verre'; Vienne - Wien, 26-31 août 1991; ©1993 - A.I.H.V. - Amsterdam.

McCANN, Jerry
720 **'1999 Fruit Jar Annual'**. Publ. by Phoenix Press, Chicago, Il., 1998.

721 **'2000 Fruit Jar Annual'**. Publ. by Phoenix Press, Chicago, Il., 2000.

McEWEN, Alan
722 **Collecting "Quack Cures"'**. ©1977. Distributors Southern Collectors Publications, Southampton.

McGREW, John R.
723 **'The Brewers & Soft Drink Bottlers of Hanover'**. Hanover, PA; Hanover Historical Society, 1991.

McGUIRE, Eric
724 **'The San Francisco Directory of Liquors Wholesale & Retail'**. Mill Valley, Ca., 1967.

McGUIRE, Timothy J.
725 **'How to Collect Antique American Bottles (Inexpensively)'**. ©1990 Timothy J. McGuire. Publ. by Leprechaun Books, Flat Rock, MI.

McINTYRE, Sylvia
726 **'The Mineral Water Trade in the Eighteenth Century'**. In 'The Journal of Transport History; New Series Vol.II No.1, p.1-19, Febr 1973. © 1973 Leicester University Press.

McKEARIN, George S. & Helen
727 **'American Glass'**. ©1941 Bonanza Books, New York.

728 **'Two Hundred Years of American Blown Glass'**. ©1949 Crown Publishers, Inc., New York.

McKEARIN, Helen
729 **'Bottles, Flasks and Dr. Dyott'**. Crown Publishers, Inc., New York. ©1970.

730 **'Notes on Stopping, Bottling and Binning'**. In CJGS, Vol. XIII, 1971, p. 120-127.

731 **'Price List of Bottles and Flasks; also a few offerings in pewter, prints, cup plates and Anglo-American pottery'**. New York.

732   *'The Story of American Historical Flasks'*. Exhibition. The Corning Museum of Glass, Corning, N.Y.; Summer 1953.

McKEARIN, Helen & WILSON, Kenneth M.

733   *'American Bottles & Flasks and Their Ancestry'*. ©1978, Crown Publishers, Inc., New York.

McMURRAY, Charles

734   *'Collector's Guide of Flasks and Bottles'*. Priv. publ. by Charles McMurray, Dayton, Ohio, USA: ©1927.

McNULTY, Robert H.

735   *'Common Beverage Bottles: Their Production, Use, and Forms in the Seventeenth- and Eighteenth-Century Netherlands - Part I★'*. In CJGS, Vol.XIII, p.91-127, 1971.

736   *'Common Beverage Bottles: Their Production, Use, and Forms in the Seventeenth- and Eighteenth-Century Netherlands - Part II★'*. In CJGS, Vol.XIV, p.141-148, 1972.

737   *'European Green Glass Bottles of the Seventeenth and Eighteenth Centuries: A Neglected Area of Study'*. In "Annales du 5ème Congrès International d'Etude Historique du Verre", Prague, 6-11 juillet 1970, Edition du Secrétariat Général, Liège, 1972, p.145-152.

MEADOWS, Cecil A.

738   *'Trade Signs and their Origin'*. Routledge & Kegan Paul, London, UK. Publ. 1957.

MECHOW, Tod von

739   *'American Sodas & Beers, The Worksheet'*. ©1996 Tod von Mechow, Phoenixville PA.

MEIGH, Edward

740   *'Notes on the Design of Glass Bottles'*. In 'Journal Society of Glass Technology', Vol. XVIII, 1934, p. 122-127. Editor W.E.S. Turner. Publ. by the Society of Glass Technology; Professor W.E.S. Turner, The University, Sheffield, 9.

741   *'The Development of the Automatic Glass Bottle Machine'*. *A Story of some Pioneers.* In 'Glass Technology Vol.1 No.1 Febr.1960, p.25-50. Publ. by The Society of Glass Technology, Sheffield.

742   *'The Story of the Glass Bottle'*. Publ. by C.E. Ramsden & Co. Ltd., Stoke-on-Trent, England; first publ. Oct 1972. © 86p.

MELLIER, A.A.

743   *'Illustrated Catalogue and Current Prices'*. St. Louis, Mo.; 1872.

MENDELSOHN, Oscar

744   *'Drinking with Pepys'*. Macmillan & Co. Ltd., London, 1963.

MENDERA, Marja

745   *'Archeologia e Storia della Produzione del Vetro Preindustriale'*. Edizioni All'Insegna del Giglio, Firenze 1991.

MENDES, José M. Amado

746   *'Santos Barosa, 100 Anos no Vidro 1889-1989'*. Publ. by Santos Barosa - Vidros, Marinha Grande, Portugal, 1992.

MERRET, Christopher

747   *'The art of glass'*. London, 1662. A translation with additions of Antonio Neri's L'Arte Vetraria, publ. Florence, 1612.

MICHAELIS, Ronald F.

748   *'Old bottle seal finds'*. In ADCG, Oct 1964, p.51-2.

MILLER, George L. & SULLIVAN, Catherine

749   *'Machine-made Glass Containers and the End of Production for Mouth-blown Bottles'*. In 'Research Bulletin', No. 171, Dec 1981. Parcs, Ottawa, Canada.

MILLER, Michael

750   *'Arizona Bottle Book'*. *A Collectors Guide to Arizona Bottles & Stoneware.* Priv. publ. by M. Miller, Peoria, Arizona, USA. ©1999.

MILLIGAN, Harry J.

751   *'Canning Jars of Canada'*. *A "Colcasea's" Record Book and Price Guide.* Printed by Haines Frontier Printing Limited, Sarnia, Ontario, Canada.

MINARD-VAN HOOREBEKE, Louis

752   *'Recueil Descriptif des Antiquités et curiosités du treizième au dix-neuvième siècle, formant la collection de Louis Minard-Van Hoorebeke, archtecte à Gand'*. Imprimerie de I.S. van Doosselaere, Gand (Belgium), 1866.

MINTON, Lee W.

753   *'Flame and Heart'*. *A History of the Glass Bottle Blowers Association of the United States and Canada.* ©1961. Merkle Press Inc., USA.

754   *'History of Glass Bottle Blowers'*. Merkle Press, Washington; 1961.

MOLYNEUX-BERRY MW, David

755   *'The Sotheby's Guide to Classic Wines and their Labels'*. Dorling Kindersley, London. ©1990.

MONROE, Loretta

756   *'Old Bottles Found Along the Florida Keys'*. Coral Gables, Fla: Wakebrook House, 1967.

MOODY, Brian E.

757   *'Packaging in Glass'*. Hutchinson Benham Ltd., London, UK. First publ. 1963. Rev. ed. 1977.

758   *'The origin of the "reputed quart" and other measures [bottles, etc.]'*. In Glass Technology, 1960, p.55-68.

MOORE, Charles G.

759   *'The Watt White Collection of Important 19th Century Ink Bottles'*. Absentee Auction 84. 11 Dec 1996 & 8 Jan 1997. New York, New York, 10022.

MORGAN, Roy

760   *'Mainly Codd's Wallop: The Story of the Great British Pop Bottle'*. Wellingborough, Kollectorama, 1974. 24p.

761   *'Mainly Codd's Wallop'*. *The Story of the Great British Pop Bottle.* ©1974. Publ. by Kollectarama, Wellingborough, Northants, England. Rev. ed. Feb 1977.

762   *'Sealed bottles: Their history and Evolution (1630-1930)'*. Research by Roy Morgan & Gordon

Litherland. Burton-on-Trent, Midlands Antique Bottle Publishing, [1976], 120p.

MORGAN, Roy

763   *'The Benign Blue Coffin, and other Life Saving bottles'*. ©1978 Roy Morgan. Publ. by Kollectarama, Wellingborough, Northants, England.

MORRISON, Tom

764   *'Root Beer – Advertising and Collectibles'*. Publ. by Schiffer Publishing, Ltd., West Chester, Pennsylvania 19380. ©1992.

MOSS, Hugh M.

765   *'Chinese Snuff Bottles of the Silica or Quartz Group'*. Publ. in London, 1971.

MOSS, Hugh/GRAHAM, Victor & TSANG, Ka Bo

766   *'The Art of the Chinese Snuff Bottle'*. The F & F Collection. *Vol. I & II.* ©1993; New York, Weatherhill, Tokyo.

MOTTER, Faye

767   *'Stories in Bottles'*. ©1966 Faye Motter, Edina, Missouri. Printed by Moss Printing, Kansas City, Missouri.

MUCHA, Maria

768   *'Die Glashütten in Grosspolen im 17. und 18. Jh. auf Grund archäologischer Untersuchungen'*. P.479-486 in 'Annales du 12e Congrès de l'Association Internationale pour l'Histoire du Verre'; Vienne - Wien, 26-31 août 1991; ©1993 - A.I.H.V. - Amsterdam.

MUCHA, Miriam E.

769   *'Solving the Mystery of Two Altered American Bottle Molds'*. In CJGS, Vol.26, p.111-119, 1984.

MUNSEY, Cecil

770   *'The illustrated Guide to the Collectibles of Coca-Cola'*. Hawthorn Books, Inc., publishers, New York; ©1972.

771   *'The Illustrated Guide to Collecting Bottles'*. Hawthorn Books, Inc., Publishers, New York; ©1970.

MURSCHELL, Dale L.

772   *'American Applied Glass Seal Bottles'*. ©1996 Dale L. Murschell. Priv. printed.

773   *'American Black Glass Seal Bottles'*. In Antique Bottle & Glass Collector, Vol.14, No.9, p.44-45, Jan 1998, East Greenville, PA 18041.

NAGEL, Fred A.

774   *'Nailsea glass'*. In Antique Bottle Collecting, Jan 1982, p.12-15.

NAMIAT, Robert

775   *'Barber Bottles with Prices'*. Publ. by Wallace-Homestead Book Co., Des Moines, Iowa; 1977.

NEEDHAM, Jack

776   *'Scheepsmodellen in Flessen'*. ©1973 Nederlandse vertaling De Boer, Bussum (NL)

NELSON, G.P.

777   *'Bottle Shapes'*. In Journal of the Society of Glass Technology, Vol. 6, 1922, Abs. 90. Sheffield (UK).

NERI, Antonii & MERRETTI, Christophori

778   *'De Arte Vitraria'* (in Latin). Henr. Wetstenium, Amsterdam, 1686.

NERI, Antonio *see* MERRETT, Christopher

NERI, MERRET & KUNCKEL

779   *'L'Art de la Verrerie'*. Paris, 1752.

NESTLE, Karl Theodor

780   *'Geschichte der Weinflasche'*. Gerresheimer Glas A.G., Düsseldorf, 1977.

NEUBURG, Frederic

781   *'Antikes Glas'*. ©1962, Eduard Roether Verlag, Darmstadt.

NEWMAN, Harold

782   *'An Illustrated Dictionary of Glass'* - 2442 *entries. . . with an introductory survey of the history of glass-making by Robert J. Charleston.* Thames & Hudson, 1977, 351p.

NIELSEN, R. Frederick

783   *'Great American Pontiled Medicines'*. 1978.

NIGHTINGALE, Mark

784   *'Variations and developments of the pontilled graduated stock medicine bottle [1820-60]'*. In Antique Bottle Collecting, May 1982, p.8-9.

NOLAN, John E.

785   *'Locating and Digging Antique Bottles in Australia'*. Crown Castleton Publishers, Golden Square, Vic., Australia. ©1992.

786   *'Locating & Digging Antique Bottles in Australia'*. Publ. by Crown Castleton Publishers, Golden Square, Vic. 3555, Australia. Reprinted July 1994.

787   *'Locating Treasure on the Victorian Goldfields'*. Crown Castleton Publishers, Golden Square, Vic., Australia. ©1993.

788   *'Locating Treasure on the Victorian Goldfields'*. Publ. by Crown Castleton Publishers, Golden Square, Vic. 3555, Australia, 1997.

NOPPEN, J.G.

789   *'A series of old English decanters'*. In AP, Jly-Dec 1935, p.74-9.

NOREEN, S.E. & GRÆBE, H.

790   *'Henrikstorp - det Skånska Glasbruket 1691-1760'*. Tre Tryckare, Cagner & Co., Göteborg 1964.

NURNBERG, John J.

791   *'Crowns - The Complete Story'*. Publ. 1953/1955/1961; Lent & Overkamp Publishing Co., Inc., Paterson 2, N.J., U.S.A.

O'FALLON, J.M.

792   *'Old English bottles'*. In CL, Dec 1921, p.778-80.

O'LEARY, Fred

793   *'Corkscrews: 1000 Patented Ways to Open a Bottle'*. Schiffer Publishing, Atglen, PA., USA, 1996.

ODELL, John

794   *'Digger Odell's Official Antique Bottle and Glass Collector Magazine Price Guide'*. *Vol.1: Barber Bottles.* John Odell, Lebanon, Ohio, 1995.

795   *'Digger Odell's Official Antique Bottle and Glass Collector Magazine Price Guide'*. *Vol.2: Bitters Bottles.* John Odell, Lebanon, Ohio, 1995.

796   *'Digger Odell's Official Antique Bottle and Glass*

Collector Magazine Price Guide'. Vol.3: Flasks. John Odell, Lebanon, Ohio, 1995.

797 *'Digger Odell's Official Antique Bottle and Glass Collector Magazine Price Guide'. Vol.4: Ink Bottles.* John Odell, Lebanon, Ohio, 1995.

798 *'Digger Odell's Official Antique Bottle and Glass Collector Magazine Price Guide'. Vol.5: Medicines.* John Odell, Lebanon, Ohio, 1995.

799 *'Digger Odell's Official Antique Bottle and Glass Collector Magazine Price Guide'. Vol.6: Colognes, Poisons, Foods, Pattern Mold, Label under Glass, Target Balls & Fire Extinguishers.* John Odell, Lebanon, Ohio, 1995.

800 *'Digger Odell's Official Antique Bottle and Glass Collector Magazine Price Guide'. Vol.7: Sodas and Mineral Waters.* John Odell, Lebanon, Ohio, 1995.

801 *'Digger Odell's Official Antique Bottle and Glass Collector Magazine Price Guide'. Vol.8: Whiskeys.* John Odell, Lebanon, Ohio, 1995.

802 *'Digger Odell's Official Antique Bottle and Glass Collector Magazine Price Guide'. Vol.9: Black Glass.* John Odell, Lebanon, Ohio, 1997.

803 *'Digger Odell's Official Antique Bottle and Glass Collector Magazine Price Guide'. Vol.10: Poisons, Drugstore & Apothecary Bottles.* John Odell, Lebanon, Ohio, 1997.

804 *'Digger Odell's Official Antique Bottle & Glass Collector Magazine Price Guide', More Inks.* Compiled and Edited by John Odell, Lebanon, Ohio, USA. ©1998.

805 *'Digger Odell's Official Antique Bottle & Glass Collector Magazine Price Guide'.* Edited by John Odell, Lebanon, Ohio, ©1998.

806 *'Indian Bottles & Brands'.* ©1997 John Odell, Lebanon, Ohio.

807 *'The Secrets of Privy Digging'.* ©1994 John Odell, Lebanon, Ohio.

OHIRA, Yoichi

808 *'Lo Scanno e la Bardella a Murano e in Altre Località Europee'.* In CJGS, Vol. 29, 1987, p. 72-80.

OJEA, Ed & STECHER, Jack

809 *'Warner's Reference Guide'.* Priv. publ. by Edward L. Ojea, Nevada City, Ca., USA. 1998.

OLIVE, Guy

810 *'Tire-Bouchons Français/Brevets 1828-1974'.* Publ. priv., 1995.

OMODEO, Anna

811 *'Bottiglie e bicchieri'.* ©1970 by: Görlich Editore S.p.A., Milano.

OPIE, Robert

812 *'The Art of the Label'.* A sumptuous, full colour hard-back containing many bottles with original labels.

OSTIER, Jacques

813 *'Champagne, Vin de France'.* Plaquette éditée par le Comité Interprofessionel du Vin de Champagne-Epernay, 1973.

OSTRANDER, Diane

814 *'A Guide to American Nursing Bottles'.* 1984. Rev. ed. by The American Collectors of Infant Feeders 1992.

OWENS BOTTLE COMPANY

815 *'Modern Bottles', A Colorful Story.* Publ. c.1930. The Owens Bottle Company, Toledo, Illinois, USA.

816 *'Want Book and Catalog of Owens Bottles', Owens Machine Made – By Owens for Druggists.* Publ. 1928. The Owens Bottle Company, Toledo, Illinois, USA.

PALMER, Arlene

817 *'Glass in Early America'*- Selections from the Henry Francis du Pont Winterthur Museum. Henry Francis du Pont Winterthur Museum, Winterthur, Delaware, 1993.

PAPERT, Emma

818 *'The Illustrated Guide to American Glass'.* ©1972 Hawthorn Books, Inc., Publishers, New York.

PAUL, John R. & PARMALEE, Paul W.

819 *'Soft Drink Bottling – A History with special Reference to Illinois'.* Illinois State Museum Society, Springfield, Ill., 1973.

PAYNE, A. & ADAMS, A.

820 *'The Bottle Collectors Dictionary – An Illustrated Identification Aid and Price Guide'.* First publ. Dec 1976. Reprinted Nov 1977 and Oct 1978. Publ. by Southern Collectors Publications, Southampton, Hants.

PELIGOT, Eugène

821 *'Le Verre, son Histoire, sa Fabrication'.* G. Masson, Paris, 1877.

PELLATT, Apsley

822 *'Curiosities of Glass Making': with Details of the Processes and Productions of Ancient and Modern Ornamental Glass Manufacture.* David Bogue, 86, Fleet Street, London; 1849. 146p.

PENZER, N.M.

823 *'The Book of The Wine-Label'.* Home & Van Thal, London; 1947.

PEPPER, Adeline

824 *'The Glass Gaffers of New Jersey – and their creations from 1739 to the present'.* Charles Scribner's Sons, New York; 1991.

PERFALL, Manuela von

825 *'Parfum, Reich der Düfte'.* Hädecke Verlag. ©1992 by AVG GmbH, D - 6952 Obrigheim/Neckar.

PERRY, Evan

826 *'Corkscrews and Bottle Openers'.* Shire Publications Ltd., Princes Risborough, Aylesbury; ©1980.

PETERS, Frank

827 *'Fruit Jar Manual & Price Guide'.* ©1973 Old Bottle Magazine, Bend, Oregon.

PETERS, Ferd

828 *'German Corkscrews Patents' [Deutsche Korkenzieher Patente (DRP)] 1877-1945, zweite Ausgabe and/und 'German Corkscrew Registrations' [Deutsche Gebrauchsmuster für Korkenzieher (DRGM)] 1891-1945, second ed.* Juli 1997.

PETERS, Roger M.
829   *'Wisconsin Soda Water Bottles (1845-1910)'*. ©1996 Roger M. Peters. Publ. by Wild Goose Press, Madison, Wisconsin.

PETERSON, Arthur G.
830   *'Glass Salt Shakers'*. ©1970 Wallace-Homestead Book Company, Des Moines, Iowa.

PETRETTI, Allan
831   *'Petretti's Coca-Cola Collectibles Price Guide'*. Wallace - Homestead Book Company, Radnor, Pennsylvania. ©1989.

PETRETTI, Allan & MUNSEY, Cecil
832   *'Official Coca-Cola Collectibles Price Guide'*. The Nostalgia Publishing Company, Hackensack, New Jersey 07601. ©1982.

PETTIT, Dwight A.
833   *'The Encyclopedia of Black Glass'*. *(Vol.I)... European Spirits & Glass Makers (Book 1) The History of... A. van Hoboken & Co. Rotterdam. Priv. printed for: Pine Tree Glass Co., Key Largo, Florida; 1980.*

PEYSER, Barbara A.
834   *'Bottles'*. In A., May 1972, p.49-50.

PHILLIPS, Glen C.
835   *'The Ontario Drug Store and Druggist List (1851-1930)'*. Aug 1989; Iron Gate Publishing Co., Sarnia, Ontario, Canada. ©1989.

836   *'The Ontario Soda Water Manufacturers and Brewers Gazetteer and Business Directory'*. ©1987 Glen C. Phillips. Publ. by Clearwater Publishing Company.

PHILLIPS, Helen V.
837   *'Antique Bottles'*. Cheyenne, Wyo.: Logan Printing, 1967.

PHOLIEN, Fl.
838   *'La Verrerie au Pays de Liège'*. Aug. Bénard, Imprimeur-Editeur, Liège, Belgium ©1899.

PILLIVUYT, Ghislaine
839   *'Histoire du Parfum de l'Egypte au XIXe Siècle'*. Collection de la parfumerie Fragonard. Denoël, Paris 1988

POLAK, Ada
840   *'Gamle Vinglass'*. 1974, C. Huitfeldt Forlag, Oslo.

841   *'Gammelt Norsk Glass'*; *with an English summary*. Gyldendal Norsk Forlag, Oslo 1953.

842   *'Glass, its makers and its public'*. Weidenfeld & Nicolson, London. ©1975.

843   *'The "IP Olufsen Weyse" Illustrated Price-List of 18th-Century Norwegian Glass'*. In CJGS, Vol.XI, p.86-104, 1969.

POLAK, Michael
844   *'Bottles - Identification and Price Guide'*; First ed. ©1994 Michael Polak. Publ. by Avon Books, New York.

845   *'Bottles, Identification and Price Guide'*. Second ed. ©1997 Michael Polak. Publ. by Avon Books, New York.

PONTIL, pseud.
846   *'Two Ravenscroft sealed goblets'*. In CONN, Jan-Jun 1933, p.200.

POSER, Karl-Heinz
847   *'Alte Trinkgläser, Flaschen und Gefässe'* - *Gebrauchsglas in und um Schleswig-Holstein*. ©1997 Selbstverlag Karl-Heinz Poser, Neumünster.

POWELL, A.C.
848   *'Glassmaking in Bristol'*. In Trans. of the Bristol Archaeological Soc., v.47, 1925.

POWELL, Harry James
849   *'Glassmaking in England'*. C.U.P., 1923, 183p., illus. Includes: Old London and provincial glasshouses, p.86-111.

PRASCH, Helmut
850   *'Waldglas aus Oberkärnten 1621-1879'*. ©1971, Selbstverlag des Bezirksheimatmuseums Spittal-Drau.

PREBLE, Glen
851   *'Impressed in Time, Colorado Beverage Bottles'*. 1987.

PRICE, R.
852   *'Notes on the evolution of the wine bottle'*. In Trans. of the Glasgow Archaeological Soc., v.6 (New Series), Pt 1, p.116.

PRICE, W.H.
853   *'The English Patents of Monopoly'*. Boston, Houghton Mifflin, 1906.

PRICE-LISTS
854   *'A Schedule of Wholesale Rates and Sizes of Green-Glass Vessels'*, annexed to the Articles Quadripartite, dated 1 Jan. 1677 (= Jan. 1st, 1677/8), between Edmond Lewin, John Bowles, Edward Dallow, and the Company of Glass sellers (Company's MSS.), London. In 'Journal of the Society of Glass Technology', Vol. 22, 1938, p. 165-205. Publ. by the Society of Glass Technology, Sheffield (UK).

855   *'Glaswarenkatalog der Compagnie Siegwart, Besitzer der Glasfabriken in Flühli Ct. Luzern und Hergiswyl Ct. Unterwalden'*. 1857 & 1872, Switzerland (A sales catalogue on bottles and hollow glassware).

856   *'Prisliste over Flasker'*. Fra Aktieselskabet Fyens Glasværk, Odense, Danmark. 1. Januar 1899 (Price-list on bottles)

857   *'Prisliste over Flasker'*. De forenede Glasværker, Danmark. 1. February 1903.

858   *'Thüringer GLAS-TAXA'* - *Nach welcher Glas-Sorten von allerhand Modellen, Namen und Maasen, sowohl wegen kostbarkeit der Materia, als auch der künstlichen Arbeit, in einem ordentlichen Preis angesetzet, und von dem Factor vor baares Geld verkaufet werden. Allzunah, 29. Juni 1735, 14. März 1736, 11. März 1737 und 26. März 1737.* (Price-lists of glassware made in Thuringian glasshouses). Photostats Willy Van den Bossche.

PROCKTER, A. & SANDOW, M.
859   *'The London Mineral Water Directory'*. 1870-1914.

PUCKHABER, Bernhard C.
860   *'Saratogas'*. ©1976 B.C. Puckhaber, U.S.A.

PUTNAM, H.E.

861 *'Bottle Identification'*. 1965 H.E. Putnam. Publ. Old Time Bottle Publ. Co., Salem, Oregon.

862 *'Bottled Before 1865'*. ©1968 P.A. Putnam. Printed by Old Time Bottle Publ. Co., Salem, Oregon.

RACE, S.

863 *'Glass container manufacturing: from the past into the future'*. In Glass Technology, Feb 1980, p.6-26.

RADEMACHER, Franz

864 *'Die deutschen Gläser des Mittelalters'*. Bruno Hessling Verlag – Berlin, 1963.

RAU, Hermann Günter

865 *'Die Spessartglashütte im Sommergrund bei Schöllkrippen'*. In 'Glastechn. Berichte' 49 (1976) Nr. 5, S.126-129.

866 *'Spätmittelalterlicher Tonmodel aus dem Nordspessart'*- *'A late Middle Age clay mould from North Spessart'*. In 'Glastechnische Berichte', Frankfurt a.M. (1973), 46.Jahrg., Heft 2, p.36.

RAVAGNAN, Giovanna Luisa

867 *'Vetri antichi del Museo Vetrario di Murano'*; *Collezioni dello Stato*. Corpus delle Collezioni Archeologiche del Vetro nel Veneto & Comitato Nazionale Italiano Association Internationale pour l'Histoire du Verre. ©1994 Comitato Nazionale Italiano dell'A.I.H.V.

RAVENSCROFT, William

868 *'Ravenscroft "sealed" goblet, c.1677'*. In AP, Jan-Jun 1943, p.161.

RAWLINSON, Fred

869 *'Old Bottles of the Virginia Peninsula'*. *Soft Drink, Milk, Liquor, Medicine and Beer Bottles (1885-1941)*. 1968. FAR Publications, Newport News, Va.

REED, Adele

870 *'Bottle Talk'*. Bishop, Calif.; Chalfant Press, 1966.

871 *'Old Bottles and Ghost Towns'*. ©1961 Adele Reed, Bishop, Calif.; Printed by Chalfant Press, Inc., Bishop, Calif.

REED, Mark

872 *'Kent Bottles'* - *An Illustrated History of Mineral Water Companies (1870-1940)*. ©1997 Mark Reed. SAWD Publications.

REIDEL, Marlene

873 *'Glück mit Glas – Von der Bierflasche bis zur Prunkvase'*. Verlag Morsak Grafenau. ©1988.

REINARTZ, Manfred

874 *'Glas aus dem Schwarzwald'*. *Die Glasabteilung des Heimatmuseums der Stadt Villingen-Schwenningen im Stadtbezirk Schwenningen*. Villingen-Schwenningen 1980.

RENSSELAER, Stephen van

875 *'Check List of Early American Bottles and Flasks'*. ©1921 Stephen Van Rensselaer. Publ. by Crocker Barrel Press, New York; 1921.

876 *'Early American Bottles and Flasks'*. Rev. ed. ©1926 Stephen Van Rensselaer. Publ. Peterborough, N.H. at the Transcript Printing Company, 1926.

877 *'Early American Bottles and Flasks'*. Rev. ed. ©1969 Stephen Van Rensselaer. Originally publ. 1926. Reprinted, with additions, 1969 by John E. Edwards, Publisher, Stratford, Conn.

REUTER, Willy

878 *'Aus der Geschichte des Glashandels'*. In Glastechnische Berichte, 30. Jahrg. Heft 12, S.514-519.

REVI, Albert Christian

879 *'American Pressed Glass and Figure Bottles'*. Thomas Nelson & Sons, London, New York, Toronto. ©1964

RICKETTS, Henry

880 *'An Improvement in the Art or Method of Making or Manufacturing Glass Bottles, such as are used for Wine, Porter, Beer, or Cyder'*. British Patent No. 4623 from 1821.

RIEB, J-P.

881 *'Vie matérielle en Alsace au Moyen Age et à la Renaissance. Verrerie'*. In 'Encyclopédie de l'Alsace, Vol.12, Ed. Publitotal Strassbourg 1986.

RIFF, Adolphe

882 *'La verrerie de Wildenstein (Haut-Rhin) 1700-1884'*. (Art Populaire de France, Recueil d'études). Strassburg 1960, S.195-208.

RINDA, Warren

883 *'History and Directory of Sodas & Beers (1846-1905)'*. Newark, N.J. Bottlers. ©1987.

RING, Carlyn

884 *'For Bitters Only'*. ©1980 Carlyn Ring. The TT Press, Wellesley Hills, Mass.

RING, Carlyn & HAM, W.C.

885 *'Bitters Bottles'*. ©1998. Publ. by William C. Ham, Downieville, CA. 95936.

RING, Carlyn & RAY Jr., Sheldon

886 *'For Bitters Only - Up-Date and Price Guide'*. ©1984.

RINGBLUM, Jeri Lyn

887 *'A Collector's Handbook of Miniature Perfume Minis, Mates and More Bottles'*. ©1996 Jeri Lyn Ringblum. Publ. by Schiffer Publishing Ltd., Atglen, PA.

RINKER, Meryle

888 *'Bottle Collector's Primer'* (*The Beginning Collector's "Answer Book"*). April 1969. Ashland, Oregon.

RIVERA, Betty & Ted

889 *'Inkstands & Inkwells - A Collector's Guide'*. Publ. 1973, Crown Publishers, Inc. New York.

ROBERTS, Kenneth

890 *' "The Bottle Collectors" Antiquamania'*. Garden City, N.Y.; Doubleday Ddoran & Co., 1928.

ROBERTS, Mike

891 *'Price Guide to all the Flasks'*. ©1981. Spencer-Walker Press, Inc., Newark, Ohio.

ROBERTSON, David

892 *'The North East Bottle Collectors Guide to Newcastle upon Tyne'*. 1996, John C. Yule, Broompark.

ROBERTSON, E.D.J.

893 *'Some notes on the variation with temp. range of the*

resistance of glass containers to thermal shock'. In 'J. Soc. Glass Tech., <u>23</u>, 95, p.17-25.

ROBERTSON, W.S.
894 *'Quantitative Morphological Study of the Evolution of some Post-Medieval Wine Bottles'*. In 'Science and Archaeology', No.17 (1976), p.13-20. Managing Editor: Dr. J.D. Wilcock, Research Centre for Computer Archaeology, North Staffordshire Polytechnic, Stafford.

ROBINSON, Jancis
895 *'The Oxford Companion to Wine'*. ©1994 Jancis Robinson & Oxford University Press, Oxford/ New York. First publ. 1994.

RODGER, William
896 *'Rodney decanters for seafarers'*. In The Times, 16 Mar 1963, p.11.

ROESDAHL, Harald
897 *'Gamle glas og karafler'*. Forum Copenhagen 1977.

ROGERS, John C.
898 *'Beginners Guide to Collecting Antique Bottles'*. ©1996 John C. Rogers, St. Petersburg, Florida, U.S.A.

ROLLER, Dick
899 *'Fruit Jar Patents'* (1853-1869) *Vol.I, Parts I-II*. Publ. by Phoenix Press, Chicago, Il., 1998.
900 *'Fruit Jar Patents'*. *Vol II - Book 1; 1870-1884*. First Printing Jun 1982. Phoenix Press, a Division of Fruit Jar Annual, Jerry McCann, Chicago, Il. ©1997.
901 *'Fruit Jar Patents'*. *Vol II - Book 2; 1885-1899*. First Printing Jun 1982. Phoenix Press, a Division of Fruit Jar Annual, Jerry McCann, Chicago, Il. ©1997.
902 *'Fruit Jar Patents'*. *Vol.III (1900-1942)*. ©1996. Publ. by Phoenix Press, a Division of Fruit Jar Annual, Jerry McCann, Chicago, Il.

ROOSMA, Maks
903 *'The Glass Industry of Estonia in the 18th and 19th Century'*. In CJGS, Vol.XI, p.70-85, 1969.

ROSE-VILLEQUEY, Germaine
904 *'Verre et verriers de Lorraine – au début des Temps Modernes'*; *(de la fin du XVᵉ siècle au début du XVIIᵉ siècle)*. Thèse de doctorat (Ph.D.). Imprimerie Bialec, Nancy, 1970.

ROSENBLUM, Beatrice
905 *'Field Guide to Orange County (New York) Bottles'*. Middletown, NY: T. Emmett Henderson, 1974.
906 *'Handbook Guide to Orange County Bottles'*. Middletown, NY: T.E. Henderson, 1974.

ROSENMILLER, Fred
907 *'Bottles & Jugs'*. *With a York, Pennsylvania Perspective*. Publ. by W.F.O. Rosenmiller, York, PA 17401

ROSTRON, Primrose R.
908 *'Antique bottles – expensive empties'*. In Glass, 54 no.12, 1977, p.562-3.

ROTH, Paul W.
909 *'Glas und Kohle'*. Bärnbach/Weststeiermark: 30 April bis 31 Oktober 1988. Leykam Verlag - Graz, 1988.

ROYCROFT, Ross & Christine
910 *'Australian Bottle Price Guide'*. *A pictorial price and rarity guide featuring Australian bottles*. New ed. and number three in a series. ©1979 and 1985. Publ. by David Westcott Antiques.
911 *'Australian Bottle Price Guide'*. *A pictorial price and rarity guide featuring Australian bottles*. New ed. and number two in a series. ©1984. Publ. by Crown Castleton Publishers, Maiden Gully.
912 *'Australian Bottle Price Guide'*. *A pictorial price and rarity guide featuring Australian bottles*. New ed. and number four in a series. ©1986. Publ. by David Westcott Antiques.
913 *'Australian Bottle Price Guide'*. *A pictorial price and rarity guide featuring Australian bottles*. New ed. and number five in a series. ©1990. Publ. by Crown Castleton Publishers, Maiden Gully.
914 *'Australian Bottle Price Guide'*. *A pictorial price and rarity guide featuring Australian bottles*. New ed. and number one in a series. ©1976, 1982 and 1992. Publ. by Crown Castleton Publishers, Maiden Gully.
915 *'Australian Bottle Price Guide'*. *A pictorial price and rarity guide featuring Australian bottles*. New ed. and number six in a series. ©1997, Broadford, Vic., Australia
916 *'One Thousand Stone Ginger Beers of Australia and their values'*. *A pictorial price and rarity guide featuring Australian stone ginger beers and demijohns*. ©1983. Publ. David Westcott Antiques, Deniliquin, NSW (Australia).

RUGGLES-BRISE, Sheelah, Lady
917 *'List of sealed bottles from seventeen museums'*. In GC, no.25.
918 *'List of sealed bottles from eighteen private collections'*. In GC, no.26.
919 *'More bottle seal discoveries'*. In CL, Oct. 1952, p.1315-16.
920 *'Sealed bottles. With illustrations by Barbara Ashley'*. Country Life, 1949, 175p.
921 *'Sealed wine bottles and bottle-decanters'*. In GC, no.24.
922 *'Symposium of bottle-decanters'*. In GC, no.69.
923 *'Wine in England through the ages'*. In GC, no.16.

RUSSELL, Mike
924 *'The Collector's Guide to Civil War Period Bottles and Jars (With Prices)'*. ©1988 Mike Russell. Russell Publications, Arlington, VA.
925 *'The Collector's Guide to Civil War Period Bottles and Jars (With Prices)'*. Third ed. ©1998. Publ. by Russell Publications, Herndon, Virginia, USA.

SACHAROW, Stanley
926 *'The Package as a Marketing Tool'*. ©1982. Chilton Book Company, Radnor, Pensylvania, USA.

SAINT-QUIRIN
927 *'Les Verriers du Languedoc 1290-1790'*. Association "La Réveillée", 34000 Montpellier.

SAITOH, Hideo
928 *'Bottle & Label Design'*. ©1990. Hideo Saitoh. First

publ. in Japan in 1990 by Atsushi Oshita, Bijutsu Shuppan–sha Ltd., Tokyo, Japan.

SAITOWITZ, Sharma J. & LASTOVICA, Ethleen

929 *'Rediscovering the Cape Glass Company at Glencairn'*. *History and archaeology of an industrial enterprise 1902-1906*. Publ. by Consol Limited, Germiston 1400, South Africa, 1998

SALDERN, Axel von

930 '*German Enameled Glass'*. *The Edwin J. Beinecke Collection and Related Pieces*. The Corning Museum of Glass, Corning, N.Y., 1965.

931 *'Gläser der Antike'; Sammlung Erwin Oppenländer*. Museum für Kunst und Gewerbe Hamburg; Römisch-Germanisches Museum, Köln; 1974.

932 *'Glassammlung Hentrich – Antike und Islam'*. Kunstmuseum Düsseldorf 1974.

SAMMLER UHREN

933 *'Mini Flacons, International'*. ©1993 SU Sammler-Uhren Verlagsgesellschaft mbH, Wiesbaden

SAMUELS, Justine

934 *'Glass decanters under £100'*. In AC, Jly 1980, p.64-6.

SANCTIS, Paolo de & FANTONI, Maurizio

935 *'The Corkscrew, a thing of beauty'*. Marzorati Editore, Milano, 1990.

SANCTUARY, C.T.

936 *'Evolution of the decanter, 1700-1830'*. In AP, Jly-Dec 1947, p.113-15.

SAUERMILCH, Curt

937 *'Nachmittelalterliche Flaschen und Glassiegel'*. In Glastechnische Berichte, 29. Jahrgang, Heft 5, Frankfurt a.M. 1956, S.202-204.

SCHAEFER, Heiner

938 *'Brasilflaschl und Tabakbüchsl'*. *Schnupftabakgläser aus vier Jahrhunderten*. Verlag Morsak Grafenau. ©1985.

939 *'Schnupf, Bruder!'*. *Prisen - Dosen - Tabakflaschen*. Verlag Morsak Grafenau. ©1985.

940 *'Schnupftabak-Gläser'*. *Kleinodien aus dem Bayerischen Wald*. ©1997 Morsak Verlag, Grafenau.

SCHALCH, E.A.

941 *'The charm of old bottles'*. In Wine and Spirit Trade Record, 1958, p.1356-62.

SCHEBEK, Edmund

942 *'Böhmens Glasindustrie und Glashandel'* - *Quellen zu ihrer Geschichte*. Reprint from 1878 original. Verlag Sauer & Auvermann KG, Frankfurt/Main 1969.

SCHEERLINCK, Karl

943 '*Jenever en Likeur in Kleur'* ('*Genièvres et Liqueurs en couleurs'*). *Belgische jenever- en likeuraffiches 1885-1940 (Affiches belges de genièvres et de liqueurs 1885-1940)*. Nationaal Jenevermuseum, Hasselt, Belgium. ©1994.

SCHLÜTER, Mogens

944 *'Danske flasker - Fra Renæssancen til vore dage'*. Nyt Nordisk Forlag Arnold Busck, København 1984.

SCHMEISER, Alan

945 *'Have Bottles Will Pop'*. Publ. Michalan Press, Dixon, Calif., 1968.

SCHMIDT, Rudolf

946 *'Die Rohstoffe zur Glaserzeugung'*. Akademische Verlagsgesellschaft Geest & Portig K.G., Leipzig, 1958.

SCHNAUCK, Wilhelm

947 *'Glaslexikon'; ein Handbuch für Handwerk, Handel und Industrie*. München, Callwey, 1959.

SCHNEIDER, Karl

948 *'Bocksbeutel. Platt-, Feld- und Pilgerflaschen. Ihre Geschichte und Verbreitung'*. Rötter Druck und Verlag, Bad Neustadt/Saale, 1999.

SCHNITZLER, Bernadette & NISTERS, Andrea

949 *'Leben im Mittelalter'*. 30 Jahre Mittelalterarchäologie im Elsaß. ©1992 Historisches Museum der Pfalz, D 6720 Speyer.

SCHNURPFEIL

950 *'World's Directory of Glassworks - 1921'*. *Complete list of all glass manufacturers, glass refiners, silverers, cutters, exporters, importers, dealers, etc*. Issued by Schnurpfeil's Review for Glass Works, Reichenberg, Bohemia.

SCHOONENBERGHE, Eric van

951 *'Jenever in de Lage Landen'*. ©Stichting Kunstboek, Belgium, 1996.

SCHROEDER, Bill

952 *'1000 Fruit Jars, Priced & Illustrated'*. Rev. Fourth ed. Collector Books, Paducah, Kentucky 42001. ©1976.

SCHUERMANS, H.

953 *'Bulletin des Commissions Royales d'Art et d'Archéologie'*. 1882-1893, Bruxelles. (Many basic articles on the history of glass and bottles in Belgium and The Netherlands).

SCIENCE MUSEUM

954 *'Descriptive catalogue of the collection illustrating glass technology by S.E. Janson'*. HMSO, 1969, 55p.

SCOVILLE Warren C.

955 *'Capitalism and French Glassmaking, 1640-1789'*. University of California Press, Berkeley and Los Angeles, 1950.

956 *'Technology and the French Glass Industry, 1640-1740'*. In 'The Journal of Economic History', (USA), Vol. 1, 1941, p.153-167.

SEAMANS, Berna Mackey, & ROBB., Mertie Mackey

957 *'Colorado Bottle History: When and Where?'*. Denver: R. & S. Publications, 1969.

SECCOMBE-HETT, G.V.A.

958 *'Label decanters'*. In GC, no.119.

SEELA, Jacob

959 *'The Early Finnish Glass Industry'*. In CJGS, Vol.XVI, p.57-86, 1974.

SEELIGER, Michael W.

960 *'H.H. Warner, His Company & His Bottles'*. ©1974 Michael William Seeliger, Madison, Wisconsin.

SEITZ, Heribert

961 *'Äldre Svenska Glas med graverad Dekor'* - *En undersökning av det bevarade 1700-talsbeståndet*. With an English summary. Stockholm 1936.

962 *'Glaset förr och nu'*. ©1933. Stockholm, Albert Bonniers Förlag.

SELLARI, Carlo & Dot

963 *'Eastern Bottles'*. 3 Vol. Waukesha, Wisconsin: Country Beautiful, 197-?; Price Guide, 197-?

964 *'The Illustrated Price Guide of Antique Bottles'*. ©1975. Country Beautiful, Waukesha, Wisconsin.

SHAND, E.B.

965 *'Glass Engineering Handbook'*. Second ed. McGraw-Hill Book Company, Inc., New York, USA. 1958.

SHAND, P. Morton

966 *'The architecture of wine'*. In Architectural Rev., Sept 1929, p.101-18.

SHANKEN, Marvin

967 *'Impact World Directory'*. *Leading Spirits, Wine & Beer Companies. Who's Who of Industry Executives*. Publ. by M. Shanken Communications, Inc., New York, London, San Francisco, 1993.

SHIMKO, Phyllis

968 *'Sarsaparilla Bottle Encyclopedia'*. ©1969, Andrew & Phyllis Shimko, Aurora, Oregon.

SHROEDER, Bill

969 *'1000 Fruit Jars. History of fruit jars. How to sell and ship'*. Paducah, Ky: Collector Books, 197-?

SIELING, Susan

970 *'Australian Fruit Jars'*.

SIMMONS, Douglas A.

971 *'Schweppes - The First 200 Years'*. ©1983. Springwood Books, London.

SIMON, André Louis

972 *'A Dictionary of Wines, Spirits and Liqueurs'*. Publ. Herbert Jenkins, London, UK. ©1958.

973 *'A Dictionary of Wines, Spirits and Liqueurs'*. The Citadel Press, New York, USA. First American ed. 1963.

974 *'Bottlescrew Days. Wine drinking in England during the eighteenth century'*. Duckworth, London, 1926, 273p.

975 *'Collecting wine: John Pierpont Morgan's cellarbook'*. In CONN, Sept-Dec 1962, p.227-30, Bottles and glasses.

976 *'Old bottles - origins of corkscrews'*. In GC, no.71.

977 *'The evolution of the wine bottle'*. In GC, no.27.

978 *'The history of the wine trade in England'*. 3v. Wyman, 1906-9. Mention of bottles and glasses.

979 *'Wine Trade Loan Exhibition of Drinking Vessels, also Books & Documents'*. Held at Vintners' Hall, London, Jun-Jly, 1933.

SLOAN, Jean

980 *'Perfume & Scent Bottle Collecting'*. Wallace-Homestead Book Company, Radnor, Pennsylvania. ©1986.

SLUIMER, J.

981 *'Twee Eeuwen Flessenindustrie in Nederland - Geschiedenis van de Nederlandse Flessenfabrieken tussen ca. 1700 en 1914'*. Doctoraalscriptie Vakgroep Economische en Sociale Geschiedenis, Universiteit van Amsterdam, 1984.

SMIT, J.

982 *'Glass bottle manufacture in South Africa up to 1944'*. Africana notes and news 24: 265-70, Dec 1981.

SMITH, Elmer L.

983 *'Bottles... A Sampler of the Collectibles'*. Applied Arts Publishers, Lebanon, PA., 6th Printing 1977. ©1971 Melvin J. Horst and Elmer L. Smith.

SMITH, R. Weaver

984 *'Bottle glass and Nailsea'*. In ADCG, Dec 1948, p.22-4.

SNYDER, Bob

985 *'Bottles In Miniature, Vol. I, II, and III'*. Amarillo, Texas; Bob Snyder, 1960, 1970, and 1972.

SOETENS, Johan

986 *'In Glas Verpakt'*. *Kunst, Kitsch en Koopmanschap*. (Very good book on bottles, c.1000 illustrations). De Bataafsche Leeuw, Amsterdam, The Netherlands, 1999.

SOMERSCALES, Simon

987 *'The Oxfordshire Ginger Beer Collectors Guide'*. BBR Publishing, Barnsley, S.Yorkshire.

SPAID, David M.

988 *'Mini World - Figural Bottle Price Guide'*. Publ. by B&K Enterprises, Los Angeles, Calif. 90050. ©1972.

989 *'Mini World - Figural Bottle Price Guide, 1973'*. Printed & publ. by B&K Enterprises, Los Angeles, Calif. 90050. ©1973.

SPIERS, Claude H.

990 *'Pharmaceutical and medical glass'*. In GC, no.126.

STANCLIFFE, Jane

991 *'Bottle Tickets'*. Victoria & Albert Museum, London; undated.

STAU, Sven

992 *'The Illustrated Stone Ginger Beer'*. *For the antique bottle collector*. ©1984. Printed by Stau Printing, Buffalo, New York.

STEENBERG, Elisa

993 *'Flaskor och Glas'*. ©1952, Nordiska Museet, Stockholm.

STEGERWALD, Hans

994 *'Formen deutscher Bierflaschen im Wandel der Zeit'*. Edited by Hans Stegerwald, 97261 Güntersleben. Publ. 1995.

STEVENS, Bob C.

995 *'Tabatières Chinoises, le Guide du Collectionneur'*, (Collector's Book of Snuff Bottles). Fribourg, Switzerland Office Du Livre S.A. 1980.

STEVENSON, Tom

996 *'Sotheby's World Wine Encyclopedia - A Comprehensive Reference Guide to the Wines of the*

World'. Dorling Kindersley, London/New York/Stuttgart. ©1988.

STIER, Wallis W.
997   *'Poison Bottles'. A Collectors' Guide.* ©1969 Wallis W. Stier.

STOCKTON, John
998   *'Victorian Bottles – A Collector's Guide to Yesterday's Empties'.* ©1981 John Stockton (Text). Publ. by David & Charles Inc., North Pomfret, Vermont, USA; 192p.

STROBL, Sebastian
999   *'Glastechnik des Mittelalters'.* Gentner Verlag Stuttgart, 1990.

STUART, L.R.
1000   *'Stuart's Book on Avon Collectables'.* Lynn R. Stuart, Gilbert, Arizona 85234. ©1970.

STUART, Sheila
1001   *'How we got the decanter'.* In ADCG, Feb 1964, p.36-8.

SULLIVAN, Catherine
1002   *'A Catalogue of the container Glass from the Machault'.* 1979. Microfiche Report Series No.93, Environment Canada – Parks, Ottawa.

SULLIVAN, Don
1003   *'Old Bottles are Fascinating and can be Profitable'. Pictures, Prices and Descriptions of over 1,000 Bottles, Jugs and Food Containers.* 1968. Wright Litho & Printing, Inc., Springfield, Mo., USA.

SUNDBERG, John
1004   *'Skånska Glasbruket 1691-1762'.* Hässleholm 1940. Editor: Utgivarens Förlag, Hyllstofta.

SWEENEY, Rick
1005   *'Collecting – Applied Color Label Soda Bottles'.* ©1995 Rick Sweeney.

SWITZER, Ronald R.
1006   *'The Bertrand Bottles'. A Study of 19th-Century Glass And Ceramic Containers.* National Park Service, U.S. Department of the Interior; Washington 1974.

TABOR, Nancy María Grande
1007   *Bottles Break'.* ©1999. Publ. by Charlesbridge Publishing, Watertown, Ma., USA.

TACKE, Eberhard
1008   *'Beiträge zur Geschichte der modernen Getränkeflaschen in Deutschland'.* Bd.21, Heft 4. (In Neues Archiv für Niedersachsen), Göttingen, Germany, 1972, S.380-382.

TAIT, Hugh
1009   *'Decanters or Wine-Bottles?'. The unrecorded private collection of the House of Sandeman.* In AC, London; Dec 1989, p.68-75.

TALBOT, Olive
1010   *'The evolution of glass bottles for carbonated drinks'.* In Post-Medieval Archeology, 8, 1974, p.29-62.

TANSLEY, June
1011   *'The Collectors Book of Ink Bottles'.* Books 1-3. Bembridge: Isle of Wight, 1976-7.

1012   *'The Collectors Book of Ink Bottles'.* Vol.1. ©1980 Southern Collectors Publications, Southampton, England.

TASKER, John
1013   *'Collecting Antique Bottles in New Zealand'* - A Guide for Beginners. 1984; A.H. & A.W. Reed Ltd., Wellington 3 (New Zealand).

1014   *'Old New Zealand Bottles and Bygones'.* © John Tasker. First publ. 1989 by Heinemann Reed, Birkenhead, Auckland.

TAYLOR, Gay LeCleire
1015   *'Out of the Mold'. A special exhibition Museum of American Glass at Wheaton Village, April 7 through October 26, 1990.* ©1990 Wheaton Historical Association, Wheaton Village, Millville, N.J.

TERLINDEN, A.M. & CROSSLEY, David
1016   *'Post-medieval Glassmaking in Brabant: the excavation of a seventeenth century furnace at Savenel, Nethen, Belgium'.* In Post-Medieval Archeology 15 (1981), p. 177-206.

THATCHER GLASS CO.
1017   *'Story of a Milk Bottle'.* 1920.

THE GLASS CONTAINERS MFG. INSTITUTE
1018   *'Billions of Bottles'.* N.Y. 1959.

THEOBALD, Wilhelm
1019   *'Technik des Kunsthandwerks im Zehnten Jahrhundert'. Des Theophilus Presbyter Diversarum Artium Schedula.* VDI-Verlag GmbH, Berlin, Germany. 1933.

THEOPHILUS
1020   *'On Divers Arts: The Treatise of Theophilus'.* Trans. J. Hawthorne and C.S. Smith. Chicago, Univ. of Chicago Press, 1963.

THEUERKAUFF-LIEDERWALD, Anna-Elisabeth
1021   *'Venezianisches Glas der Kunstsammlungen der Veste Coburg'.* (Venedig - A la façon de Venise - Spanien - Mitteleuropa). Especially p.367-484 and p.501-524 on bottles, perfume bottles, jars & decanters. Kunstsammlungen der Veste Coburg; Luca Verlag Lingen 1994.

THOMAS, David & MARCHANT, Bob
1022   *'When Milk Came in Bottles - A History of Toronto Dairies'.* ©1997. Cowtown Publications, Port Hope, Ontario, Canada.

THOMAS, John L.
1023   *'Picnics, Coffins, Shoo-flies'.* Weaverville, Cal.: 1974.

1024   *'Whiskey Bottles and Liquor Containers from The State of Washington'.* ©1998 by John L. Thomas, Capitola, CA 95010-2655.

1025   *'Whiskey Bottles of the Old West'.* ©1977. Publ. by Maverick Publications, Bend, Oregon, USA.

1026   *'Wine and Liquor Containers of the State of Oregon'.* ©1998 by John L. Thomas, Capitola, CA 95010-2655.

THOMPSON, James H.
1027   *'Bitters Bottles'.* ©1947: Century House, Watkins Glen, N.Y.

THORPE, William Arnold

1028 **'A History of English and Irish Glass'**. *(2 Volumes)*. The Medici Society, London. ©1929.

1029 **'The evolution of the decanter'**. In CONN, Jan-Jun 1929, p.196-202, and 271-81.

1030 **'The Glass Sellers' Bills at Woburn Abbey'**. In 'Journal of the Society of Glass Technology'. Vol.22, 1938, p.165-205. Publ. by the Society of Glass Technology, Sheffield.

TIBBITTS, John C.

1031 **'1200 Bottles Prices'**. *A Bottle Price Guide, Catalogue, and Classification System*. ©1964 John C. Tibbitts. Publ.by The Little Glass Shack, Sacramento, Calif.

1032 **'1200 Bottles Prices; a bottle price guide, catalog, and classification system'**. New ed. Sacramento, Cal.: Little Glass Shack, 1964; 2 vol. new ed. with up-dated prices, and index. Vol.II by J.C. Tibbitts and Don Smith. 1970-73.

1033 **'Chips from The Pontil'**. ©1963. Publ. by John C. Tibbitts, Sacramento, Calif.

1034 **'How to collect Antique Bottles'**. ©1969 John C. Tibbitts. Publ. by The Heirloom Press, Santa Cruz, Calif.

1035 **'How to Collect Antique Bottles'**. Sacramento, Cal.: Little Glass Shack, 1969.

1036 **'John Doe, Bottle Collector'**. Sacramento, Cal.: Little Glass Shack, 1967.

TOCHTERMANN, Ernst

1037 **'Spessart-Glashütte des Hans Ziroff, 1627-1631'**. Ed. Heimatkundliche Schriftenreihe Bischbrunn, Germany; ©1979

1038 **'Von der Pilgerflasche zum Bocksbeutel'**. In 'Glück und Glas', p.77-92. Verlag Kunst & Antiquitäten, München, 1984.

TOOLEY, Fay V.

1039 **'The Handbook of Glass Manufacture'**. *(2 Volumes) A book of reference for the plant executive, technologist and engineer*. Books For Industry, Inc., New York. ©1972.

TOULOUSE, Julian Harrison

1040 **'A Primer on Mold Seams'**. 1969. Western Collector, Part I, vol.7, no.11 (Nov.), p.526-35; Part II, Vol.7, no.12 (Dec.), p.578-87. San Francisco.

1041 **'Bottle Makers, and their Marks'**. ©1971 Julian Harrison Toulouse. Publ. in Camden, N.J. by Thomas Nelson Inc. and simultaneously in Don Mills, Ontario, by Thomas Nelson & Sons (Canada) Limited.

1042 **'Empontilling: a History'**. 1968. The Glass Industry. Part I (Mar), p.137-142; Part II (Apr), p.204-205. New York.

1043 **'Fruit Jars'**. ©1969 Julian Harrison Toulouse. Publ. by Thomas Nelson & Sons, Camden, N.J. and Everybodys Press, Hanover, Pennsylvania, and simultaneously in Canada by Thomas Nelson & Sons (Canada) Limited, Don Mills, Ontario.

TOUSSAINT, Jacques

1044 **'Patrimoine Verrier en Namurois'**. Société Archéologique de Namur, Belgium, 1997.

TRENCHARD, C.

1045 **'English glass bottles'**. In AC, 1935, p.185-6.

TRIFFON, James A.

1046 **'The Whiskey Miniature Bottle Collection'** - *Scotch Whisky. Vol.2*. ©1981 James A. Triffon. Publ. by Brisco Publications, Palos Verdes Peninsula, Calif.

TUCKER, Donald

1047 **'Collector's Guide to the Saratoga Type Mineral Water Bottles'**. Publ. 1986 Donald & Lois Tucker, Inc., North Berwick, ME.

TURNER, W.E.S.

1048 **'The Early Development of Bottle Making Machines in Europe'**. Publ. in the Journal of The Society of Glass Technology, Vol. 22, p. 250-258, 1938.

TUTTON, John

1049 **'Udder Delight'**. *A Guide to Collecting Milkbottles and Related Items*. ©1980 John Tutton, Marshall, Va.; Printed by Commercial Press, Stephens City, Va.

1050 **'Udderly Beautiful'**. A Pictorial Guide to the Pyroglazed OR Painted Milkbottle. ©1996 John Tutton, Front Royal, VA.

1051 **'Udderly Delightful'**. *A Guide to Collecting Milkbottles and Related Items*. ©1994 John Tutton, Front Royal, Va.; Second ed. 1994; Printed by Commercial Press, Stephens City, Va.

1052 **'Udderly Fantastic'**. *A Pictorial Guide to the Pyroglazed or Painted Milkbottle*. ©1992 John Tutton. Printed by Commercial Press, Inc. Stephens City, Va.

TWAINE CO.

1053 **'Story Behind Mineral Water Bottles'**. Dublin, 1769-1959.

TYSON, Scott

1054 **'Glass Houses of the 1800's'**. ©1971 Scott Tyson, Pottstown, Pa.; Priv. publ. by Scott Tyson.

UMBERGER, Art & Jewel

1055 **'Collecting Character Bottles'**. Tyler, Tx.: Corker Book Co., 196-? (500 figural bottles).

1056 **'Corralling the Corkers'**. ©1967. Corker Book Company, Tyler, Texas, USA.

1057 **''It's a Bitters!'**. *Bitters Price Guide*. ©1967 Art and Jewel Umberger, Tyler, Texas. Publ. by Corker Book Company, Tyler, Texas.

1058 **'It's a Bitters!'**. *Bitters Price Guide, Vol. II*. ©1969 Art and Jewel Umberger, Tyler, Texas. Publ. by Corker Book Company, Tyler, Texas.

1059 **'It's a Corker!'** *Bottle Price Guide*. Tyler, Tx.: Corker Book Co., 1966; rev. ed. 1968. (Over 400 bottles).

1060 **'It's a Sarsaparilla!'**. *Price Guide*. ©1968 Art and Jewel Umberger, Tyler, Texas.

UNITED STATES, Patent Office

1061 **'Improvements in Molds for Making Bottles'**. Letters patent No.22, 129, dated November 23, 1858.

UNITT, Doris & Peter
1062 **'Bottles in Canada'**. *The Collectors' Guide to seeking, finding, dating, pricing, and researching bottles*. Publ. by Clock House, Peterborough, Ontario, Canada. ©1972 Doris and Peter Unitt.

UNITT, Peter & WORRALL, Anne
1063 **'Unitt's Bottle Book & Price Guide'**. Clock House Publications, Peterborough, Ontario, Canada. ©1985.

URQUHART, O.
1064 **'Bottlers and Bottles, Canadian'**. ©1976, S. & O. Urquhart, Toronto, Ontario (Canada).

UTT, Mary Lou & Glenn & BAYER, Patricia
1065 **'Lalique Perfume Bottles'**. ©1990 Mary Lou Utt. First publ. in Great Britain by Thames and Hudson Ltd., London 1991. Originally publ.by Crown Publishers, Inc., New York.

VADER, John & MURRAY, Brian
1066 **'Antique Bottle Collecting in Australia'**. Publ. by Paul Hamlyn Pty Limited, Sydney, Auckland, London, New York. ©1975.

VALENTE, Vasco
1067 **'O Vidro em Portugal'**. Portucalense Editora, Porto, Portugal. 1950.

VAN DEN BOSSCHE, Willy
See: BOSSCHE, Willy Van den

VERBOVEN, Hilde
1068 **'Een Schatkist vol Jenever'**. Nationaal Jenevermuseum, Hasselt/België, ©1993.

VERHOEF, B.
1069 **'Bier Encyclopedie'**. ©1997. Publ. Rebo Productions b.v., Lisse, The Netherlands.

VERHOEVEN, Isabelle
1070 **'Art & Parfum'** - *Histoire des Flacons*. Pierre Mardaga Editeur. ©1989 4020 Liège, 1000 Bruxelles.

VIENNEAU, A.
1071 **'The Bottle Collector'**. Petheric Press, 1969.

VINCENT, Keith
1072 **'Nailsea glass'**. David & Charles, 1975.

WADE, A.G.
1073 **'A 17th century Bishop's seal'**. In CL, 26 Dec 1947.

WAGONER, George
1074 **'Restoring Old Bottles'**. West Sacramento, Calif.; Gorman's Stationary, 1966.

WALBRIDGE, William S.
1075 **'American Bottles Old & New (1607 to 1920) – A Story of the Industry in the United States'**. ©1920. Frontier Book Co., Publisher, Fort Davis, Texas.

WALLIS, Fletcher
1076 **'British Corkscrews Patents from 1795'**. Vernier Press, Brighton, 1997.

WALTER, Jr. Leo G.
1077 **'Walter's Inkwells of 1885'**. *Book 1*. ©1968 Leo G. Walter, Jr., Akron, Ohio.

WALTERS, Jeff
1078 **'Classic Soda Machines'**. *2nd ed. A Field Reference and Price Guide*. ©1992, 1995. Publ. by Memory Lane Publishing, Pollock Pines, Cal., USA.

WARMAN, Edwin G.
1079 **'Bottle Collector's Treasury; a collection of information about classic and common bottles'**. Uniontown, Pa: E.G. Warman, 1972.

WASILEWSKI, Andreas
1080 **'Heilkunst im Spiegel von Apothekenstandgefäßen und ihren Signaturen'**. *Eine historische Betrachtung*. Verlag Dr. Schmellenkamp GmbH, Blaustein, 1991.

WATNEY, Bernard M. & BABBIDGE, Homer D.
1081 **'Corkscrews for Collectors'**. Sotheby Parke Bernet, London & New York; 1981.

WATSON, George & SKRILL, Robert
1082 **'Western Canadian Bottle Collecting'**. Hume Compton in Nanaimo, British Columbia, Canada, Jly 1971.

WATSON, George & SKRILL, Robert & HEIDT, J.
1083 **'Western Canadian Bottle Collecting'**. *Book Two. With a special section on Ink Bottles by Gerard & Joan Bentryn*. Printed in B.C. by Evergreen Press Limited. Undated.

WATSON, Richard
1084 **'Bitters Bottles'**. ©1965 Richard Watson. Publ. by Thomas Nelson & Sons in New York and simultaneously in Toronto, Canada by Thomas Nelson & Sons (Canada) Ltd.

1085 **'Supplement to Bitters Bottles'**. ©1968 Richard Watson. Publ. by Thomas Nelson & Sons in Camden, N.J. and simultaneously in Toronto, Canada by Thomas Nelson & Sons (Canada) Ltd.

WATTERS, Pat
1086 **'Coca-Cola – An Illustrated History'**. Doubleday & Company, Inc., Garden City, New York, 1978.

WEARIN, Otha D.
1087 **'I Collect Character Bottles'**. Iowa; Nishona Vale Press, 1957

1088 **'Statues that Pour – The Story of Character Bottles'**. ©1965 Otha D. Wearin. Publ. by Wallace Homestead Book Company, Des Moines, Iowa.

WEEDEN, Cyril
1089 **'The Bristol bottlemakers. . .'**. In Chemistry & Industry, 3 Jun 1978, p.378-81.

WEISS, Gustav
1090 **'The Book of Glass'**. Praeger Publishers, New York, 1971.

1091 **'Ullstein Gläserbuch'** - *Eine Kultur- und Technikgeschichte des Glases*. ©1966, Ullstein Berlin Frankfurt/M Wien.

WENDT, Dr. Ralf
1092 **'Das Waldglas'** - *Volkskundliche Sammlungen Bauernkultur in Mecklenburg - Band IV*. Herausgegeben vom Historischen Museum Schwerin 1977.

1093 **'Glashütten in Mecklenburg'** - *Beitrag zur Sozialgeschichte und Volkskunde eines ländlichen Gewerbezweiges (1. Hälfte 17. bis Ende 19. Jahrhundert)* - Dissertation zur Erlangung des Doktorgrades an der Philosophischen Fakultät der Humboldt-Universität zu Berlin. Berlin, 30.9.1968.

WENZEL, Johann Heinrich Gottlieb

1094 **'Thüringer GLAS-TAXA'** - *Nach welcher Glas-Sorten von allerhand Modellen, Namen und Maasen, sowohl wegen kostbarkeit der Materia, als auch der künstlichen Arbeit, in einem ordentlichen Preis angesetzet, und von dem Factor vor baares Geld verkaufet werden. Allzunah, 29. Juni 1735, 14. März 1736, 11. März 1737 und 26. März 1737.* (Price-lists of glassware made in Thuringian glasshouses). Photostats Willy Van den Bossche.

WENZEL, Mathias

1095 **'Original German document dated 1659 with a poem and a line drawing of a handled "Bocksbeutel"'**. Collection: Thomas Stauner, Dettelbach, Germany.

WESTCOTT, David

1096 **'Early Historic and Rare Bottles'**. *Westcott Collection; Sales Catalogue Sept. 1979.* David Westcott, Deniliquin, NSW.

WESTON, Mike

1097 **'Northern California Bottles'**. ©1997 Mike Weston (USA).

WESTROPP, Michael

1098 **'Irish glass: an account of glass-making in Ireland from the sixteenth century to the present day'**. H. Jenkins, [1920], 206p.

WEYL, Woldemar A.

1099 **'Coloured Glasses'**. Society of Glass Technology "Thornton", Sheffield, England; 1951/1992, 541p.

WEYSE, Ip Olufsen

1100 **'De Kongelige Allernaadigste Octroierede Norske Glas Fabrique Producter'**. A fully illustrated catalogue on 1087 glass products and bottles produced in the glasshouse of Nøstetangen/Norway. Also known as the "Nøstetangen Catalogue", publ. in Kiöbenhavn, 1763.

WHITALL TATUM and Company, 1880

1101 **'1892 Catalog. Colognes, drug mills, bottles, scales, cork presses'**. Edited reprint. Millville, NJ: S.R. Bailey, 1969.

1102 **'1902 Catalog'**. Edited reprint. Millville, NJ: S.R. Bailey, 196-? Chattanooga, Tenn: 1967.

1103 **'Flint Glassware, blue ware, perfume and cologne bottles, show bottles and globes, green glassware, stoppers, druggists' sundries'**. Catalog reprint, with introduction. Princeton, NJ: Pyne, 1971.

WHITE, Helen H.

1104 **'New views of old glass: English and American wine bottles of the seventeenth century'**. In A, Jly-Oct 1933, p.26, 68, 108 and 146.

1105 **'Snuff Bottles from China'**. *The Victoria and Albert Museum Collection.* Bamboo Publishing Ltd., London. ©1990.

WHITE, James Seeley

1106 **'Diving for Northwest Relics'**. *Identification and Dating of Bottles, Pottery and Marine Hardware.* Binford & Mort, Thomas Binford, Publisher, Portland, Oregon; 1979.

1107 **'The Hedden's Store Handbook of Proprietary Medicines'**. Printed in U.S.A. by Durham & Downey, Portland, Oregon. ©1974.

WHITEHOUSE, David

1108 **'Glass: A Pocket Dictionary Of Terms Commonly Used To Describe Glass And Glassmaking'**. The Corning Museum of Glass, Corning, N.Y. ©1993.

WHITWORTH, E.W.

1109 **'Wine Labels'**. ©1966 E.W. Whitworth. Publ. by Cassell & Company Ltd., London; 1966.

WICHMANN, Jeff

1110 **'Antique Western Bitters Bottles'**. Publ. by Pacific Glass Books, Sacramento, Ca., 1999.

1111 **'The Best of the West – Antique Western Bitters Bottles'**. Publ. by Pacific Glass Books, Sacramento, Cal., USA. ©1999.

WIEGAND, Konrad

1112 **'Strukturwandel und Entwicklungstendenzen in der deutschen Hohlglasindustrie unter besonderer Berücksichtigung der Flaschenglasindustrie'**. Diss. Erlangen/Nürnberg, 1965.

WIEREN, Dale P. van

1113 **'American Breweries II'**. Eastern Coast Brewiana Association, West Point, PA; 1995.

WILEY, Harvey W.

1114 **'Beverages and Their Ancestory'**. Philadelphia, Pa.; Blakiston & Co., 1906-1907.

WILLS, Geoffrey

1115 **'Bottles: from 1720'**. *10 - English and Irish Glass. A Guinness Signature.* ©1968. Guinness Superlatives Ltd., Guildford, Surrey, England.

1116 **'English and Irish glass'**. Guinness Signatures, 1970. Contents: Bottles to 1720; Bottles from 1720.

1117 **'English Glass Bottles 1650-1950, for the Collector'**. ©1974 Geoffrey Wills. Publ. by John Bartholomew & Son Ltd., Edinburgh/Bromley, 1974.

1118 **'Ewers and Decanters, English and Irish Glass - A Guinness Signature'**. *No. 4 of a Series of 16.* © Guinness Superlatives Ltd., Guildford, England, by McCorquodale & Co. Ltd., London. 1968.

1119 **'Sealed glass bottles'**. In Connoisseur Concise Encyclopedia of Antiques, v.4, 1959, p.257-60.

1120 **'The Bottle-Collector's Guide'**. ©1977 Geoffrey Wills. First publ. in Great Britain 1977 by John Bartholomew & Son Limited, Edinburgh/Bromley.

1121 **'The Bottle Collector's Guide'**. Edinburgh, Bartholomew, 1978.

WILSON, Bill & ASKEY, Jim

1122 **'Pioneer Soda Water Companies of BC'**. 1986. © Bill Wilson and Jim Askey. Publ. by Tamahi Publishing, New Westminster, B.C.

WILSON, Bill & Betty

1123 **'19th Century Medicine in Glass'**. Amador City, Cal.: 19th Century Hobby and Publishing, 1971.

1124 **'Spirits Bottles of the Old West'**. ©1968 William L.

Wilson. Reprinted by Antique & Hobby Publishing Co., Amador City, Calif.

1125   *'Western Bitters'*. ©1969 William L. Wilson. Printed by The Northwestern Printing Company, Santa Rosa, Calif.

WILSON, Kenneth M.

1126   *'The Glastenbury Glass Factory Company'*. In CJGS, Vol.V, p.116-132, 1963.

WILSON, Rex L.

1127   *'Bottles on the Western Frontier'*. The University of Arizona Press, Tucson, Arizona, in collaboration with Southwest Parks and Monuments Association, 1981.

WINBOLT, S.E.

1128   *'Wealden Glass: The Surrey-Sussex Glass Industry, 1261-1615'*. Hove, Combridges, 1933.

WINCHESTER, Alice

1129   *'Wine Trade Loan Exhibition [Catalogue, ed. by André Simon]'*. London, 1933. An exhibition at the Vintners' Hall, 1933.

WOLFENDEN, Ian G.

1130   *'Victorian decanters: the early Victorian period c.1835-1865'*. In AC, Dec 1979, p.20-3.

WOOD, Mabel C.

1131   *'Chemung County, New York: Bottles, Bottlers, and Their Stories; an interesting study and history of the area'*. Elmira Heights, NY: Golos Publishers, 1973.

WOOD, Serry

1132   *'The Old Apothecary Shop'*. Watkins Glenn, N.Y.; Century House 1956.

WOOD, Zang

1133   *'Colored Hutchinsons'*. ©1999. Publ. by Sunbelt Publications, New Mexico.

1134   *'New Mexico, Blobs - Hutchs, Mineral Waters'*. ©1998. Flora Vista, NM 87415.

WOODHAMS, John

1135   *'Have you got the Bottle?'*. Publ. by London League Publication, 1998.

WORLIDGE, J.

1136   *'Vinetum Britanicum or a Treatise of Cider'*. London 1676.

WRIGHT, Barry

1137   *'Embossed Glass Soda Water Bottles in Nova Scotia'*. Publ. by: Barry Wright & Stuart Graphics and Printing, Nova Scotia (Canada).

WYATT, Victor

1138   *'From sand-core to automation'* - *A history of glass containers*. ©1965/1978. Glass Manufacturers Federation, London, England.

WYNN-JONES, B.

1139   *'Mineral Water Bottles'*. Edited by Andy Payne. ©1978, Southern Collectors Publications, Bitterne, Southampton (U.K.).

WYNNE-THOMAS, R.J.L.

1140   *'Relics of the Marsala trade'*. In CONN, Mar 1975, p.211-15. Discusses glasses and bottles.

YATES, Donald

1141   *'American Stone, Ginger Beer and Root Beer - Population Guide and Check List'*. Issue Number 1, September 3, 1996. Strongsville, Ohio.

YATES, Donald & Elizabeth

1142   *'American Stone, Ginger Beer & Root Beer (1790 to 1920)'*. June 1996; Don & Betsy Yates, Strongsville, Ohio.

YOUNG, Anne Mortimer

1143   *'Antique Medicine Chests - or Glyster, Blister & Purge'*. Publ. 1994, Vernier Press, London/Brighton.

YOUNG, James Harvey

1144   *'The Toadstool Millionaires'*. *A Social History of Patent Medicines in America before Federal Regulation*. Princeton University Press, Princeton, New Jersey, USA. 1961.

YOUNG, Sidney

1145   *'History of the Worshipful Company of Glass-Sellers of London'*. London, Barker, 1913.

YOUNT, John T.

1146   *'Bottle Collector's Handbook & Pricing Guide'*. ©1967 John T. Yount. Publ. by Educator Books, Inc., San Angelo, Texas.

1147   *'Bottle Collector's Handbook and Pricing Guide'*. Rev. ed. San Angelo, Tx: Action Printing, 1967; rev. ed. San Angelo, Tx: Educator Books, 1970.

ZECCHIN, Luigi

1148   *'Vetro e Vetrai di Murano'*. *Studi sulla storia del vetro. Volumes I-II-III*. ©1987 Arsenale Editrice s.r.l., Venezia.

ZIMMERMAN, Mary I.

1149   *'Sun-colored Glass, Its Lure and Lore; the facts and the hobby of old purple glass'*. Amarillo, Tx: 1964.

ZISCHKA, Ulrike

1150   *'Die anständige Lust'*, *von Esskultur und Tafelsitten*. Edition Spangenberg bei Droemer Knaur. ©Münchner Stadtmuseum 1993.

ZUMWALT, Betty

1151   *'Ketchup, Pickles, Sauces - 19th Century Food in Glass'*. ©1980 Ernest & Betty Zumwalt. Publ. by Mark West Publishers, Fulton, CA., USA.

433

INDEX

Page numbers in *italics* refer to Glossary entries. Words written in CAPITALS refer to indications on bottle such as on labels, seals or embossings.